PRAISE FOR *BECOMING DR. SEUSS*

LONGLISTED FOR THE ANDREW CARNEGIE MEDALS FOR
EXCELLENCE IN NONFICTION

"*Becoming Dr. Seuss* is more compelling than mere pop hagiography; it is sweeping in scope, unstinting in detail, and willing to criticize or contextualize when needed."

—*THE NEW YORKER*

"Nuanced, profoundly human, and painstakingly researched, this 496-page biography is perhaps the most complete, multidimensional look at the life of one of the most beloved authors and illustrators of our time. . . . While it is a standard biography in general terms, Jones goes above and beyond to contextualize Geisel in the larger picture at every moment of his life. [A] fascinating read that discusses the origin of the humorous, simple rhymes, bizarre creatures, and magic that characterized Geisel's books while also showing the author's more radical side as an unemployed wanderer who abandoned his doctoral studies, a successful advertising man, and a political cartoonist."

—*NPR*

"A rich, anecdotal biography . . . Whether readers are familiar with Dr. Seuss books or not, they will find this biography absorbing and fascinating."

—*KIRKUS REVIEWS* (STARRED REVIEW)

"This attractive biography should be on the bedside reading table of thousands of Dr. Seuss lovers, and deservedly so."

—*LIBRARY JOURNAL* (STARRED REVIEW)

"A warm, defining biography of one of the most beloved writers of this or any time."

—*LITHUB*

"One of the most anticipated books of Spring 2019."

—*PUBLISHERS WEEKLY*

"While acknowledging Geisel's flaws and debts to others, Jones convincingly shows him as a transformative figure in children's publishing, both as an author and cofounder of the Beginner Books imprint. Fans of Dr. Seuss will find much to love in this candid but admiring portrait."

—*PUBLISHERS WEEKLY*

"One of the buzziest books being released this May 2019."

—*O, THE OPRAH MAGAZINE*

"Enjoyable. Lively."

—*THE WALL STREET JOURNAL*

"Profiling cultural empires and their instigators is familiar territory for Jones, who also wrote *Jim Henson: The Biography* and *George Lucas: A Life*. It's clear that Jones is experienced in extracting details from the most innocuous letter or interview, fleshing out the lives of cultural groundbreakers we've long admired. As all successful biographers should do, Jones doesn't cheerlead his own writing style by adding unnecessary flourishes or similes; he lets the subject's actions and quotes energize the book. Thankfully, Geisel is a hilarious and insightful character whose love of literature is almost as infectious as his timeless rhymes."

—*THE WASHINGTON POST*

"A loving portrait of a singularly creative man whose influence is as strong today as ever."

—*AV CLUB*

"Finally! The solution to the mystery of where Dr. Seuss earned his PhD. Brian Jay Jones also reveals the true identity of Chrysanthemum Pearl; the etymology of the word *nerd*; the political leanings of Horton and Yertle; and the relationship of Krazy Kat to the one in the hat. It comes as no surprise that Theodor Geisel was a born storyteller; prying truth from fact, Jones pins our favorite fabulist nimbly, colorfully, and splendidly to the page."

"Readers of *Becoming Dr. Seuss* may be astonished to learn in this rollicking ride of a biography that Theodor Seuss Geisel—progenitor of the most anarchic animals of all time—was himself a radically bizarre creation, every bit as strange and emotionally uncoordinated as a Snoo or a Sneetch. Childless, chain-smoking, and cocktail-swilling, bawdy and argumentative, Geisel got his unlikely start promoting Standard Oil's fly-killing insecticide (his ad campaign featured the immortal tag line 'Quick, Henry! The Flit!'); drawing coarse political cartoons (sometimes racist or misogynist); and serving as a World War II understudy to Frank Capra, making films teaching grunts to evade death and mosquitoes. His epic transformation into one of the most beloved and bestselling children's writers of all time, winner of Oscars and a Pulitzer, is a poignant, affecting tale of a man who mastered the art of concision through imagination and sheer toil yet could never bring such exactitude to his own life, callously replacing his wife and editor of forty years, a suicide, with her rival. In Jones's telling, the Seussian legacy emerges triumphant, elevating the power of children's literature. 'I no longer write for children,' Geisel said proudly at the end of his life. 'I write for people.'"

"Once again, Brian Jay Jones takes us on a beguiling deep-dive into the life of one of the leading lights of American popular culture. Written with verve and warmth and a close attention to both the life and the times in which it was lived, *Becoming Dr. Seuss* brims with charm and humor from beginning to end."

"Brian Jay Jones offers a richly detailed, admiring biography of Theodor Geisel, the man whom children and adults the world over would come to love as Dr. Seuss, and goes on to say [Jones] provides a meticulously detailed yet thoroughly engaging look at the life and artistry of this American original."

—*BOOKPAGE*

"How the Seuss found his juice. The real-life tales that sparked America's favorite children's author."

—*THE NEW YORK POST*

"Worthy of a complete read."

—*NEW YORK JOURNAL OF BOOKS*

"An important and interesting book about an author who greatly influenced our culture and most certainly our educational system."

—*THE MISSOURIAN*

"What this biography does best is account for Geisel's demanding creative habits. He was dedicated to work and, when he had the power and leverage, he fussed over every detail of his books, from the size of the page and the font to the placement of text and picture. He insisted on the exact colors he required, and his longtime publisher, Random House, usually sensibly let him have his own way; his titles eventually sold in the hundreds of millions."

—*CHRISTIAN SCIENCE MONITOR*

ALSO BY BRIAN JAY JONES

Jim Henson: The Biography

George Lucas: A Life

Washington Irving:
An American Original

BECOMING
DR. SEUSS

· · · · · · · · · · · · · · · · ·

THEODOR GEISEL AND THE
MAKING OF AN AMERICAN
IMAGINATION

BRIAN JAY JONES

DUTTON

DUTTON

An imprint of Penguin Random House LLC

penguinrandomhouse.com

Previously published as a Dutton hardcover edition in 2019

First trade paperback printing: May 2020

Excerpts *from Dr. Seuss & Mr. Geisel: A Biography* by Judith and Neil Morgan, copyright © 1995 by Judith and Neil Morgan. Used by permission of Random House, an imprint and division of Penguin Random House LLC. All rights reserved.

THE LIBRARY OF CONGRESS HAS CATALOGUED THE HARDCOVER EDITION AS FOLLOWS:
Names: Jones, Brian Jay, author.
Title: Becoming Dr. Seuss : Theodor Geisel and the making of an American imagination / Brian Jay Jones.
Description: New York, New York : Dutton, [2019] |
Includes bibliographical references.
Identifiers: LCCN 2018059288 | ISBN 9781524742782 (hardcover) |
ISBN 9781524742805 (ebook)
Subjects: LCSH: Seuss, Dr. | Authors, American—20th century—Biography. |
Illustrators—United States—Biography.
Classification: LCC PS3513.E2 Z687 2019 | DDC 813/.52 [B]—dc23
LC record available at https://lccn.loc.gov/2018059288

Dutton trade paperback ISBN: 9781524742799

Printed in the United States of America
1   3   5   7   9   10   8   6   4   2

BOOK DESIGN BY LORIE PAGNOZZI

FOR MOM AND WAYNE

CONTENTS

CHAPTER 17
OFF AND AWAY

PART I

AND THAT IS A STORY THAT NO ONE CAN BEAT

CHAPTER 1

MINNOWS INTO WHALES

1904–1921

n paper, Mulberry Street doesn't look like much. It's just another residential street on the city map of Springfield, Massachusetts, a slightly bent capital letter *L* lying on its back, not much more than a pass-through between the busier streets of Union and Maple. The street itself is quiet and relatively nondescript, with very little indication that it's a major destination on a map of the American imagination.

But sure enough, it was here—at least as told in the tale by Springfield's own Dr. Seuss—that a little boy named Marco used his imagination to transform a simple horse and wagon into a colorful spectacle, with a brass band pulled by an elephant-riding sultan, flanked by motorcycle policemen and confetti-dumping airplanes, while enthusiastically being reviewed by the top-hatted mayor and the town aldermen. Modern-day pilgrims still flock to Mulberry Street, slowly trolling the neighborhood, windows down, hoping to catch a glimpse of something—anything—that inspired the magnificent imaginations of Marco and Dr. Seuss. Residents smile knowingly, pausing over lawn mowers and trunks still filled with groceries to answer the same question from visiting wayfarers.

"Where did Dr. Seuss live?"

The answer, it seems, is as disappointing as discovering London's

221B Baker Street is actually home to a bank, and never was home to Sherlock Holmes. Dr. Seuss didn't live on Mulberry Street at all. Instead, pilgrims are directed to another spot on the map, another inverted L about two miles south: Fairfield Street. This is where Dr. Seuss grew up, and the house he lived in for nearly twenty years, at number 74, is still there, looking much as it did during his lifetime.

Parts of Springfield, in fact, look as they did during Dr. Seuss's day—or at least the places that shaped his imagination and influenced his art can still be seen if one knows where to look. A few blocks from Fairfield on Howard Street stands the old armory. Its curved stone turrets are reflected in the castles populating so many Seuss books. Over in Forest Park, the Barney Mausoleum—built with a family fortune earned by inventing and selling clamp-on ice skates—looms two stories above the pavement, with the curving staircases and pillared archways that would show up in *The 500 Hats of Bartholomew Cubbins*. And the nearby Forest Park Zoo? That was where "[I tried to] draw the animals," said Dr. Seuss later. "I didn't know how to draw, so they'd come out strange."[1]

Dr. Seuss didn't produce Springfield's only creations. Founded by the Puritan William Pynchon in 1636 on a high bluff overlooking the Connecticut River, Springfield has been nurturing and stirring American imaginations for nearly three hundred years. American independence was won with the reliable ammunition and gun carriages produced at the Springfield Armory beginning in 1777. (A decade later, Daniel Shays—spouting a different kind of idealism—would attempt to steal muskets and ammunition from the same armory in a thwarted attempt to overthrow the government of Massachusetts.) By 1795, Springfield Armory would regularly be producing the muskets that would be carried on the shoulders of American soldiers all the way through the War of 1812 and on into the Civil War.

Weaponry wasn't Springfield's only specialty; true, local businessmen Horace Smith and Daniel B. Wesson, who developed the firearms company that bore their last names, had roots in the town—but so, too, did Charles Goodyear, who discovered and patented the process for making vulcanized rubber in a small Springfield factory in 1844. A year earlier, two industrious Springfield publishers, brothers Charles and George Merriam, acquired the rights to publish Noah Webster's *An American Dictionary of the English Language*, marking the founding of another iconic American brand.

There was Milton Bradley, who would launch the American board game industry by cranking out the earliest incarnations of The Game of Life in his lithography studio in 1860. Over on State Street, the beloved and reliable Indian motorcycles would roll out of the company's Springfield factory from 1901 until 1953. Even modern sports would find their origins in the town when in 1891 a Canadian-born physical education teacher named James Naismith, looking to keep his classes occupied through the long, cold Massachusetts winters, mounted a peach basket on a ten-foot pole in the gymnasium at the International YMCA Training School and—opting not to name the game after himself—christened the new game *basketball*.

Springfield, then, could unequivocally and rightly stake a claim as a major landmark on the frontier of American inventiveness and imagination. Dr. Seuss himself was a construct of one of those unique American minds: a comfortable coat regularly shrugged on and off at will by one of Springfield's most famous sons, Theodor Seuss Geisel. The dropped *e* at the end of Theodor would forever perplex journalists and copyeditors, but to Theodor—Dr. Seuss himself—it wouldn't much matter. Everyone would always call him Ted.

••••

Theodor Seuss Geisel could trace his roots back to the German town of Mühlhausen, a tiny village squatting on the western shore of a hairpin turn in the Enz River, in what is now the German state of Baden-Württemberg. It was here, in 1650, that Joseph Geissel married Catharina Loth; the extra *s* would be dropped in later generations, and well before Ted's grandfather was born in July 1844. Born Theodor Adolph Geisel in Mülhausen, T. A. Geisel moved to nearby

Pforzheim at age fourteen to enter into a six-year apprenticeship with a local jeweler. From there, he joined the German cavalry—T. A. Geisel would always have a love for horses, and even at only five feet six, he stood tall in the saddle—and served in the German army for the seven-week Austro-Prussian War that quickly sparked, flared, and burned out in the summer of 1866.

"My grandfather was a German cavalry officer who decided he didn't want to be one," Ted said[2]—and in 1869, twenty-five-year-old T. A. Geisel stepped onto the steamship *Ohio* at the port in Bremen, bound for the United States, where members of his extended family had secured him a job in the store of Springfield jeweler J. B. Rumrill. If Geisel missed his homeland, he seemed only ever looking forward, never back. In 1871, he married Christine Schmaelzle, another recent German immigrant four years his junior. Two children would follow shortly. In 1875, he became an American citizen.[3]

T.A. built a reputation as a talented jeweler—in his five years in Springfield, he had become Springfield's go-to designer for brooches—but in 1876 he abandoned brooches for booze, giving up the jeweling trade entirely to begin a new career as a brewer ("a slight jump," his grandson said archly).[4] Pooling his savings with those of a young brewer's apprentice named Christian Kalmbach, T.A. purchased a small brick brewing plant located way out on Boston Road on the east side of town, right at the last stop on the horsecar line.

While the facility they purchased was primitive and deemed "feeble" by locals[5]—just a few wooden buildings that produced barely a thousand barrels of beer annually—the proprietors of the new Kalmbach & Geisel Brewery proved remarkably ambitious and adept both as businessmen and brewers. Under the guidance of T. A. Geisel, who had a knack for property and structures, the wooden brewery quickly expanded into one of the largest in the region, becoming a "magnificent" compound of redbrick buildings surrounding a central courtyard and eventually taking up twelve grassy acres.[6]

For a while, the Geisels lived on the grounds of the brewing compound, then took a small cottage directly across from the brewery on

State Street. It was here, in the shadow of the smokestack of the Kalm-bach & Geisel Brewery, that T.A. and Christine Geisel had their fourth child and first son, Theodor Robert Geisel—Dr. Seuss's father—on June 28, 1879.[7] In the coming decade, there would be two more surviving children, Adolph and Christine[8]—but as the first son and name-sake, it was T.R. who was expected to follow in his father's footsteps in the brewing industry.

Before T.R. was three, the brewery that once produced less than a thousand barrels of beer in a year was delivering at least that much in a *single day*, fanning a small army of beer wagons out across Spring-field every morning, each distinctive black and gold wagon drawn by majestic four-horse teams. As a boy, T.R. would rise early to head off to school; his father, meanwhile, had already been up for hours, over-seeing the several hundred barrels of Kalmbach & Geisel beer that were loaded onto trains to ship daily through all of New England.[9] "It was good beer, too," said Ted—so good, in fact, that Kalmbach & Geisel would be fondly referred to by locals as "Come back and guzzle."[10]

And guzzle the locals did—so much so that the brewery would con-tinue to grow and thrive over the next decade, prompting T.A. to add an enormous icehouse and replace their compound of buildings with a brand-new state-of-the-art three-story brick structure. In 1893, with profits soaring and more than 400,000 barrels of beer rolling out annually, T.A. bought out Christian Kalmbach, renamed the busi-ness the Highland Brewing Company, and immediately designated himself as the new organization's president, treasurer, and manager.

Five years later, the still-growing Highland Brewing Company was sold and incorporated—along with several local rivals, including the Hampden Brewing Company, just up the river in Willimansett—to form the Springfield Breweries Company. T.A. pocketed his profits but insisted on remaining as manager of the Highland facility, and jockeyed to have his nineteen-year-old son T.R. hired as treasurer for the entire organization. Despite the lofty title and elevated responsi-bilities, T.R. Geisel would modestly list his occupation simply as "bookkeeper."[11]

T.A., however, would always proudly identify himself as a *brewer*, a title anyone of German extraction would bear with particular satisfaction. As the proprietor of one of New England's most successful breweries—and an active member of some of the leading German clubs of Springfield—T.A. was understandably a proud man. Devoted to family—he would insist his children live under his own roof until they married—T.A. had only one real hobby: his beautiful team of horses, which he kept decked out in the finest gear. With his broad shoulders, a wide mustache that curled slightly at the ends, and piercing blue eyes that seemed set in a perpetual squint, T.A. was imperial in bearing, though not imposing—he was a bit too short for that. His grandson, however, would always remember him in a slightly mythic manner, recalling his *Großvater* as wearing "boiled white shirts and diamond studs and [who] sat in deep leather chairs with Persian rugs at his feet."[12]

By 1901, T.A. was ready to become his own boss again, and enlisted twenty-two-year-old T.R. as his partner for his newest start-up endeavor, the Liberty Brewing Company, with riverside offices at the busy corner at Liberty and Charles Streets.[13] This time, T.R. was appointed as both treasurer and secretary of the company, titles he was proud to boast of and which he hoped would impress the young woman he'd been wooing for a year, a twenty-three-year-old baker's daughter named Henrietta Seuss.

Like T.R., Henrietta—called "Nettie"—was a first-generation Springfielder. Born May 13, 1878, she was the daughter of George and Margaretha Seuss, who had emigrated from Bavaria and established a successful bakery in their new hometown. Like the Geisels, the Seusses were active in Springfield's German community. George Seuss, in fact, had been a founder of the popular Springfield Turnverein, a social club and gymnasium with a heavily German clientele, and also served as a city alderman. Seuss's popular bakery, located in the heart of downtown Springfield, was hard to miss—one only had to follow one's nose to find it on Howard Street, practically in the shadow of the massive Springfield Armory. If brewing was a family business for the Geisels, the bakery was similarly a Seussian family affair; Nettie, in fact, had worked at the bakery since the age of fifteen, her loyalty to the family firm overriding her desire to attend college.[14]

T.R. and Nettie made an attractive, if somewhat intimidating, couple. Both were six feet tall and athletic in build. Nettie, a dark-haired beauty, weighed nearly two hundred pounds, was an expert diver, and in a town that took marksmanship seriously—it was the home of Smith & Wesson, after all—was a crack shot with a rifle. Like his father, T.R. was dark-haired and dark-eyed, with a regal bearing. He also was an accomplished horseman, as well as one of the very best sharpshooters in the region; in 1902, he would hold the world record for shooting at two hundred yards.[15]

The two seem to have met some resistance to their relationship. On August 31, 1901, the young couple sneaked away to New York and covertly married, a secret they seem to have kept until the news finally trickled into the pages of the *Springfield Republican* nearly a year later. "The announcement was as much a surprise to their closest friends as to others," the *Republican* reported. "[N]o one had been given an inkling of what had happened."[16]

The announcement of the marriage also sparked some tut-tutting from those in the burgeoning temperance movement—a crusade that would soon have far-reaching consequences for the Geisels—who disapproved of the matrimonial merging of the Seuss and Geisel businesses. "Seuss the baker puts the staff of life in people's mouths," commented one wag, while "Geisel the brewer takes it out and pours beer there instead, causing the children of drinkers to suffer the pangs of hunger."[17]

Such criticism aside, the secret likely couldn't have been kept much longer anyway; by the time of the marriage's revelation in March, Nettie was visibly pregnant with their first child—and on July 4, 1902, gave birth to a daughter they named Margaretha Christine Geisel.[18] T.R. would dotingly call her Marnie, a nickname that would stick. That same year, T. A. Geisel—now officially a *Großvater* himself—would move from his modest cottage on State Street to a spacious house at 162

Sumner Avenue, the grandest street in Springfield, lined with large Victorian houses and bordering the gigantic Forest Park on the park's short north end. The house had plenty of room for family, but T.R. and Nettie seem to have preferred living with or near her parents in Howard Street instead, perhaps because the Seusses lived within walking distance of T.R.'s offices at the Liberty Brewing Company.

It was here, in the Seuss house at 22 Howard Street—just down the street from the Seuss family bakery—that T.R. and Nettie Geisel had their second child and first son on March 2, 1904, a cold but fair-weathered Wednesday. Like his father and grandfather before him, the boy was named Theodor, with the middle name Seuss—pronounced *Soyce*, in proper German fashion—affixed as a recognition of his mother's side of the family.

Before his baby son was two years old, T.R. moved his family into a respectable home at 74 Fairfield Street, an address in the Forest Park district of Springfield, just a short walk from T.A.'s home on Sumner Avenue. For T.R., commuting to his Liberty Street office was now as simple as catching the new electric streetcar that ran down to Main Street from Belmont Avenue, practically right behind the house. While it wasn't necessarily as fashionable as the Sumner Avenue address occupied by the eldest Geisel, the Fairfield neighborhood, and the house at number 74, both had their charms. Fairfield was a short stretch of tree-lined lane, running due west from its terminal point at Litchfield Street for several hundred yards before bending a gentle dogleg down to connect with Garfield Street to the south. In the bend of this leg was a small triangular grassy lot, lit by a gas lamp, which Ted and his friends would dub "the Soccer Field" and make the focal point of neighborhood games.

The Fairfield house was a light gray three-story; with its irregularly spaced windows on the second floor and one gabled window at the top, it looked like a child's drawing of a house. Ted and Marnie each had a bedroom at the back of the second floor, with a bathroom between them. Upstairs, under the eaves, was a room for a young nanny and housekeeper named Anna, who would terrify Ted by locking him in her closet when he misbehaved. And in the backyard was an element that was something of a Springfield novelty: a free-standing brick garage, large enough for two carriages, but which the Geisels kept filled mostly with bicycles and various equipment until the mid-1920s, when T.R. would park a gleaming Hudson Super Six automobile behind the roll-down door.

Ted had two vivid memories of his early childhood in the Fairfield house. The first involved a large brown stuffed dog given to him by his mother. Ted named it Theophrastus, after the ancient Greek writer and philosopher, and would keep it with him throughout his life, perching the worn and frayed stuffed dog on his drawing table or on an office shelf, where it would serve as mascot and muse.

The other early memory was more melancholy than merry. On August 17, 1906, Nettie gave birth to another daughter they named Henrietta. Several months later, the newborn developed pneumonia; Marnie, though only four, never forgot the "terrible sounds of her cough that we heard all through that three-story house."[19] After Henrietta died on December 19, 1907, a grieving T.R. moved his Pooley record cabinet out of the family's music room on the first floor to make space for Henrietta's little casket. Though he was only a little more than two and a half, Ted was forever haunted by the memory of the casket in the front room. Even after the casket had been removed and the Pooley cabinet returned to its rightful place, Ted would always eye the piece of furniture warily. "I always saw Henrietta in her casket in the place where the Pooley cabinet was," he recalled.[20]

T.R. and Nettie would have no more children, but the extended Geisel family was already large, loud, and close-knit, spending weeknights over huge dinners of bratwursts and "countless bolognas,"[21] as Ted remembered, and weekends at endless parties and social events. "In 1905, while Albert Einstein was discovering relativity," Ted wrote later, "I, at the age of one, was going to German clambakes on Sunday afternoons in my diapers."[22]

The German population in Springfield wasn't large—it made up less than one percent of the city's total population in 1910[23]—but it was active and enthusiastic. Apart from the Seuss-established Turnverein, where there were formal dress balls between exhibitions of gymnastics, there was also the Schützenverein riflery club—T.R. and Nettie weren't the only ones who took shooting seriously. Ted would be raised in a household where German was spoken regularly, and remembered eavesdropping from the top of the stairs on Saturday nights, listening to his family talk and sing and argue in colorful language that tumbled and rolled, growing louder as the evening wore on and the liquor flowed. On Sunday morning, if anyone wished to atone for the previous night of drinking, the Trinity Evangelical Lutheran Church still held services in German.

Ted's parents were neither overly devout nor sticklers for services in German, for Nettie chose instead to take Ted and Marnie to services at the Episcopal Church, where Ted preferred the music and ceremony over the sermon. He was especially captivated by the sight of the local druggist walking slowly up the center aisle, swinging a smoke-seeping metal container burning incense—which, Ted noted with some surprise, "never hit anyone."[24]

But apart from its underlying morality, religion would always be more obligation than inspiration, though as a child, Ted took an obvious delight in making up rhyming verse as a mnemonic device to remember the books of the Old Testament:

> The great Jehovah speaks to us
> In Genesis and Exodus;
> Leviticus and Numbers, three,
> Followed by Deuteronomy.[25]

It was a suggestion of the kind of playful Seussian wordplay to come, as well as a hint of the careful parsing and agonizing over his work that would become a later habit—for Ted subsequently admitted to inserting the word *three* into the poem's third line simply to make it rhyme properly.

Nettie, too, would directly influence Ted's ear for the beat and intonation of words. As she put her son to bed each evening, Nettie would chant a refrain she had often sung behind the counter at the Seuss bakery to inform patrons of the day's pie flavors: "Apple, mince, lemon . . . peach, apricot, pineapple . . . blueberry, coconut, custard and SQUASH!"—at which point she would playfully squash a giggling Ted down into his mattress. Ted later credited his mother "for the rhythms in which I write and the urgency with which I do it."[26]

Both Nettie and T.R. would inspire and encourage Ted's love for books. Reading was a pastime the entire family took seriously, leaving well-thumbed books casually on side tables, and the pages of the *Springfield Republican* newspaper folded carefully over the arm of a chair. "Teaching a child to read is a family setup," Ted said later. "It's the business of having books around the house, not forcing them. Parents should have twenty books stacked up on tables or set around the living room. The average kid will pick one up, find something interesting. And pretty soon he's reading."[27]

That was certainly the case with Ted, who in a 1979 interview with *Parents* magazine swore he was reading the works of Jonathan Swift, Robert Louis Stevenson, and Charles Dickens at age six.[28] There may have been an element of Swiftian satire in his retelling of this memory—it wasn't the first or last time Ted would give a dramatic retelling of his own childhood—but Ted did have a detailed memory of other children's books that struck his fancy. He distinctly recalled, for instance, reading *The Brownies: Their Book*, stories of child-sized spirits from English and Scottish folklore, written and drawn by the poet Palmer Cox, as well as *Goops and How to Be Them*, a humorous book of manners and social mores by the writer and artist Gelett Burgess. "My parents bought them and I read them and loved them," Ted said later. The Goops, he thought, with their emphasis on polite behavior, "were a little too moralistic for me, but I loved the Brownies—they were wonderful little creatures. In fact, they probably awakened my desire to draw."[29]

Ted also took great delight in books with clever concepts or conceits—and one of the cleverest of writers and artists around was Peter Newell, whose *The Hole Book* made a deep impression on six-year-old Ted. The book opened with a verse Ted could quote from memory, even seven decades later:

> Tom Potts was fooling with a gun
> (Such follies should not be),
> When—bang! The pesky thing went off
> Most unexpectedly!

Every page of the book—including the cover—had a small round die-cut hole meant to trace the trajectory of the bullet as it made its way from page to page, cutting the rope on a swing, puncturing a water heater, and popping balloons. "It just raised hell," Ted remembered fondly.[30]

Nettie quickly came to realize the power that books had over her son and would use them to coax him into good behavior. In particular, Ted recalled his mother using books in Arthur M. Winfield's series of Rover Boys novels to bribe him into focusing on his piano lessons with the church organist. "The most mighty book in my life was one of the Rover Boys series," Ted said. "I've forgotten just which one, precisely, because, as a preadolescent, I gobbled down more than thirty in a row." The Rover Boys were three brothers—Tom, Sam, and Dick Rover—who attended boarding school together and spent most of their time playing pranks and, to modern eyes, engaging in obnoxious and slightly dangerous behavior. But Ted adored the stories and their matching hardcovers. "The Rovers are the boys who made me want to read," he said.[31]

And yet it was an imperfect reading experience. The Rover Boys stories were full of stereotypes typical of the era: there was Hans Mueller, a fat German who was often the butt of the joke, and Alexander Pop, an African American handyman whose face, as described by Winfield, "shone like a piece of polished ebony," and who spoke in a

Stepin Fetchit patois: "Yo' is a sight fo' soah eyes, 'dccd yo' is, boys . . . I can't tell yo' how much I'se missed yo'!"[32] Even among the otherwise charming work of Newell's *The Hole Book* is an illustration in which the errant bullet leaves a hole in a watermelon as an African American family reacts in shock, eyes wide, lips protruding. It was the kind of thoughtless ethnic typecasting that had been and would be the norm for generations—stereotypes that would find their way into some of Ted's early work as well.

•••

At four years old, Ted Geisel entered kindergarten at the Sumner Avenue School in thc fall of 1908. The nearly brand-new, brick-red building was a fifteen-minute walk away, a little more than half a mile from their home on Fairfield, and Ted was instructed to hold Marnie's hand tightly as they crossed the wide and sometimes busy Sumner Avenue. Beyond that, Ted had few memories of his elementary school years; by all indications, he was a typical if unexceptional student. His real interests lay outside the school's walls: playing with his toy soldiers on his front steps, engaging in ear-wiggling and pull-up contests out on the neighborhood Soccer Field (Ted, never the athlete, won at the former and lost at the latter), or eagerly reading the comics in the pages of the *Boston American* newspaper that his father brought home each evening.

Even when T.R. Geisel wasn't delivering the comics page, Ted was still fairly certain that his father was a wise and great man. Although T.R. would be expected to dole out any appropriate punishments—Nettie rarely raised her voice in anger—he was a level-headed man who imparted to his son both a sense of discipline and a foundational decency. While Ted would never be a good shot with a rifle or even fully undcrstand his father's obsession with marksmanship—he later said it was "an all-consuming hobby that . . . was silly and unproductive"—Ted came to appreciate the considerable discipline and commitment it took for his father to hone such an expertise. Ted remembered watching each morning as his father held his rifle steadily over his head for ten minutes, strengthening his arms and shoulders and thus ensuring the barrel of his rifle never faltered in the slightest when he aimed and shot. "He was an inspiration," Ted said warmly. "Whatever you do, he taught me, do it to perfection."[33] Decades later, even after he had become one of the most famous and successful writers in the world, Ted still hung one of his father's paper shooting targets in his office, with multiple bull's-eyes shot out of its center—a constant reminder to do the work necessary to achieve excellence, regardless of the task.

In 1909, when Ted was five years old, his father was appointed by Springfield mayor William Sanderson to fill a vacancy on the park board.[34] The board oversaw all public lands in the area, including the 500-acre Forest Park on the south side of Springfield, stretching away expansively from Sumner Avenue on its northern border. The park had been created in 1884 with land donated by several wealthy Springfielders, including Everett Barney—he of the clamp-on ice skate fortune—and had been developed by Frederick Law Olmsted, the visionary designer of New York's Central Park. Olmsted brought the same fashionable practicality to the Springfield project, installing plenty of shady walking paths and places to picnic, fish, ice-skate, and swim—Springfield, in fact, would boast one of the earliest public swimming pools.

But to both T. R. Geisel and his son, the best part of Forest Park was its zoo, a small and well-maintained facility in the park's north end, crammed with a large assortment of birds and animals, including alligators, monkeys, swans, lions, and even its own herd of elk.[35] For most of Ted's childhood, Sunday afternoons would be the best time of the week—for that was when T.R. would stand just inside the small foyer of the Geisel house, his hand on the knob of the carved Dutch front door, and call out, "Come on, son, let's go over to Forest Park and count the animals."[36]

It was likely he would never have to ask more than once. "[E]very Sunday I would go to the zoo with him and I'd come back home and try to draw the animals," said Ted.[37] Try as he might, he found that realistic drawings of animals just weren't his forte: eyes went wide, with arched eyebrows over them; knee joints appeared in the wrong places; tails ended up tufted. Even a change of media didn't matter. "I was always drawing with pencils, pens, crayons, or anything," said Ted. "And nearly always it was animals, goofy-looking ones. My mother overindulged me and seemed to be saying, 'Everything you do is great. Just go ahead and do it.'"[38]

But T.R., too, was supportive of his son's artistic efforts. "Ted always had a pencil in hand," T.R. said later, and recalled encouraging Ted to submit a few of his drawings to the instructors at an art correspondence course, who would evaluate the drawings for a small fee. "I got him to send one of his drawings and staked him the fifteen dollars [fee]," T.R. explained. "Yes, they said, he had talent—but heck, they were after the fifteen bucks, and they told that to everybody!"[39] Ted thought it had been worth the money. "As a matter of fact, it wasn't a bad investment," said Ted. "I think I picked up a lot of technical points that really helped get me started."[40]

T.R. also had a quiet sense of humor his son would come to appreciate. Ted would later love telling a story of spending a long day fishing with his father, without catching a thing. On their way home, T.R. stopped at Deegel's hatchery, which raised fish for local restaurants, and "bought the most beautiful mess of uncleaned trout you ever saw," recalled Ted. "When we got home, he showed them to the neighbors and got a reputation around there as one of the greatest trout fishermen in the world."[41] Thirty years later, Ted would open his book *McElligot's Pool*—the tale of a boy fishing in a tiny swimming hole—with a warm dedication to his father: "This book is dedicated to T. R. Geisel of Springfield, Mass., The World's Greatest Authority on Blackfish, Fiddler Crabs, and Deegel Trout."

Besides his expertise in store-bought trout, T.R. was also something of an aspiring inventor, regularly poking around in his basement workshop, where he worked on solving simple tasks with complicated-looking devices that would, to later eyes, appear . . . well, appropriately *Seussian*. Among the more practical was a biceps-strengthening machine, as well as a device that could be attached to the spigots of the beer barrels, with a snapping spring clip to shoo away flies. But Ted's favorite invention was the one his father called the Silk-Stocking-Back-Seam-Wrong-Detecting-Mirror, a complex apparatus for spot-checking the alignment of women's stockings. Ted's love of weird and clever contraptions, which did weird and clever things, would largely come from his early experiences in T. R. Geisel's workshop.

When he wasn't tailing along after his father in the workshop, Ted just plain loved listening to his father *talk*, whether he was dispensing advice or telling stories. Ted remembered the two of them lying on their backs in the field directly behind their house on the night of April 20, 1910, talking in hushed tones as they scanned the sky for Halley's Comet. Other times, they would take long walks together while T.R. entertained his son with stories of life in a brewery. T.R. would get considerable mileage out of a story about a local attorney he had hired to collect brewery debts in Northampton, Massachusetts: a modest and quiet young man named Calvin Coolidge. One day, on their way to visit a client, T.R. and Coolidge stopped in a saloon that sold two martinis for 25 cents. As T.R. quickly disposed of his two drinks, Coolidge slowly drank his first, then picked up his briefcase and informed the bartender, "I'll be back tomorrow for the other one."[42] T.R. always howled with laughter at the story, though perhaps some of Coolidge's famously silent demeanor had rubbed off on him as well. "You will never be sorry," T.R. told his son, "for anything you *never* said."[43]

One thing the two of them would never share was a love of shooting. When Ted was nine, T.R. tried one last time to interest his son in guns and marksmanship, taking him along to see Buffalo Bill's Wild West show when it stopped in Springfield in May 1911—advertised as "positively the last" tour of the showman's career, and guaranteeing the aging cowboy "positively appears at every performance!"[44] Ted was skeptical to begin with, but when inclement weather turned the event into a muddy, rain-soaked mess, Ted decided he was done once

and for all with "all that shooting."[45] Still, it wouldn't be the last time
T.R. would fail to convince his son to take an interest in an organized
sport or physical activity.

• • • •

Middle school at Forest Park School was just around the corner from
their house in Fairfield—there was no need to cross the busy Sumner
Avenue—but Ted had grown more interested in practical jokes than
practical knowledge.

By his own admission, Ted had become something of a rabble-
rouser and a smartass on Fairfield Street, but he thought in all fair-
ness that some of his colorfully named neighbors had it coming.
Living close by were the Bump and Haynes families, sanctimonious
teetotalers who annoyed even the mild-mannered T. R. Geisel. Much
kinder was their neighbor directly across the street, Maurice Sherman, editor of the *Springfield Union,* and down on the corner at number 90, the dentist Dr. Leonard Stebbins, whose surname was perhaps
Ted's favorite among his neighbors—second only to that of business-
man Norval Bacon, a name Ted would file away and use several times
in his career as a cartoonist.

If Ted had a nemesis among the adults on Fairfield, however, it was
probably Horace Clark, the humorless secretary of a packing case
company who lived at number 36, near the Soccer Field. It was Clark
who had thwarted Ted's effort to hang a kite string telephone line between Ted's window and that of his best friend, Bill King, who lived
next door to Clark—but their antagonistic relationship reached its
nadir on Halloween of 1912, when Ted and his friend Charles Napier
were playing pranks on neighbors up and down the street. That night,
as Ted was at Clark's parlor window "rattling a cricket"—a rapidly
spinning spool that vibrates loudly on a flat surface—Napier brazenly
urinated on Clark's front porch. Napier escaped unseen, but Ted—
whose faux cricket had the desired effect of startling Clark—was
nabbed when the annoyed Clark sped out the front door and collared

Ted at the side window. Even as he recounted the story sixty years later, Ted was still smarting at the injustice of the situation:

> I am afraid my father never believed me when for many years after I protested my innocence . . . Horace nabbed and blamed me for the nuisance that C.N. had committed at least half an hour before. He then dragged me to my house, rang the doorbell and told my father what I had not done to his porch, using, of course, the dignified sentence, "Theodor wetted my stoop."[46]

T.R.'s response to this talebearer was never recorded.

Ted's antics aside, T.R. was beginning to have his hands full with work. In 1914, Ted's recently widowed grandfather sold his business to the Springfield Breweries Company—the very same company he had sold his Highland Brewing Company to in 1898—and promptly retired. T.R. was promoted to manager at a salary of $100 per week—about $2,000 in today's dollars. The senior Geisel, meanwhile, took his money from the sale of the company and began investing in real estate, and found he was just as good at land as he had been at lager. Hotels were bought and sold, and the stables in Sumner Avenue in which Ted's grandfather had once kept his horses now held two Packards, carefully maintained and regularly polished by a private chauffeur.

Still, there were signs of distress on the horizon. On May 7, 1915, the English passenger ship *Lusitania* was torpedoed by a German U-boat and sank off the southern coast of Ireland, killing 1,198 people, including 128 Americans. Despite public outrage and amped-up cries for the United States to enter what was, at that moment, still a largely European conflict, President Woodrow Wilson refused to declare war. But as the United States and Germany eyed each other warily across the Atlantic, anti-German sentiment began to fester in many American communities—and Springfield was no exception. Ted began to hear himself and his family members referred to derisively as Huns, while classmates pointed him out nervously as "the German brewer's kid."[47]

The Geisels did their best to shrug it off—but it is probably no coincidence that the Geisels spent much of 1915 on extended vacations and road trips away from Springfield. That spring, T.R. and Nettie took the train west to San Francisco for a month-long visit to the Panama–Pacific International Exposition. Years later, Ted loved to tell a story of his father's adventures at the expo, reporting with excitement that T.R. had taken advantage of an exhibit that permitted fairgoers to make a free long-distance phone call—a very new phenomenon—to any city in the United States. As Ted told it, his father gleefully phoned Springfield mayor Frank Stacy, and even remembered their conversation had been reported in the newspaper under the large-type headline "Geisel Calls Mayor." Ted could even quote the story down to the letter.[48]

Unfortunately, Ted's enthusiasm for the story aside, there is little evidence the dramatic phone call actually happened—for one thing, no such newspaper story ever appeared. Years later, Ted's young narrator Marco in *And to Think That I Saw It on Mulberry Street* would be warned by his father to

"Stop telling such outlandish tales.
Stop turning minnows into whales."[49]

But for Ted himself, turning minnows into whales was all part of the fun. There would always be a bit of Marco, the teller of outlandish tales, in Theodor Seuss Geisel—and in Dr. Seuss.

• • • •

Ted spent much of that long summer of 1915 vacationing with his mother and sister in a beach house near the coast in Clinton, Connecticut. Ted loved clamming in the cold New England waters, and he and Marnie competed in endless tennis matches, a game Ted played well enough, but which Marnie—two years older and with a hard serve—almost always won. With the summer beach house excursions, and a grandfather who drove a gleaming Packard and lived at one of Springfield's most prestigious addresses, Ted was aware that the Geisels were among the town's more affluent families. Yet he was also aware that his family's German heritage meant they would never truly attain the social status of the long-established families like the Wessons.

Ted tried to put the best face on it. "Our fathers did get into some clubs, like the Elks," said Ted, "and they took us kids to Elks' clambakes where we ate lobsters and Quahog clams and corn-on-the-cob and our fathers drank beer until our mothers made them stop and we all came home on the trolley car singing and wildly happy."[50] But while Ted would accept the status quo, he would never be wildly happy about it. As a cartoonist, standing up to systemic injustice—whether it wore the face of racism, anti-environmentalism, or just plain meanness— would be a central theme in much of his best work.

For the most part, the Geisels' status would be elevated by genuine success. Business at Springfield Breweries continued to boom; the company was now moving more than half a million barrels annually across New England. T.R.'s new offices were in a building situated at Fort and Water Streets in the center of downtown,[51] with easy access to both the railroad and the river, and still easily reachable by streetcar. T.R. had been promoted quickly, moving from manager of the Liberty branch over to the larger Hampden branch. While Ted rarely expressed any interest in joining his father in the brewing business, he could be persuaded to take odd jobs from time to time—and in late 1916, he spent several weekends accompanying his father out to the frozen Springfield Breweries pond to oversee a team of French Canadian workers as they harvested ice.

On one of those cold weekend mornings, Ted watched as one of the workers suddenly fell through the ice, and joined his father and the work crew in the mad scramble to fish the man out. As the laborer was finally pulled to safety and draped with blankets, his hands went to his head in a panic. *"Mon chapeau! Mon chapeau!"* he exclaimed, and threw himself back into the frigid water to retrieve his missing hat. Ted loved this story, though he would shake his head in wonder that anyone would "risk his life for his hat."[52] Decades later, one of Ted's characters would similarly risk his life because of a hat.

And yet even as Springfield Breweries prospered, the nerves of brewers everywhere that winter were on edge about the increasingly vocal and active temperance movement; there was a very real concern that there might be a call for the all-out prohibition of the sale of any form of alcohol. Ted's father had followed stories in the *Springfield Republican* about the march on Washington by the Women's Christian Temperance Union and the Anti-Saloon League in 1913 with interest. While Woodrow Wilson had remained quiet on the issue of Prohibition during the 1916 election, the newly elected Congress leaned strongly in favor of a constitutional amendment prohibiting the sale of alcohol.

The debate erupted into the open on Fairfield Street, with the Geisels' Prohibition-minded neighbors, the Bumps and the Hayneses, now actively lobbying for a liquor ban. Ted remembered sitting at the top of the stairs listening to his father and Uncle Will as they drank whiskey in the first-floor living room, laughing and plotting revenge on the Bumps and the Hayneses by arranging to have one of the Springfield Breweries delivery wagons pull up in front of the teetotalers' homes to drop off several kegs. Both men would recant by the morning light of sobriety, but Ted sympathized with his father's feelings; he would never be entirely trustful of so-called moral crusaders who tried to impose their agendas on their fellow citizens.

Anti-German sentiment was also continuing to fracture communities around the country, further decaying with President Wilson's February 3, 1917 announcement that the United States would be severing diplomatic relations with Germany over that nation's continued use of U-boat warfare—a threat to the "freedom of the seas," said Wilson. The Geisels and Seusses and their German neighbors would curtail many of their public activities at the Turnverein or at the

Schützenverein riflery club, even as behind closed doors they would continue to dine on German food, drink German beer, and converse and sing loudly in the German language. Some evenings Ted's father and grandfather would retire to the front music room to listen to classical music or opera, playing the Victrola a bit too loudly. "You really should try to see a Wagnerian opera sometime," Ted recalled his grandfather telling his father, nearly shouting to be heard over the music. "That German music is not as bad as it sounds." It was a perhaps too-frank appraisal of the famous German composer that always made Ted laugh.[53]

Things would go from bad to worse on April 6, 1917, when the United States formally declared war on Germany. As a wave of nativism and xenophobia swept the country, all things German became taboo: Frankfurters became hot dogs. Hamburgers became liberty sandwiches. German-sounding street names were changed, and the town of Berlin, Michigan, would change its name to Marne. In a suburb of St. Louis, Missouri, a thirty-year-old German immigrant named Robert Prager was lynched.[54] Frightened, many recent immigrants—whether Irish, German, Italian—would try to emphasize their pride in their adopted country by assuming a hyphenated modifier, such as "German-American." Former president Theodore Roosevelt, sounding like many Americans at the time, was having none of it. "There is no room in this country for hyphenated Americanism," he had told a whooping Carnegie Hall crowd.[55]

The Geisels would experience some harassment during the war—they weren't just German but also brewers, pretty much playing to the stereotype. It was in this atmosphere of xenophobia that Ted began his freshman year of high school that fall, enrolling at Central High School on State Street, across from the Springfield Library. For Ted, the harassment would continue throughout his freshman year. "During the fever of World War I, when I was about fourteen, everyone was angry at the Germans," Ted said later. "I was not only known as the 'Kaiser,' but because of my father's job at the brewery, the 'Drunken Kaiser.' I sometimes fled home with coals bouncing off my head."[56]

The Geisels did their very best to demonstrate their American patriotism, with T.R. teaching marksmanship for the Massachusetts Volunteer Militia, while Ted, as a member of Boy Scout Troop 13, dutifully sold Liberty bonds to support the allied cause. The Liberty bond sale would in fact be the source of one of Ted's most traumatic childhood memories—even if it never really happened.

As Ted related the story, his grandfather—also feeling he had to prove his patriotism—had purchased a supply truck for Springfield's militia and, when he learned his grandson was selling Liberty bonds, made a point of purchasing $1,000 worth. Thanks largely to his grandfather's largesse, Ted's Boy Scout troop had the second-highest sales in the region—and Ted himself was among the top ten individual fundraisers. As such, he would be receiving a medal from Theodore Roosevelt when the former president came to Springfield on Wednesday, May 1, 1918, as part of his New England speaking tour to rally support for Liberty bonds.

"We all put on our Scout uniforms and marched to City Hall," Ted recalled, "and after Roosevelt had given a fiery speech, we lined up onstage to be decorated." With his family and thousands of denizens of Springfield watching, Ted stood at the end of a line of nine other boys, awaiting his medal. Colonel Roosevelt slowly made his way down the row, pinning medals on chests and shaking hands. "But somebody had made a mistake," said Ted, "and there were ten boys and only nine medals." And so when the colonel arrived at Ted at the end of the line, "Roosevelt had nothing to pin on me," Ted said, wincing at the memory. "He just stood there, nonplussed. Then a Scoutmaster ran up and said there had been a misunderstanding, and shoved me off the stage."[57] For the rest of his life, Ted would attribute his frequent bouts of stage fright and dread of "platform appearances" to Teddy Roosevelt and the missing medal.

While this is a good story, it's probably not entirely true. Over the years, Ted would continue to polish it, heightening the drama to make his embarrassment even more palpable. "I can still hear it now," Ted said in 1965 as he recounted the story to *The Saturday Evening Post*.

"Teddy Roosevelt looking around and asking, 'What is this little boy doing here?' And all those eyes from the audience staring right through me, the people whispering, 'Ted Geisel tried to get a medal and he didn't deserve it.' I can hear them saying, 'What's he *doing* there?'"[58]

Colonel Roosevelt was certainly in Springfield on May 1, at the invitation of the Hampden County Improvement League—and the following day the *Springfield Republican* ran a front-page photograph of him standing in the rain, speaking to the Boy Scouts on the steps of the auditorium. But there is no stage, no sign of a medal ceremony; Roosevelt, in a dark coat, simply stands on the steps, facing the crowd, while several Scouts are visible to his left.[59] According to the contemporaneous report of the events in the *Republican*, "[b]efore entering the hall, he [Roosevelt] delivered a short address to the scouts, thanking them for their service and congratulating them upon engaging in training that is the basis of sound citizenship in the future."[60] Still, while it remains unclear whether there was a medal ceremony that day—and whether it went awry in the manner described by Ted—it's obvious *something* happened that day that forever spooked Ted of public appearances. Perhaps, at age fourteen, Ted was simply terrified by the mere thought of appearing in public—and Roosevelt was incorporated into Ted's panic merely because of his proximity. To Ted, the details wouldn't matter much anyway; he had his story—and a good one—that would be related and dramatically retold countless times throughout his life, a minnow forever turned into a whale.

• • • •

When Ted entered Central High School in the fall of 1917, it was considered to be the school where the upwardly mobile sent their children to prepare them for college. For the Geisels, that certainly seemed to be the case for Marnie, who got great grades, struggling only with math, and excelling in French, German, and Latin. She would graduate in 1919 magna cum laude and go on to attend Smith College. For Ted, however, school was something to be endured, not mastered, though he later boasted of maintaining a B average "without working."[61] Like Marnie, he was baffled by math—even basic arithmetic would so frustrate him that for his entire life, he refused to even balance a checkbook—and while he enjoyed foreign languages, he loathed Latin so much that he preferred to simply skip the class altogether. He would make fun of it mercilessly in the pages of the school's student newspaper, the *Central Recorder*.

"[I]n high school you had to go out for some kind of activity," Ted said later. "I looked at these bruisers who were playing football and I decided to do something with a pencil. It worked and I enjoyed it."[62] For most of his high school years he would write—and draw a little—for the *Recorder*, serving as the newspaper's official "live wire" and then as boys' news editor.[63] Ted was never one to take his duties *too* seriously, however—and almost immediately he was making a name for himself among his classmates by writing short one-line jokes known as grinds. The dreaded Latin class drew Ted's fire early, serving as the butt of the joke for a one-liner about the newly enacted federal daylight saving time: "It'll be just our luck to be in Latin class when they turn back the clocks."[64]

He was also getting his first taste of writing clever rhyming verse for an audience, penning parodies of famous poems, most notably spoofing Walt Whitman's ode to Abraham Lincoln, "O Captain! My Captain!" which Ted—again training his eye on the despised Latin class—repurposed as "O Latin" ("O Latin! my Latin! that study hour is done").[65] His name was spelled wrong on the piece—they credited him as Theodore Geisel—but Ted would be off and running with one variation on his name after another over his four years, signing pieces as Ted Geisel, Theo S. Geisel, T. S. Geisel, T.S.G., and when the mood struck, as T. S. LeSieg. Ted wasn't the first Geisel to craft a pseudonym by spelling his surname backward; he had stolen the trick from his father, who had a weakness for playing the numbers—a bit of illegal gambling—and would sign his betting slips as "LeSieg" to avoid embarrassment in the event they were ever publicly discovered.

Ted would also submit several cartoons to the *Recorder* during his time at Central, some attributed to "Pete the Pessimist," and most of which are unremarkable. His earliest known cartoon—a joke about classmate "Frawncis" Blinn, who took six years to graduate—shows a bald and aged Blinn leaning over a cane, with a rolled-up paper helpfully labeled *diploma* tucked under his arm. It's a simple line drawing of the character in profile, with some crosshatched shading at Blinn's feet. Mostly, Ted seemed to be aping the styles he saw in the forgettable comic strips in the *Springfield Union*, such as Frederick Leipziger's gag-a-day *Doings of the Van Loons* and Charles Wellington's *That Son-In-Law of Pa's!*, both of which relied on easy jokes about henpecked, put-upon husbands.

His drawing would improve over the next three years, though Ted would have very little formal art instruction—he could recall taking only one art class in high school, and didn't remain in it long. As Ted remembered:

> [A]t one point during the class, I turned the painting I was working on upside down—I didn't know exactly what I was doing, but actually I was checking the balance: if something is wrong with the composition upside down, then something's wrong with it the other way. And the teacher said, "Theodor, real artists don't turn their paintings upside down." . . . I somehow felt I wouldn't learn much from that teacher, so I left the course.[66]

As his work evolved, Ted would continue to be more influenced by the comic pages than by formal instruction. A cartoon drawn during his senior year, for example, highlighting his class trip to

Washington, D.C., has an innovative layout that recalls Winsor McCay's *Little Nemo in Slumberland*, with hotel windows framing a central drawing of President Warren G. Harding shaking hands with Ted's classmates. The cartoon has some other nice moments. There's a decent caricature of Harding, a self-portrait of Ted playing ukulele in a hotel window, and a student feeding a dinosaur skeleton as a policeman rushes into the frame, billy club raised, ready to make an arrest. Figures have large, well-defined feet, and detailed clothing—polka-dotted trousers, pinstriped pants and dark waistcoats—reminiscent of George McManus's *Bringing Up Father*, which had debuted in 1913. "He was as good an artist then as he ever was," said classmate Walter Whittum—a statement that gave Ted either too much or too little credit.[67] Ted's high school art, while competent, would give very little indication of the unique and whimsical style to come.

• • • •

The hard stares and thrown coals of Ted's freshman year ended late in the autumn of his sophomore year, when World War I came to a close on November 11, 1918. Anti-German sentiment would, for the most part, fade in Springfield—and Ted, no longer lying low, would take a more active role in rabble-rousing, cheekily proposing in the pages of the *Recorder* that students unionize into a "Pupil's Union," on a platform of "extra pay for homework" and "[e]ntertainment, [such] as dancing and movies, in all study rooms."[68] And Ted *did* love the movies and movie stars. In the winter of 1917, he had read in a film magazine that Douglas Fairbanks, his favorite movie star, shaved naked every morning. Ted decided to take up the same habit, carefully scraping away with a razor in the cold bathroom in the house on Fairfield Street. "I almost froze to death," Ted said later. "[I] nicked myself with my father's razor, and lost faith in Douglas Fairbanks, who was doing all his naked shaving in sunny California."[69]

Ted's father, perhaps sensing that his son needed more physical activity than he would find as a reporter for the *Central Recorder*, insisted that Ted enroll in dance classes from Mr. McCarty in the opulent ballroom of the Hotel Kimball. Ted hated it from the start. He felt slightly embarrassed by the act of dancing; he was already tall and slightly gangly in high school, and would eventually top out at more than six feet. Worse, he hated wearing the dancing shoes that he lugged back and forth in a green flannel bag. Dancing was purely an obligation to his father, and Ted loathed every moment of it. He would soon quit attending classes.

But his father would keep trying. Next, Ted was enrolled in fencing at the Turnverein, where instructor Chris Neubauer subjected his young student to what Ted called "hour-long agonies." The course necessitated calisthenics and rope climbing—activities Ted openly detested—and he was mortified by the pink jersey Neubauer required him to wear. Ted would make it through seventeen classes before T.R. finally permitted his visibly exasperated son to stop attending classes altogether. Later, Neubauer—who informed T.R. that his son had "no pectoral muscles at all"[70]—recommended T.R. give his son a canoe so that he could row it to develop his upper body strength. T.R. complied, buying Ted an eighteen-foot canoe for his fifteenth birthday. Ted would do little more than push it onto the water at Watershops Pond and sit in it, never touching the oars.

On December 5, 1919, Ted's grandfather, Theodor Adolph Geisel, died at age seventy-nine, after a prolonged illness. While the eldest Geisel had been out of the brewing industry for years, he'd kept a close eye on the Prohibition debate, and had been astute enough to recognize that a constitutional day of reckoning was at hand. Following the passage in late 1919 of the Volstead Act, which defined "intoxicating liquors" that would be prohibited under federal law, T.R., too, had been trying to come up with solutions that might keep the Springfield Breweries company afloat in an age of temperance. He even went so far as to change the recipe of the company's Extra Tivoli Beer—which had won an international competition for its high quality—to give it a lower alcohol content that he hoped would bring it under the definition of "non-intoxicating liquors."

It wouldn't be enough. On January 17, 1920, Prohibition officially went into effect under the sledgehammer weight of the Eighteenth Amendment. For his efforts to keep Springfield Breweries solvent, T.R. was promoted to president of the company, occupying his new office the very week the sale of intoxicating liquors became illegal. That was it for Springfield Breweries. "My father was rather angry about that turn of events," Ted said, with considerable understatement.[71]

For weeks, T.R. sat in the Geisels' darkened living room, head in hand, muttering, "son of a bitch . . . son of a *bitch*." "[H]e became very cynical," said Ted, ". . . he didn't know what to do with himself."[72] For more than a year, T.R. would mourn the loss of the industry he had grown up in, dutifully reporting to work and sitting at his desk in his offices on Fort Street, even as the company was picked to pieces around him, its assets, such as they were, slowly liquidated.

Prohibition wasn't the only new component of societal upheaval in 1920. That summer saw the formal adoption of the Nineteenth Amendment, giving women the right to vote. Ted's views on feminism would evolve slowly. While he would go for cheap laughs about women in his college humor magazine and would later be criticized for the absence of female protagonists in his work, Ted quietly idealized women and craved their attention and acceptance. He would always consider himself publicly awkward and something of a wallflower, but during his high school years he exhibited a determined effort to land himself a serious girlfriend, serving on the school's social committee and prom committee and as assistant manager of the Friday-night dances. His first kiss, however, with classmate Libby Elsborg, would be something of a disappointment for both of them. "I don't know why I kissed Libby," Ted said, "and neither did she."[73] Much better was his first real crush, on a girl in his class named Thelma Lester, "whom I loved right down to the bottom of my boots,"[74] he said fondly.

And for a young man who would always swear his traumatic experience with Teddy Roosevelt and the missing medal had given him an aversion to appearing on stage, Ted was very involved in social activities, including those that required public speaking. He was an officer in the debate club—it was one of the clubs where he could see Thelma Lester—and the secretary of the student senate. By all accounts he performed ably in productions of *The Mikado* and *Twelfth Night*. In fact, in his final semester at Central, Ted would write and perform in a two-act minstrel show in the school auditorium, serving as the sole author of the show's opening one-act comedy called *Chicopee Surprised*. After an intermission, Ted performed in the minstrel show with the rest of his classmates, strumming a tenor banjo in a five-piece jazz band,[75] and even soloing—while made up in "blackface" common to minstrel shows of the era—on recent comedy novelty songs like "Sweet Marimba."[76]

Several years later, Central High School principal William C. Hill would describe Ted as "a young man of upright character and good ability":

> Ted comes of a good family with high ideals for the
> success of their children, and I have sometimes thought
> that it was this influence which kept his head from being
> too much turned by the popularity which his natural gifts
> of good fellowship and humor brought him . . . he has
> qualities of leadership which can be steadied and turned
> to serious purpose.[77]

For all his modest talk, Ted was well liked in high school by classmates and teachers alike. He was good looking—his dramatically lit yearbook photo in the 1921 *Pnalka* shows him with a far-off stare, with no touch of a smile, in a stiff white collar, looking very much a serious young man. This may have been a private joke, since it was his sense of humor that had made him one of the most popular boys in the school. Indeed, in one of the final issues of the *Recorder* that would appear during Ted's senior year, there was a description of the "ideal boy" at Central as having "Don Benson's grin, / Ralph Walsh's build, / Dayton Phillip's oratorical powers, / [and] Ted Geisel's wit."[78] His classmates voted him Class Artist and Class Wit, and next to his very serious yearbook photo, Ted had inserted as his benedictory quote: "Next comedy appeared with great applause."[79]

It was important both to T.R., who hadn't attended college, and to Nettie, who had given up a higher education to work in the family bakery, that their son go to college. For Ted, the only question was where. Like many students at Central High School, Ted had been very impressed with and strongly influenced by his English teacher, Edwin A. Smith, an outgoing twenty-three-year-old whom everyone, even the students, called by his nickname "Red." "[R]ather than being just an English teacher, [Smith] was one of the gang," said Ted, "—a real stimulating guy who was probably responsible for my starting to write."[80]

It was Smith, in fact, who had encouraged Ted to read the work of Hilaire Belloc, the French-born, English-raised poet who wrote outlandish and often violent books of verse for children, including 1896's *The Bad Child's Book of Beasts* and the 1907 satirical moral guide, *Cautionary Tales for Children*. Artist Basil Temple Blackwood often graphically illustrated Belloc's tales of comeuppance for bad children—one bit of verse ends with a boy being devoured by a lion, leaving behind only his wide-eyed head—but Ted was more intrigued with Belloc's writing. The poet had a knack for silly names—Charles Augustus Fortescue, Godolphin Horne—and knew how to get a laugh out of an unexpected use of long, unusual words:

> The Microbe is so very small
> You cannot make him out at all,
> But many sanguine people hope
> To see him through a microscope.[81]

Ted would remain a lifelong fan and admirer, and he had Red Smith to thank for introducing him to Belloc's unique voice—a voice that would shape his own verse. Smith was also a graduate of Dartmouth College in Hanover, New Hampshire—and Ted also fondly recalled that Smith's family had run a candy store in White River Junction, Vermont. It was enough to help Ted, and others, make up their minds on where they wanted to go to school. "We all said, 'Let's go where Red Smith went,'" Ted recalled.

Encouraged by Smith, Ted and several classmates submitted their applications to Dartmouth. Decades later, in a bit of typical false modesty, Ted would downplay his ambitions to attend Dartmouth and Smith's role in it. It had all seemed so unintentional and random, he told *Dartmouth Alumni Magazine*. "I had a good friend at Springfield High who planned to attend Dartmouth, and so I became interested and finally applied," he said. "My friend never did go, but I wound up here anyway."[82]

CHAPTER 2

THE SLOB GENERATION

1921–1925

L ate in the summer of 1921, Ted Geisel waved goodbye to his family at Springfield's Union Station depot—an impressive structure with peaked gables, about half a block from T. R. Geisel's darkened offices on Fort Street—and boarded a train bound for Dartmouth College, more than 130 miles up the Connecticut River in Hanover, New Hampshire. For the next four hours, the train wove along both the eastern and western shores of the Connecticut before finally depositing Ted at White River Junction, Vermont. Here a taxi conveyed him and his suitcase the final five miles to the Dartmouth campus.

Sitting on more than 250 acres of waterfront wilderness in the little town of Hanover, Dartmouth had been quietly turning out reliable business leaders, researchers, and politicians since its founding in 1769. It was considered a small college—its enrollment when Ted attended there was around 1,800—but its students and alumni were, and are, devoted to it with a nearly religious passion. As perhaps its most famous alumnus, Daniel Webster, had explained in 1818, Dartmouth was "a small college, and yet there are those who love it."[1]

And yet to some Dartmouth administrators, the school had been growing too large, too quickly. As one Dartmouth historian later bemoaned, "it became very evident . . . that some step must be taken to control this inflow of students and to prevent the institution from being overwhelmed by the mere weight of numbers."[2] In response, president Ernest Martin Hopkins had implemented a policy of selective admissions, setting up an application process that permitted faculty to cultivate higher-achieving students and encouraged the admission of students who were neither wealthy nor the sons of Dartmouth alumni or were the first in their families to attend college.

Ted was in nearly all of the latter categories. On his Dartmouth application, he had listed his father's occupation as "Temporarily retired—Brewer," and while a bit of money from his grandfather's estate had made Ted's $250 tuition attainable, T.R.'s perilous employment status meant money would remain tight for the Geisels. On the academic side of things, while Ted's grades at Central weren't exceptional, his application had likely prevailed mostly on the strength of Red Smith's endorsement. Suitably inspired by Smith, Ted planned to major in English. As a freshman, then, he enrolled in English I, filling out the rest of his schedule with prerequisite courses in Latin, chemistry, citizenship, and—to his likely revulsion—physical education. With his fluency in German, he also was permitted to enroll in German 11 as a freshman, a class in which he would receive his only A of the academic year. It was the beginning of what would continue to be for the most part an unremarkable academic career. Ted's mind would usually be elsewhere.

For his freshman year, Ted took room 416 in Topliff Hall on East Wheelock Street, just down the street from the sprawling Dartmouth Green, the enormous park-like space at the heart of the campus. It was a decent-sized room, meant to house two students—but Ted would have the place, with its view overlooking the street, all to himself. Ted quickly made friends among his floor-mates, but as Pledge Week approached in early fall for Dartmouth's various fraternities, Ted was disappointed none of the Greek organizations attempted to recruit him—a slight he believed was due to anti-Semitism. "With my black hair and long nose, I was supposed to be Jewish," Ted said. "It took a year and a half before word got around that I wasn't."[3]

To his surprise, he was elected class treasurer, and was one of two freshmen selected as art editors for the annual *Green Book*—but it was a floor-mate at Topliff who would help Ted find his true passion. Across the hall from Ted's room was L. Bronner Jr., an upperclassman who worked as a staff member for *Jack-O-Lantern*, the Dartmouth humor magazine. With Bronner as his wingman, Ted began spending more and more time in the offices of *Jack-O-Lantern*—*Jacko,* as it was always called—in Robinson Hall, on the west side of Dartmouth Green. The snubbing by Dartmouth's fraternities was instantly forgotten; Ted knew where his people were, and what he wanted to do. "I think my interest in editing the Dartmouth humor magazine began . . . that Pledge Week."[4]

He was also cheered on by a seasoned but intense-looking *Jacko* staffer named Norman Maclean, an aspiring novelist from Montana and the son of a Presbyterian preacher. With Maclean's enthusiasm steeling his nerves, Ted began submitting cartoons to *Jacko*—and when the first issue of the fall semester was published in late October, Ted found, to his delight, that he had four cartoons featured inside. "That was an extension of my activities in high school," he said[5]—and his early cartoons are much like those he drew for the *Central Recorder*, trying to land the joke with pithy one-liners, such as a drawing of two homely young men in beanies and ties, over the caption "Two Arguments Against Matrimony." Some of Ted's better freshman-year cartoons take great delight in interpreting phrases or lingo literally, such as his drawing titled "The Pied Piper," showing a flute player getting shellacked by several thrown pies, or one of his favorites, "The Fatted Calf," a cartoon of a clearly overweight woman's balloon-like calves, her feet crammed into bulging high heels.[6] Ted would proudly sign his work as Ted G., Ted Geisel, T. Geisel, and at one point, Fish.

Most of Ted's freshman year, however, seems to have been devoted to working on the *Green Book*, as after making his debut in *Jacko* with four cartoons in October 1921, he would only have four more cartoons published for the rest of his freshman year. Doing homework and studying was a slog, too; while he liked the atmosphere and sturdy redstone facade of the Wilson Library, he much preferred frequenting a cheap local eatery called Scotty's, where his favorite menu item was a "toast side"—two pieces of toast served with a generous scoop of peanut butter on the side. "He was always raising hell and laughing a lot," recalled classmate Frederick Blodgett, "and didn't study worth a damn."[7] Blodgett's memory was accurate; Ted's grade-point average would slide from a 2.6 his first semester to a 2.4 the second. It would rarely tick much higher.

But grades were beside the point; Ted, like Daniel Webster, immediately warmed to Dartmouth itself, finding a sense of purpose and sense of belonging—though rarely inside a classroom. He enjoyed having his name in print in *Jacko*, worked hard at *Green Book*, and began making friendships he would keep and value for the rest of his life. For Ted, there would be no higher testament to a man's character than to learn he was a *Dartmouth man* (and they were all men—Dartmouth would not admit women until 1972, the last of the Ivy League schools to do so). As a Dartmouth man, then, Ted began to carry himself with a bit more flash and swagger, cheering enthusiastically at football games, adding bow ties to his wardrobe, and lounging on the Green—but there would still always be just a bit of reserve, a hint of that slightly nervous Boy Scout who'd been embarrassed by Teddy Roosevelt. "In person, Ted could appear to be somewhat reserved, but he was always sunny," classmate Radford Tanzer remembered. "You never heard him grump."[8]

Ted spent the summer after his freshman year back in Springfield, working odd jobs while his father dabbled at investments in real estate. While some investments paid off, most didn't—and T.R. cautioned his son that the Geisel family's finances were on shaky ground. Getting a college education and broadening one's prospects were critical in light of the new family economics. T.R., with an eye on his son's skidding grades, urged Ted to take his schooling more seriously.

Likely at his father's behest, then, Ted's course load for his sophomore year seems to reflect the intentions of a young man deliberately trying to apply himself. Besides the required English courses for his major and the relative safety of German classes—though despite his facility in the language, after his first year, Ted would never attain anything higher than a B—there were classes in zoology and botany, psychology and, in a deliberate nod to his father, two semesters of economics. But the work was hard, and Ted struggled to attain a C even in his English classes; the second semester of his sophomore year would represent the nadir of his academic career when a D in economics bottomed his GPA out at 2.0. That same semester, his botany professor, sensing his misery, promised to raise him one letter grade if Ted learned the Latin names of four trees that had been studied in class. With his ear for odd names, Ted complied and squeaked out a C.

No longer smarting from the freshman year slight that had kept him from pledging a fraternity, Ted became a member of Sigma Phi Epsilon, and would also pledge Pi Delta Epsilon, the honorary journalism fraternity. While he had lobbied hard to get into Sigma Phi Epsilon—and his work on *Jacko* had made him a desirable pledge— Ted, by his own admission, was a lackadaisical fraternity member and declined to live in the frat house at 11 Webster Avenue. "I wasn't a good brother," he admitted. "I didn't live in the frat house. [It] didn't change the way I thought."[9]

Instead, he found his real brotherhood over on the upper floor of Robinson Hall—the so-called Publications Row, where the offices of both *Jacko* and *The Dartmouth*, the daily student newspaper, were located. This was his true fraternity, a place where the staffs of *Jacko* and *The Dartmouth* mingled freely, critiquing one another's work and playing cards late into the evening. It was over the card table, in fact, that he got to know a fellow sophomore named Whitney Campbell from Oak Park, Illinois, who regularly wrote for *The Dartmouth*. A short fellow, Campbell was a good student, well read in history and the classics. And yet there was still something impish about Campbell that belied his otherwise serious demeanor—photos from the period show him with a wry smile on his face, as if he's perpetually trying to stifle a laugh. Ted liked him almost immediately.

Ted and "Whit" were quickly inseparable. Campbell even managed to get Ted to regularly engage in physical activity, taking him out on the golf course, where they would play for a nickel a hole. Other times, they'd wander the streets of Hanover at night, collecting empty bottles to trade in for soda pop at Scotty's, eat popcorn for dinner, then stay up all night talking in the offices in Publications Row or in Campbell's room. During one of these late-night bull sessions, Ted casually mentioned that he wanted to be editor of *Jacko* his senior year. "Good," Campbell replied. "I intend to become editor of *The Dartmouth*."[10] Both Ted and Whit would pursue their parallel goals with a similar fervor, though with different mindsets, reflective of their personalities. Whit, always the multitasker, could successfully juggle any number of obligations; for Ted, *Jacko*, and *Jacko* alone, would be the main priority.

Ted's sophomore year *Jacko* cartoons are a slight improvement over those from his freshman year, at least in terms of the illustrations themselves. There's a bolder use of blacks, the figures are less flat, and there was even an effort at some black-and-white watercoloring, though the effect reproduced so badly on *Jacko*'s paper that Ted never attempted it again.[11] The jokes, however, are still variations on wordplay—probably the best of which is "Tucked in Tight," in which Ted plays on *tight* as a slang word for *drunk*, drawing a disheveled gentleman passed out in a mussed-up bed, a bottle still tightly clutched in one hand. "All you had to do was say 'gin,'" Ted said later, "and everybody would laugh."[12]

There were also cannibal jokes, hunting jokes, and—in a nod to his miserable days under Chris Neubauer at the Turnverein—even a groaner of a fencing joke ("So you've taken up fencing?" asks one gentleman, to which the other replies, "Oh, I made a stab at it"). Still, the work was good enough that in January 1923, Norman Maclean offered Ted an official spot on *Jacko* as a member of the art staff. Ted's name would now officially appear in the magazine's masthead, and as far as Ted was concerned, he was on his way to the editor's chair.

Maclean may have thought so, too. At the beginning of Ted's junior year in the fall of 1923, Maclean—who'd been appointed as editor of *Jack-O-Lantern* for his senior year—almost immediately took Ted under his wing as his junior partner and heir apparent. "He found that I was a workhorse," Ted said later, "so we used to write practically the whole thing ourselves every month."[3] At this point, Ted practically lived on Publications Row—he had even given up his single room in Topliff Hall to live with Robert Sharp, a fellow junior and fellow Springfielder, in South Massachusetts Hall, directly across from Robinson Hall and the offices of *Jacko*.

Ted loved working with Maclean, and the two of them developed what Ted admitted was a "rather peculiar" method of writing together. "Hunched behind his typewriter, he would bang out a line of words," recalled Ted. "Sometimes he'd tell me what he'd written, sometimes not. But then he'd always say, 'The next line's yours.' And always, I'd supply it." It could sometimes make for "rough reading," Ted admitted, "but it was great sport writing."[4] More and more, however, Ted was writing alone, as Maclean seemed to always be at work on a novel—"and the further he got with his novel," said Ted, "the less time he had for his *Jack-O-Lantern*. So pretty soon I was essentially writing the whole thing myself."[5] While Maclean would later become an acclaimed writer best known for his 1976 novella *A River Runs Through It*, Ted was never sure exactly what Maclean was working on in the winter of 1923; the evening Maclean finished his book, he and Ted were out celebrating when Maclean's boardinghouse burned to the ground, taking the novel with it. "I don't think he ever rewrote it," Ted said.[6]

Ted's art was continuing to slowly evolve. His human figures were still awkward, with big feet and rubbery limbs aped from the comic pages, with no real distinctive style—but in the November 1923 issue of *Jacko* came a piece written and illustrated by Ted that looked like nothing he had done before: a one pager called "Who's Who in Bo-Bo," featuring descriptions and drawings of "Bo-Bobians," which can fairly be called the earliest ancestors of Seussian menageries to come. There's a grinning plaid-patterned cowlike creature with a sagging udder captioned *The Heumkia*—Ted's ear for odd names isn't yet as finely tuned as it would become—which Ted calls "the moron of the animal kingdom," and a wide-eyed seallike creature wearing a bow tie, identified as *The Dinglebläder*. But perhaps most "Seussian," at least for the moment, was an ostrichlike creature termed *The Panfh*, wearing red cleats and ribbons at the knees and staring intently at the reader with enormous, penetrating eyes.

The Bo-Bobians were crudely drawn, but there is no mistaking some of the elements that would make their way into Ted's later distinctive style; there are wide eyes and knowing grins—and rather than hooves, the Heumkia appears to be wearing footed pajamas, with one foot casually cocked over the other, while the Panfh's legs resemble tightly wound coils.[17] Looking back, Ted appreciated that he was simply learning by doing. "I began to get it through my skull that words and pictures were yin and yang," he said later. "I began thinking that words and pictures, married, might possibly produce a progeny more interesting than either parent . . . [though a]t Dartmouth, I couldn't even get them engaged."[18]

But Ted's writing was getting better, and funnier, too. Ted was the instigator, for instance, behind the exploits of a group of recurring characters with the surnames Zylsch and Zimkowitz—much more Seussian-sounding names than Panfh and Heumkia. In one particularly inspired piece, Ted created a box score for the annual baseball game between the East Lebanon Zimkowitzes and the West Lebanon Zimkowitzes, in which all the names in the lineup and in the game stats are Zimkowitz ("Home run—Zimkowitz, 2 base hits—Zimkowitz"). The final score is given as "Zimkowitz 14—Zimkowitz 10." In a later issue, there would appear a wedding announcement in which a Zimkowitz married a Zylsch, while later, in a full-page article on winter sports gear, an Otto Zimkowitz loudly checks in to give his opinion on the best brand of skis.[19]

Ted attributed his improved writing to the influence of a relatively new English professor at Dartmouth, W. Benfield "Ben" Pressey, a Harvard-educated thirty-year-old who taught an advanced writing course. "He was very kind and encouraging," Ted said of Pressey, "my big inspiration."[20] Pressey wanted his students writing accessible, rather than academic, prose, an attitude Ted found refreshing. "I don't think much of creative writing courses, because I think it is almost impossible to teach anyone how to write," Ted said, "but Ben Pressey's course did help me."[21]

He also liked Pressey's more informal approach to teaching. Instead of sitting for hours in the classroom, Pressey took to hosting seminars in his own home, where students were encouraged to read their work aloud as Pressey's "very beautiful" wife served steaming mugs of cocoa. Ted thought most of the writing produced by him and his classmates was "trash," but appreciated that Pressey "seemed to like the stuff I wrote." At one point, he and Pressey engaged in a good-natured but heated debate in which Ted argued that great writing was more about style than subject matter. To prove his point—that good writing could transcend even the most mundane of subjects—Ted wrote a book review of the Boston & Maine Railroad timetable that treated its various schedule changes and service announcements like serious literature:

> The only other bad feature of the book is found in
> Chapter 14, "Springfield, Greenfield and White River."
> This is well written, to be sure, but horribly slow in
> moving, especially from Brattleboro on. Obviously, this is
> directly due to the poor motivation of the engineer's
> character, though the author lays the blame to a "big
> washout down the line."[22]

"Nobody in the class thought it was funny," recalled Ted, "except Ben and me."[23]

Pressey did have a good sense of humor and admired Ted's quickness with a joke. Over cocoa one night, Pressey asked his class if any of them had read a play called *The Yoke*. "Ah, the triumph of the egg," muttered Ted[24]—a pun Pressey could appreciate, and Ted basked in the approval of his mentor. Pressey, said Ted warmly, "was important to me."[25]

It didn't take long for Ted to change his mind about the merits of style over substance. On December 8, 1923, the famed orator and anti-evolutionist William Jennings Bryan spoke at Webster Hall to deliver a fiery rebuke of Dartmouth's mandatory freshman course on evolution. Like many of his fellow students, Ted found Bryan and his rhetoric spellbinding—"one couldn't hold back a swelling admiration for [Bryan's] compelling powers," wrote the student editors at *The Dartmouth*.[26] And yet Bryan's passion never persuaded; he seemed to Ted to be all flash and no substance. "Nothing but oratory,"[27] sniffed *The Dartmouth*, and Ted agreed. Ted felt so strongly that Bryan had failed to make his case, in fact, that when the captain of Dartmouth's track team casually mentioned to Ted that he thought Bryan had been right, an offended Ted vowed never to "look at any track event" ever again.[28]

Despite his fondness for Pressey, Ted would still only manage to attain a C and a B in Pressey's writing class over its two semesters. Still, his grades had improved somewhat, to the likely relief of T. R. Geisel: on the strength of an A in Sociology I—and one of his half-hearted but regular Bs in German—Ted's GPA crept up to 2.8 for the first semester of his junior year, the highest GPA he would attain at Dartmouth. His other English class for his junior year was a course in comparative literature—covering English literature in the first semester, German in the second—taught by William K. Stewart, a well-traveled scholar who regaled his students with stories of his adventures in Europe. Ted would end up with a B in Stewart's classes for each of the two semesters, keeping his GPA holding at 2.6.

••••

On May 15, 1924, Ted was appointed editor in chief of *Jack-O-Lantern* for his upcoming senior year—and at the same time, just as they had vowed two years earlier, Whit Campbell was appointed editor in chief of *The Dartmouth*. Ted had worked hard to get there; his work in *Jacko* had gotten consistent laughs, and both he and his art were recognized around the campus. He had earned the editor's chair—and yet he also knew he could thank Norman Maclean for his support and endorsement. "My big desire . . . was to run that magazine," said Ted later. "If Mac hadn't picked me, my whole life would have been a failure."[29] The final issue of Ted's junior year welcomed him into the editor's chair with a notice hailing him as the writer "who has been responsible all year for the atrocity of the Zimkowitz family and who has used *Jacko* for three years as a publicity agency for certain lady friends."[30]

Ted spent that summer back home in Springfield, doing odd jobs—mostly washing bottles at the newly opened Wawbeek Spring Water plant, whose ginger ales and root beers had replaced the more potent ales and beers that had once rolled out of the warehouses of the Springfield Breweries—and counting down the days until he could return to Dartmouth and slide back into his *Jacko* editor's chair. His sister, Marnie, was home as well, a master's degree from the University of Wisconsin firmly in hand, and preparing to pursue a doctorate at Radcliffe in the fall.

Meanwhile, T.R., still in search of full-time employment, turned a short-turnaround real estate investment into a stunning $30,000 profit—about $400,000 in today's money. "Luck entered into it somewhere," Ted snickered, though T.R. always insisted it had been "clever business management."[31] Whether due to providence or proficiency, the windfall was substantial enough to finally give the Geisels some much-needed financial peace of mind.

On his return to Dartmouth for his senior year, Ted chose once more to live with Robert Sharp, this time in new quarters at the Randall Club, an elegant two-story boardinghouse at 13 West Wheelock. To his delight, he'd been elected as a member of Casque & Gauntlet, Dartmouth's highly selective senior honor society—and while he wouldn't live at the organization's Federalist-style brick house on Main Street, Whit Campbell did, which meant Ted spent nearly as much time at the Casque & Gauntlet as he did at the Randall Club.

But Ted's real headquarters for the year would, as always, be the

Jacko offices in Publications Row. Here, Ted ruled over his pages with a mock seriousness, laying down edicts prohibiting his staff from writing any jokes that would "ridicule the incoming freshmen"—at least in the first issue—and writing pithy editorials, including a long piece on the upcoming 1924 presidential election where he urged his classmates to "Vote for Somebody":

It is not that JACKO is interested in who shall be President. What he desires is that one vote for a man about whom he really knows something. JACKO has little desire to vote for a man like Mr. Coolidge, a man whose method of governing approximates absent treatment in its most abstract form.

But to get down to the more serious half of our editorial, JACKO certainly hopes that Dartmouth wins all of its games by enormous scores, don't you?[32]

Apart from targeting freshmen, Ted and his *Jacko* staff also found they could get easy laughs at the expense of women. Misogynistic jokes were a mainstay of college humor and would continue to be for generations to come, and *Jacko* was no exception. Even as early as his freshman year, Ted had indulged in the kind of randy humor typical of the era. One of his cartoons from February 1922 shows an attractive woman standing before a balding hotel desk clerk who eyes her lecherously, a cigarette burning in his mouth. "O, clerk," says the woman, "there's something the matter with the keyhole in the door to my room." "That so?" responds the clerk. "I'll look into that tonight." (The same page also featured a cartoon by a different artist, in which a woman exclaims, "I've got an idea!" to which her male colleague replies, "Treat it carefully. It's in a strange place.")[33] In one of Ted's first chatty pieces as editor in chief, he took considerable glee in relating a story of a group of college-age Springfield men mercilessly teasing teenage girls on a train. "For what is more pleasant," Ted wrote, "than to see five husky college men make some silly girls realize how insignificant and helpless they are?"[34]

It was partly an act—the swagger of a young man fancying himself as a swashbuckling, rebellious leader of the counterculture, staring down the elites and the prigs of the status quo. "As a sworn enemy of Culture," wrote Ted, "*Jacko* from his grimy office viewed with displeasure the spread of Courtesy, Good Manners and Respect for Women." It was also an extension of the "nagging wife and henpecked husband" cartoons Ted had read on the comics page, as well as the often jarring misogynistic humor that would later pervade the movie work of comedians like the Marx Brothers—who in 1924 were already honing their act on the New York City stage—and W. C. Fields. But that context still doesn't make it any easier to read—and even Ted cringed as he reconsidered his work in *Jacko* five decades later. "You have to look at these things in the perspective of 50 years ago," he said in 1976. "These things may have been considered funny then . . . but today I sort of wonder. The best I can say about the *Jacko* of this era is that they were doing just as badly on the [rival college humor magazines] *Harvard Lampoon*, the *Yale Record*, and the Columbia *Jester*."[35] Still, it's a bad look for Ted—and it wouldn't be the last time he'd be asked to reexamine the portrayal of women in his work.

••••

Besides his perch atop the masthead of *Jacko*, Ted also was elected to the editorial staff of *The Dartmouth*, a position he likely accepted mostly so he could have an official excuse to goof around with Whit Campbell. The two enjoyed their roles as publishing magnates, sharing offices across the hall from each other on Publications Row, where they cheated each other at cards all night while waiting for Whit's daily issue of *The Dartmouth* to go to press. Ted also relished the opportunity to leap in and help Whit out when "one of Whit's news stories turned sour"; he thrived when the deadline clock was ticking. "We'd put our royal-straight flushes face down on the table, rewrite the story together, and then pick up our royal-straight flushes again, and raise each other as much as a quarter," said Ted. "This did little to affect the history of journalism in America. But it did cement the strongest personal friendship I made at Dartmouth."[36]

Outside of their offices in Robinson Hall, Ted and Whit were regulars at the Dartmouth football games, bracing against the New Hampshire cold to cheer on their team at their newly completed Memorial Field facility. It was easy to be a fan; Dartmouth had gone 8–1 during Ted's junior year, led by its tough-playing senior captain Cyril Aschenbach, the favorite player of Ted's father. Now, in Ted's senior year, they continued clobbering the competition, holding five teams scoreless during the season on their way to a 7–0–1 record. When Dartmouth took on archrival Harvard late in October 1924, Ted and Whit drove Whit's 1914 Ford 130 miles to Cambridge to watch Dartmouth squeak out a 6–0 win.

Afterwards, caught up in the fever, the rival editors put together a football game pitting the staffs of *Jacko* and *The Dartmouth* against each other. Reporting on the game, *The Dartmouth*—which won 13–7— noted that, "Geisel, playing a stellar game at left tackle, made a brilliant wrestle for the final play of the game. He dove for the fleet legs of Cliff Randall, quarterback for *The Dartmouth*, and found he had those of Sleepy Jones, his own art director."[37] Ted's athletic prowess had clearly not improved in his four years of college.

To his credit, Ted had hunkered down academically for his final year, loading up on the English courses he needed to complete his degree, including classes in Romantic and Modern English poetry, nineteenth- and twentieth-century prose, and—his favorite—seminars in writing and criticism, taught by the flamboyant professor David Lambuth. Lambuth was nothing short of a character; he drove a gigantic cream-colored Packard, which he steered across campus while wearing a matching jacket with a flaming red lining. As he lectured, he would slowly fill the classroom with cigar smoke—and Ted found him intriguing and exotic, even as he struggled somewhat with Lambuth's seminar. "Ted was an average student," recalled roommate Robert Sharp. "I wouldn't say that he was studious—not enough to get into the Phi Beta Kappa—but his grades were always good."[38]

But it was still *Jacko* that mattered the most—and when Ted wasn't writing snarky editorial copy, his cartoons were now featured regularly in *Jacko*. It was his drawing of the pumpkin-headed *Jacko* mascot that usually appeared at the top of each issue's front page, and his art was used in everything from house ads to column filler. There were more weird animals showing up in his art as well. A November 1924 cartoon with the caption "Why is it when one sees animals like this one never has a gun along?" shows a winged goat—Ted loved drawing cows and goats—a two-legged elephant wearing dress shoes, and a doglike creature with three catlike animals stacked up on its back.

Ted was signing his work as Ted LeSieg, T.G., Geisel, or just plain Ted—and sometimes his work appeared without any signature at all, perhaps because he was concerned that it might seem he was inserting his own cartoons simply because he was the magazine's editor. One of his best *Jacko* jokes, in fact—a cartoon of a well-dressed young man eyeing two boys playing marbles, with the caption "Mr. John Keats sees the Elgin Marbles for the first time"—went completely unsigned. By March 1925, he was signing his work with completely new pseudonyms, often using his aliases to enhance the underlying joke, such as a drawing of an amorous, frolicking cow with the signature *L. Burbank,* after Luther Burbank, a botanist known for crossbreeding. Ted had apparently learned *something* in his botany class.[39]

It was likely on the strength of his work in *Jacko* that Ted was voted Class Wit by his senior Dartmouth classmates. "He made a point of looking at the humorous side of things," said Sharp, "and while it's hard to say offhand how much other people enjoyed his witticisms, he certainly had a lot of friends and was good company."[40]

On the other hand, his fellow Casque & Gauntlet members would unanimously vote him Least Likely to Succeed. "He never seemed serious about anything,"[41] said classmate Frederick Blodgett, though Kenneth Montgomery, another Casque member, thought that was all part of Ted's charm. "He was not gregarious in the sense of hail-fellow-well-met; there was no sense of self-importance about him," said Montgomery. "But when he walked into a room it was like a magician's act . . . Everything became brighter, happier, funnier. And he didn't try. Everything Ted did seemed to be a surprise, even to him."[42]

The fun would come to an end on Saturday, April 11, 1925.

That evening—the night before Easter—Ted was hosting a party in his room at the Randall Club for a group of about ten friends, including Curtis Abel, the business manager of *The Dartmouth*. As the evening wore on, a pint of bootleg gin appeared—whether it was Ted's, no one would ever say—and the party grew louder and more uproarious. As the evening reached its crescendo, Ted and Curtis Abel urinated onto the tin roof outside Ted's window—a distinctive sound that caught the attention of "Pa" Randall, proprietor of the Randall Club, who angrily called the chief of police.

Ted would always decry the entire affair as a bum rap. He would forever claim that no one at the party was drunk—"we had a pint of gin for ten people, so that proves nobody was *really* drinking," he said—and would swear that he and Abel had merely discharged the contents of a seltzer bottle onto Randall's roof. Pa Randall, he suggested, simply "hated merriment."[43] Regardless, Ted and his fellow partiers were hauled before Dean Craven Laycock, who put the entire crew on probation and ordered them each to write contrite letters to their parents. Ted's father was mortified. "While I do not object to your taking a drink," he wrote back to his son, "I do object to your taking one in Hanover, while in college, if the rules of the college do not permit it." He urged Ted to quietly accept whatever punishment Dean Laycock might dole out. "Abide by the decision of the authorities . . . and . . . serve your full sentence conscientiously. While . . . you are soon to graduate, make an attempt in the next few weeks to eradicate this blot from your good record."[44]

Ted didn't like it. "We were all put on probation for defying the laws of Prohibition, and especially on Easter Evening," he groused.

Likely because the party was in his room, the terms of Ted's probation were even more severe than those of his classmates—and Laycock's final added penalty hurt the most. Effective April 19, 1925—the
day his probation went into effect—Ted would no longer be permitted
to serve as editor of *Jacko*. While his name would remain at the top of
the letterhead until a new editor was selected at the end of the month,
Ted was prohibited from including any of his work in the final two
issues of his senior year.

Ted took it hard and personally. It was a generational bias, he
insisted—those in charge just didn't understand the young men of his
era, raised during a world war and coming of age during Prohibition.
Through no real fault of their own, he insisted, he and his classmates
were considered a "slob generation." "I came up through the Roaring
Twenties, when everybody had a hip flask, went to football games and
got drunk in the afternoons," Ted said later. "Adults despised us. We
were considered a lost generation of fools."[45] Whit Campbell, writing
in the pages of *The Dartmouth*, was less inclined to give his own generation the benefit of the doubt. In an editorial titled "This Generation of Ours" that appeared two days before Ted's drinking incident,
Campbell and his editorial team were scathing in their assessment of
themselves and their classmates:

> This generation of ours has lost humility. We do not
> recognize our own insignificance. We take the present as
> ours, instead of preparing for our heritage of the future.
> We assume the superman demeanor, to veil callow minds
> beneath.
>
> [. . .]
>
> This generation of ours is cowardly. We do not face life
> with courage, but try to escape. We flutter under the

illusion of forgetting. We dodge the questions of life. We
do not play square, because we are afraid to stake
ourselves against life.

In the midst of both this personal and generational existential crisis, the April issue of *Jacko*—which had gone to press a few days before Ted's party at the Randall Club—arrived on newsstands across Hanover. Ted had several cartoons inside, all signed with brand-new pseudonyms. A large drawing of a couple leering at each other over the back of an equally lecherous-looking milk cow was signed *L. Pasteur*, the chemist responsible for the pasteurization of milk. A prison joke appeared with the signature *Thos. Mott Osborne*, a nod to the noted prison reformer of the same name, while a drawing accompanying an "Unpublished Adventure of Baron Munchausen" is signed *D. G. Rossetti*, after the British painter and founder of the Pre-Raphaelite Brotherhood.

But by far the most noteworthy cartoon appeared on page 24 of the April issue, with the caption *"Financial Note:* Goat Milk Is Higher Than Ever." Here Ted drew yet another of his goats—this one with curling antlers and a wide-eyed stare—standing on a mountaintop helpfully labeled "Alps," with its back legs up on an outcropping, thus raising its udders that much higher. It's a fairly decent joke—but more important is the pseudonymous signature in the cartoon's bottom right corner: *T. Seuss*. It was the first time Ted had ever used his full middle name as part of his alias; ten pages later, under a cartoon of a couple riding side by side on horseback, the signature is simply *Seuss*.

In the years and decades following Ted's suspension from the pages of *Jacko*, Ted, and others, would perpetuate the myth that he had adopted several pseudonyms—most notably Seuss—as a way to escape Dean Laycock's penalty on a technicality: if *Ted Geisel* wasn't allowed to have work in *Jacko*, the reasoning went, then *Seuss* and others would. "To what extent this corny subterfuge fooled the dean,

I never found out," Ted said later. "But that's how 'Seuss' first came to be used as my signature. The 'Dr.' was added later on."[46] It's another one of Ted's really good stories that's also entirely untrue. Ted had been submitting cartoons to *Jacko* under various pseudonyms—Fish, L. Burbank, Thos. Mott Osborne, and even T. Seuss—*before* Laycock's formal directive, not because of it.

In fact, it appears that Ted's *real* strategy to avoid the dean's penalty was to publish his work in *Jacko* with no credit at all; the next issue would feature several uncredited short written pieces and at least one unsigned cartoon. It was only after learning of *this* particular workaround that the newly elected editor—C. H. Frankenberg, Class of 1926—was instructed not to permit *any* unsigned work into the final issue. Ted's *Jacko* days were over. But Dr. Seuss—at least in his most primordial form—had been spawned in its pages.

• • • •

On June 23, 1925, Ted graduated from Dartmouth, finishing his academic career with a 2.454 GPA, and ranked 133rd out of 387 students. Unlike many of his classmates, Ted wasn't entirely certain what to do next. Whit Campbell had been accepted to Harvard Law School, on his way to what would be a long and successful career in corporate law, while roommate Robert Sharp was off to graduate school to study English, the beginning of a professorial track that would make him the chair of the English Department at Wheaton College. Unlike some of his classmates, Ted had no family business to return to and wasn't sure his English degree would be good for much of anything, calling it "a mistake" that taught "the mechanics of getting water out of a well that may not exist."[47] With a shrug, then, he decided to head for graduate school to get his doctorate in English, with vague ambitions of becoming an English professor.

But not just any graduate school. Back in February, Ted had decided to apply for the prestigious Campbell Fellowship in English Literature, which sent its recipient to England to study at Oxford

University. As part of the application, Ted pried letters of support out of several professors—but the accolades didn't exactly come thundering in. "I have little to say," wrote Professor Hewette Joyce matter-of-factly. "He was a student of mine . . . and a rather good one, though by no means exceptional. He is bright and has a ready wit, is personally attractive and, I think, a hard worker, but more than that I cannot say."[48] Ben Pressey's endorsement was more encouraging, if unenthusiastic. "I have great admiration for his cleverness, the quickness and shrewdness of his mind," wrote Pressey. "He is not profound, but he makes the fullest possible use of the abilities he has, which are not inconsiderable."[49] Better was the letter he received from Maurice Sherman, editor of the *Springfield Union*, who still lived across the street from the Geisels. Ted, he wrote, "is in every sense a fine type of young man, industrious and alert, both mentally and physically . . . As to his personal character and sense of responsibility, I can speak in the highest terms."[50]

Ted informed his father of his plans to apply for the Campbell Fellowship, caging the information in vaguely optimistic language that convinced T.R. his son had already won the prize. According to Ted, his father ran across the street to inform Maurice Sherman of the good news—and Sherman, "being a staunch Dartmouth man," announced the news in the *Union* the next day. Unfortunately, the current holder of the Campbell Fellowship had opted to remain at Oxford for another year and had been granted an extension—and thus Ted's application, along with any others, was shelved. "So my father," said Ted, "to save face with Maurice Sherman and others, had to dig up the money to send me to Oxford anyway"[51]—or as T.R. Geisel later explained, "I had to send him to Oxford just to keep the story accurate!"[52]

Maurice Sherman was also kind enough to provide Ted with a bit of employment during his summer break, offering him the opportunity to exercise his newly earned English degree before leaving for Oxford. In this case, Sherman hired Ted to step in for vacationing contributor R.P.M., who regularly wrote a breezy column titled On the Firing Line. Ted's professional debut was announced on July 6, 1925, as R.P.M.

informed his readers he was leaving them "to the tender mercy of a substitute while we frolic through two weeks of vacation."[53]

Ted spent the next two weeks making pithy observations about politics, social mores, and national stories like the Scopes Trial, pitting William Jennings Bryan—whom Ted had already skewered in *Jacko*—against Clarence Darrow in a legal battle over the teaching of evolution in public school. Some jokes landed better than others— one of the best described the football team at a "rigidly classical"[54] university as calling its plays in Roman numerals—but in his first real appearance as a professional journalist, Ted comported himself well, providing reliably entertaining copy, delivered on time.

With the return of R.P.M., however, Ted's days at the *Union* were numbered; he would submit a final piece, a theater review, for publication on July 26. Then he began to pack his bags and readied himself for the trip to England and Oxford, where he was certain he'd acquire the advanced degree he needed to become an English professor. Dr. Geisel, he thought, had a good ring to it.

CHAPTER 3

STRANGE BEASTS

1925–1926

n Monday, August 24, 1925, Ted sailed from Boston on the ship *Cedric*, bound for Liverpool. His father had booked him into first class for the weeklong trip, and Ted was pleased to put down on the ship's manifest that his final destination was "Lincoln College, Oxford." On his arrival in Liverpool on August 31, Ted took the train 170 miles southeast to Oxford, then caught one of the black Morris Cowley taxicabs to the large wooden door marking the entrance to Lincoln College on Turl Street.

Established in 1427, Lincoln was Oxford's ninth oldest college, founded by Richard Fleming, bishop of Lincoln, to train theology students in the skills needed to contest what he regarded as the heretical teachings of the philosopher and priest John Wycliffe—and by the time Geisel arrived in 1925, one of its most famous graduates was John Wesley, the founder of Methodism. It was also one of the smaller and poorer of the Oxford colleges, with fewer children from well-to-do or titled English families—but that also meant that its stone buildings hadn't been renovated or updated in decades or even centuries, giving Geisel a feeling he was stepping back in time to the eras of Shakespeare, Sir Philip Sidney, or John Dryden. Even his room, No. 11, seemed appropriately medieval: a large square space in the rear of the college, with a stone fireplace and three windows overlooking adjacent Brasenose College. For a young man with ambitions of becoming a college English professor, it seemed an ideal atmosphere in which to immerse oneself.

Unfortunately, it didn't take Ted long to realize he was in over his head. As a mediocre student who had struggled to attain a C in a general English seminar at Dartmouth, a deep drill into Germanic philology at Oxford—even if taught by the brilliant new professor J.R.R. Tolkien—was bound to be a struggle.[1] He quickly sought out tutoring, and was paired with seventy-two-year-old Alexander Carlyle, the nephew of the Scottish essayist Thomas Carlyle. "I was surprised to see him alive. He was surprised to see me in any form," Geisel said later. "He was the oldest man I've ever seen riding a bicycle. I was the only man he'd ever seen who never should have come to Oxford."[2] Still, Geisel respected Carlyle's brilliance and dutifully wrote essay after essay for the aged scholar as part of his studies, reading them aloud for Carlyle to critique. "He realized I was getting stultified in English schools," said Ted. "I was bogged down with old High German and Gothic and stuff of that sort, in which I have no interest whatsoever—and I don't think anybody really should."[3]

Unlike many of his classmates, Geisel wasn't the kind to lounge in the grassy quad discussing the poetry of Wordsworth—such conversations, he thought, were pretentious and slightly silly. Nor did he sit in the Junior Common Room sipping tea while thumbing through the pages of the erotic French magazine *La Vie Parisienne*, which students had cheekily subscribed to, using Lincoln College as its delivery address. Instead, he preferred getting outside the walls of the college to have tea and anchovy toast at Fuller's tea shop, or to browse for hours either in Blackwell's bookstore or the reading rooms at the iconic Radcliffe Camera library in the middle of campus.

"My big problem at Oxford," Geisel said later, "was who to talk to."[4] Making friends could be tough. Although he was a graduate student, because he was in his first year at Oxford, he was consigned to sitting in the dining hall with the first-year students, most of them four years younger than him. Geisel looked instead for other Americans, eyeing the Rhodes Scholars—considered by the English to be the *good* Americans—for a sympathetic face. He finally found one in a graduate student from the University of Cincinnati named Joseph Sagmaster, a distinguished-looking young man with a prim mustache who shared his interests in newspapers and writing. Ted also attached himself to a fellow Dartmouth graduate, Donald Bartlett, who was a year older and attending nearby Exeter College.

Among his British classmates, Geisel tended to gravitate toward those who could transcend the traditionally stiff upper lip. He was already giving the English a wide berth anyway; he had quickly run afoul of Lincoln College's rector, the humorless John Arthur Ruskin Munro, who had invited Geisel—as he did all new students—for a personal meeting in his lodgings at No. 15. Ted knocked on the rector's door, and was informed Munro and his wife were at tea and was turned away. Mildly annoyed, Geisel returned several days later and was this time ushered into Munro's quarters, where the rector spent their entire conversation asking Geisel about his participation in English sports like rugby or cricket. Ted, never the athlete, could only confess to playing tennis with Bartlett, a response that did little to endear him to Munro. Geisel was, however, especially fond of a young Englishwoman he refers to in his correspondence only as Mirabel, an undergraduate who shared his affinity for practical jokes and horseplay. When a classmate of theirs got his hands on a movie camera, Ted and Mirabel took every opportunity to leap in front of it, hamming it up. During the spring boat races for Eights Week, the two of them donned fezzes and "staged a love affair"[5] at the river's edge, vamping in front of classmates and professors—including an unamused Munro, "who took the thing," said Geisel, "as an American insult against English respectability."[6] From here on, Munro would routinely and intentionally ignore Ted.

There were times, too, when Geisel really did seem determined to be equally as unforgiving of his English hosts. When he was invited to a social event in St. James's Square in London, hosted by the glamorous American-born viscountess Nancy Astor, Geisel turned down the invitation because the viscountess had addressed his invitation to "T.S. Giesel." "Misspelled," Ted wrote haughtily across the top of the card, "that's why I turned her down, the lout!"[7] Perhaps Geisel had an even more personal reason for turning down the viscountess: Astor was well known for spurning alcohol and had introduced legislation in Parliament to restrict its sale to minors. Ted would always have a policy of prohibition against prohibitionists.

Despite Carlyle's best efforts, Geisel's academic performance wasn't improving—and even Geisel confessed his interest in most of his English literature classes was flagging. "I started to draw pictures on my notes as that was practically the only thing that could keep me from going crazy," he admitted later. "They were merely the ideal wanderings of a mind numbed by too many semi-colons."[8] Indeed, the loose-leaf notebook Ted had taken with him to Oxford for recording notes offers a revealing and fascinating look into Ted's state of mind during his year at Oxford.

At first Geisel was clearly trying to perform his obligations as a student, taking relatively careful notes that fill most of the page, with only a few small doodles scribbled in the margins or used to highlight a particular word or phrase. On one page, the title "Bacon's Essays" is written on drapery; on another, notes on poetry in the Bible are decorated by two non-biblical figures, one of which is a gentleman in a top coat and top hat, peering off the page, a cigar clenched in his teeth. Several pages later, birds begin to show up, marching in the corner of the page—one carries a sign that reads BARTLETT—and gliding on the water. A section of notes on Sir Walter Raleigh features a drawing of Raleigh himself, with a thick mustache and beard, glaring fixedly back at the reader.

As the days pass, figures begin to take more prominence, pushing Geisel's minimal notes off the page, his handwriting crabbed and nearly unreadable. A page on the works of John Dryden features Geisel's carefully shaded self-portrait—labeled "Self Portrayte" in mock Middle English—drawn in profile, his eyebrows dark and nose comically long (the first effort, just above it, is darkly scribbled out). Notes on

Keats are filled with dogs in various positions—sitting, prancing, up on two legs—while notes on the Romantics are surrounded by various figures, heads in profile, busts, and a drawing of Joan of Arc.

Even Shakespeare couldn't hold Geisel's interest for long, as a man in a tall hat and waistcoat is crammed in next to his notes on *Comedy of Errors*, while another page on the Bard is taken up almost entirely by a gigantic unshaven figure in a vest, leaning up against the right side of the page, a cigar smoldering in one hand. A brief page of notes on Alexander Pope features a drawing of the poet in a pope hat, with "by special appointment" scribbled beneath him. Another page on the poet Thomas Shadwell is filled with knights, dogs, and what seems to be a flying cow, though Ted helpfully labeled it *Flying Ibex*. "I think this demonstrates that I wasn't very interested in the subtle niceties of English literature," said Geisel. "As you go through the notebook, there's a growing incidence of flying cows and strange beasts. And finally, at the last page of the notebook there are no notes on English literature at all. There are just strange beasts."[9]

In fact the flying cow and strange beasts were what caught the eye of a young woman seated next to him in a lecture, who watched closely as Geisel did everything in class but take notes. "You're not very interested in the lecture," she told him plainly—then leaned in and pointed at one of his drawings. "I think that's a very good flying cow," she said. Geisel was intrigued and mentioned the encounter to Sagmaster, who informed him that the young woman was a Wellesley College graduate from Brooklyn named Helen Palmer—and if Geisel wanted, Sagmaster would be more than happy to make a more formal introduction.

Helen Marion Palmer was born in Brooklyn, New York, on September 23, 1898, which made her nearly six years older than Ted. As a child, Helen had contracted polio—a condition she recovered from, but which would leave her with what she referred to as a "lopsided smile."[10] When Helen was eleven, her father, a successful ophthalmologist, died of a heart attack, leaving her in the care of her headstrong mother, Marie, who suddenly had to raise Helen and her thirteen-year-old brother Robert as a single parent in a little apartment on Brooklyn's Ocean Avenue. In 1916, at age eighteen, Helen began attending Adelphi College, then transferred to Wellesley College just outside Boston after her freshman year. After graduating with honors in 1920, Helen returned to Brooklyn and spent the next three years teaching English at Girls High School—but she longed to try for her master's degree at Oxford, a dream her mother not only encouraged but in which she also intended to fully participate. When Helen left for England to attend the Society of Oxford Home-Students (now St. Anne's College) in 1924, Marie went with her, and the two of them now shared quarters on Woodstock Road.

Playing the role of matchmaker, Sagmaster invited both Helen and Ted to his rooms for an informal dinner of anchovy toast. "You never saw a better case of love at first sight," Sagmaster recalled. "They completely ignored the host, talked together for hours, left together, had dinner together, and spent as much time together during term as the Oxford rules allowed."[11]

They were an attractive couple; Helen, at five foot three, was nine inches shorter than Ted, but carried herself in such a confident manner that most swore she was taller. Her shoulder-length brown hair was usually carefully coiffed—though often hidden under a hat—in marked contrast to Ted's hair, which, when left on its own, often stood on end and looked as if he'd just woken up. Both smiled easily, particularly when engaged in conversation with each other—and if anything, the smile that Helen always called lopsided was even broader than Ted's. Sagmaster would later say that bringing Helen and Ted together was "the happiest inspiration I've ever had."[12] Indeed, the two of them were immediately inseparable; in late October, when Helen's mother returned to the United States, Helen immediately moved into Frewin Cottage, a charming apartment with a bathroom window that wouldn't close, only a few minutes' walk from Ted's room at Lincoln College.

But Ted and Helen's interest in each other went deeper than purely physical attraction. Ted might acknowledge that Helen had "a certain grace,"¹³ but he also liked that she was smart—and not just in a "well read in the classics" sort of way, though she was certainly that. Talking with Helen about books, said Ted, he was "horrified . . . to find that while I loved Swift, Defoe, Shaw and Beerbohm, I knew absolutely nothing about literature."¹⁴ Helen was also passionate and opinionated, with a strong sense of how things should be—and Ted liked that, too. "Helen brought me to the realization that I wasn't soundly grounded in any subject," said Ted, "[and] that I had merely been playing writer and scholar."¹⁵ What Helen saw in Ted, then, was both talent and potential—both of which, as far as she was concerned, were being wasted on English literature. "You're crazy to be a professor," she told Ted flatly. "What you really want to do is draw."¹⁶

And so Ted Geisel would draw, paying only middling attention to his studies. Almost in spite of himself, he took an interest in the works of John Milton, and began illustrating "great hunk[s]" of *Paradise Lost*—especially the places, said Geisel, where "Milton's sense of humor failed him."¹⁷ Thus Milton's line "Thither came Uriel, gliding through the even / On a sunbeam" became a cartoon of a cherubic Uriel sliding down a wide sunbeam, an oil can in his hand to help "lessen the friction on his coccyx."¹⁸ Geisel bundled this drawing together, along with several others of Adam and Eve, and took them over to Blackwell's, the famed bookstore and publisher in Broad Street, to see if there would be any interest in hiring him to illustrate the entirety of *Paradise Lost*.

There wasn't. "I was thrown out," Geisel recalled.¹⁹

• • • •

Ted and Helen would be apart only briefly, during the 1925 Christmas break when Helen joined her family in the United States while Ted roamed through France with Sagmaster, Bartlett, and another friend. When Helen returned in 1926, she moved into a cottage at 14 Ship Street, just around the corner from the main entrance of Lincoln College—and it was here that Geisel would spend most of his remaining months at Oxford, doodling in his notebooks, reading the assigned text only when the mood struck him, and taking side trips into the countryside with Helen.

To that end, Geisel decided the day trips would be easier and a little more fun if he had a motorcycle. Unfortunately, Oxford's policies prevented first-year students from owning or even driving motorcycles—an impasse that was resolved when Helen reminded him that while he might be in his first year, she was in her *second*. The two of them pooled their money and bought a motorcycle with a sidecar and rumble seat. And lest anyone see him rumbling around Oxford on the motorcycle and report this violation of the rules to the sobersided rector Munro, Geisel always disguised himself as a poultry delivery boy, dangling plucked ducks from the handlebars or visibly stuffed into the saddlebags.

By early April, Geisel had made a decision—or as far as he was concerned, a decision had been made for him by an Oxford don whom he called "Sir Oliver Onions," actually Professor Charles Talbut Onions, a Shakespearean scholar and one of the editors of the *Oxford English Dictionary.* "That was the man who really drove me out of Oxford," recalled Geisel. Onions, an obsessive lexicographer, could devote hours to Shakespearean punctuation, and Geisel had been driven nearly mad by a two-hour lecture on the nuances of punctuation in various versions of *King Lear.* "He had dug up all of the old folios, as far back as he could go," said Geisel. "Some had more semicolons than commas. Some had more commas than periods. Some had no punctuation at all. For the first hour and a half, he talked about the first two pages in *King Lear* . . . It got unbelievable. I got up, went back to my room, and started packing."[20]

While Geisel would stay for the remainder of the semester, he was ready to be done with academia. "I decided that if I stayed and got my degree, I'd be equipped to teach other people about semicolons and commas," he said sardonically.[21] He later admitted that he had been "lazy of mind" during his year at Oxford. "I'm afraid I went through another freshman stage of utter astonishment and mental prostration at the stupendous amount of learning that I had never suspected to exist," he wrote to Whit Campbell. "[I] have managed to reconcile myself to man's limitations—and am all through trying to 'know life whole.'"[22]

His professors didn't try to talk him out of it. Carlyle, his tutor, "very correctly told me I was ignorant," recalled Geisel, and encouraged him instead to "just travel around Europe with a bundle of high school history books and visit the places I was reading about—go to the museums and look at pictures and read as I went."[23] An extended trip to Europe would take place at the end of the semester—but first, he decided, it was time to propose marriage to Helen.

His proposal ended up being spectacularly impromptu—and typical of Geisel, the story would change with the telling over time.

In the first version, Ted and Helen were driving home from an evening party on their motorcycle—Ted driving, Helen in the sidecar—when Ted took a turn too quickly and spun the bike into a ditch, spilling both of them into the mud. As they sat in the ditch, unhurt but spluttering, Ted suddenly asked Helen to marry him. In a later version of the proposal story, Ted claimed he'd proposed to Helen while they were still speeding around on the motorcycle, with Ted shouting his proposal loudly over the noise of the motor—and Ted wrecked the bike in a ditch when Helen told him yes. Whichever version of events is true—if any—by the spring of 1926, Ted Geisel and Helen Palmer were officially engaged.

"The engagement is not, I must say, one of my annual Spring announcements," he wrote sassily to Whit Campbell. He had apparently notified his family of his engagement, but told Campbell that he was "disappointed in not getting the report of my family's reaction."[24] As for informing Helen's mother, Marie, of their pending nuptials, Ted and Helen intended to take their motorcycle to France during their extended Easter break and meet Marie in Paris. Here in Paris, Ted told Campbell, he and Helen "broke the news to her in a dazzling fashion."[25]

They had gotten off to a bad start. On their first night together in town, Ted took Helen and her mother to dinner, where Marie "took no serious notice" of Ted and informed him in no uncertain terms that she equated drinking alcohol with "feeding the devil." The conversation ground to a halt. Things seemed to improve the next night when Ted and Helen escorted her mother to an opera—but without understanding any French, Ted could see that his future mother-in-law quickly "began to get unhappy." At intermission, then, Ted and Helen left their seats to each take a stiff drink to steel their nerves, then returned to Marie, where Helen tried to steer the conversation toward their announcement.

"Mother," said Helen, "what do you think of this"—and here she gestured toward Ted—"as a husband?"

Marie's mouth hung open in disbelief as she fanned herself frantically with her program. Finally she gathered herself.

"But my dear girl," Marie said breathlessly to her daughter, "why, I don't even know his name!"

Ted went for his wallet and admitted he "fumbled" for a moment before dramatically brandishing a small piece of cardboard.

"Madam," he said with a small bow, "my card."[26]

It was hard to tell if Marie was pleased with the news. Ted noted that the three of them watched the rest of the opera in silence. Afterward, they stopped in a nearby restaurant and sat down at a table to drink lemonades—Marie's drink of choice—and Ted noted somewhat acidly that Helen and her mother spent the evening engaged in side conversations about "the 'little ones to come' and that sort of rot." When Marie finally turned her attention to Ted, she urged him to return to the United States as quickly as possible to look for a job. But Ted waved off her recommendation and informed her he was all but certain he'd be teaching in Vienna—where, at least at that moment, he was considering going to study nineteenth-century German drama— or pursuing "a newspaper job, also abroad."[27] Later Ted drove Helen and a still-skeptical Marie Palmer back to her hotel, with Marie jangling in the motorcycle's sidecar as they bounced over cobblestone roads. "She hasn't thought the same of me since," Ted confessed to

Whit.[28] It would take some time for Ted to earn his mother-in-law's endorsement.

As Easter break ended, Geisel dreaded abandoning Paris for Oxford. "When I look back from the Continent, and remember English tradition, I have shooting pains in my buttock," he wrote.[29] "I really think I have had enough University study. I like to come and go as I please in my reading," he told Campbell.[30] "I have said 'to hell with the whole of English literature'—and I am now reading for ideas—wherever they may be found."[31] He had abandoned his idea of studying German drama in Vienna—but for a moment, he was very nearly persuaded by the scholar Émile Legouis, an authority on Jonathan Swift, into pursuing a PhD with him at the Sorbonne in Paris.

Geisel was skeptical from the start—"I discovered that one had to speak French, and I couldn't"[32]—but visited Legouis at his home in Paris "to find out exactly what he wanted me to do." Legouis told the young man that he had a premier assignment, explaining that there was a very brief period in Swift's career—between the ages of sixteen and a half and seventeen—in which it appeared Swift had never written a thing. Legouis, recalled Geisel, had challenged him to "devote two years to finding out whether he *had* written anything. If he had," Geisel further explained, "I could analyze what he wrote as my D.Phil. thesis. Unfortunately, if he hadn't written anything, I wouldn't get my doctorate."[33] Geisel stood up and walked out and—as he related the story nearly fifty years later—"I threw in my doctoral towel and took the next freighter to Corsica."[34]

Helen, however, completed her master's degree at Oxford. Much to her disappointment, she would be with Ted in France when degrees were formally bestowed. While Ted could be dismissive of formal education, Helen never was—and she was unhappy that her graduating record had been designated as Class III, little better than a 2.0 GPA. Her teachers had clearly noticed that Ted had distracted her. "Missed classes . . . engaged to American," wrote one tutor. Helen found it embarrassing. "I should have done better," she admitted to one of her Oxford tutors. "It is as bad to disillusion others as to disillusion oneself."[35] Helen's devotion to Ted, often at the expense of her own ambition or happiness, would be characteristic of their life-long relationship.

••••

In June 1926, Ted's parents and his sister, Marnie, joined him in England, their first stop on an extended trip through Europe as a family. His parents may have viewed his engagement to Helen as rash, but—unlike Ted's experience with Marie Palmer—Helen quickly made a good impression on the Geisels. She would remain behind in Oxford for a few weeks before meeting her mother and the Geisels in Paris. The Geisels, meanwhile, traveled through England, Paris, and Switzerland—"about which I am mad," wrote Ted—before making a trip to Bavaria to visit relatives in Mühlhausen, the birthplace of Ted's *Großvater*. For Ted, it was not the happy experience his father likely hoped it would be.

Ted's grandfather had a brother named Robert, now seventy-five years old and still living in Mühlhausen with his wife. Ted was surprised to learn that, at about the time T.A. had immigrated to Spring-field, Robert and his wife had also moved to the United States, "starting along the well-known road of prosperity," wrote Ted, but then returned to Germany at the urging of Robert's homesick wife. Instead of the successful life Ted's grandfather had built back in America, Robert Geisel still worked eight hours a day in a forge, subsisting on a diet of "sour blackbread and beer." Ted pitied the "lean and grey old man" before him, and was dismayed to learn that a "misanthropic wife who found no joy in American life" had denied Robert the same opportunities for achievement as his more successful brother.

Their final night in town, Ted's father hosted a dinner for more than thirty members of the extended family—and Ted, as he ate and chatted with his own relatives, thought he had "never had such a pathetic experience." His cousins, all "intense and bright" were "mostly illiterate . . . stuck for the rest of their lives in the Black Forest—all suffering from the false step Robert made in returning to Germany."[36] It made Ted appreciate his grandfather's achievements, and his own life, all the more—and he pitied his cousins for what he saw as their missed opportunities. "When I think of the distance these folks could have gone—had they stayed in America," he wrote to Whit Campbell. "But oh hell."[37]

Later, the Geisels drove to the little town of Kleinschwarzenbach—a tiny hamlet of farmers living in thatched-roof cottages—to visit relatives from the Seuss side of the family. Ted found the experience "far more pathetic than that at my Father's relations," though for different reasons. Once again, T. R. Geisel hosted a large dinner; while Ted was amused that sixty-seven people showed up "claiming to belong to the clan of Seuss," the gathering itself depressed him. "There were tears to go with the beer," he wrote in a letter to Whit, and told how he had wept as one relative after another showed him photographs of family members killed in the war—"cousins who had been called [into service] and went," Ted wrote sadly. Ted took his twenty-four-year-old cousin Alvin for his first ride in a car, and the young man was struck almost speechless by the amazing new technology. "He showed a tremendous desire to go to America," Ted wrote. And yet, he told Whit sadly, "no one in his family will ever leave the farm—unless, perhaps, they are called to serve in another war."[38]

It all made Ted profoundly sad—and a little angry. "Some day," he told Campbell, "I shall endow two fellowships. One will take men from [Alvin's village] and ship them around to the different capitals for two years travel and tutorial." The other, he explained, would be given to the statesmen and politicians who send young men to war and consign their parents to lives of quiet oppression. "This fellowship will entitle them to spend six months in a thatched-roof shack . . . to examine a few of the war memorials, look through the family albums, and sit down on a rock to watch the peasants digging turnips to pay the national debt."[39]

Ted had his own debts to contend with as well. He informed Whit that he planned to spend some time in Vienna late in the fall, which might burn through his grandfather's money faster than perhaps he intended, but he wasn't about to slow down. He admitted that he was reading more, was becoming more interested in history and European politics and "unfortunately, too many things." Still, he told Campbell he had come to accept that "I shall never teach school—so I decided to quit and come to the continent where people, if less 'cultured' are a bit more intense—and less insular." He signed off with what was becoming his regular signature: *Seuss*.[40]

Returning to Paris with his parents, the Geisels were reunited with Helen, who'd been vacationing with her mother in Dinard since early summer. On one of their final evenings together before the Geisels returned to the United States, Ted and Helen took his parents out to the Folies-Bergère, the cabaret music hall, to see the singer Maurice Chevalier. True to its reputation, the evening featured not just Chevalier but "gorgeous girls and jiggling breasts"—and T. R. Geisel promptly stood up and announced they were all returning to the hotel, since "there's nothing here but tits and music."

"So, you don't like music?" Ted asked.

T.R. was not amused. The Geisels returned immediately to their hotel, depositing Helen at her boardinghouse en route. With Nettie tearfully settled into bed, T.R. poured his son a stiff drink, then whirled around on him purposefully. "If you're going to make pronouncements like that, wait until we are man-to-man."[41] Suitably admonished, Ted would watch his mouth—and never again would he and his father speak of it.

••••

With the departure of the Geisels for home, Helen returned to her mother for a tour of Italy, leaving Ted alone in Paris for the fall. He walked the streets slowly and deliberately now, lounging away the afternoons in coffeehouses, museums, and bookstores, taking "futile French lessons," gazing blankly at art, and people-watching over one café au lait after another. At Sylvia Beach's famed Shakespeare and Company bookshop, he bought a blue-bound copy of James Joyce's *Ulysses*, which was still banned in the United States, and did his very best to read it. "James Joyce irritated me," Ted said later. "I thought he could have made more sense if he'd wanted to."[42]

He became a regular at the crowded La Closerie des Lilas—a popular watering hole and salon for literary American expatriates—where he often spotted Ernest Hemingway seated at a table, writing and smoking a pipe. "He always wore a turtleneck sweater and accumulated saucers," Geisel recalled.[43] "What he was writing I never knew. I was scared to walk over and ask him, lest he ask me what *I* was writing. I was a twenty-two-year-old kid writing knock-kneed limericks about goats and geese and other stuff that I couldn't sell. He was probably writing *A Farewell to Arms*."[44]

Another evening, while prowling the Boulevard Saint-Michel with Don Bartlett and another Oxford friend, Geisel spotted the American novelist Theodore Dreiser—Geisel said he recognized him "by his surly face and blubberous mouth"—walking with the anarchist Emma Goldman ("the fat Jewish lady"), who'd been deported from the United States for her vocal political views in 1919. The friends followed them to a café in the Sorbonne and sat close enough to eavesdrop on the conversation. Ted was unimpressed. While Dreiser was currently basking in the success of his novel *An American Tragedy* and Goldman was always a controversial personality, Ted found their conversation mundane. "Never before have I sat in on such rapid fire stuff," he wrote to Whit Campbell, practically rolling his eyes on the page. As a joke, the young men bribed a bellhop into presenting Dreiser with a pair of blue suspenders and pretending they were a gift from the French Academy. Goldman, who understood French, laughed out loud; Dreiser, who spoke no French, could only gape and repeatedly ask, "What? WHAT?" Ted shook his head in annoyance. "Dreiser is one of these ponderous chaps," he told Whit. "He will puzzle over it for years and then write another book."[45]

Not every excursion was literary in nature. He returned to the Folies-Bergère to catch the new revue *La Folie du Jour*, featuring the African American entertainer Josephine Baker, who danced, strutted, made faces, and flirted with rowdy audience members, while wearing nothing more than a skirt made of bananas—"which serve to vivify, rather than to conceal, her Alabama vulva," Ted told Whit in a coarsely worded letter.[46] Geisel may have hooted along with the crowd—as he told Campbell, "I always go [to Folies-Bergère] to release imprisoned sex instincts"—but he was also concerned that the bare-breasted, hip-shaking performance by this "American Nigger," as he crudely put it, was giving his countrymen a bad name. "Unfortunately, the Europeans are all the more convinced of the crassness of the U.S.A. by this," he told Campbell, "—and it adds just one more proof to their claim that we are jazz and money mad." As he told Whit later, "one is close to ashamed—ashamed of what the U.S.A. seems to stand for. The States are damn unpopular at the present moment. In France, [Americans] breeze about ruthlessly while the French are going hungry."[47] But that still wasn't going to stop Geisel from leering at Baker as she twirled and danced the Charleston naked, breaking hearts and putting on a show that became an international sensation. Ernest Hemingway, too, was a big fan.

Still, he promised Campbell he was trying to do some serious work. "I have started a complete study of the modern German drama," he reported. "I hope to correlate it up with the modern English and American literary movements (and later with the Russian) and see what kind of theses I can do. Then, for diversion I am taking a course in Goethe and reading a bit of 18th Century English." His enthusiasm lasted three days; he spent more time and effort growing and grooming what he called "a convincing moustache."[48]

He reunited with Helen in Italy, where she was still vacationing with her mother—and scandalized Marie Palmer and her "retrograde tendencies" by taking Helen with him to look at Michelangelo's statue of the naked David. His future mother-in-law had "fainted dead away," he told Campbell. "All art," he told his friend impishly, "should wear jock straps." He watched and listened to the dictator Benito Mussolini warily, reading his speeches in the newspaper and seeing his face papered on nearly every surface. "I cannot write what I think on the subject," he wrote to Campbell. "Intellectually, I am considered a dangerous radical." Still, he wasn't sure whom he mistrusted more: Mussolini, or an unnamed Harvard man he had recently met at a party in Florence. "He is an ass," declared Ted. "He will buy his way into an ambassadorship before he is 35."[49]

Having abandoned his studies of German drama and the writings of Goethe—and looking for his next project—Geisel began writing what he hoped would become the next Great American Novel. ("Who hasn't?" he asked fifty years later.)[50] It, too, quickly became a mess. "I was heavily influenced at that time by [novelist and photographer] Carl Van Vechten, who often lapsed into Italian during the course of his books," said Ted later.[51] "There's a chapter in [my novel] with people conversing in Italian. I don't know any Italian. I don't know how that got in there."[52]

Still, he managed to complete a massive first draft—Ted once claimed it ran for two volumes—"and when it wouldn't sell," he said years later, "I condensed it into one volume. When that didn't sell, I boiled it down into a long short story. Next I cut it to a short, short story. Finally I sold it as a two-line gag. Now I can't even remember the gag."[53]

Around Christmas of 1926, Helen returned to the United States, heading for her mother's home in New Jersey while she looked for a teaching job. Ted remained in Italy for another six weeks, moving slowly through Rome, Naples, Sicily, and Palermo, where, he admitted, he wasn't doing much of anything. Eventually, even sleeping late and shopping all day became tiresome—and on Sunday, February 13, 1927, Ted boarded a ship at Palermo bound for New York.

His year at Oxford had been a bust, and his plans for a teaching career had dissolved with his unattained doctorate. His future was uncertain, and his prospects for employment were cloudy at best.

Helen, however, typically thought she knew exactly what Ted should do. "Ted's notebooks were always filled with these fabulous animals," she said. "So I set to work diverting him. Here was a man who could draw such pictures; he should earn a living doing that."[54]

CHAPTER 4

THE FLIT

1927–1936

n the spring of 1927, after nearly six years away from Springfield, Ted Geisel was living back under his parents' roof again—
and he wasn't happy about it. "I am sick and tired of being a
Springfield boy," he grumbled.[1] Since returning home from Europe in late February, he and Helen had lived apart; with her
master's degree in English, Helen had quickly landed a teaching job
at a private school for girls in Orange, New Jersey—but she and Ted
were engaged, not married, which meant no living together. With no
job, no teaching certificate, and few prospects, Ted really had little
choice but to return to Springfield, bunking in his old second-floor
bedroom and setting up his drawing board and a typewriter at his
father's desk in the little office just off the master bedroom. At age
twenty-three, he certainly didn't want to be there.

With Helen's encouragement, he was determined to make it as an
illustrator—and that meant pounding out endless letters to book and
magazine publishers in New York; sending around samples of his
work, some of which might be returned, most of which might not;
and endlessly pitching one idea after another. Very early on, Ted was
sending letters and cartoons to Alexander K. Laing, a poet, writer,
and fellow Dartmouth man who also happened to be a contributor to
The New Yorker. Geisel very smartly proposed to Laing an ongoing series of cartoons—a successful series meant being paid for several

cartoons, as opposed to just one—featuring something he was calling a *Hippocrass*, a creature with a long neck, a dog-like face, wings on its back, and two legs ending in boxing gloves. (While Hippocrass was a perfectly Seussian-sounding name, it was a classic reference that perhaps only a third-generation brewer would know, as *hippocras* actually refers to an ancient Greek spiced wine.) As envisioned by Geisel, the Hippocrass was a kind of mascot for drinkers everywhere, first shown locked up on Ellis Island, where Jimmy Walker, the anti-Prohibition mayor of New York, sympathetically frees him. From there, Geisel drew Hippocrass frolicking in the city, doing interviews, getting drunk, and being lectured by a stern-looking President Calvin Coolidge, who wears a sombrero with a swastika on it. As was true of his father, there would never be anything subtle about Ted's views on the prohibitionists.

Laing agreed to write the text accompanying Geisel's Hippocrass cartoons, but the project failed to gain any traction with editors at *The New Yorker*. Geisel could see the writing on the wall. "Not having received any checks, letters of praise or telegrams of disapproval, I take it that the Hippocrass has not been housebroken," he wrote to Laing—and then gamely proposed another series of cartoons he called "Emminent [*sic*] Europeans," featuring a stoic Croupier—the person in charge of a gaming table, who clears the table with a long rake—and a clueless Palace Guide. The Croupier was the funnier of the two ideas; Geisel proposed they "play up on his complete detachment from worry, his placid indifference to whatever happens"—and one cartoon shows a distraught gambler standing at the game table with a pistol to his head, eyes clenched tightly shut, as the blasé Croupier absently rakes in his money. "Kindly write me your opinions post haste," Geisel begged Laing—but Laing found no takers for the Eminent Europeans series, either.

Taking matters into his own hands, Geisel caught the train for New York City in April, convinced that a more personal touch with publishers would push open the doors to publication. In this, too, he was disappointed. "I have tramped all over this bloody town," he wrote Whit Campbell from his room in the Hotel Woodstock on 43rd Street, and explained that he had been "tossed out" of the offices of two publishers, two movie studios, three advertising agencies, and the offices of *Life* and *Judge* magazines. *Life*, at least, had promised to "consider more carefully" one of his cartoons, while a local magazine had asked for "half a dozen grocery store cartoons," which he grudgingly promised to deliver. But he remained slightly embarrassed by his ongoing efforts to "consciously cultivate" Laing at *The New Yorker*. "Key-ryst!" wrote Geisel. "What is this world coming to?"[2]

He had also had dinner in the city with five Dartmouth classmates—a gathering that depressed him, as all five had real jobs and appeared to be on their way to real careers (except for one, noted Geisel, who would get somewhere only "if they don't shoot him first"). As for his own prospects, he told Whit he was playing it by ear. "What comes up will come up, and will determine my future life," he explained matter-of-factly. "I rather think it will be free-lancing for a while. I've been steered in that direction by all the great publishers and editors in New York." He continued:

I don't know. But I know one thing.

My policy is to laugh my god damned head off, be the provocation ever so slight. Occasionally I depress myself and work myself into one of those delightful funks . . . And I seek out subway tracks on which to toss myself. And then it strikes me as very comical—and I laff instead.[3]

He signed off as Seuss, putting a flourish on the serifs of the *S*, then noted parenthetically that he was, "a damn fool and proud of it."[4]

Despite his darkening spirits, his persistence paid off. In early summer, an editor at *The Saturday Evening Post* purchased one of his cartoons for $25—about $350 today. It wasn't a princely sum, but when pooled with his savings, it was enough that he could announce to his parents that he was moving immediately to Manhattan. "I informed my parents that my future was assured; I would quickly make my fame and fortune in *The Saturday Evening Post*," Geisel said.[5] His parents were delighted, though Geisel said later that his father was mostly happy because he was "hoping I'd become self-sufficient and get out of the house, because I was working at his desk."[6] Regardless, Ted boarded the New York, New Haven, and Hartford Railroad, "and I invaded the Big City," he said, "where I knew that all the editors would be waiting to buy my wares."[7]

They weren't. The piece for *The Saturday Evening Post*—a Lawrence of Arabia joke drawn in a more traditional, less exaggerated style— ran on July 16, and was signed *Seuss*. It would be the last piece he would place in the *Post* for thirty-seven years.[8]

Geisel moved to Greenwich Village that summer, taking a room with John Clarke Rose, a former *Jacko* artist. Their one-room studio at 133 Washington Place was over a lively club and restaurant called Don Dickerman's Pirate's Den, where servers dressed as pirates staged fights every hour on the hour. While the Pirate's Den would become a fashionable night spot over the next decade, Geisel remembered only the overfed rats that he and Rose would shoo away by whacking them with brooms. "God, what a place," he said later, shuddering at the memory.[9]

Still, it was exhilarating to live in New York City—especially in the era of the speakeasy at the height of the Jazz Age. With booze in his blood, Geisel never for a moment considered giving up drinking, and he and Rose regularly sought out underground restaurants and clubs where the alcohol flowed freely—or barring that, found restaurants where greased palms ensured the police looked the other way. The nightlife in New York in 1927 was particularly thrilling; new clubs like the Onyx—started by the bootlegger Joe Helbock—were opening across the city, bringing jazz and bathtub gin to previously peaceful neighborhoods.

In Harlem, Duke Ellington and his orchestra would take up residency at the Cotton Club, the beginning of a highly creative and productive three-and-a-half-year gig. This was also the year Babe Ruth would become the first baseball player to hit sixty home runs in a season, leading a team of hard-hitting New York Yankee sluggers in a batting lineup known as Murderers' Row. In film, 1927 would see the release of the first full-length talkie, *The Jazz Singer*, as well as Fritz Lang's groundbreaking silent science fiction film *Metropolis*. And that June, New York would shower aviator Charles Lindbergh with a gigantic ticker-tape parade, a hero's welcome celebrating his successful solo flight across the Atlantic.

The world was becoming a whole lot bigger and louder—and Geisel, in his apartment in lower Manhattan, was in the middle of it all. But Helen wasn't. To Geisel's disappointment, she rarely visited his dirty bachelor pad, preferring to spend the summer with her mother on the New Jersey shore. When Helen was in the city with Ted, however, she was, in nearly every sense, the epitome of the new American woman— one who danced and drank and voted and earned her own money. Even with her modest pay as a schoolteacher, she was significantly out-earning Ted.

Despite making endless rounds of the magazines, Ted was still having a hard time finding anyone who was interested in his work. "I tried to do sophisticated things for *Vanity Fair*," he recalled. "I tried unsophisticated things for the *Daily Mirror*."[10] Nothing seemed to work until one fall evening, between sessions of rat-whacking, John Rose mentioned that a former Dartmouth classmate named "Beef" Vernon had been hired to sell advertising for the humor magazine *Judge*—and Rose thought perhaps he and Ted could "con him" into an introduction to editor Norman Anthony.

In no time, Ted found himself hustled in front of thirty-two-year-old Norman Anthony in the offices of *Judge* on East 48th Street. Anthony, in the lingo of the era, was a certified rake. A hard-drinking, rambunctious womanizer—he would later report being married "three or four" times—Anthony had overcome an early life as a New

York City street thug to become a successful journalist and editor.[11] After several years at the *New York Herald,* he had been hired as the editor of *Judge*—a satire magazine that called itself "the world's wittiest weekly"—and had rapidly turned it into the most successful humor magazine in the nation.

Founded in 1881 to challenge the political humor magazine *Puck, Judge* had eventually driven *Puck* out of business—and under the leadership of Anthony, it also regularly outsold *Life* and its newest rival, *The New Yorker.* While *Judge* featured both text pieces and cartoons, Anthony was savvy enough to understand it was cartoons his readers wanted, and had scaled back the text in favor of illustrations and cartoons—an editorial decision that sent sales soaring from 30,000 to 100,000 copies weekly. With its full-color front and back covers and a double-page centerfold, *Judge* made its artists look good—and cartoonists longed to have their work featured in its pages. And now, thanks to the maneuverings of Beef Vernon, Geisel was here in Anthony's office, knocking on the door of the big leagues.

With his rapidly receding hairline and round wire-rimmed glasses, Norman Anthony might almost have been mistaken for a banker or insurance salesman, were it not for the sly, slightly crooked grin almost perpetually on his face that gave away his sense of humor. It was perhaps little wonder, then, that he and Geisel hit it off immediately— and it speaks to Geisel's patter and power of persuasion that he left Anthony's office with an offer to join the staff of *Judge* in October, at a salary of seventy-five dollars per week—about $1,000 today. Ted and Helen celebrated the good news with a spaghetti dinner at a speakeasy.

Geisel's first cartoon for *Judge*—his second for a national publication— appeared in the October 22, 1927 issue. It was yet another henpecked husband joke, this time featuring two married circus performers on tall unicycles. ("And to think!" says the wife, "I could have been the wife of a six-day bike racer—if I hadn't listened to your rot about Higher Art!") As he had with the piece in *The Saturday Evening Post,* Ted signed this one *Seuss* as well.

Even with *Judge*'s large monthly circulation, editor Norman

Anthony was always convinced his magazine was on the verge of bankruptcy, and was always on the lookout for any way to keep up his cash flow. Lately, he had implemented a policy permitting his staff and other contributors to be paid with "due bills" from advertisers. What this meant was that if *Judge* was owed $250 in advertising revenue from Barbasol shaving cream—and Anthony owed one of his cartoonists $250—Anthony could have the cartoonist collect a "due bill" directly from Barbasol in the amount of $250. Translated into practice, however, what tended to happen was that Barbasol and other advertisers would simply pay their due bill with an equivalent amount of product instead of cash. It was essentially a barter system—and Geisel recalled that he was indeed once paid for his work with $100 worth of shaving cream. Another time, recalled Geisel, "I was once paid in Little Gem nail clippers—a hundred gross of them, which they thought I could sell for a profit. I finally gave up trying to sell them."[12] Still, Geisel thought the system had its advantages. "I sort of loved trading my stuff for their stuff. I was happier in one way under the barter system than I've ever been since. When you get paid in money, it leads to accountants and lawyers."[13]

Now that he was officially employed and bringing in a somewhat stable income—whether partially comprised of nail clippers or not— Ted decided that he and Helen should be married—and the sooner, the better. Ted proposed they marry before the end of the year, preferably in early November, a timeline that Helen eagerly agreed to. But that vaguely defined date was vetoed by Nettie Geisel, since Ted's sister, Marnie—now married to lawyer Lloyd Dahmen—was due to deliver their first child on or about the first of November. When Marnie delivered a healthy baby girl—whom they named Margaretha, but whom everyone would call Peggy—precisely on November 1, Ted and Helen set their date for the Tuesday after Thanksgiving, exactly four weeks later.

On November 29, 1927, Ted and Helen were married at five P.M. in Westfield, New Jersey, in the home of Helen's brother, Robert. Helen was given away by her mother, while Whitney Campbell—who had driven more than two hundred miles from Cambridge, Massachusetts, to New York—served as best man. Ted choked up with emotion as he thanked Campbell for standing with him. "It was a long way for you to come just to toss a ring onto a Bible," he wrote to Whit several days later. "But it was a gesture that I will remember as long as my cerebral textures remain healthy and intact." He told his friend he was trying to find an appropriate thank-you gift that was "an outward and comical sign of an inward and spiritual grace"[14]—about as poetic a thank-you as Ted would ever manage.

A formal reception of punch and cake followed—but the real post-wedding party was thrown later that evening by Ted's father, who hosted a champagne dinner at a nearby speakeasy. "The champagne supper cheered up my mother," said Ted. "And the party saw everyone in a very pleasant frame of mind."[15] Ted took some good-natured ribbing from a few Dartmouth men who expressed shock that Ted and Helen hadn't already gotten married in Europe—an accusation at which Ted would only grin and wink cheekily. The evening ended on a high note, when one of Ted's Casque & Gauntlet brothers did a drunken impression of Lady Astor—the very same English socialite whose party invitation Ted had spurned two years earlier for spelling his name incorrectly.

Ted and Helen spent their honeymoon in a hundred-dollar-a-night suite at the Hotel Traymore in Atlantic City, paid for with—what else?—due bills. "[I]t is fun," he told Whit. "The Traymore (if you don't know it) serves perfect food and we are growing stout and catering to our predispositions toward laziness."[16] During their first year of marriage, Ted and Helen would, in fact, spend many long weekends enjoying hundred-dollar suites at the Traymore, courtesy of more of *Judge*'s due bills.

It was certainly better than the apartment the newlyweds had taken at West 18th Street in New York's Chelsea neighborhood. For one thing, the neighborhood stunk. The apartment was located across the street from a stable, from which dead horses were frequently dragged into the street to be disposed of later. It was also unsafe, and if Geisel wanted to make the two-mile walk uptown to the offices of *Judge*, he made certain he left the house carrying what he called his "loaded cane"—a walking stick fitted with a spring blade in one end—to ward off would-be muggers.[17] Other times, he might sprint for the subway station at Broadway and 23rd, ride to the stop at 49th Street, then walk the two-and-a-half blocks to the *Judge* offices at 18 East 48th.

Within a month of working at *Judge*, Geisel was already producing a regular ongoing series called "Boids and Beasties: A Department for Indefatigable Naturalists," a text-heavy feature with lots of smiling Seussian animals, many of which could trace their roots back to the pages of his Oxford notebook. In the first installment, published in the November 19, 1927, issue, the piece is credited to Dr. Theophrastus Seuss, a nod to Ted's beloved stuffed dog, while the signature at the bottom of the page was *Seuss*. Geisel hadn't settled on Dr. Seuss yet, but he was getting closer.

Geisel's art was getting more stylized, though there was still a lot of crosshatching and the outlining of figures with short parallel lines, an artistic conceit lifted from the comic pages. Nearly every creature, from human to bird to lion to fish, is also a bit bug-eyed, with visible eyelashes. Men tend to have beards or mustaches and wear hats or smoke cigars; a clueless-looking Calvin Coolidge was a favorite target as well. Ted also struggled to draw animals even somewhat realistically—his kangaroo was particularly terrible, with a face like a French bulldog—but he excelled at elephants, which managed to radiate charm and personality while still keeping their basic anatomy intact.

When he could get fanciful with his creatures, things got better. There was a written piece about "The Waiting Room at Dang-Dang: Where the D.T. Animals Stay When They're Not Out on Jobs," profiling Mr. Fronk, the Superintendent of the Beasts of Delirium Tremens, Inc., who sends out a wild menagerie of animals to romp through the booze-soaked hallucinations of drunks. The accompanying cartoon shows an assortment of weird Seussian animals seated around

Fronk—including an elephant with a cigar, a polar bear playing the bass viol, and a rabbit-like animal with eight legs.[18]

Prohibition and alcohol-related jokes, in fact, were the easiest for him, as well as the inspiration for some of his most popular cartoons. College students, in fact, would pore through *Judge* each month, looking for Geisel's soused elephants or staggering drunks. "When I think about the twenties, I realize that so much of my work was about drinking," Ted said later.[19] "Humor is a funny thing. You pick something out of the air. If the air changes, it's not funny any more."[20] For Ted, booze jokes would almost always be funny; even the Hippocrass, neglected but not forgotten, would make an appearance in a Christmas 1927 full-page piece called "Christmas Spirits"—yet another drinking joke—as the embodiment of the alcoholic spirit "Green Chartreuse."[21]

Still, some topics were taboo. "As far as humor [in the 1920s] was concerned, sex had not been invented," Geisel said later. "Dirty words were illegal as hell."[22] And yet he still couldn't resist making at least two jokes featuring the naked Lady Godiva on horseback, though both times the joke was about the horse, rather than more obvious sniggering about Godiva's state of undress.

He would also sneak the names of his friends into his prose pieces: there was Whit Campbell flicking ashes into the open trunk of an elephant, Joseph Sagmaster in a Santa suit hunting reindeer, and former roommate John Rose wielding a snake to blackmail millionaires. Geisel also wasn't above a bit of obvious product placement, using the names of real products in his drawings or as punch lines, which sometimes resulted in appreciative packages showing up on his desk at *Judge*; when Geisel name-checked White Rock soda in one piece, the company sent him forty-eight bottles of their soft drinks. This would not be the last time Ted's use of a brand name would pay dividends.

By early 1928, Geisel was quickly becoming one of *Judge*'s most popular artists—Teddy Roosevelt Jr. would even write to the magazine asking for one of Ted's originals, a request that Geisel thought more than made up for his supposed humiliation at the hands of the late president on a Springfield stage all those years ago. And *Judge*, despite Anthony's playing fast and loose with the bottom line, would continue to outsell the competition, on the strength of both Geisel's work and text pieces by writers like S. J. Perelman, who would later write for the Marx Brothers and *The New Yorker*. It was *The New Yorker*, in fact, that was *Judge*'s closest national competitor—even Geisel would admit that the *New Yorker*'s proficiency with one-liners could often make *Judge*'s "He-She two-line gags" sound "square."[23]

Like the prolific Perelman, Geisel, too, was producing his share of long prose pieces, hauling out his typewriter to place it on the sloped surface of his drawing table and banging away as a cigarette burned in the ashtray. Smoking, a common habit of the era, was a habit Geisel himself would never be able to shake. When working, he would often chain-smoke, lighting one off the last, then stubbing out the old one in a deep ashtray sitting on his drawing table. Geisel would try and fail to kick the habit countless times throughout his life.

Drinking, however, would never fall out of favor—throughout his life, Geisel would almost always makes time for cocktails. Finding a reliable drinking establishment in New York during Prohibition was something of a sport, and Ted and Helen had found their favorite evening hangout in a speakeasy called the Dizzy Club, hidden in a loft at 64 West 52nd Street.[24] "A great place," Ted told Campbell, and he particularly liked that the club stayed open all night, not shutting down until six A.M.—at which point Ted could blearily walk to the offices of *Judge*, about ten minutes away.[25]

Lately Ted and Helen had taken to meeting another couple at the Dizzy, a fellow Dartmouth man named Al Perkins and his wife who, like Ted and Helen, had "[no] conscience about staying up all night." Perkins was both a rambunctious drinker and practical joker—"the funniest fellow I have ever met," said Geisel—who could induce similarly bad behavior in Ted. Geisel related to Campbell how he had one evening locked a "nigger waiter"—Geisel's casual use of that term as a young man remains horrifying to modern ears—in a walk-in refrigerator. "Some ten minutes later, I released the poor chap, thinking he would thank me for my kindness," he told Whit. "[But h]e wasn't that kind of nigger."[26]

Out-of-control drinking would also ruin his twenty-fourth birthday celebration. Ted and Helen had invited Ted's parents and Helen's mother to their tiny apartment "for a nifty little party" to commemorate the occasion. Two of Ted's Dartmouth buddies, Paul Jerman and Courtney Brown, showed up on his doorstep "most horribly stewed." Jerman spent most of the evening vomiting in the small bathroom, then passed out. "It rather spoiled the evening for the family," Ted said, "and gave them the idea that all my time is spent in being ill with Jerman."[27]

• • • •

The February 11, 1928, issue of *Judge* featured a long prose piece by Geisel on "The Origin of Contract Bridge," tracing the card game back to a croquet-type sport created by three Druids named Aethelstan, Beowulf, and Flloyd-Jones—one of whom, in Ted's accompanying illustration, holds up a sign reading NO BEER, NO WORK. While the cartoon is signed with an all-capital-letters SEUSS, the byline on the article is, for the first time, Dr. Seuss.

Still, Geisel would continue to sign his cartoons with a simple SEUSS for another two and a half months, until the April 28, 1928, issue of *Judge*. There, on page 15, was a cartoon featuring two distinctly Seussian creatures: the Japanese Makaraskiijip—a camel-like creature on roller skates that ferries around children—and the Bvorlyjk of the North Pole, a winged catlike creature on snowshoes that delivers babies to frigid regions where the stork won't go. Beneath the skates of the Makaraskiijip and under the snowshoes of the Bvorlyjk, Geisel has signed his cartoons—for the first time ever—as *Dr. Seuss*. While it would take several more months before Geisel would use it exclusively, six months after joining *Judge*, he had arrrived at the pseudonym that would define him for the rest of his life.

Why Dr. Seuss? Perhaps predictably, Geisel's tale would evolve with the telling. In the preferred version of the story—the one Geisel told over and over—he adopted the designation of *Dr.* because, as he explained in 1934, "I always wanted a PhD but never got it, so I assumed my own doctorate."[28] The story would become slightly more nuanced over time, with Ted incorporating into the narrative a bit of reverence for T. R. Geisel, who had paid for his son to pursue an ultimately unfulfilled doctoral degree. "I ended up saving him thousands of dollars by giving myself my own doctorate," Ted said in 1979. "I just took the title, because I was going crazy earning it."[29] Perhaps there was a bit of guilt behind Ted's decision to assume the mantle of Dr. Seuss.

And yet there was also another completely different version of the story. Geisel had debuted the designation *Dr.* with the first installment of his "Boids and Beasties" feature—and had chosen that particular byline to give the pseudoscientific pieces a bit of scholarly credibility. "It was a mock zoological thing," he explained in 1975, "and I put the 'Dr.' on the Seuss to make it sound more professorial."[30] It made sense, then, that he would use the same professorial designation for his mock history of contract bridge and, later, for a reimagining of Arthurian legends—the byline was almost always attached to pieces that could be made all the funnier with a bit of faux erudition. Geisel, who had always tinkered with pseudonyms, may have liked the sound of Dr. Seuss enough to stick with it. But it's also feasible that the real story contained a bit of both tales: perhaps Ted had initially adopted the title *Dr.* to give his mock-serious pieces a bit of ersatz gravitas, then retained the title out of deference to his father and the doctorate that never was.

One could also ask why the pseudonym was adopted at all. Geisel had begun his stint at *Judge* as an unknown artist. He could have chosen to sign his name any way he wanted—he could even have signed his work as Geisel or Ted G., as he had done in high school. Geisel later offered two explanations for his decision to cloak himself in a pseudonym. "I wanted to write the great American novel," he explained to *The Dartmouth* in 1934. "And I wanted to keep the name of Geisel clean in case that day should ever come."[31] But there was more to it than that; in a letter to Whit Campbell, Geisel stated that he was slightly embarrassed to be working for *Judge*, and felt more comfortable hiding behind a pen name. "I am writing for *Judge*, and must dumb things up," he wrote to Campbell in March of 1928, then added parenthetically, "(hence the assumed name)."[32]

Even worse, he told Campbell, there were times when he worried he was falling into a creative rut. "I still eke out an existence from *Judge*," he wrote in March 1928. "Perhaps it is bad for me to eke it out so easily. For it keeps me abed late of mornings, and allows me to cavort in the evening." He told Campbell he had just put together a series of cartoons based on the stories of King Arthur, and begged his friend to "please write and tell me frankly what you think of them." To his credit, Geisel was trying something new with the piece, writing the text in Old English rhyme. But he and his editor had argued about that particular setup and Geisel had been asked to rewrite the piece "into American slang." Worse, he said, his editor "took out all the humor . . . and inserted his own little jests instead." Geisel was worried the cartoons carrying his name were now an unfunny mess. "I think it rotten from a humorous point of view," he told Campbell, "but I still maintain that the ed[itor] may be right, just being as it is."[33]

Ted's instincts were mostly correct. The series "Ye Knights of Ye Table Round: Being the Inside Dope on King Arthur's Court" began running in *Judge* in late March 1928—and they weren't all that funny. The cartoons were still heavily inked and crosshatched, though there were still some inspired moments, such as an "apartment castle" fitted out with segmented towers stretching upward at odd angles, held in place by brackets and struts, and looking very much like some of Dr. Seuss's later cartoon architecture. Still, Geisel knew it wasn't his best stuff, though he was hoping the cartoons might be amusing to readers of "the average point of view." "I grant you they are terrible," he sighed to Whit. "I am a commercial sort of fellow, though, and am playing it for all I am worth."[34]

The admitted "commercial sort of fellow" was also still intentionally dropping in plenty of references to brand names in his work—and a cartoon appeared in the January 14, 1928, issue of *Judge* that Geisel would rightly say "changed my whole life." In the cartoon, a knight sits bolt upright in a canopy bed, knees drawn up to his chest, armor stacked on the floor next to him, as a Seussian dragon—which looks more like a gigantic cat than a lizard—pokes its head menacingly under the canopy, very nearly in the knight's lap. "Darn it all, another Dragon," says the knight. "And just after I'd sprayed the whole castle with Flit." As an insecticide joke, it was hardly a thigh-slapper—but while writing the gag, Ted had fussed over which of the two major brands of insecticide—Fly-Tox or Flit?—to use in his punch line. In the end, he had simply flipped a coin. "It came up heads, for Flit," said Ted.[35]

It would be the luckiest coin toss of Ted Geisel's life. The January 14 issue of *Judge* was picked up in a beauty salon by the wife of Lincoln Cleaves, the executive in charge of the Flit insecticide account for the McCann-Erickson advertising firm. Mrs. Cleaves brought Geisel's Flit cartoon to the attention of her husband and suggested McCann-Erickson bring Ted in to talk about creating more Flit ad campaigns.[36]

Lincoln Cleaves was definitely interested and seems to have connected with Ted fairly quickly, promising to try him out on a Flit advertising campaign. But it was taking Cleaves a long time to make up his mind, and Ted complained to Whit Campbell that the Flit people were "dickering" with him, dangling before him what he thought was surely a too-good-to-be-true promise of $1,200 for twelve Flit cartoons. "God pray it go through," Ted wrote fretfully.[37] Perhaps as a reminder to Cleaves that he was still waiting for a response, Ted inserted a cartoon in the March 31 issue of *Judge* in which a derby-wearing, mustachioed gentleman—with a suitcase label reading "Miracle Bug Company"—blasts a flea circus using a pump bug sprayer clearly labeled FLIT.[38]

Cleaves and Ted eventually connected, and Ted was put under contract to create a series of Flit cartoons for McCann's client, the Standard Oil Company of New Jersey, which produced Flit and marketed it through its subsidiary, Stanco Inc. Ted's first ad would appear in the May 31, 1928, issue of *Life* magazine, showing a concerned father looking out the window as his son gargles loudly below. "Don't worry, Papa," his daughter says reassuringly. "Willie just swallowed a bug, and I'm having him gargle with Flit."[39] Ted would create a total of six cartoons for the 1928 campaign, with a new one running every other week from May through August, the height of mosquito season.

In an era when most print ads were heavy with text or featured large photographs of the product, Geisel's Flit advertisements didn't look like any other ads. For one thing, they were intentionally funny—a nearly foreign concept in advertising at that time. In some cartoons—such as one early ad featuring a judge sentencing a somber-looking man to prison for refusing to let his wife use Flit—the product itself was mentioned but not shown. Other ads involved Flit visibly being used in creative ways, such as a four-panel cartoon in which a mosquito-plagued cellist rigs a Flit gun to spritz repellent with every movement of his bow. Over time, Ted would draw increasingly wilder-looking insects getting their comeuppance with Flit in outlandish ways, including one ad titled "The Suicide" in which a mosquito holds a Flit gun against his body, preparing to finish himself off with a blast of the fatal spray.

But Ted's most lasting contribution to the Flit campaign was the memorable four-word punch line he used over and over again: "Quick, Henry! The Flit!" The catchphrase would be squawked, for instance, by a ventriloquist dummy as he leapt away from his performer to escape an enormous mosquito, shrieked by a ghost at a séance as it waved away a swarm of insects, and spelled out in cursive by four snakes as advice to a mosquito-bothered snake charmer. The phrase became a national phenomenon, so popular that it would show up not only in full-page magazine ads but also on billboards, in subway stations, and at bus stops. The catchphrase eventually became so embedded in the culture of the era that it was used as a punch line by comedians for an easy laugh or referenced in the lyrics of popular songs. In the first year of Geisel's Flit campaign, the advertising trade magazine *Printers' Ink* noted, in its year-end assessment, that "[t]he most momentous theme of the summer of 1928 was not Prohibition, presidential election, aviation, or world peace. It was mosquitos."[40]

Geisel had created a juggernaut of an ad campaign—and he had also found a steady source of income that would make him a lot of money. In the first years of his contract, Geisel estimated he made about $12,000 annually from advertising—nearly $200,000 today. The Flit campaign would prove so popular, in fact, that Ted would do work for Stanco for the next seventeen years. "That toss of a coin determined my whole career," he said later.[41] More important, the money Geisel earned through his advertising work would buy him his artistic freedom. There would be no more frantic pitching of projects to *The New Yorker* or merely eking out an existence with *Judge*. What would eventually become the Dr. Seuss empire would be laid on a foundation built and paid for with Standard Oil money.

With his Standard Oil contract in place, as well as a bit of unexpected money from Helen's late father's trust, the Geisels felt secure enough in September 1928 to abandon their apartment in the seedy Chelsea neighborhood for a more upscale and uptown address at 393 West End Avenue. "There were many fewer dead horses," Ted said, with some relief. He also quickly learned their new phone number was only one digit away from that of the neighborhood fish market, and Ted took great delight in wrong numbers. If a customer mistakenly dialed the Geisel apartment asking for a delivery of two pounds of haddock, Ted would draw a cartoon of a two-pound haddock on a piece of cardboard, and have the drawing delivered to the baffled customer.

While Ted and Helen liked their new address, they would have their heads turned by yet another new location late in November. To celebrate their first anniversary, the Geisels took a vacation to the West Coast to visit Ted's old New York City roommate John Rose in the little seaside town of La Jolla, California. Ted was immediately smitten with the place, with its Spanish missionary style buildings, exotic flora, and perpetually sunny skies. The Geisels decided then and there they would save up to relocate to La Jolla. On their return to New York, Helen and Ted began to curtail their spending, cutting back most notably on the time and money they invested in going to speakeasies. "When I saw La Jolla, I thought, 'This thing is too good to be wasted on old people,'" Ted said later, reflecting on the memory. "One of my life ambitions was to get to live [t]here before I grew old."[42]

• • • •

Standard Oil clearly knew it had struck pay dirt in Geisel's Flit campaign. The cartoons had been so popular in 1928, in fact, that Stanco decided to launch its 1929 ad campaign five months early, releasing Ted's first ad in January instead of May—and then ran new cartoons every three weeks for the entire year. And for those who couldn't get enough of the Flit ads, Stanco would even release a collection of the cartoons in a small paperback book in September 1929—the first-ever collection of Dr. Seuss cartoons. Geisel, however, wouldn't make a dime off it.

Judge, too, seemed to recognize they had a celebrity in their midst; the March 23, 1929, issue would sport a cover by Dr. Seuss—his first national magazine cover—featuring a mustachioed gentleman with a butterfly net hunting a Seussian menagerie of animals, including a giraffe, a turtle, several birds, and an elephant with a long, curling trunk. The beautiful full-color cover would be his first of five for the magazine. And almost as if Geisel appreciated that he now had a reputation—that he no longer had to "dumb things up"—even his prose pieces for *Judge* became cleverer and more experimental, especially as he began poking fun at and deconstructing the English language.

One of his best pieces would run in April 1929, a full-page titled "Ough! Ough! Or Why I Believe in Simplified Spelling," in which Ted took great delight in playing with the various possible pronunciations of *-ough* in American English. Ted's narrator, for instance, lands a job performing chores on the farm of Mr. Hough, who spends his days lounging in the bough of a tree that dangles into a horse trough. "Mr. Hoo!" shouts the narrator, "Your Boo is in the Troo!" In another, Ted's narrator takes a beating at the hands of a boxing champ and cries out, "Eno! Eno! I'm thruff!"[43]

And yet Geisel would still produce his share of racial jokes, both in *Judge* and in his ads for Flit. The humor wasn't intentionally cruel— there were no jokes about slavery, lynching, or other kinds of violence—but Geisel's art and language played squarely into the negative racial stereotypes so pervasive in the mainstream culture of the era. One 1929 Flit ad features a black husband leaning lazily back in his chair, smoking a pipe, while his wife—up to her elbows in laundry— berates him for his inability to find a job. "You hold a job, Worthless?" she says derisively. "Say, nigger, when you all hold a job a week, mosquitoes will brush their teeth with Flit and like it!" Geisel likely regarded it as yet another joke about a hen-pecked husband—one of his most-used tropes—rather than as a commentary on race; the offensive stereotype was the backdrop for the joke rather than the punch line itself. Still, it's not one of Geisel's better moments as an adman.

More shocking was a full-page cartoon in the June 7, 1929, *Judge* in which Geisel drew a "Cross-Section of the World's Most Prosperous Department Store," where patrons could acquire items needed for clichés: a fly to put in the ointment, for example, or a needle for a haystack. The final joke on the page—in a reference to a figure of speech common to the time—was a large room where shoppers could take home a "nigger for your woodpile."[44] Ted's drawing shows the store's tuxedo-clad owner proudly gesturing to a room full of black men— drawn in the big-lipped, wide-eyed, ink-black caricature typical of the time—who smile and chat among themselves, waiting patiently for purchase. The careless reference to slavery can't be missed—the smiling men are for sale, after all—and yet, to Geisel, the joke was likely never intended to be at the expense of black men. Rather, it was about the frequently used idiom, which has since rightly fallen out of use, replaced mainly by *skeleton in the closet.*

As far as Geisel was concerned, he was working within the norms of the era, relying on the language and cartoon stereotypes he'd been reading and seeing in the mass media since childhood. Pop culture of the era portrayed nearly every ethnic group—and even some white nationalities—as overtly negative caricatures, whether it was buck-toothed Chinese workers, slovenly besotted Irishmen, or parsimonious Jewish bankers with impossibly long noses. Two years earlier, the year's most successful motion picture, *The Jazz Singer,* had featured Al Jolson performing "Mammy" in blackface—and Ted's cartoons of black men and women would almost always resemble the predominant blackface negative stereotype perpetuated on film and in print.

Further, the stereotypical patois spoken by Geisel's black characters came straight out of the *Amos 'n' Andy* radio show and his beloved Rover Boys books; meanwhile, the casual usage of the pejorative *nigger* could be found in the Hardy Boys books and in the Western novels of Zane Grey. Even the celebrated cartoonist George Herriman, who was of mixed race, had sometimes relied on racial stereotypes for easy laughs in his various newspaper strips. Over the course of a career that would span seven decades, Geisel drew tens of thousands of cartoons, of which only a small number are truly racially insensitive—there are probably more misogynistic cartoons and cartoons about drinking. And yet the fact that as a young man, Ted perpetuated negative racial stereotypes cannot be denied. He would evolve—but it would take time.

••••

Nineteen twenty-nine was a good year for Geisel—but for millions of Americans, the decadent, booze-soaked 1920s would come crashing to an end in a single day. On Tuesday, October 29, 1929—so-called Black Tuesday—the stock market collapsed in a devastating meltdown that sent fortunes plummeting and plunged large swaths of the American economy into a near perpetual free fall. Almost overnight, New York went from celebratory to solemn as the encroaching Great Depression slowly shuttered factories, put families out onto the street, and shattered millions of American workers.

Ted and Helen would not go completely untouched; Helen's brother, a securities analyst, would be among more than a million unemployed New Yorkers. The relative steadiness of the advertising industry meant Ted's work remained stable and his income stayed moderately secure. But knowing his own prospects were sound didn't make it any easier to watch as jobless and homeless New Yorkers formed long breadlines and thronged soup kitchens. "[All] these people who have nowhere to go," he said sadly.[45]

Ted worried, too, about his father, who had managed to successfully live off real estate investments for most of the past decade, but hadn't had a paying job since Prohibition had closed down the family business in 1920. Looking for employment in the public sector, T.R. had ambitiously sought the Republican nomination for mayor of Springfield in 1929, but hadn't made it past the primary. Ted, a Democrat, had done his best to follow the election in a nonpartisan silence as his father lost the vote by a wide margin and returned to his post on the Springfield park commission, where he'd been seated, without pay, since 1909.

T.R's professional fortunes would suddenly improve in early 1930, when his colleagues on the commission asked him to serve as park commission chairman—one step away from the post of park superintendent, which came with it not only control over the park system but also a regular salary. Then, in the summer of 1930, Superintendent Charles M. Ladd resigned, and T.R. was elevated to the post of superintendent—a position he would hold for the next thirty-eight years.

Ted was proud and slightly relieved that his father now had both an income and a purpose. Over the next decade, Ted's father would help steer Springfield through the Depression, dispensing park funds and federal Works Progress Administration money to employ local workers and improve the park system. "He built tennis courts, trout streams, three golf courses, bowling greens," Ted recalled later. Some of his projects would even bear his name, as grateful Springfielders called one picnic area in Forest Park "Geisel Grove." "He changed people's lives more than he would have done if he'd been a millionaire. He used WPA funds and government money to put people to work. So he ended up a very worthwhile guy."[46]

Meanwhile, Ted's sister, Marnie, found her marriage to lawyer Lloyd Dahmen rapidly deteriorating—and in the autumn of 1929, she and Nettie Geisel, with two-year-old Peggy in tow, traveled to Reno, Nevada, to establish the state residency needed to end her marriage quickly. Once the divorce had been finalized, Marnie and Peggy moved in with T.R. and Nettie in Springfield. While Marnie took a job as a substitute teacher of German, she was already beginning to spiral into alcoholism—a cruel and difficult disease to suffer in a family full of brewers and day drinkers.

While Ted's contract with Standard Oil prohibited him from working on any other national campaigns, his advertising work in 1930 expanded to include several local and regional campaigns, including ads for desk fans sold by General Electric. The Flit ads were continuing to run all year long, with many now appearing in full color and showing up in the pages of *Life*, *Judge*, *The Saturday Evening Post*, *The New Yorker*, *Time*, and *Collier's*. The ads would also run in more than 3,600 newspapers, including the *Springfield Union*, where it was well known that the *Dr. Seuss* signed on each cartoon was actually local boy Theodor Seuss Geisel.

Ted had also extended his freelance work into other magazines beyond *Judge*, placing some of his most charming pieces in *Life*, where he would have a number of covers and begin a popular series called "Life's Little Educational Charts," featuring Seussian animals like the Mnpf and the Pflupf. And still there were the booze jokes, such as a beautiful full-page cartoon in *Life* featuring more of Ted's fanciful "D.T. Beasts"—including a pair of elephant birds—being loaded into the Ark by Noah's "dissolute brother, Goah," who counts the animals with a jug of moonshine dangling from one hand.[47] It was no wonder so many of Ted's fans were beginning to call him "Dr. Souse."

That winter, Ted and Helen spent Christmas in Springfield, staying in the house on Fairfield not only with his parents, but also with his sister, Marnie, and her daughter, Peggy. The house was crowded but warm, and Ted took an immediate shine to his three-year-old niece. On Christmas Eve, he sneaked to the attic over Marnie and Peggy's room and began stamping loudly and ringing sleigh bells. "Everyone would be asleep and he would tromp around and ring Christmas bells and make noise like Santa and his reindeer," said Peggy's son Ted Owens. It was a tradition Ted would continue for years. "My mom enjoyed it immensely," said Owens, "even when she no longer believed in Santa."[48]

Always the proud Dartmouth man, Geisel would take part in campus events when he could, and in 1931 he was pleased to be asked to provide the art for Dartmouth's annual Winter Carnival program. Ted attended the festivities with Helen in February, where he was delighted to see the Phi Gamma Delta fraternity house had created a Dr. Seuss–inspired catlike snow sculpture, with a tail that wound its way in through the front door, through the house, and out into the backyard. "It went into the fireplace and melted, and they had pledges replenishing the tail for three days," Ted said.[49]

As a token of their appreciation, the fraternity gave Geisel some odd-shaped antlers they'd found. Geisel was enchanted, and when he returned to his office in New York, he began sculpting animal heads to mount them on. "I can thank the Phi Gams for starting me in my career as a taxidermist," he told *The Dartmouth*.[50] He would receive other animal horns from the Springfield Zoo, courtesy of his father, and would eventually use them to perch atop several Seussian animal trophy heads, which he sculpted himself and hung proudly on the walls of his office. "They are his main hobby," a somewhat exasperated Marnie explained to one reporter, noting also that the heads, with their smiling faces and wide eyes, gave her nightmares.[51] A photo of Ted from this time shows him sitting at his desk, wearing a matching striped jacket and tie, pencil clamped tightly in his mouth—an ashtray littered with cigarette butts sits at his right elbow—inking a drawing of a unicorn he would eventually turn into one of his sculptured heads. Later, Ted would have his animal heads mass-produced and sold as "rare and amazing" trophies from the Bobo Isles, a nod to the Bo-Bobians he had once drawn in the pages of *Jacko*.

February 1931 would also see the publication of *Boners*, the first mainstream book to feature cartoons by Dr. Seuss.[52] *Boners* was a collection of unintentionally funny bits of student writing—featuring nuggets like "A polygon is a dead parrot"[53]—lifted from real school exams and term papers. Geisel was brought in by Viking Press to provide twenty cartoons, and was given a prominent credit on the book's cover and spine, a sure sign of his growing name recognition. To Geisel's surprise, *Boners* was an immediate hit, selling out of six printings in four months, pushing its way onto the *New York Times* bestseller list, and inspiring a second volume—aptly titled *More Boners*, also illustrated by Dr. Seuss—only two months after the release of the first volume. Sales were brisk, and reviewers were particularly effusive about Geisel's cartoons. "The drawings by Dr. Seuss are hilarious,"[54] wrote *The New York Times*, while another reviewer called the cartoons "simply swell."[55]

Geisel saw none of the profits from it. "I was money-worried," he said. "The two [*Boner*] books were booming and I was not."[56] As the artist for the book, Geisel had been work for hire, and he'd been paid a flat fee for his twenty cartoons. In most cases, it was the writer, with his royalties, who made far more from a successful book than the work-for-hire illustrator. It was at this point, Ted later explained, that he came to realize "there was no sense in just illustrating books."[57] To make any real money in publishing, he'd have to be both the writer *and* the artist.

It was an attractive idea, both financially and creatively. Geisel's work for Stanco and the Flit campaign paid well and didn't take up much of his time. "I'd get my year's work done in about three months," he said later, and as a result, "I had all this spare time and nothing to do."[58] That wasn't quite true; Geisel actually had plenty to do, with his commercial work for non-national campaigns, and the cartoons and prose pieces he was still regularly producing for magazines. But he *was* looking to expand his creative repertoire—and if he could get paid for it, so much the better.

Geisel would usually overstate the restrictive nature of his contract with Standard Oil—outside work was permitted, within reason—but he *did* have to be careful. The exclusive nature of his contract with Standard Oil, he explained, "forbade me from doing an awful lot of stuff."[59] Writing and illustrating children's books, however, wasn't a forbidden activity. "I would like to say I went into children's book work because of my great understanding of children," Geisel said later. In truth, "I went in because it wasn't excluded by my Standard Oil contract."[60]

His first children's book, he decided, would be an ABC primer, featuring Seussian animals illustrating each letter of the alphabet. But Geisel was experimenting with colored inks for the project, which he knew was going to make it difficult to reproduce cheaply for the mass market. "It had about seventeen different blues in it and three kinds of red," Ted said. "It would have cost about $150 a copy."[61] Geisel shopped the book around to several publishers, including Viking, the publisher of *Boners*. No one took it. He would keep working.

• • • •

During visits to Springfield in late 1930 and early 1931, Ted had noticed that his mother's health was declining. Nettie Geisel was enjoying life with her daughter and granddaughter in the house—each evening, she would sing to Peggy the same baker's song she had sung to Ted—but she had been complaining of headaches for several months. However, Nettie had recently converted to Christian Science, which meant there would be no calls to doctors, no consulting with physicians. Illness, she was certain, was something that would leave the body of its own accord.

Early in 1931, Nettie alarmed her family when she nodded off in the middle of a bridge game and lost consciousness for some time. Still she refused medical attention. Finally, in early March, over Nettie's objections, T.R. took his wife immediately to Peter Bent Brigham Hospital in Boston, where doctors discovered a fatal brain tumor. Shortly thereafter, on March 8, 1931, Nettie Seuss Geisel died at age fifty-two. She was buried at Oak Grove Cemetery in Springfield two days later.

T. R. Geisel was devastated; Ted was nearly inconsolable. He and Helen would travel in Yugoslavia for seven weeks over the summer to give Ted the opportunity to mourn his mother and "to clear the air and get new ideas." Marnie, meanwhile, would do her best to take over the Geisel household. There would be no more substitute teaching of German. "Marnie had to give up everything to keep house for her father and to take care of her daughter, who was then still a little girl," said her grandson Ted Owens.[62] Her alcoholism would remain largely hidden from neighbors, and the Geisels would never speak of her condition publicly, cloaking her condition as agoraphobia. Marnie would rarely venture far beyond the door of 74 Fairfield Street.

Despite Ted's grumblings about money, he was doing well enough that he and Helen could vacate their apartment on West End Avenue in August to move into an even larger place at 17 East 96th Street, less than a block from Central Park. For Ted, the move had been somewhat strategic, for the new location was more convenient to the uptown publishers to whom he still hoped to pitch his projects. But there was also an element of ego involved: the Upper East Side neighborhood was more prestigious, and Ted would almost always gauge success by address. Yet Ted would never feel entirely at home in a Park Avenue neighborhood, a state of mind revealed in a bit of hastily scribbled verse:

> Mrs. Van Bleck
> Of the Newport Van Blecks
> Is so goddamn rich
> She has gold-plated sex

Whereas Miggles and Mitzi
And Bitzi and Sue
Have the commonplace thing
And it just has to do.[63]

Through a frequent dinner companion named Hugh Troy—a fun-loving, six-foot-five practical joker and Cornell graduate—Ted and Helen began to be invited to some of New York's more fashionable dinner parties, thrown at some of New York's more fashionable addresses. It was through Hugh Troy that the Geisels found themselves at the exceptionally posh dinner table of Frank A. Vanderlip, the wealthy president of National City Bank and a co-creator of the Federal Reserve—and here again, Ted refused to take the evening too seriously. Before dinner, he and Hugh Troy snuck into the kitchen and slipped a fake pearl into one of the dozens of oysters sitting on an enormous dinner platter, waiting to be presented to the evening's guests. When dinner was finally served, a Wall Street broker discovered the pearl in his oyster, prompting a lengthy deliberation over who was entitled to the pearl: Vanderlip, who had purchased the oyster, or the broker who had found it? Helen, who thought Ted let the argument go on far too long, finally forced her husband to confess to the practical joke. Ted would tell the story for years, and was later somewhat annoyed to learn that author John Cheever—a friend of the Vanderlips—had been telling the fake pearl story as his own.

By early 1932, Geisel's contract with *Judge* had expired, but at this point, he hardly needed the work or the exposure; even Walter Winchell was a fan of Dr. Seuss, declaring "I think Dr. Seuss is grand!" in his nationally syndicated column.[64] Apart from his work for *Life*, Ted was also being published in *College Humor* and *Liberty*—a magazine he liked because it paid a staggering rate of $300 per page—and would soon show up in *University Magazine*, *New York Woman*, *Collier's*, and *Ballyhoo*. "[I was] the Typhoid Mary of magazines," Geisel later joked, "every magazine I've ever worked for had gone bankrupt, and it's not my fault."[65] Lately, however, he was slowly moving away from magazine work to focus instead on advertising and other projects.

Those other projects still included the ABC book, for which Geisel was even more determined to find a home. He was still sending the finished art around to publishers—who, he complained, often mishandled his pages and smudged them with "thumb prints, footprints, grease, muck, and rubble."[66] At the same time, there had been some interest from an exhibitor who also hoped to display the finished art at Dartmouth as part of a showcase of Dr. Seuss art—but Geisel was hedging his bets on that one, still holding on to the hope the book might be picked up by a mainstream publisher. By May 1932, however, any hope for a publishing deal was abandoned when his pages went missing, lost in the mail. To this day, the ABC book remains an enigmatic entry in the Seuss oeuvre.

That autumn, Ted cast his vote for Franklin D. Roosevelt for president. For the most part, Ted's cartoons had remained generally free of politics—the exception was a cartoon in the otherwise apolitical *Liberty* suggesting the Republican party swap its elephant mascot for any number of winged, horned Seussian creatures—but his vote for FDR was seen by the staunchly Republican T. R. Geisel as an act of willful political defiance. As the 1932 election approached, Ted and his father had quarreled over politics and candidates, and the tenor of their debate had gotten so heated that Ted and T.R. vowed to table any further discussions of politics—at least until after the next election. Ted also promised to refrain from doing any overtly political cartooning—a vow he was destined not to keep.

• • • •

Geisel's work on the Flit campaign had turned Flit into one of the most recognizable brands in the nation, and transformed Ted—or rather, Dr. Seuss, whose name appeared at the bottom of every Flit ad—into one of the nation's best-known artists. *Vanity Fair* even ran a brief profile of him, calling Dr. Seuss the "Czar of the Insect World" for his "insecticide dramas, the Flit advertisements, which have made his name famous among cartoonists."[67] Dr. Seuss had made insecticide *funny*—and now the Standard Oil Company, through its affiliation with Esso, was hoping he could do the same thing for another otherwise uninspiring product, their Essolube 5-Star Motor Oil.

For the Essolube campaign, Geisel created a series of creatures called Moto-Monsters that preyed on cars and could be thwarted by the use of Esso's motor oil: the monkey-like Karbo-nockus, the catlike Moto-raspus, or the Zero-doccus, a gigantic, fuzzy snow creature that targeted automobiles in freezing temperatures. "Foil the Karbo-nockus!" would never become the same pop culture phenomenon as "Quick, Henry! The Flit!" However, Ted's Essolube campaign would be even more omnipresent than the Flit cartoons, showing up not only in newspapers but also in brochures, on subways, on gas station walls, and even in jigsaw puzzles. "It wasn't the greatest pay," said Ted, "but it covered my overhead so I could experiment with my drawings."[68]

The Essolube work did indeed cover the Geisels' overhead; with the earnings from the Karbo-nockus, Ted and Helen were able to move again, this time to a fourteenth-floor apartment at 1160 Park Avenue, about two blocks south of their apartment on East 96th Street—and a much more prestigious address. While Ted would joke that "we moved when we discovered we could live just as cheaply on Park Avenue,"[69] there was no denying that the Geisels had officially arrived. The dinner parties and evening drinking sessions would start again—and now that Prohibition had been repealed, there was no more need for speakeasies. Drinking was legal again.

Also arriving at 1160 Park Avenue was a housewarming gift from Ted's father, a gigantic stone slab encasing a fossilized dinosaur footprint. The gift was partly a joke and partly a tangible metaphor for T. R. Geisel's own competitive nature. In this case, the competition had sprung from a dinner Ted had arranged with him, his father, and Cyril Aschenbach, T. R. Geisel's favorite Dartmouth football player. T.R. had wanted to talk football with the former team captain, but

Aschenbach, a collector of rare antiques, had only wanted to discuss sconces and other recent acquisitions. T.R. had been visibly annoyed, and at the end of the evening warned his son, "I'm going to send you an antique that will shut Cyril Gaffey Aschenbach up forever." The dinosaur print had been extracted from a shale pit near Holyoke, and T.R. had ordered it delivered to his son. Ted loved it—"My father, as you see, had an unusual sense of humor"—and would keep it with him, moving it from place to place, for the rest of his life. "Half of the people I show it to think I've made it myself," he said later, laughing.[70]

Ted enjoyed playing the role of man-about-town from his Park Avenue apartment, and in May 1934, when *The Dartmouth* sent a young reporter named Bob Warren to New York to write a profile of the former *Jacko* editor whose name was now on billboards across the country, Ted couldn't resist playfully yanking the young man's chain. When Warren showed up in the late afternoon, Geisel made a point of answering the door in his pajamas, hair standing on end, looking "as if he had just climbed out of bed." In his most world-weary tone, he told Warren, "I get to bed around three in the morning and about ten someone calls and says, 'We need that stuff right away. Can you hurry it up?' It's a bad life." As he lit a cigarette and sat down for the interview, Ted casually asked Warren, "Truth or fiction?" Warren, who understood and appreciated exactly what Ted was up to, gave an answer worthy of Dr. Seuss himself: "A little bit of both ought to do quite well," the young man replied.

The resulting interview was a good-natured mess, more fiction than truth, with Geisel ping-ponging from one subject to another, changing subjects in the middle of answers or ignoring some questions altogether. Geisel talked about visiting angry llamas in Peru (that one was partly true, as he and Helen had recently visited South America), studying animals in Africa, and being disappointed to discover there were no longer any Dalmatian dogs in Dalmatia. The session did, however, result in one perhaps unintentionally beautiful nugget of wisdom: "I've discovered one thing, and that is that God has turned out more ridiculous creatures than I have."[71] The interview did much to convey the reputation Geisel was cultivating as a whimsical and well-traveled devil-may-care genius, knocking off clever cartoons and advertisements as easily as he knocked back cocktails. After publication of the interview in *The Dartmouth*, Geisel was so pleased with the piece that he happily began providing his alma mater with original art to use in its annual fundraising literature, while *Jacko*—finally lifting Dean Laycock's 1925 injunction on his work—would publish some of Ted's new cartoons.

Jacko wouldn't be the only paper running new Dr. Seuss cartoons. In early 1935, Geisel had the opportunity to realize a longtime dream by producing a weekly color comic strip called *Hejji* for several of publishing magnate William Randolph Hearst's newspapers. Hearst took the comics pages seriously—many of his papers printed thirty-two pages of comics in full color, and he permitted some comics to take up an entire page—and Geisel used the opportunity to create a surreal, gorgeously colorful strip, crammed with jokes and situations he would use again later. The vaguely Arabian-influenced strip follows the adventures of Hejji in the Land of Baako—a land where whales live in water-filled craters of volcanoes, located in a place at such a high altitude that only Baakonese eagles can carry *other* birds into its airspace. And yet, in the first strip—published April 7, 1935—Hejji enters Baako riding on the back of a camel, and is immediately captured. He's then brought before the Mighty One—the turbaned, mustachioed leader of the kingdom—and Hejji and the Mighty One begin roaming the kingdom in a series of adventures that would run from week to week.

Geisel's art on *Hejji* is bright and clean—the self-aware crosshatching and shading are now gone—and very Seussian. It's some of Geisel's best work to date, with story elements and funny ideas that would show up in later work: a stack of turtles, an abandoned egg that needs to be sat upon, and Seussian castles with bent windows and intricate archways supported by struts. Geisel loved the comic strip format, both as an artist and as a reader. "At its best, the comic strip is an art form of such terrific *wumpf!* that I'd much rather spend any evening re-reading the beautifully insane sanities of George Herriman's *Krazy Kat* than to sit myself down in some opera house or hear some smiling Irish tenor murdering Pagliacci," he said later.[72]

Unfortunately, *Hejji* would be canceled by Hearst after twelve weeks, ending on a cliffhanger just as Hejji and the Mighty One are about to be jumped by the masked Evil One. Geisel insisted that he had been fired from the strip—it made for a better story. "A telegram came from William Randolph Hearst saying, 'Fire the last three people you hired,'" said Ted. "I was one of them, so that was the end of that career." But "[i]t's just as well," Ted added. "I didn't know where the story was going next."[73]

What he did know, he said later, was that "Flit was pouring out of my ears and beginning to itch me."[74] Fortunately, Standard Oil would assign him yet another unglamorous product, which he would once again promote with his usual fervor and flair. This time, the assignment came from executives at Essomarine—which manufactured oil for boat engines—who gave Geisel the task of providing the illustrations for a boating safety manual called *Secrets of the Deep, or The Perfect Yachtsman*. Geisel delivered a cover and several drawings, while *Yachting* magazine editor Bill Taylor—writing as "Old Captain Taylor"—provided the practical safety tips. The guide was full of good advice, but the art of Dr. Seuss, coupled with Taylor's spry writing, made the manual so popular that Standard Oil asked Geisel to create a special campaign for the upcoming 1936 National Boat Show in New York.

What Geisel created wasn't quite an advertising campaign for a specific product; his idea rarely even *mentioned* engine oil. Instead, he created an exclusive club that promoted the Essomarine *brand*, in the same way that Walt Disney had created the first Mickey Mouse Clubs in 1930 to promote the Disney name, and not just individual Disney cartoons. Working with several representatives of Esso, Geisel proposed creating the Seuss Navy, which came with its own letters of introduction, registration cards, and membership certificates—all busily and beautifully illustrated by Ted, who created a certificate overflowing with sailors and sea monsters, and affixed with the official seal, on which Ted had drawn a seal he would later name Nuzzlepuss. Every member of the Seuss Navy would have the rank of Admiral, except for Ted, who declared himself Admiral in Chief and Cartographer Plenipotentiary.

Esso initially printed only a few certificates to distribute at the 1936 boat show, limiting enrollment to owners of boats with inboard motors, but also smartly providing certificates to several high-profile boat owners. "[Sailor Vincent] Astor and [bandleader] Guy Lombardo and a few other celebrities hung these things in their yachts," recalled Ted. "And very soon everyone who had a putt-putt [boat] wanted to join the Seuss Navy."[75] What people really wanted were Ted's certificates—and eventually anyone, even those without boats, could join the Seuss Navy.

And join they did, attracting more than 75,000 members in the first two years of the program.[76] Esso was delighted—and so was Geisel, as every boat show presented another opportunity to throw a big Seuss Navy party where food was plentiful and booze flowed freely. "It was cheaper to give a party for a few thousand people, furnishing all the booze, than it was to advertise in full-page ads," Geisel said. For the print ads, he would go on to create a series of sea creatures similar to his Moto-Monsters called Marine Muggs—like the Sludge Tarpon, a fish with a long pointed nose that took great joy in clogging boat engines—but the Moto-Monster ads would be secondary to the parties themselves, which received plenty of attention in the press, "and then they would have to explain it by talking about Essomarine," said Ted.[77]

As the campaign wore on, Ted would create short dramas to be performed at boat shows—or would show up at the Seuss Navy in full admiral costume, hamming it up for the party crowds and the cameras. "We used to get the Bayway refinery band to play for dances," said Ted. "One night they played four notes and walked off the stand, just to attract press attention."[78] Things also became more and more elaborate; eventually Ted would lead all of his new Admirals in a ceremony swearing an oath of allegiance to Mother Neptune. "The Seuss Navy was a rather corny outfit," Geisel said affectionately, but he was proud of it[79]—and for years, his official biography would include the Seuss Navy as one of the societies, clubs, and fraternal orders to which he belonged. Ted liked to claim that by the time World War II started, the Seuss Navy was one of the largest in the world. "We commissioned the whole Standard Oil fleet, and we also had . . . the *Queen Mary* and most of the ships of the U.S. lines."[80]

Geisel was enjoying his time with the Seuss Navy so much, in fact, that he began to dread returning to the relatively mundane Flit campaign. As he later explained, "I was on the [Flit] account for seventeen years, using exactly the same caption by drawing a different picture each time. Flit was my important account, and it was a seasonal product that sold during the summer, so I got all my work done in the first six months of the year." But now, he said, "I was really wanting something more to do."[81] He was still playing with the animal trophies—Geisel would call them the Seuss System of Unorthodox Taxidermy—and there would be other side projects: cartoons for sports magazines and women's fashion monthlies, and more jobs illustrating books, including Austin Ripley's adult-oriented *Mystery Puzzles*, featuring a cover by Ted with a genuinely frightening knife-wielding killer, and an interior cartoon of an innocent-looking little boy carrying an axe in one hand and a man's decapitated head in the other. But these were still work-for-hire jobs, generating no real ongoing income, and—worse for Ted—they just weren't that much fun to do.

He was, however, still intrigued by the idea of writing and illustrating children's books. "I'd like to say I got into children's books because I had a burning passion, a great message to bring to the youth of the world," Geisel said later, "but it was because I was going nuts."[82] Four years earlier, he had abandoned the ABC book for good—even had the pages not been lost in the mail, there had been a lack of enthusiasm for the project by publishers. Now he was ready to try his hand again at another children's book—but he had no idea what to write about. The inspiration wouldn't come.

As he would often do when stuck for ideas, Ted suggested taking an extended vacation, and he and Helen left for Europe in the summer of 1936. The two of them lounged for several weeks in the Bavarian Alps, taking long bus tours up into the mountains and drinking on open patios. Ted sketched the jagged mountain peaks, hoping for something, anything, to spark his imagination. But it was hard to be creative; war was in the air that summer, and as Ted traveled through the homeland of his *Großvater*, he was troubled by the oppressive Nazi presence and propaganda, and wary of Hitler as he watched him *"Sieg Heil!"* athletes at the Summer Olympic Games in Berlin. On August 29, as Ted boarded the Swedish American steamship MS *Kungsholm* at the Swedish port of Gothenburg, his notebook was still empty. The vacation had been a creative disappointment.

The trip back didn't make things any easier. Bad weather rocked the *Kungsholm* as it slowly made the weeklong trip back across the Atlantic toward New York. The 1,575 passengers were largely confined to indoor activities; with the rough waters, no one was permitted to linger on deck. Passengers were invited to "dance to the lively tempo of a modern dance orchestra," said the ship's promotional literature, "or merely enjoy an adventure in cracked ice and tall glasses."[83] Geisel, perhaps predictably, chose the latter. As he sank back into one of the sofas in the first class lounge, vodka on the rocks in hand, he became aware of the sound of the ship's engines thrumming in a distinctive, regular rhythm: bah-dah *bum* bah-dah *bum* bah-dah *bum* bah-dah *bum* . . . over and over again. It was inadvertent anapestic tetrameter—the same rhythm as Clement C. Moore's poem "A Visit from St. Nicholas"—and it was making Geisel crazy. "Finally Helen suggested I think up nonsense rhymes to be said to the rhythm of the damned engines," said Ted, "just to get rid of it."[84]

Using several sheets of the *Kungsholm*'s stationery, Geisel began scribbling down nonrhyming snippets of ideas for a narrative:

> A stupid horse and wagon
> Horse and chariot

Chariot pulled by a flying cat
Flying cat pulling a Viking ship
Viking ship sailing up a volcano
Volcano blowing hearts, diamonds & clubs

"Those are the first words I ever wrote in the field of writing for children," Geisel said later. "I put them down in the bar of the MS *Kungsholm*, sometime during the summer of 1936. I wrote them for only one reason. I was trying to keep my mind off the storm that was going on."[85] Next, as if trying to finally reckon with the pulsing rhythm of the ship's engines, Ted wrote a rhyming couplet:

I saw a giant eight miles tall
Who took the cards, 52 in all

Stuck, he then began reciting silly words and phrases, bouncing them to the rhythms of the engines, trying to make one stick. And then, "out of nowhere," as Geisel recalled, he suddenly had it:

And this is a story that no one can beat
I saw it all happen on Mulberry Street.[86]

CHAPTER 5

BRAT BOOKS

1936–1940

he MS *Kungsholm* docked in New York City on Tuesday, September 8, after ten days at sea. Geisel couldn't get off the boat fast enough; since his evening in the lounge listening to the throb of the ship's engines, he'd been playing with the same bouncing stanza over and over again:

And this is a story that no one can beat
I saw it all happen on Mulberry Street.[1]

"When I finally got off the ship, this refrain kept going through my head," he said. "I couldn't shake it."[2] But the story he would tell at that pulsing, rollicking pace wouldn't come quickly. Apart from his handwritten pages of random situations—"Flying cat pulling a Viking ship"—Geisel had no real idea what his story was or where it would go. In fact, he was probably not even certain he had the beginnings of a children's book on his hands. In his work so far, Geisel had shown no real disposition for writing for kids; children in his work tended to be the butts of jokes, taking the pie in the face rather than delivering it. In a 1928 *Judge* cartoon titled "Making Our Daughters Less Irritating," Ted created a device—worthy of T. R. Geisel and Rube Goldberg—that removed the pout from a young woman by swinging down a mallet "and socko" smacking her in the mouth.[3]

Geisel kept coming back to his handwritten list, which began with "A stupid horse and wagon," and became progressively more fanciful as the list went on. As he hunched over the drawing table in his apartment, Ted wrote out more and more verses, printing in pencil on yellow sheets of paper, and read them aloud to Helen, asking for her opinion. Helen, as Ted would quickly discover, had an ear for clunky rhymes and a knack for character; while Ted would never shy from asking for opinions on his work, there were few whose opinions he valued more than Helen's. With Helen both encouraging and editing him, Ted slaved over every word, every line, every beat, and every drawing. "I wrote the book to get it out," Ted said later. "Self-psychoanalysis."[4]

If it was self-psychoanalysis, then there was a bit of regression going on—for Geisel would dig deep into his Springfield upbringing for inspiration, giving his book some of the look, feel, and emotion of his own childhood. Ted's narrator would reflect his own fondness for exaggeration, his proclivity for "turning minnows into whales" in the name of "a story that no one can beat." For his "stupid horse and wagon" that his young narrator eventually turns into a parade of elephants, airplanes, and motorcycle policemen, Ted was influenced by the look of the horse-drawn beer delivery wagons that had rolled out of the various Geisel brewing companies. And those motorcycles ridden by the police escort as the tale gets wilder? They closely resemble the famous Indian motorcycles manufactured in Springfield, all the way down to their red bodies and white-walled tires. The Mulberry Street of Ted's book wasn't literally the Mulberry Street of Springfield, of course—there can be no traffic jam at the intersection of Mulberry and Bliss, for example, because in Springfield, those two streets never cross each other.[5] Instead, Ted had distilled his own gut and memories through the filter of imagination to turn a very real place into something larger and more magical than itself. Like the setting of any good children's story, Mulberry Street exists on an atlas of infinite imagination.

Geisel wrote and drew throughout the winter of 1936 and into early 1937, filling one trash can after another with discarded yellow pages and crumpled-up drawings. "Six months later, I found I had a book on my hands," he said. "So, what to do with it?"[6] As a freelancer, Geisel had no literary agent to shop his book around New York on his behalf; if he wanted his book in the hands of publishers, he was going to have to do it himself. So Ted hit the streets, lugging around his book—now called *A Story That No One Can Beat*—as he visited the offices of New York publishers. Other times, he mailed his original art to editors, waiting anxiously for weeks for a response, and—if the response was negative—hoping his art would be returned to him none the worse for wear.

To his increasing distress, the responses were all negative. Geisel would later recall being rejected by twenty-seven publishers, though that number would vary with the telling, ranging from as low as twenty to as high as forty-three. Regardless, no one was biting. While editors knew the Dr. Seuss name, it wasn't enough to overcome some initial skepticism. Some editors expressed concern that *A Story That No One Can Beat* had no real moral lesson for children—that the narrator, as a result of choosing *not* to share his tall tale with his father, had suffered no consequences. ("What's wrong with kids having fun reading without being preached at?" Ted groused.)[7] Others argued that he should leave the rhyming verse to Mother Goose. Mostly, said Geisel, "[t]he main reason they all gave was there was nothing similar on the market, so of course it wouldn't sell."[8]

In the late spring of 1937, Geisel decided he was done with it. After one last rejection, he was walking up Madison Avenue toward his apartment on East 96th Street, with his book tucked under one arm, determined "to burn it in the incinerator" when he got home. The walk back uptown would lead to one of the luckiest breaks of his career. "I'm a great believer in accidents," Geisel said later. "Everybody gets into things accidentally."[9] As he reached the 400 block of Madison Avenue, he ran into Marshall "Mike" McClintock—a fellow Dartmouth man, Class of 1926—who asked him what he was carrying.

"That's a book no one will publish," Geisel told him. "I'm lugging it home to burn."[10]

McClintock told Geisel he'd just started a job as the juvenile book editor for Vanguard Press—housed in the very building they were standing in front of at 424 Madison Avenue—and asked Geisel if he'd like to come inside to show his book to Vanguard president James Henle. "So we went inside," reported Geisel, ". . . and he took me to the president of Vanguard Press." Henle, a former labor reporter for the *New York World*, was a publishing crusader unafraid to embrace one of Vanguard's founding philosophies of publishing "unpublishable" books. While that sometimes meant gambling on controversial, socially relevant books like James T. Farrell's Studs Lonigan trilogy, it also meant taking a chance on books like Geisel's that didn't look like anything else on the market.

Henle turned Geisel over to editor Evelyn Shrifte, who agreed to formally acquire *A Story That Can't Be Beat*. According to Geisel, the entire meeting, from first hello to the signing of contracts, had taken only twenty minutes. Whether that was another of his dramatic embellishments is uncertain; what mattered was that a chance encounter with Mike McClintock on Madison Avenue had led to Geisel getting his first book published. "That's one of the reasons I believe in luck," Geisel said later. "If I'd been going down the other side of Madison Avenue, I would be in the dry-cleaning business today!"[11]

Even with the book in the hands of Henle and Shrifte, there was still a little work to be done. In general, said Shrifte, Henle's editorial approach was laissez-faire, offering lots of advice, but keeping his hands mostly off of it. And for the most part, Henle *did* leave his author alone, though he did ask Geisel to come up with a "snappier" title than *A Story That Can't Be Beat*, finally accepting Geisel's revised title, *And to Think That I Saw It on Mulberry Street*. Geisel also made one minor change in the text, naming the narrator after Mike McClintock's eight-year-old son, Marco. On the book's first page, he would dedicate *Mulberry Street* to Mike's wife, Helene McClintock, "Mother of the One and Original Marco."[12]

Once it was officially in the hands of Shrifte and the production department at Vanguard, however, Geisel still couldn't leave it alone. He was obsessed with the colors and the quality of the inks that would be used to mass-produce his art. "There was a great to-do with Ted about color samples," said Shrifte. "He knew what he wanted."[13] It was a refrain that would be fairly leveled at Ted Geisel for the rest of his life. By the end of August, however, with Shrifte ready to send the book to print, Ted finally had to let it go. He and Helen retreated to Maine for a short vacation at Blue Jay Bay. On arrival at their hotel, Ted found a telegram from Shrifte waiting for him: EVERYTHING OKAY DON'T WORRY.[14]

And to Think That I Saw It on Mulberry Street was published in September 1937, to only minimum fanfare. Vanguard worked hard to promote it, gambling on a full-page ad in *Publishers Weekly*, announcing the publishing debut of "the good Dr. Seuss."[15] And yet, even with the book taking up a full page in its own publication, *Publishers Weekly* refused to review it. Word of mouth seemed to help—and naturally, the book blew out of stores in Springfield, where residents swarmed Johnson's Bookstore on Main Street the night before the book's official release, banging on the store's locked doors and windows, begging clerks to sell them copies.[16]

The real breakthrough for *Mulberry Street* came in the pages of *The New Yorker*, where the esteemed writer and intellectual Clifton "Kip" Fadiman gave the book a brief but enthusiastic notice: "They say it's for children," wrote Fadiman, "but better get a copy for yourself and marvel at the good Dr. Seuss's impossible pictures and the moral tale of the little boy who exaggerated not wisely but too well."[17] Geisel was beside himself with excitement. "If the great Kip Fadiman likes it," he enthused, "I'll have to do another."[18]

The New York Times also reviewed the book favorably, calling it "highly original and entertaining," while *The Atlantic* called it "so completely spontaneous that the American child can take it to his heart on sight." Ted's old Dartmouth acquaintance Alexander Laing would review the book for the *Dartmouth Alumni Magazine*, writing his piece in spry though somewhat terrible rhyme, where he comically addressed the issue of the pronunciation of Ted's famous pseudonym:

You're wrong as the deuce
And shouldn't rejoice
If you're calling him Seuss.
He pronounces it *Soice*.[19]

The one opinion Ted craved, however, he'd never get; Nettie Geisel had died nine years earlier. "My mother would have loved it," Ted said later.[20]

Despite Vanguard's marketing efforts and the positive press, it would take a while before *Mulberry Street* would sell through its initial print run of 15,000 books. Geisel had worried, perhaps rightly, that *Mulberry Street*'s $1 cover price—"a lot of money" he said warily[21]— would be too expensive for Depression-era readers. Sales seemed to bear that out; by 1943, it had sold 31,600 copies—a respectable number to be sure, but one that would earn only about $3,500 in royalties over seven years.[22] It was clear that he hadn't yet found a new full-time profession. But even Geisel wasn't sure he *wanted* to be seen solely as a writer of books for what he called "the Kiddie-Kar and Bubble Gum Set." Writing for the children, he said, "was not a sign of going forward. This was a step down. A loss of face . . . literary slumming." Most children's books, he continued, "insulted the intelligence not only of the child, but also of the people who wrote them."[23]

And yet Geisel was on the leading edge of authors creating a new generation of respectable children's books, moving away from generic books heavy on morality or steeped in fairy tales, and toward creator-driven stories centered on character and identified with an author's particular artistic style or point of view. The year before Vanguard's publication of *Mulberry Street*, Viking Press had released *The Story of Ferdinand*, by writer Munro Leaf and artist Robert Lawson, a book with a likable, quirky main character and such strong crossover appeal—children and adults loved it—that it had raced to the top of the bestseller list, at one point outselling even *Gone with the Wind*. Two years after *Mulberry Street* came the first appearances of two iconic characters, in Ludwig Bemelmans's *Madeline* and H. A. Rey's

Cecily G. and the Nine Monkeys, featuring Curious George. Kids' books *would* get better and smarter—and Ted would consistently lead the way, inventing, revising, and reinventing them again over the next five decades, with the perpetually in print *Mulberry Street* as his calling card.

Still, with longevity comes reexamination and scrutiny—and as one generation after another continued to read *Mulberry Street*, so, too, would some of its blemishes, cracks, and outright biases come to be exposed. In the mid-1970s, Ted and *Mulberry Street* would draw the fire of the nascent women's movement for Marco's—and Ted's—dismissiveness of the female point of view. Early on in *Mulberry Street*, as Marco's tale gets taller, he rejects including in his story something as commonplace as a reindeer pulling a sleigh, arguing that anyone, "even Jane," could come up with something so obvious.[24]

Confronted in 1977 with Marco's dismissal of Jane, Geisel, at age seventy-two, seemed slightly exasperated at being taken to task over words he had written at age thirty-three. "Suddenly, after all these years, I'm deluged with protests over that one line," he told *The Saturday Evening Post*. "They say that line will cause boys to grow up feeling superior to their sisters. They demanded I change the line." Geisel was sympathetic to the argument and said he knew the request was "well-intentioned." But he also insisted that it was nothing personal—that Marco was merely expressing the same sort of sibling rivalry that had beset brothers and sisters, including him and Marnie, for eons. "The boy in my story *did* feel that way about his sister," he explained, "and I wasn't about to change a word."[25]

Equally as problematic was his use of a derisive term for Asians in *Mulberry Street*'s final two-page spread, where Ted had drawn a massive parade of characters, which included, as originally written, "A Chinaman who eats with sticks." The accompanying drawing reflected the stereotypical 1930s portrayal of Asians, depicting a man with a conical straw hat, chopsticks, and slanted slits for eyes. For most of his life, Geisel would never quite see the problem with this sort of cartoon portrayal. As he saw it, he was working within the established norms of the era—just as, in the same book, he had drawn a rajah with pointed slippers, a jeweled turban, and a thick upturned mustache, a look straight out of films like the 1938 Raymond Massey movie *The Drum*. For Geisel, it made the character immediately identifiable as a rajah, in the same way that all of Geisel's elected officials tended to wear striped trousers, tailcoats, and top hats. Seventy years on, however, the stereotypes typically haven't aged well, and remain a grating point of contention with many modern readers.

In 1937, however, the only real controversies surrounding *Mulberry Street* involved Geisel's unwillingness to personally promote it. Asked to speak about his book at the New York Public Library—Anne Carroll Moore, the children's librarian, was a fervent fan—Geisel made it as far as the front steps of the majestic building before losing his nerve and going home. Another time, Vanguard arranged for him to make a public appearance at a small college in Westchester County—an engagement he tried to squirm out of before Helen told him not to be rude. On the morning of his speech, Ted left the apartment on time, then never showed up at the venue. A panicked Helen called Shrifte, then friends, then family. Finally, expecting the worst, she called area hospitals, looking to see if Ted had been in an accident. As Helen sat anxiously by the phone into the evening, Ted finally showed up back at their apartment and sheepishly admitted he'd been hiding out at Grand Central Station all day. He had never even gotten on the train to Westchester.[26]

• • • •

With *Mulberry Street* proving slow to earn out, Geisel would have to continue to earn the bulk of his income through his advertising work. While Essomarine motor oil would remain his largest client—and the Seuss Navy would continue to take up much of his time—Geisel was having fun with some of his new accounts. He had picked up Schaefer Beer, doing his first work for an alcoholic beverage since the end of Prohibition. For one of the Schaefer ads, he managed to incorporate another of his hobbies, showing a taxidermied goat's head thirstily eyeing a tray of frothing beer glasses. He would also create an unconventional campaign for Hankey Bannister whisky, sculpting a Hankey Bird—a Scottish black bird in a kilt, vest, and tam, explained Ted, "developed after years of painstaking cross-breeding in the Seuss Laboratories"[27]—that could be attached to the whisky bottle with a spring clip. Customers would end up buying the whisky just so they could keep the sculpted bird.

In a brief self-penned biography Geisel submitted to the Dartmouth alumni magazine in March 1938, he hinted at a number of unrealized projects that may or may not have been in the works. "A sheaf of poems, musical comedy scripts, articles, etc. give evidence to the fact that Ted, one of these days, will characteristically break into a new field," he wrote in a third-person profile. "His ambition is to write, and his next venture might well be in movie scenarios." He also mentioned a new favorite hobby: "mummy-digging in South America."[28]

Lately, he had picked up an actual new hobby: collecting hats. "Why, he must have several hundred," Marnie admitted to one journalist years later. The hats—nearly a hundred of them, including fire hats, a feathered admiral's cap, and a particularly ornate Czech army helmet—were stored in his office closet, just close enough to the dining room that he could run in during parties to grab a handful for an impromptu bit of performing for guests. Recently, however, he had gone to them for another bit of motivation—for hats would play a key role in a new children's book he was working on for Vanguard.

The plot was partly inspired by a bit of real-life resentment. Geisel recalled that he'd been riding in a train, "and there was a fellow sitting ahead of me, who I didn't like." While Geisel didn't know who the man was, he couldn't take his eyes off of his "real ridiculous Wall Street broker's hat." There was something about the man that rubbed him the wrong way. "Very stuffy," said Geisel, "and I just began playing around with the idea of what his reaction would be if I took his hat off and threw it out the window. And I said, 'He'd probably just grow another one and ignore me.'"[29]

From there, the idea evolved into a story about a little boy named Bartholomew Cubbins, who offends a snooty king when he can't deferentially remove his hat because another one automatically materializes in its place. As Geisel was plotting his story, the number of hats troubling Bartholomew kept increasing, going from 48 to 135 and finally to 500. Geisel opted to write his new book in straight narrative prose, as opposed to the rhyming verse of *Mulberry Street*. Further, he had decided to make his story more like a fairy tale, plumbing old stories for characters and motifs. "I knew nothing about children's books," he admitted later. "Traditional fairy tales were still in order. I thought perhaps that was the thing to do."[30]

That didn't mean it was going to be any easier to write, however; in fact, there were times it made things even harder. Working within the fairy-tale setting provided Geisel with almost too much territory, too many different directions in which to take his story, too many characters and settings to play with. "I began to think of appurtenances around the castle, and one of them would be a bowman, and then it occurred to me there would also be an executioner," he said. "And I said, 'We've gotta get a little bastard of a crown prince in here.' And I would draw and semi-write that sequence up. Then I would . . . see how they fit. I'm not a consecutive writer."[31]

Geisel had adopted a regular work routine, sitting down at his desk in the second bedroom of their apartment at more or less the same time every morning—usually around nine A.M.—and working all day. If he needed a break, he would take a short walk or play a bit of handball or squash, then return home to work late into the evening, a cigarette constantly burning in his ashtray. Hanging on one wall of his office was the paper rifle target of his father's. "To remind me of perfection," said Ted—a standard, he said, he feared he would never attain.[34] At the end of the evening, he would finish off with a nightcap, usually a straight vodka, then go to bed to start the whole process over again the next morning.

By the summer of 1938, it was finished—or at least it was ready to go to Evelyn Shrifte for final edits and production. As in the case of

Mulberry Street, Geisel still couldn't leave it alone, fussing over the colors and scribbling his comments all over the mocked-up pages. Geisel was meticulous about the layout, penciling in the precise spacing he expected between the margins and the text, then phoning Shrifte in her office to make sure his directions had been followed or giving her yet another correction to the text.

The 500 Hats of Bartholomew Cubbins was published in the fall of 1938—and it sold slowly. The reviews were still good—*The New York Times* thought it "a lovely bit of tomfoolery"—but like *Mulberry Street*, its price tag probably kept it out of reach of some readers; Vanguard had priced it at $1.50 because of its higher page count. Alexander Laing, always one of Geisel's favorite reviewers, once again reviewed Ted's book for the *Dartmouth Alumni Magazine*. While always enthusiastic—maybe even overly so—Laing was particularly prescient as he speculated on Geisel's creative future: "Dr. Seuss . . . has given strong evidences that his several other occupations, madly fascinating as they are, may have been only the preludes to a discovery of his proper vocation," wrote Laing. "I do not see what is to prevent him from becoming the Grimm of our times."[33]

Overlooked by readers and reviewers of *Bartholomew Cubbins* was Ted's enigmatic dedication to the book:

To

Chrysanthemum-Pearl

(aged 89 months, going on 90)[34]

Who was the mysterious Chrysanthemum-Pearl? The answer was personal—and heartbreaking.

While Dr. Seuss would be loved by millions—perhaps billions—of kids and young readers around the world, Ted and Helen Geisel themselves would never have children. For the rest of his life, in one interview after another, Ted would find himself faced with the inevitable question "Why don't you have any children of your own?" His well-rehearsed response was a casual one: "You have 'em," he'd say, "and I'll entertain 'em." But the publicly flip remark masked the Geisels' own private sadness. "It was not that we didn't *want* to have children," Ted explained later. "That wasn't it."[35]

Seven years earlier, around the time the Geisels had moved into their new apartment on East 96th Street, Helen had begun complaining of severe abdominal pains. Ted was concerned enough to take her to the hospital, where doctors determined she needed an immediate oophorectomy—a removal of both ovaries. While the actual diagnosis remains unclear, such a drastic medical remedy seems to indicate that doctors may have been concerned about severe ovarian cysts. Regardless, in 1931, only four years into their marriage—Ted was twenty-seven, Helen thirty-three—the Geisels knew they would never have children. Helen was devastated; she and Ted agreed to keep their grief private, restricting knowledge of Helen's condition to their immediate family.

Unable to have any real children, then, Ted and Helen created a fictional one: Chrysanthemum-Pearl, born at about the time of Helen's surgery (hence her age was given as eighty-nine months, or a little more than seven years, in 1938), and a precocious child whom the Geisels could good-naturedly discuss at dinner parties when the conversation turned to children. Friends were in on the ploy—though as far as they knew, Ted and Helen had simply *chosen* to remain childless and had made up Chrysanthemum-Pearl for some genial competitive fun. And thus, any time a friend told a story about one of their children, Ted—in a tactic worthy of *Mulberry Street*'s Marco— would one-up the tale with a story of the miraculous feats of Chrysanthemum-Pearl, who could, for example, "whip up the most delicious oyster stew with chocolate frosting."[36] Everyone would laugh, and the conversation would usually move on to a different subject. In fact, Ted and Helen talked for years about Chrysanthemum-Pearl in such convincing terms that, for a while at least, their niece Peggy thought she was real. Even she wouldn't know the full story behind Chrysanthemum-Pearl for decades.

••••

On Saturday, December 17, 1938, Geisel sat down at a table at the prestigious 21 Club on West 52nd Street. He knew the place well—it was a former speakeasy, after all—but as one of the more upscale dining rooms in New York City, the 21 was rarely the setting for a run-of-the-mill lunch meeting. This meal would be no exception—for sitting across from Geisel that afternoon was the man who'd invited him to lunch: Bennett Cerf, the rich, witty forty-year-old cofounder of the Random House publishing company.

A native New Yorker and the son of well-to-do Jewish parents, Cerf was clever, good looking, and something of a rake—three years earlier, he'd been married to the glamorous actress Sylvia Sidney for exactly six months. As a young man, he'd attended Columbia University, where he was editor of the *Jester*, Columbia's humor magazine— although unlike Geisel, Cerf was more interested in incorporating book reviews than booze jokes into the magazine. After college, Cerf had worked briefly as a reporter and a Wall Street broker before founding Random House with Donald S. Klopfer in 1927. With no fear of controversy and a natural knack for publicity, Cerf in 1933 had hauled the U.S. government into court over the right to publish James Joyce's controversial—and banned—"work of obscenity," the novel *Ulysses*. Cerf had prevailed, and *Ulysses* quickly became one of Random House's first bestsellers. And the publicity hadn't hurt.

But Joyce wasn't Cerf's only catch. Cerf had both taste and an instinct for talent; he would, over the course of his career, publish William Faulkner, Eugene O'Neill, and Truman Capote, to name just a few. And now, as he and Geisel dined on hamburgers while a drizzle of rain fell outside, Cerf told his lunch guest which author he was hoping to land next.

He wanted Dr. Seuss.

Dr. Seuss was definitely interested. Geisel liked Henle and Shrifte at Vanguard, but he knew Vanguard couldn't compare to Random House when it came to the resources needed for printing, promotion, and publicity. Moreover, Geisel *really* liked Bennett Cerf. He found him entertaining and urbane, quick with a joke—and it didn't hurt that they had both edited their college humor magazines; that had elevated Cerf significantly in Ted's eyes. Writing for *Jester*, Cerf explained, "[taught me] how to write a quick story, how to put it down in as few words as possible . . . I learned not to clutter up my mind with a lot of useless information because an intelligent man doesn't need to carry all that stuff in his head. He has only to know where to find what he needs when he needs it."[37] That was the kind of thinking Geisel could get behind, too.

Random House, Cerf told Geisel, didn't have a large catalogue of children's books—but he liked what he had seen from Dr. Seuss, and asked Geisel if he had any other projects in mind. "Not especially," Ted told him. "Maybe an adult book with naked ladies."

Cerf never blinked "Great! I'll buy it," said the publisher. "You come with me and I'll print anything you do."[38] The two left lunch that afternoon with a handshake of an agreement—though no formal contract—to work together. "I felt [Bennett Cerf] was the kind of star I wanted my wagon hitched to," Geisel said later. "You could tell that Bennett was going somewhere."[39] Geisel's hunch would be right.

What Cerf may not have suspected as he bounded up the steps of the 21 Club and out into the rain was that Geisel wasn't kidding about his next project. He really *did* have an idea for a book with naked ladies in it—an adult-oriented fairy tale, updating the story of Lady Godiva and Peeping Tom. That all sounded fine to Cerf, whose main concern was that, whatever Ted chose to do, he just do it quickly. "It is extremely important that we have complete books in hand by early summer," Cerf wrote to Geisel, "so that our salesmen can do a proper selling job on their early fall trips."[40]

Cerf's faith seems to have inspired Geisel—for he went immediately to work writing and drawing not just one book for Cerf and Random House, but *two*.

First up was the naked-lady book. *The Seven Lady Godivas* was a reimagining of the historic figure who—at least according to legend—had ridden naked through the streets of Coventry in protest of oppressive taxes, and went unseen by everyone in town except for a voyeuristic tailor named Peeping Tom. "History has treated no name so shabbily as it has the name Godiva," Geisel wrote in the book's foreword—and in his reimagining, it was actually the story of the seven Godiva sisters—Lulu, Gussie, Teenie, Hedwig, Dorcas J., Arabella, and Mitzi—and their suitors, the Peeping brothers: Tom, Jack, Harry, Dick, Frelinghuysen, Sylvester, and Drexel. In Geisel's telling, the nudity of the Godivas was incidental; the sisters were simply so smart that they had no time for "frivol and froth," which included things like jewelry and clothing.

This wasn't entirely new territory. Geisel had made a number of Lady Godiva jokes in the pages of *Judge*, where he had also drawn women in various states of undress. But Geisel's particular style of drawing wasn't suited to drawing women. "I tried to draw the sexiest-looking women I could, and they came out just ridiculous," he said later.[41] "I think their ankles came out wrong, and things like that."[42] In fact, anyone looking for anything scandalous in *The Seven Lady Godivas* is bound to be disappointed; apart from a few bare butts, Geisel's women are usually drawn from the side or in three-quarter view to keep their pubic areas hidden, and exposed breasts are devoid of nipples. Other times, his women are discreetly covered by a conveniently placed fence or bale of hay. Nudity aside, the Godivas are the proactive heroes of the book, smart and sympathetic in their individual quests to find their "horse truths"—after a painful bite, for example, Teenie Godiva learns never to look a gift horse in the mouth. Geisel would be assailed in years to come about his lack of female protagonists, but in the pages of his first book for Cerf, he'd have seven of them.

As he had with *Bartholomew Cubbins*, Geisel chose to write *The Seven Lady Godivas* in unrhymed prose. This time, however, he wouldn't be working in full color; it was likely Cerf, eyeing the bottom line, who had gently suggested working only in shades of a single color. And so Geisel had drawn with black ink, using a gray ink wash for shading, and a reddish orange for highlights—which, when applied lightly, could be used to provide skin tones, or used heavily to tint the bright red sails of a ship. The different look was likely deliberate; Geisel was trying something new with *Godivas*, intentionally aiming for more adult readers. Geisel claimed it had been "to escape the monotony of writing about nothing but 'men folks and children, dragons or fish.'"[43]

While Cerf was looking for a children's book more along the lines of *Bartholomew Cubbins*, the publisher was happy to indulge Geisel's experiment if it would bring him under the roof of Random House. "I quite understand why you don't want to sign any definite contract now for future juveniles," wrote Cerf, ever the dutiful suitor. "I do hope, though, that after your present commitments are fulfilled, we will be able to work out a contract whereby we will become the publishers of every book that you write."[44]

Geisel had high hopes for *The Seven Lady Godivas*, believing he had created a new kind of literature—a comic aimed at more adult readers. "At that time, I was groping for a way to get out of what I was doing," he said later. Unfortunately, *Godivas*, on its publication in 1939, "was my grope that didn't work. It was my first adult humor book and my last. It was a complete failure."[45] Geisel would blame the book's cover price partly for its tepid reception—at two dollars, it was his most expensive book yet—and he also thought his decidedly nonerotic naked women had disappointed adult readers who might have been looking inside for . . . well, something different. He had equally confused—and, in some cases, angered—parents who found *The Seven Lady Godivas* shelved alongside *Mulberry Street* and *Bartholomew Cubbins*. "Kids would take it out with the other Dr. Seuss books," said Geisel, "and their parents were shocked."[46] Many libraries either discarded the book or refused to carry it at all.

Random House would sell only 2,500 copies of *Godivas* out of its initial print run of 10,000. The unsold books would be remaindered— sold in bulk and at a cut rate—and Geisel loved to tell the story of finding them at Schulte's Cigar Stores in New York, where they were sold for a quarter apiece to a more adult clientele. It was "the most expensive failure of my career,"[47] he said later, though he tried hard to learn a lesson from it. "I think it all went to prove that I don't know anything about adults," he said plainly.[48] Still, Geisel would dream for years of turning the book into an animated feature.

Dr. Seuss's first book for Random House had been a dud. But Bennett Cerf was hanging in there. "[*Godivas* was] intended for an adult audience, which I am sad to say it never found," he said generously. Geisel's editor at Random House, Louise Bonino—"one of the best juvenile editors in the country," said Cerf[49]—told Geisel he needed to shake off *Godivas* and write another kid's book right away.

Fortunately, Geisel's other book in the works for 1939, *The King's Stilts*, was much more what Bonino was looking for. Geisel was firmly back in fairy-tale territory, using prose to tell the story of the good and dutiful King Birtram, whose kingdom begins to decline only when the evil Lord Droon denies the king his regular evening of fun on his red stilts. "[I]t's hard work being King, and he does his work well," say Birtram's subjects. "If he wants to have a bit of fun . . . sure! . . . Let him have it!"[50] The same could have been said of Geisel. "I think his ability to see humor everywhere in everyday life is one reason why Ted is so well and enjoys life so," his sister, Marnie, told the *Springfield Union-News*.[51]

Ted had worked hard on this one, too, and had relied heavily on Helen for her editorial input and aptitude for plot. Each day, he would read his manuscript aloud to Helen, then hand the typewritten pages over for her to correct or add her own suggestions. Like *Godivas*, *The King's Stilts* was drawn in black and white, with a gray wash for shading and orange for highlights. Using yellow notepads, Ted would mock up and lay out each two-page spread carefully; thus he could determine exactly which drawings were facing each other, where the colors would go, and how much space the text should take up. Helen would mark these pages up as well, writing her remarks in the margins or beneath Ted's own handwritten notes—and when Ted got the pages back, he would often write his new comments directly over hers, thickly doubling up his letters so his comments would all but obliterate Helen's handwriting beneath.

The King's Stilts was a charming book, with a likable main character—King Birtram was *much* nicer than King Derwin of *Bartholomew Cubbins*, who seemed all too eager to cut off a little boy's head—and a fun, fully realized story, with not a hint of nudity in sight. Yet, while it seemed Dr. Seuss had gotten back to form, *The King's Stilts* also bombed on release, selling only 4,648 copies in its first year.

Still, it had sold better than *The Seven Lady Godivas*. Cerf was determined to show Geisel he still believed in him, sending him by Pullman train car on an all-expenses paid book-signing tour that took Geisel through Rochester, New York, then into Ohio, where he visited Cincinnati, Columbus, Dayton, and Cleveland. To his likely surprise, he had no trouble with appearing in public at any of these venues. He gamely signed books at the fifth-floor bookshop in the gigantic Higbee's department store in Cleveland, then headed for Columbus, where he was put up at the Deshler-Wallick Hotel. Here he dashed off an impromptu letter to Lew Miller, the sales manager at Random House, letting him know he'd sold "a mess of books." Ted loved sending notes to people—many times just a quickly scribbled line about something that struck him as funny. Letters would arrive unexpectedly, containing perhaps a scrap of a newspaper article with Ted's editorial annotations, a postcard with a short, pithy comment—or in the case of his letter to Miller, a note on the Deshler-Wallick's stationery, which featured a line drawing of the hotel with one of its pointed towers. On Miller's letter, Ted couldn't resist adding a quick couplet just below the picture of the hotel tower:

> Here I sit in the Hotel Wallick.
> You'll notice that the spire is Phallick.[52]

The slow sales didn't mean *King's Stilts* didn't have its fans. The *New York Herald Tribune* called it "the best Seuss so far, and that's no small praise."[53] Meanwhile, over at *The New York Times*, children's book reviewer Ellen Lewis Buell thought the book was "a little anticlimactic" when compared with *Mulberry Street* and *Bartholomew Cubbins*, but nonetheless warmly welcomed a new Dr. Seuss book, adding that "Dr. Seuss at his second best is much better than no Dr. Seuss."[54]

At the moment, however, Geisel wasn't certain there would be another Dr. Seuss book; with *The King's Stilts* selling slowly, Geisel was still having a hard time making a living off of what he called "the brat book business."[55] Fortunately, the Flit campaign had picked back up again, paying him good money to essentially use the same punch line over and over again. By then "I'd drawn them by the millions," sighed Geisel.[56] He'd also been fiddling for nearly a year with a gadget he'd hoped to unveil to great fanfare and profit at the 1939 New York World's Fair, which had opened in Queens, New York, on April 30, 1939. Forty-five million people were expected to pass through its entrance, strolling through exhibits centering around the theme of the World of Tomorrow. Ted's invention, called the Infantograph, wasn't a lofty gadget for a better tomorrow; instead, it was a bit of carnival hucksterism—but that didn't make it any less clever.

Geisel envisioned setting the Infantograph up in a tent on the main concourse—he'd already designed it—with a banner out front beckoning couples inside with a tantalizing come-on: *If you were to marry the person you are with, what would your children look like? Come in and have your INFANTOGRAPH taken!* The unsuspecting couples would then come inside the tent, sit in front of the Infantograph, and, after the click of a camera shutter, would receive a photograph of their features blended together into a single composite image.

In concept, wrote Geisel, the resulting photograph would be "instructive, entertaining, and amusing."[57] In practice, however: not so much. "All the babies tended to look like William Randolph Hearst," he said sadly.[58] Ultimately, Geisel would never get the camera to work in a way he was happy with; the idea was scrapped, and plans for a pavilion at the fair were abandoned. The only Infantograph photo that remains is a publicity shot of Ted and Helen demonstrating the machine, each staring blankly ahead, with their heads locked into wooden collars. Ted would hold on to the idea as long as he could, finally dissolving his Infantograph Corporation in 1944. Still, he would always insist, "it was a wonderful idea."[59]

••••

In autumn of 1939, even as both *Seven Lady Godivas* and *King's Stilts* were landing to a relative lack of interest, Geisel was at work on yet another children's book, his fifth in three years. This time, he was abandoning the fairy-tale conceits he'd used in both *Bartholomew Cubbins* and *King's Stilts* to return to the realm where he was more comfortable: the animal kingdom. Whether in the pages of *Jacko*, *Judge*, or *Life*, or in countless ad campaigns, the work of Dr. Seuss was filled with animals, from grinning cows and goats on mountaintops, to whales in craters, turtles on tables, and drunken elephants on roller skates. And it was an elephant Geisel was playing with now, in fact—an elephant he'd put up a tree, without a clear idea yet about how to get him down.

For his entire life, Geisel would claim that *Horton Hatches the Egg* had been born of a happy accident. As he initially told the story, "I was just sitting doodling on some transparent paper. I had drawn a tree, and I had drawn an elephant. When one paper lighted on top of the other, it looked as if the elephant were sitting in the tree."[60] As Geisel told and retold the story over the next four decades, he would—like Marco—add new embellishments, eventually settling on a version of the story that had the breeze from a serendipitously open window blow a sketch of an elephant on top of a drawing of a tree. "All I had to do was figure out what the elephant was doing on that tree," Ted said in 1972. "I've left my window open for 40 years since that, but nothing's happened."[61]

In truth, there were elements of Horton's story that Geisel had covered before. A year earlier, in the pages of *Judge*, Geisel had written and drawn a one-page Dr. Seuss Fable called "Matilda, the Elephant with a Mother Complex." In this story, an abandoned chickadee egg is found on the side of a trail by an elephant named Matilda, an old maid who lingered at the back of her herd, watching families through eyes "dim and misty with tears." When Matilda finds the egg, she's determined to sit on it, even as she eventually eats all the food within her reach and other animals come out of the woods just to make fun of her. Eventually she hatches a healthy chickadee, which flies away in terror, leaving Matilda to roam the jungle "alone and friendless . . . with nothing at all to show for her pains but a very bad case of lumbago." Dr. Seuss's moral was as dark as his ending: "Don't go hatching other folks' eggs."[62]

It also wasn't the first time Geisel had put an unusually large or unfit animal in a tree. In the past, he'd put whales and walruses in treetops, and had even shown elephants sitting on eggs. Now he had an elephant on an egg *in* a tree—and it had taken some time before he could figure out how the elephant had gotten there in the first place. As Geisel initially plotted it, Horton the Elephant—Ted had discarded the names Osmer, Bosco, and Humphrey—would volunteer to sit on the egg for Mayzie, a devoted mother bird who was concerned that Horton would accidentally crush her egg under his weight. However, once Geisel decided that Mayzie was a lazy bird who was actually abandoning her egg—and that Horton was sitting on the egg because he had given his word he'd take care of it—Geisel knew he'd found his story.

As Geisel worked on *Horton Hatches the Egg* throughout the fall of 1939, he was more and more pleased with how it was coming together—and was stunned at how easy it all seemed to be. "The new book is coming along with a rapidity that leaves me breathless," he wrote to Louise Bonino at Random House.

It is a beautiful thing.

The funniest juvenile ever written. I mean, being written.

Never before have I stood before myself and pointed so

proudly, saying, "Genius you are." I feel certain it will sell

well over a million. . . . P.S. I like my new book.[63]

After the failures of *Godivas, Cubbins,* and *King's Stilts,* Geisel had decided to go back to the narrative format that had succeeded for him with *Mulberry Street,* and was writing this one in rhyming verse. And he was at getting to work in *two* colors this time, green and orange, giving the book more vibrancy and pop. Narratively, Geisel had created in Horton a likable main character who suffers stoically through one terrible situation after another—bad weather, mockery, even threat of death—and all because he makes a principled stand, determined to live up to the book's (and Horton's) moral and poetic refrain:

> I meant what I said,
> And I said what I meant. . . .
> An elephant's faithful
> One hundred per cent![64]

The ending of the story, however, was proving problematic—and Ted was looking to Helen for help in getting Horton down. "She's a fiend for story line," said Ted.[65] Indeed, Helen was taking their plot problem seriously, and had spent the better part of a class reunion luncheon explaining to her former classmates that now "there was a book overdue at the publisher's, and Ted had an elephant up in a tree and couldn't figure out what to do with him."[66] Cerf was also providing help where he could, and for this book had wisely paired Ted with a new editor, Saxe Commins—"one of the great men of Random House," said Cerf[67]—who had worked with playwright Eugene O'Neill and was similarly a stickler for a cohesive story. In the end it was Helen, not Ted or Saxe Commins, who figured out how to bring Horton down: Horton comes off the egg when it hatches an elephant bird, and—unlike Matilda in Ted's *Judge* story—he is rewarded with a happy ending.

Geisel completed *Horton Hatches the Egg* in the spring of 1940 and sent it off to Random House, already certain he had a winner on his hands. Cerf was delighted with it, and immediately sent Ted a $500 advance, as well as a contract increasing his royalties. The contract, Cerf told Ted warmly, was "not the usual formal business document; it is a declaration of love."[68] Such enthusiasm, however, didn't translate into spectacular sales for this one, either. By brat-book standards, *Horton* was a success, selling 5,800 copies in its first year and 1,645 in its second, but these still weren't the kinds of sales Ted could live off of—nor were they even close to the kinds of sales he'd seen with *Mulberry Street*. But Cerf was happy; he felt that Geisel, after two false starts, had finally found his footing—and his voice—as Dr. Seuss.

Reviews, too, were generally positive—though *The New York Times* noted somewhat curiously that Dr. Seuss had nearly bogged down his story with a moral message—and cartoon producer Leon Schlesinger paid $200 for the rights to turn the book into a ten-minute animated version, which would be released in 1942. Alexander Laing, once again writing for the *Dartmouth Alumni Magazine*, was predictably overly effusive in his praise, at one point comparing Dr. Seuss, with an absolute straight face, to Henrik Ibsen. Unlike *The New York Times*, Laing thought the messaging of *Horton* was one of its strengths and believed Geisel might have intended Horton's tale as "a symbolic parable for our times," expressing an intentionally political point of view. "The symbolism is as clear as day," wrote Laing. "It is, among other things, a parable against appeasement . . . remember that the way to attain the little winged pachyderm of happiness on earth is to stick to your principles, no matter who else is sticking to his guns."[69]

While Geisel would always maintain—with a few exceptions—that his children's books were never intended to be political or allegorical, the war in Europe was very much on his mind as he paced his office, working through Horton's story. "Paris was being occupied by klanking tanks of the Nazis and I was listening on my radio," Ted wrote later. "I found that I could no longer keep my mind on drawing pictures of Horton the Elephant."[70] But while Ted wasn't ready to wear his politics on his sleeve in one of his kids' books, he *had* been flexing his political muscles elsewhere—if readers knew where to look.

In early 1939, Ted had agreed to take up editorial cartooning in earnest for Hearst newspapers like the *New York Journal-American*—and perhaps hoping to keep his editorial cartooning separate from his Dr. Seuss persona, Geisel signed his political work as *Tedd*. While Geisel remained a supporter of Franklin Roosevelt, the president's economic policies—especially when they hit Ted in his own pocketbook—were frequent targets. Tedd regularly griped about high taxes—a gigantic canary labeled TAXES gobbles up an enormous meal as its taxpaying owners dine on a pittance of birdseed—and took to task the expensive New Deal (which he called "Goofy Economics"), to the likely delight of his Republican father. He would, however, save his hardest punches for Adolf Hitler. As the führer's tanks steamrolled through Europe, Geisel portrayed him as an ugly suitor with a bouquet of dead fish that he hands out to women in homes labeled AUSTRIA and CZECHOSLOVAKIA, asking, "What lucky girl gets the next bouquet?"[71]

Geisel's stint as a Hearst editorial cartoonist came to an end in late 1939, at about the time he was struggling to find a way to bring Horton down from his tree—and for Ted it was just as well. He and his editors at the *Journal-American* were squabbling over whether the United States needed to enter the war in Europe, with Geisel hinting at the need for American intervention in his cartoons. Without his knowledge or consent, his editors were tagging on additional exposition to give them a distinctly isolationist point of view. Geisel quit.

October 1939 would mark his final appearance as Tedd—and the last time he would work under a different pseudonym. The next time Ted Geisel had anything to say about politics, he would say it as Dr. Seuss.

CHAPTER 6

COCKEYED CRUSADER

1940–1943

n August 1940, Ted and Helen drove out to California and made a down payment on two acres of hillside property in La Jolla, California. Since visiting the seaside town on their November 1928 anniversary trip, the Geisels had been determined to find a way to make La Jolla either their summer home or permanent residence—and this hillside tract, they hoped, would be the ideal place to start. Ted and Helen spent six weeks in California that summer, walking their property and visualizing the house they hoped to build among the boulders and flowering trees. Helen, who managed both their checkbook and their finances—Ted's one attempt at balancing their checkbook ended in failure when he insisted on rounding every line item up or down—estimated the house would cost around $8,000. Until the brat books started paying, then, Ted was going to have to keep his day job as an adman.

Fortunately for the Geisels' finances, there was still plenty of work from Standard Oil, both with the Flit campaign—which was now sprawled colorfully across the sides of subway cars—and the always entertaining Seuss Navy. There was a new client, too, in the Narragansett Brewing Company of Rhode Island, run by the colorfully named Rudolf Haffenreffer Jr. Rudy Jr. was a keen marketer with a fondness for cigar store Indians, and Ted had run with that idea, creating a new mascot for the company named Chief Gansett. The chief was a cigar store Indian who whizzed around on wheels, delivering foaming glasses of bock beer, usually accompanied by a little black cat who reacted expressively and reminded readers that Narragansett beer was "Too Good to Miss!" The chief would boost the sales of Narragansett beers—the company would later credit Dr. Seuss's ad campaign as a key part of its financial turnaround—and remain the iconic face of the company for decades.[1]

Even though *Horton Hatches the Egg* was proving slow to earn out, Cerf was still sending Ted on book signings and autograph tours. Despite the success of his last book tour, Geisel still dreaded the very idea of public events, but he went to each of them without complaint, out of deference to Cerf. In November, Geisel would even attend a Random House party at the Philadelphia Booksellers Association, penning a poem for Cerf called "Pentellic [*sic*] Bilge for Bennett Cerf's Thirty-Ninth Birthday," which he had beautifully printed on card stock and read aloud to partygoers. It didn't even matter to Geisel that Cerf wasn't thirty-nine (he was forty-two) nor that it wasn't his birthday (that was in May). Cerf howled at all of the jokes anyway. For Geisel, that was always enough.

Cerf's open display of amusement aside, it was getting harder to find things to laugh about. Each morning, before sitting down at the drawing table in his office, Geisel would read through the newspapers—out of the eight daily newspapers in New York City, *The New York Times* was his paper of choice—and was becoming more and more alarmed by what he was reading about the war in Europe. During a vacation in Germany in 1936, Ted had been shocked by Hitler's policies and propaganda—and now he was equally as distressed by the Italian propaganda machine propping up the despotic strongman Mussolini, whose rise Geisel had watched warily since visiting Italy in 1926.

For most of autumn 1940, Geisel kept seeing one name in the paper over and over again: Virginio Gayda, editor of *Il Giornale d'Italia*, and one of Mussolini's fascist mouthpieces of preference. All fall, Gayda bullied his way through one story after another, with a playground swagger worthy of Mussolini himself. In September, Gayda warned the United States that if it attempted to provide any assistance to Great Britain, it would be attacked "from the sea, land, and air by the concentrated forces and the warlike wealth" of the Axis.[2] By November, he was accusing the United States of "ideological political conflict, which is skidding toward belligerency;"[3] in late December, he was back to issuing veiled threats about the United States sparking "a spread of the conflict . . . to the Western Hemisphere."[4]

By winter, Geisel decided he'd had enough of Virginio Gayda's tough-talking fabrications. "Almost every day, in amongst the thousands of words that he spews forth," Geisel wrote with some annoyance, "there are one or two sentences that, in their complete and obvious disregard of fact, epitomize the Fascist point of view, such as his bombastically deft interpretation of a rout as a masterly stroke of tactical genius."[5] Using pen and brushstrokes of thick black ink, Geisel drew a cartoon showing Gayda dangling from a hook, his feet barely touching the ground, as he bangs his propaganda out on a steam-powered typewriter, punching the keys hard enough to break them. As Gayda's message rolls out on a long paper banner, a naked winged Mussolini approvingly holds up the other end, one palm raised in the fascist salute.

It was hardly insightful political commentary, but Geisel was pleased enough to show it to Virginia Vanderlip Schoales, the daughter of Frank Vanderlip, the very same banker whose party Geisel had enlivened years earlier with the fake pearl in a dinner oyster. The thirty-two-year-old Schoales was a liberal reformer—little surprise, considering her mother had been a suffragette—and had recently joined the staff of a new progressive daily newspaper in New York called *PM*. Schoales asked if she could show the cartoon to *PM*'s editor, Ralph Ingersoll. Geisel said she could.

Ingersoll liked what he saw, and on January 30, 1941, the cartoon was published in *PM*, accompanied by a note from Ted:

Dear Editor—If you were to ask me, which you haven't, whom I consider the world's most outstanding writer of fantasy, I would, of course, answer: "I am." My second choice, however, is Virginio Gayda. The only difference is that the writings of Mr. Gayda give me a pain in the neck.

This morning, the pain became too acute, and I had to do something about it. I suddenly realized that Mr. Gayda could be made into a journalistic asset, rather than a liability . . . Anyhow, I had to do a picture of Gayda.[6]

Unlike his political cartoons for Hearst, both the Gayda cartoon and its accompanying note were signed *Dr. Seuss*. And with that, Geisel assumed he was done with political cartooning again. Gayda had annoyed him, and he'd gotten it off his chest.

And yet, there was another public figure, this one American, who Geisel disliked as much if not more than Gayda, who would spur him to pick up his ink brushes again. "I got irritated into becoming a political cartoonist," said Ted, "by one of our nation's most irritating heroes, Col. Charles Augustus Lindbergh."[7]

Lindbergh, the thirty-nine-year-old aviation hero whose 1927 solo flight across the Atlantic had turned him into an international celebrity, was a vocal supporter of American isolationism. In Lindbergh's view, America needed to build up its army purely for its own defense— and should leave the war in Europe to European armies and politicians. "We are in danger of war today not because European people have attempted to interfere with the internal affairs of America," Lindbergh said in 1940, "but because American people have attempted to interfere with the internal affairs of Europe."[8] Lindbergh had advocated for American neutrality in the war and believed peace could be achieved in Europe through negotiation. But Geisel thought Lindbergh was being both unreasonable and unrealistic. No one liked war, Geisel said, but Lindbergh "was pushing non-preparedness."[9] "A Gallup Poll established the fact that 70 to 85 percent of all Americans were strongly opposed to any involvement in the war," Geisel said later. "And so was I. But I also believed that we had absolutely no choice in the matter and had better by God get prepared for a war that sure as hell was going to sock us."[10]

Geisel's own views had been bolstered in part by the increasing boldness of Franklin Roosevelt. In his 1941 State of the Union Address, the president had called for "the full support of all those resolute peoples everywhere," and asked Congress to approve the Lend-Lease Act to permit the United States to more easily ship aid to Britain and other allies. In the same speech, Roosevelt openly derided Lindbergh's politics of "appeasement"—and though he never called out the colonel by name, it was clear who he was referring to when he advised Americans to be wary of those who "preach the 'ism' of appeasement" and cater to the whims of "that small group of selfish men who would clip the wings of the American eagle in order to feather their own nests."[11]

On April 17, 1941, Lindbergh appeared at a rally in Chicago, where he announced that he had formally joined the America First Committee, a conservative organization whose stated purpose was "to make America impregnable at home, and to keep out of those wars across the sea."[12] Six nights later, on April 23, Lindbergh was at New York's Manhattan Center, trying to rally an already raucous crowd that *PM* described as "a liberal sprinkling of Nazis, Fascists, anti-Semites, [and] crackpots."[13] Geisel was appalled. "I got mad at Charles Lindbergh," he said. "We were obviously going to have a war . . . So I began drawing pictures against the America First movement. Nobody wanted to publish them because it was unpopular to say we'd be in conflict."[14]

In a New York of conservative Hearstian newspapers, there was really only one newspaper where he could go with such left-leaning cartoons. Geisel invited *PM* editor Ralph Ingersoll to dinner and showed him a few of the cartoons he was working on, most of which went after Lindbergh and his fellow isolationists. Ingersoll was interested—but this time he wanted to do more than just dribble out a few Dr. Seuss cartoons that Geisel would draw only when the mood struck. Ingersoll wanted Dr. Seuss as *PM*'s full-time editorial cartoonist.

Ralph M. Ingersoll, Connecticut born and Yale educated, was one of publishing's most progressive editors, both politically and professionally. Early in his career he had worked as a reporter for Hearst and a writer for *The New Yorker* before being hired away in 1929 by publisher Henry Luce, who put him in charge of the struggling *Fortune* magazine. Ingersoll was one of the first editors to grasp the importance of photographs and graphics, and his visual overhaul of *Fortune* made the magazine profitable. An impressed Luce then asked Ingersoll for his assistance in launching a magazine that was built almost entirely around its photographs, and the two men created *Life*, which would become one of the most successful magazines of the era. It was so successful, in fact, that Luce chose to edit the magazine himself and moved his editor with the Midas touch over to the struggling *Time* magazine. It was a post Ingersoll hated, mostly because of what he saw as its conservative editorial bent that loathed Roosevelt, denounced the New Deal, and promoted isolationist policies.

It was while he was still seething at *Time* that Ingersoll began drafting a treatise for a new kind of daily New York newspaper—one that would serve as a liberal crusader, in direct counterpoint to the conservative Hearst-owned newspapers. For *PM*—no one would ever be certain what the letters stood for, and Ingersoll would never say[15]— Ingersoll wanted writers with distinctive voices who were great storytellers and who had a progressive point of view. "Journalists serve two things larger than themselves," wrote Ingersoll. "The first is the truth as it exists. The second is the idea of a better mankind."[16] When the first issue of *PM* was published in June 1940, its politics were markedly left leaning: anti-fascist, pro-intervention, pro-labor, and pro–New Deal. "We are against fraud and deceit and greed and cruelty," wrote Ingersoll. "We are against people who push other people around."[17] That was just the sort of credo Geisel could get behind. "I liked that," he said.[18]

Geisel liked Ingersoll, too—and for Geisel, that was always one of the most important criteria when it came to deciding who he would do business with. Only three years apart in age—Ingersoll was older—Ted Geisel and Ralph Ingersoll had similar senses of humor, similar New England sensibilities, and—perhaps most important—a similar visceral dislike of Charles Lindbergh. In one of *PM*'s early issues, Ingersoll had run a gigantic front-page headline that screamed "Denouncing Charles A. Lindbergh." Inside, Ingersoll ran excerpts from Lindbergh's speeches alongside remarks from Nazi propaganda minister Joseph Goebbels, effectively reflecting their similar points of view. There was nothing coy about *PM* or Ingersoll, and Geisel liked that, too. The two men shook hands. "The next day," said Ted, "I was on the PM staff."[19]

On April 25, two days after Lindbergh's Manhattan Center rally, Ingersoll ran the first of Geisel's cartoons—proudly signed as *Dr. Seuss*—this one depicting Lindbergh flying a child-sized plane with a banner fluttering behind it reading, *It's smart to shop at Adolf's. All victories guaranteed.* And with that, Ted was on the record; Dr. Seuss had taken his first swing at an American hero in a very public forum. Three days later, on April 28, came his second jab at Lindbergh, mocking his isolationist policies with a depiction of the "Lindbergh Quarter"—a coin featuring an ostrich with its head buried in the sand, under the motto "In God We Trust (And How!)." From here on, Ted would depict Lindbergh and other America Firsters as ostriches—a kind of political branding that could only have come from one of Standard Oil's finest admen. The gloves were off; Dr. Seuss was in the fray—and he was pulling no punches.

In his first months at *PM*, Dr. Seuss would make Lindbergh and his fellow America Firsters—especially Senators Gerald Nye of North Dakota and Burton Wheeler of Montana, and the anti-Semitic Roman Catholic priest and radio host Father Charles Coughlin—the constant targets of his cartoon derision. "Lindbergh and his America Firsters and their sour-note choir leaders . . . seemed to be on the radio or at a Madison Square Garden rally every night preaching the gospel that we must not get involved because we were licked before we were started," Geisel explained in an unsent letter. "Father Coughlin, from his pulpit in the Church of the Little Flower, was poisoning the air of the entire middle west with radio sermons right out of *Mein Kampf.*"[20] There would be cartoons of American eagles kicked back in rocking chairs, talking but doing nothing, and Uncle Sam insisting he and a sickened Europe sleep in separate beds so there was "no chance of contagion" from "Blitz pox" or "Nazi fever."[21]

Geisel also understood that having the charismatic Lindbergh as the face of America First made isolationism an attractive political position—which is why he made such a point of going after Lindbergh personally. If Dr. Seuss could take down Lindbergh, he could take the air out of the America First movement as well. Sometimes Lindbergh seemed to be making it too easy. When the colonel made a speech in May accusing Roosevelt of wanting to provide aid to Europe and Asia as a step toward "world domination," a Dr. Seuss cartoon appeared in *PM* days later depicting Lindbergh patting a Nazi dragon kindly on the head. "'Tis Roosevelt, not Hitler, that the world should really fear,"[22] Lindbergh says reassuringly.

"I was *PM*'s political cartoonist in charge of Lindbergh, Wheeler, and Nye," Geisel said later—but at times, it was a lonely post. While *PM* had been pushing for American intervention since 1940, most Americans remained opposed—or at best, wary—of entering a war an ocean away. Despite the newspaper images of a shattered and smoking London following the first days of the German Blitz, Americans seemed more content to send aid and supplies, rather than troops. Geisel, like Ingersoll, understood that isolationism was larger than Lindbergh, and began submitting cartoons showing Republican politicians in bed with the isolationists, creating an elephant with an ostrich body, which Geisel clumsily called a "GOPstrich."

Things were better and funnier when Geisel let Dr. Seuss shine. In a June 23 cartoon, he showed an American eagle sitting complacently in an easy chair as bombs exploded around him, and mocked the isolationists with some punchy Seussian verse:

> Said a bird in the midst of a Blitz,
> "Up to now, they've scored very few hitz,

So I'll sit on my canny
Old Star Spangled Fanny . . ."
And on it he sitz and he sitz.[23]

In another, Ted portrayed America Firsters as a kangaroo carrying in its pouch a joey labeled NAZIS—which in turn carried in *its* pouch a smaller roo marked FASCISTS, which in *its* pocket carries an even smaller kangaroo labeled COMMUNISTS. "Relatives?" the largest kangaroo says, grinning at the reader. "Naw . . . just three fellers going along for the ride!"[24]

• • • •

For nearly a year, contractors and workmen had cleared and improved the Geisels' two-level property in La Jolla, to make way for the house that was slowly being built throughout late 1940 and early 1941. In June, Ted and Helen moved into the newly completed house—at the moment, it would serve mostly as a summer property—where Ted could swim in the morning and have lunch with Helen on the patio in the afternoon. Ted was surprised to learn West Coasters knew his name. "All the enlightened members of this community know about my books . . . but nobody in Southern California seems to keep 'em in stock," he wrote to Evelyn Shrifte—still a friend, despite his move to Random House. "I gotta go out now and fight rattlesnakes, bees and man-eating rabbits in the patio, then go fight Lindbergh."[25]

Under his contract with Ingersoll, Geisel had to produce three, sometimes four, cartoons weekly. Every morning he would pore through the newspapers, looking for inspiration in the headlines. Once he had an idea, he worked quickly, and his cartoons from this time are drawn in broad strokes, with big gestures. With a daily deadline hanging over him—Geisel would airmail his cartoons back to Ingersoll in New York each evening—he had little time to redraw, revise, or rethink. For an artist who could fill a trash can with one discarded draft after another in the course of an afternoon, resisting the urge for perfection was perhaps the hardest part. "Looking back at them now, they're embarrassingly and sloppily drawn. And they're full of snap judgments that every political cartoonist has to make between the time he hears the news at 9 a.m. and sends his drawings to press at 5 p.m.," Geisel said later. "The one thing I *do* like about them, however, is their frantic honesty."[26]

He was still annoyed with Virginio Gayda, tearing into the propogandist twice in two weeks, and Mussolini himself was now making appearances, usually drawn as a thuggish, petulant little boy. Adolf Hitler, too, was showing up regularly—but at the moment, no one, it seemed, could get Ted's political and creative juices flowing like Lindbergh. The famed aviator's isolationism was one thing; quite another was his increasingly vocal anti-Semitism. Lindbergh already had been accused of having Nazi sympathies—his 1938 acceptance of the Reich's Order of the German Eagle with Star hadn't helped—and some of his most active followers were loudmouthed bigots like Father Charles Coughlin, who spewed anti-Semitism in his weekly radio addresses. In a September speech to America Firsters in Des Moines, Lindbergh had finally gone all in with a lecture he called "Who Are the War Agitators?" in which he made a sharp distinction between Americans, the British people, and the "Jewish race":

> I am saying that the leaders of both the British and Jewish races, for reasons which are understandable from their viewpoint as they are inadvisable from ours, for reasons which are not American, wish to involve us in the war. We cannot blame them for looking out for what they believe to be their own interests, but we also must look out for ours.[27]

The backlash was immediate. "The most un-American talk made in my time," said former Republican presidential nominee Wendell Willkie, while over in the pages of *Liberty*—one of Geisel's old stomping grounds—Lindbergh was derided as "the most dangerous man in America.[28] In *PM*, Geisel depicted a gas-mask-wearing Lindbergh standing atop a garbage pile in the back of a "Nazi Anti-Semite Stink Wagon" from which he was "Spreading the Lovely Goebbels Stuff" by the shovelful.[29]

Two days later came one of Dr. Seuss's most memorable political cartoons, showing an American eagle—with a sign reading I AM PART JEWISH dangling from his beak—sitting with his feet and winged hands locked in stocks; at his feet leans a card announcing *This bird is possessed of an evil demon!* with Lindbergh's name among the arresting officers.[30] A week after that came one of Ted's hardest-hitting cartoons, in which a bespectacled woman with an America First sweater reads aloud to two children from a fairy-tale storybook titled *Adolf the Wolf.* "And the wolf chewed up the children and spit out their bones," says the woman, reading from the book as the children's eyes go wide. "But those were *Foreign Children* and it really didn't matter."[31] The political tide was turning against the American Firsters, the isolationsists, and Lindbergh—one political columnist noted that the aviator had gone from "Public Hero No. 1" to "Public Enemy No. 1" almost overnight[32]—and Dr. Seuss was helping to lead the charge. "I was intemperate, unhumorous in my attacks," Geisel said later, "and I'd do it again."[33]

Not everyone was amused. Some conservatives threatened to boycott Flit, Essomarine, and other Standard Oil products, arguing that the company's favorite adman was a communist. Others were offended by the way Ted drew his American eagle. "Much as I admire the work of Dr. Seuss," wrote one *PM* reader, "I question the fitness of continuing to picture our Uncle Sam as an ostrich."[34] That might have been a fair criticism; in true Seussian style, Ted's eagle *did* have a lengthy beak and, at times, a long neck that made it look more like a buzzard than an eagle. Ingersoll responded by printing one of Ted's drawings of an eagle in a Stars and Stripes top hat, with a rifle slung over one shoulder, ready for action. "He looks pretty perky to us," wrote Ingersoll.[35]

Ted and Helen left La Jolla and returned to New York by train in late November 1941, missing Sterling Holloway's reading of *Mulberry Street* on CBS Radio's *Family Hour* on November 30. Originally, Holloway was to have read the story to the accompaniment of an original Deems Taylor score called *Marco Takes a Walk*, but the composer wouldn't complete the score for another year—at which time it would be performed by the New York Philharmonic exactly one time. Ted would miss that performance, too.

As winter approached and the Geisels settled back into their Park Avenue apartment, Ted, as he scanned the headlines each morning, rightly seemed to sense there was something in the air involving Japan. He began drawing cartoons warning of Japanese aggression against Siam (now Thailand) and even the United States; a November 28 cartoon shows an angry Japan asking the United States for "a brick to bean you with."[36] Ted also suspected that isolationists were losing steam, as a November 25 cartoon shows one of Dr. Seuss's isolationist ostriches stuffed and mounted in a museum exhibit labeled HALL OF THE EXTINCT.

On Sunday, December 7, Ted and Helen were listening to classical music on radio station WQXR in the New York apartment when the broadcast was interrupted for a report that the Japanese had attacked Pearl Harbor. Whatever cartoon Ted may have had on his drawing board that morning immediately got set aside. On the afternoon of Monday, December 8, *PM* ran a large Dr. Seuss cartoon with the gigantic word WAR exploding upward, blasting one of Geisel's isolationist ostriches skyward, with *X*s for eyes, clearly down for the count. *He never knew what hit him*, read the caption.

For editor Ralph Ingersoll, *PM* had just seen one of its foundational editorial policies realized: Lindbergh, Wheeler, Nye, Coughlin . . . all the isolationists were as cataleptic as Dr. Seuss's ostrich. That same afternoon, Ingersoll rallied the *PM* staff and readers with a new mission. "Today," he wrote, "we begin a new task . . . WINNING THE WAR."[37] Now the real work would begin.

It was a responsibility Geisel was determined to take seriously. On

December 9, *PM* ran the Dr. Seuss cartoon "The End of the Nap," depicting an eagle in a rocking chair being awakened by miniature Japanese officers, who hit him with a mallet, zing him with a slingshot, and even give him a hotfoot.[38] For Geisel, who had started his career at *PM* as the "angry cartoonist in charge of Lindbergh, Wheeler and Senator Nye,"[39] there was now no longer any need to convince Americans to enter the war. Americans were in. Their long nap was over. Now Dr. Seuss saw it as his job to keep them awake.

• • • •

While Ted would do most of his cartooning at his apartment, he often visited the headquarters of *PM* on Dean Street in Brooklyn, climbing up two flights of rickety stairs to reach Ingersoll's offices on the top floor. He almost always found someone interesting around to talk to, and there was no shortage of political conversations that might serve as inspiration for the next afternoon's cartoon. Ingersoll was an editor who appreciated his editorial staff and encouraged them to write in their own voices, rather than imposing a stilted house style. It was "a newspaperman's newspaper," said one *PM* journalist, "as well as a newspaper that spoke the language of the people."[40] That made *PM* an attractive place for writers. In its brief existence, *PM* would see bylines by Dorothy Parker, Tip O'Neill, and Ernest Hemingway; Dashiell Hammett had served briefly as a proofreader. For Geisel, being in the top floor offices of *PM* was a lot like hanging out in the offices of *Jacko,* and he would always feel a special bond with the men and women of *PM.* "We were . . . a bunch of cockeyed crusaders," Geisel said warmly, "and I still have prideful memories of working alongside such guys as Ralph Ingersoll and dozens of other hard working souls."[41]

But Ingersoll's editorial approach would literally cost him. Ingersoll refused to accept any advertising in *PM* out of concern that his reporters might slant their own personal points of view in deference to advertisers. While reporters loved this policy—"we were blazing a new trail—no advertising pressures," crowed one writer[42]—it meant

Ingersoll had to look elsewhere for revenue. That was one reason *PM* was more expensive than most daily newspapers, costing five cents per day instead of the more usual three—but even that wasn't enough to keep *PM* solvent. From its inception, *PM* had been propped up with the generous support of progressive donors like chewing gum manufacturer Philip K. Wrigley, women's rights activist Elinor S. Gimbel, and the department store magnate Marshall Field III, who would eventually be floating the newspaper almost single-handedly.

With a cartoon in nearly every issue, Dr. Seuss remained one of *PM*'s most visible and popular contributors. More than once, rival publications tried to woo him away; the managing editor of the left-leaning *Nation* thought Dr. Seuss might be a good fit for his magazine, though he acknowledged that Geisel's particular style of cartooning was "pretty far removed from anything we have attempted in the past, but that might well be all to the good."[43] An editor at *The New Republic* gave up trying to hire Dr. Seuss and just wrote him an admiring fan letter instead, telling him, "You are merely the greatest man that ever lived. I don't see how you can be really so funny day after day. I wonder if you enjoy your stuff as much as a reader can enjoy it."[44] A February 1942 article in *Newsweek* praised Dr. Seuss for "blasting away at his political hates with razor-keen satire," alongside a photo of Geisel, dapper in a suit and round-rimmed glasses, smoking at his drawing table.[45]

Sometimes the satire was *too* razor sharp. In mid-January 1942, Geisel began a series of cartoons called "The War Monuments," in which he sarcastically paid tribute to those who hurt the war effort. Usually the targets were metaphorical—there was "Walter Weeper," who complains and wrings his hands, leaving the actual fighting and sacrifices to others, and "Dame Rumor, Minister of Public Information"—but on January 13, Geisel went after a real-life target, the pacifist minister John Haynes Holmes. The well-respected Holmes was a man of genuine conviction—he was a cofounder of both the NAACP and the ACLU—and in December 1941 had offered to resign as minister of his church rather than "bless, sanction, or support the war."[46] But Geisel's main objection to Holmes wasn't his isolationism, but rather the minister's suggestion that the Japanese people, while mortal enemies of the United States, were still "our brothers" in humanity. Geisel bristled at the comment. Then he hit Holmes hard, drawing a statue of the minister with one arm draped over the shoulder of a grinning Japanese fighter who holds the decapitated head of an American soldier.[47]

It was a cheap shot—and the blowback was immediate. *PM* received hate mail over several days, much of it addressed to the attention of Dr. Seuss. "I protest the Dr. Seuss cartoon on John Haynes Holmes," said one angry letter. "Beyond the sheer bad taste is something even deeper. That is, the implied rejection of the basic Christian principle of the universal brotherhood of man." One reader berated *PM* for its "grotesque incitement of hatred," while another suggested that such bad taste was typical of Geisel's sense of humor: "Dr. Seuss has long been a thorn in PM's pages," said the letter writer.[48]

On January 21, Geisel responded testily on the Letters page of *PM*:

> In response to the letters defending John Haynes Holmes . . . sure, I believe in love, brotherhood, and a cooing white pigeon on every man's roof. I even think it's nice to have pacifists and strawberry festivals . . . in between wars.
>
> But right now, when the Japs are planting their hatchets in our skulls, it seems like a hell of a time for us to smile and warble: "Brothers!" It is a rather flabby battlecry.

"If we want to win," concluded Ted, "we've got to kill Japs, whether it depresses John Haynes Holmes or not. We can get palsy-walsy afterward with those that are left."[49]

The ugly language and wariness of the Japanese was typical of the time, especially in the months immediately following the bombing of Pearl Harbor. Like many Americans—and especially as a part-time Californian—Geisel was worried the Japanese might strike the West Coast. Indeed, there were already whispers that Japanese submarines had been spotted within sight of the beaches of California. Lieutenant General John L. DeWitt, head of the Western Defense Command and an advisor to President Roosevelt, had already seen to it that the 1942 Rose Bowl game was moved from Pasadena, California, to North Carolina, fearing such a large crowd might attract the interest of Japanese bombers.

Now, in early 1942, DeWitt was arguing for the forced relocation and incarceration of hundreds of thousands of Japanese Americans, to thwart any internal sabotage by disloyal Japanese American citizens—the so called fifth column. DeWitt had no real evidence or government intelligence to justify such a drastic measure; it was mostly his own racism driving his recommendation—"a Jap's a Jap" he would later tell a subcommittee of the House Naval Affairs Committee.[50] Evidence or not, such incendiary rhetoric was enough to stir uneasiness even among Americans who, in the days following the attack on Pearl Harbor, had stood by their Japanese American neighbors and coworkers, never once questioning their loyalty.

Unfortunately Geisel also bought into DeWitt's narrative. On February 13, *PM* ran a Dr. Seuss cartoon with the caption "Waiting for the Signal from Home," depicting a long line of Japanese Americans—shown stretching along the entire Pacific coast—queuing up to receive bricks of TNT from a building labeled "Hon. Fifth Column."[51] From the stereotypical portrayal of the Japanese—each one is drawn exactly alike, in bowler hats and black jackets, eyes represented by small slits—to its underlying distrust of his fellow citizens, it's one of the lowest moments in Dr. Seuss's career. Further, it's a shockingly tone-deaf message coming from Ted Geisel, who had experienced bigotry by association during World War I when he was pelted with coal and mocked for no other reason than a shared heritage with the enemy. By his own experience, he should have known better.

PM received no angry letters about Ted's cartoon, nor did the liberal Ingersoll ever address the issue. On February 19, six days after the publication of "Waiting for the Signal from Home," DeWitt's scare tactics finally prevailed; President Roosevelt signed Executive Order 9066, permitting the forced relocation and incarceration in camps of nearly 120,000 Japanese Americans. Prejudice was now officially policy—and Geisel and millions of other Americans hadn't even blinked.

And yet both Geisel—and Dr. Seuss—continued to fight anti-Semitism and fascism, training their fire on Father Charles Coughlin. He was an easier target than Lindbergh; the priest didn't have the aura of a national hero about him, and his politics were blatantly anti-Semitic and pro-Nazi. In his *PM* editorials, Ingersoll lit into Coughlin with relish, calling out Coughlin's *Social Justice* magazine as "seditious" and daring the U.S. Department of Justice to remove its religious exemption from taxation or close it down altogether. Dr. Seuss, too, jumped into the fight with zeal, producing a number of anti-Coughlin cartoons, including one of Hitler reading *Social Justice* as he talks to Coughlin on the phone. "Not bad, Coughlin," says the führer, "but when are you going to start printing it in German?"[52] Coughlin, with his reputation increasingly tattered, would fade away before the end of the year. Ingersoll, with Dr. Seuss as his standard-bearer, declared victory. Cockeyed crusaders indeed.

It was Ingersoll, perhaps more than anyone, who would help Geisel find his voice on matters of race, equality, and social justice. On March 27, *The Saturday Evening Post* ran a long piece by writer Milton S. Mayer called "The Case Against the Jew." Mayer had likely pushed Ingersoll's buttons before; in 1939, he had made the case for isolationism in a think piece titled, "I Think I'll Sit This One Out." Now, two years later, Mayer was back again, accusing Jews of being the source of all national and international distress. "The Jews of America are afraid that their number is up," wrote Mayer. "They know that every war since Napoleon has been followed by collapse, and they know that the postwar collapse will remind a bitter and bewildered nation that 'the Jew got us into the war.'"[53]

The following day, a stunned and angry Ingersoll went after Mayer in a *PM* front-page editorial. Calling Mayer's article "a glove slapped across the American mouth," Ingersoll spent three pages vivisecting Mayer and his argument. "America is great . . . because of the fact that not races or creeds, but the people themselves are what is important," wrote Ingersoll. "Neither the colors they come in nor the creeds their fathers handed down to them shall be allowed to hinder nor to help them in their pursuit of happiness."[54]

It would be one of Ingersoll's most widely distributed and re-printed editorials, and Geisel seems to have been impressed with and inspired by it. It would reflect a turning point in his work. He would begin to draw more cartoons not just about anti-Semitism, but about racism and bigotry against *all* people. And while he would con-tinue to go after Japan as a member of the Axis, he would never again advocate for the internment of Japanese Americans. Nor did he por-tray the Japanese as inhuman, as did many editorial cartoonists of the time, who often depicted the Japanese as monkeys. While Geisel would continue to rely on caricatures to make the point, he seems to have also taken John Haynes Holmes's philosophy to heart: the Japa-nese were the enemy, but they were still human beings. It was the same humane sentiment Horton the elephant would voice, with a memorable turn of phrase, a little more than a decade later: "A per-son's a person, no matter how small."

Some of Dr. Seuss's finest cartoons on racism came in the weeks immediately following Ingersoll's evisceration of Mayer. On April 1, only four days after Ingersoll's editorial, *PM* published a cartoon of Geisel's with Uncle Sam being led by a figure labeled U.S. NAZIS toward a hooded, axe-wielding figure marked ANTI-SEMITISM. "Come on Sam," says the Nazi. "Try the great German manicure!"[55] Two weeks later came a Dr. Seuss cartoon with a "Discriminating Em-ployer" astride a tank, looking derisively over his shoulder at two smaller tanks labeled JEWISH LABOR and NEGRO LABOR. "*I'll* run De-mocracy's War," says the Discriminating Employer. "*You* stay in your Jim Crow Tanks!"[56]

By June, Geisel was able to poke a little fun at himself, paying homage to his old Flit campaign with a cartoon titled "What This Country Needs Is a Good Mental Insecticide." In this case, instead of Flit, a determined-looking Uncle Sam blasts "mental insecticide" into a man's right ear that blows a "racial prejudice bug" out his left. "Gracious!" says the man. "Was *that* in my head?"[57] Perhaps Geisel had come to understand that he'd had a few bugs in his own head as well. He was working to exterminate them.

One of his best cartoons on racism would be inspired by civil rights leader A. Philip Randolph's June 13 plea—in front of 18,000 African Americans jammed into Madison Square Garden—for an end to discrimination in the military, labor unions, and government contracting. Two weeks after Randolph's demand came Dr. Seuss's eloquent commentary: as a tuxedoed piano player marked WAR INDUSTRY sits at a pipe organ, Uncle Sam taps him on the back, a disappointed frown on his face. "Listen maestro," says Sam, "if you want to get *real harmony*, use the black keys as well as the white!"[58] Dr. Seuss, in the pages of *PM* for all to see, was officially a proud progressive.

• • • •

When it came down to it, *PM*'s major political agenda during the war was fairly simple: Adolf Hitler was incredibly dangerous and had to be stopped. For Ingersoll, that meant that all of the U.S. allies had to be embraced, even Russia—and here was the source of the main political/editorial split among Ingersoll's staff. Some viewed the Russians as a slave state under the thumb of Stalin; others thought Communism was working. Geisel leaned toward the former. He refused to be charmed by the Soviet leader, drawing him only six times in twenty months; the most heroic he would ever make Stalin look was when he portrayed him serving a Christmas Eve dinner of a roasted pig wearing a Nazi officer's cap.[59]

Hitler would earn most of Ted's ink, showing up in more than a hundred of the nearly four hundred Dr. Seuss cartoons in *PM*. "I had no great causes or interests in social issues until Hitler," said Geisel.[60] His version of Hitler wasn't the tightly wound, hotheaded führer common to so many of the cartoon portrayals at the time. Instead, Geisel's Hitler was frightening simply because he was so *calm*, usually depicted with his nose haughtily in the air, eyes closed, and eyebrows disdainfully raised, carrying out atrocities in a matter-of-fact, businesslike manner.

One of Ted's more popular regular features was one he called "Mein Early Kampf," depicting the adventures of Hitler as an infant. The first installment, in late January 1942, showed a stork delivering the newborn Hitler—complete with a mustache and a shock of black hair—who reaches over with a lighted match to give the stork the hot-foot.[61] The following day, Hitler appeared as a toddler throwing his milk bottle at his nanny, "reject[ing] milk from Holstein cows as non-Aryan."[62] Geisel would discontinue the series after a third install-ment, perhaps realizing that Hitler worked better as the bogeyman than as the instigator of the joke.

Geisel often used Hitler as a gleeful observer of American dis-unity, who cackled with joy as American journalists smeared Eleanor Roosevelt, or cocked an ear attentively as gigantic gears labeled OUR INTERNAL WRANGLES caught and ground. "I hear the Americans are stripping their gears again," hoots the führer.[63] But it's when Geisel used Hitler as a genuine terrorizing force—though always with the look of smug calm on his face—that Dr. Seuss's cartoons could become truly chilling. In July 1942, Geisel showed Hitler standing in a forest, an arm around the shoulders of the capitulating head of the new French government, Pierre Laval—another politician Geisel loathed—singing, "Only God can make a tree / To furnish sport for you and me." Around them, the trees are filled with hanged corpses, all labeled JEW.[64] It's one of Geisel's most haunting cartoons.

There were other times when Geisel chose to depict Germany as a dachshund, sometimes giving it Hitler's mustache and haircut, or a collar with swastikas. Oddly, it was *this* depiction of the Reich that earned Dr. Seuss another blast of hate mail, this time from dachs-hund owners, who resented Dr. Seuss using their pets as a stand-in for the Nazis. "If this insidious campaign continues, I am afraid people will begin to consider it their patriotic duty to kick my little darling around," wrote one concerned reader. "Sorry, friend," Geisel responded on *PM*'s letter page. "And if anyone kicks you around, sue me. You've got an excellent case!"[65]

• • • •

In Geisel's view, winning the war was all about rallying around American ingenuity, maintaining a positive attitude, and diligently contributing to the war effort through conservation, rationing, and the buying of war bonds. That meant a lot of cartoons zinging naysayers, hand-wringers, war profiteers, hoarders, and those who actively worked to undercut American morale. As Geisel saw it, one of the biggest offenders in that final category was the hyperconservative clergyman and demagogue Gerald L. K. Smith, whose monthly magazine, *The Cross and the Flag,* advocated a fascist agenda in highly inflammatory language. "I'm against permitting Jews to dilute our Christian tradition," Smith would later tell *The New York Times.* "I don't think our country should be mongrelized by the weaker elements."[66]

Geisel was appalled by Smith—but he was even more disgusted that Smith's message and magazine were being propped up and vocally endorsed by two United States senators: his old nemesis, the America Firster Gerald P. Nye, and Robert Reynolds of North Carolina, a rabid Nazi apologist. Geisel found it galling to hear Nye talk about Smith in such fawning terms—there was always something about Nye in particular that really annoyed Geisel. After listening to the senator give yet one more depressing, fatalistic anti-Semitic radio speech, Ted informed Helen he was going to take down that "horse's ass" Nye.

Helen was not amused. "Don't use language like that."

"But he *is* a horse's ass," Ted insisted. "I'll draw a picture of him as a horse's ass and put it in *PM*!"

"You can't," said Helen. "It's a vulgar idea."[67]

Ted would do it anyhow. On April 26, he delivered to Ingersoll a cartoon of Smith—under a hooded Ku Klux Klan robe—wielding a sword labeled DEFEATISM as he rides two men in a pantomime horse costume. Across the horse's front end is the name *Senator Reynolds*; across its rear is emblazoned *Senator Nye*. As promised, Geisel had literally turned Nye into a horse's ass.

Ingersoll, who rarely, if ever, provided Geisel with cartooning advice, may well have raised an eyebrow. "You're going to get us in a million-dollar lawsuit," he warned, "and you'll be sued yourself."[68] The cartoon ran anyway, without any changes, in that afternoon's edition of *PM*.

Several days later, a letter from Nye, directed to Dr. Seuss, arrived at the *PM* offices. "The issue of Sunday, April 26th carried a cartoon," began Nye, "the original of which I should very much like to possess. May I request its mailing to me?" Geisel, trying to salvage the last laugh, refused to send it, hanging it in his own home office instead. "Whatever I lacked—and it was plenty—as a polished practitioner of the subtle art of caricature," he said later, "I did become prolifically proficient in venting my spleen."[69]

Axe sufficiently ground, Dr. Seuss now turned to larger themes of preparedness, productivity, and optimism. Trying to keep up the American spirit, Geisel drew cartoons about getting off the sidelines, getting American businesses working, and warning against over-confidence or complacency. One week, there was an American eagle in a boxing ring, wearing one boxing glove while the other hand is pampered by a manicurist at a table reading THE OLD EASY LIFE. "Champ," beckons his trainer, "ain't it about time we tied on the other glove?"[70] Another week, Seuss's cartoon featured a turtle labeled DAWDLING PRODUCERS, with two columns of turtles stacked on its back, leaning slightly away from each other to make a *V* shape. "You can't build a substantial V[ictory] out of turtles," Geisel warned in the caption.[71] (It wouldn't be the last time he would stack turtles.) There were also cartoons urging Americans to conserve and ration resources, one showing a thoughtless family hot-rodding down a winding road, hats flying, even as a soldier sits in his stalled-out tank. "The gas you burn up in your car in one whole year," explains Dr. Seuss, "would only take a light tank 653 miles!" Ted gives the last word to the stranded tank driver, who addresses the reader directly: "So save it, pal! *My* trips are more important."[72]

Geisel's cartoons to encourage reduced gasoline usage were considered so effective, in fact, that in May he received a civilian War Savings Commendation from the government—and was asked to provide similar cartoons about salvaging and recycling for the War Production Board. At the same time, the U.S. Department of the Treasury approached Geisel about producing cartoons to encourage Americans to buy war bonds and stamps, rather than wasting money on luxury items. When Ted and Helen drove across the country for their annual retreat to California—Ted might preach gas conservation, but he and Helen still had places to be—Ted brought along armloads of sketches and incomplete drawings he was working on for various government projects. "This is in no sense of the word a vacation," Helen assured one correspondent in July. "Ted has endless government work to do besides his daily cartoon. But the working conditions are so beautiful!"[73] Helen had good reason to be concerned about Ted's productivity; after producing five books in three years, Ted hadn't brought any new work to Random House since completing *Horton Hatches the Egg* in 1940. But the brat books would have to wait; Ted was too busy being a cockeyed crusader.

That summer, California was taking preparedness seriously. There were blackout drills each evening, and every week, the Geisels' hillside retreat seemed to be the focal point of countless military drills. "Once a week, the marines invade and usually capture our hillside," Helen wrote Evelyn Shrifte:

> We are dive-bombed at 5:30 a.m.—then we look out of
> the window to see hundreds of little boats, amphibious
> tanks, etc., rushing to shore. In a few minutes, our house
> is in the midst of it all—tanks, jeeps, trucks, bayonets
> bared right on the driveway. The din of blank cartridges

is so terrifying that I can't even conceive of what the real thing must be like![74]

Geisel continued to airmail his cartoons back to New York that summer, filing cartoons regularly addressing the need to buy war bonds and the dangers of disunity and of Georgia's racist governor Eugene Talmadge, at that time trying to segregate the University of Georgia. (Talmadge would be defeated later that year.) There was still Hitler taunting Pierre Laval, this time depicted as an insect-sized, capitulating louse. And early that autumn, a Dr. Seuss cartoon included a billboard asking, *IF all of us were fighting as hard as YOU are . . . WHO would win the war, and how soon?*

It was a question Geisel had lately given considerable thought. For more than a year, he had been encouraging the United States to enter the war—and, once they were in, he had tried to keep their spirits up and remind them what they were fighting for. But now that didn't seem like it was enough.

At age thirty-nine, Geisel was too old to be drafted. So in October, he applied for a commission from Naval Intelligence, which required a lengthy approval process. But the Naval gears turned so slowly, in fact, that by the time Geisel received notice in December that he'd been cleared for service in Naval Intelligence, he'd already accepted a commission from the U.S. Army. "They [the Army] didn't want me," Geisel later joked, "but they had to have me."[75]

On January 7, 1943, Captain Ted Geisel reported for active duty in Fort MacArthur, California. Dr. Seuss was going to war.

PART II

IT IS FUN TO HAVE FUN BUT YOU HAVE TO KNOW HOW

CHAPTER 7

SNAFU

1943–1946

eisel had joined the Army—or so he would say for years—mostly "to save face."[1] "I got a letter to the editor [at *PM*] saying, 'Dr. Seuss, who is so old he can't be drafted, got us into this war,'" he explained with not a little amount of stretching. "I thought maybe I *had* started the war, so I better join up."[2]

What Geisel usually omitted in his retelling of the story is that he had been actively recruited to join the Army by a savvy lieutenant colonel named Frank Capra, the three-time Academy Award–winning director who was now in command of a unit within the Signal Corps, tasked with producing training films, informational brochures, and other educational materials. In late 1942, Capra had dispatched one of the writers in his unit, Leonard Spigelgass, to New York to look for potential writers, artists, and filmmakers. Spigelgass had immediately zeroed in on Geisel. "He has a remarkably good brain," the young writer reported to Capra, "and seems to me useful infinitely beyond a cartoonist."[3]

That was good enough for Capra. Geisel was offered a temporary appointment with Capra's unit, effective December 31, 1942—and when he was informed days later of his acceptance by Naval Intelligence, Ted declined their commission. "I told the Navy, 'Thanks, but I can't go,'" said Ted. "And they said to me, 'You're AWOL.'"[4] On

January 7, 1943, Theodor Seuss Geisel—serial number 09214057—was sworn into the U.S. Army. Three days later, he would be commissioned as a captain and board a train for Fort MacArthur, California, to take his place in Capra's Signal Corps unit.

Dr. Seuss was officially an Army man—and he was glad to be there. "The only good thing Adolf Hitler did in starting World War II," Ted said later, "was that he enabled me to join the Army and finally stop drawing, 'Quick, Henry, the Flit!'"[5] It also meant the end of his editorial cartoons for *PM*. Ted's final cartoon for Ingersoll ran on Tuesday, January 5, 1943, two days before his induction into the Army. It was one of his reliable cartoons about complacency, featuring a grizzled old man regaling his grandchild with stories of "The Battle of 1943"—but explaining that even as the Germans closed in, he simply "sat in this chair and groused about the annoying shortage of fuel oil!"[6] Ted had joined the Army largely because he didn't want to be *that* guy. He was proud of his work at *PM*—"I think I helped a little bit," he would say later[7]—but like many men of the era, he was itching to do his part in uniform.

Frank Capra felt much the same way. Brilliant, brooding, and frequently bothered, Lieutenant Colonel Capra, like Captain Geisel, was too old to be drafted and signed up instead. Unlike Geisel, however, the forty-six-year-old Capra had been in the Army before, serving as a second lieutenant during World War I, where he was mostly confined to a desk. After the war, he'd helmed one successful film after another—taking home Oscars for directing *It Happened One Night*, *Mr. Deeds Goes to Town*, and *You Can't Take It with You*—until the bombing of Pearl Harbor had spurred him to answer the call of duty again. Capra had barely finished editing *Arsenic and Old Lace* when he reported for active duty.

Capra didn't intend to be a desk jockey again. Initially he had lobbied to oversee a combat photography unit, hoping to witness firsthand the kind of glorious action he was convinced rival director John Ford was seeing in the field. But George Marshall, the U.S. Army chief of staff, thought Capra was too valuable for that. American soldiers, Marshall explained, unlike their German counterparts, didn't have a "faith" they were fighting for—as Stewart Alsop put it, "something for which they would gladly die."[8] Capra's job, said Marshall, was to make films that not only showed young men *how* to fight, but also "explain to our boys in the Army *why* we are fighting, and the *principles* for which we are fighting."[9] And so, Capra had been put in charge of the Army's 834th Signal Service Photographic Detachment, Special Services Division, Film Production Section, tasked with motivating, instructing, and inspiring American soldiers. His first command: move the 834th from Washington, D.C., to Hollywood, "both for production and for political reasons," insisted Capra.[10]

Capra took control of his unit on July 13, 1942, setting up briefly in a temporary space, then moving over to the vacant Fox Studio at 1421 North Western Avenue, leased from mogul Darryl F. Zanuck at the cost of one dollar per year. For the remainder of the war, Capra, Geisel, and nearly everyone associated with the unit would fondly refer to their site as "Fort Fox." Initially set up with 8 officers and 35 enlisted men, Capra's unit would eventually swell to around 150 men by the time of Geisel's arrival in early 1943.

Because Geisel was stationed in California, his duties at Fort Fox were essentially his day job; he and the other men were free to go home at the end of each day and sleep in their own beds. For the period of Ted's military service, then, the Geisels relocated from New York to California, taking a spacious three-bedroom home at 3595 Wonder View Drive, "high on a mountaintop" overlooking Hollywood.[11] The address was apt, for it truly was a wonderful view: from their perch on the windy hillside, the Geisels could see the Warner Bros. movie lot out their back door and the sparkling Hollywood Reservoir through the front; meanwhile, just to the east was the famous Hollywood sign, still reading HOLLYWOODLAND in early 1943.

To keep Helen company while he went off to work at Fort Fox each day, Ted bought her an excitable Irish setter from a breeder down the hill, and took great delight in dumping the gigantic dog in Helen's lap and announcing, "Here's your lapdog!"[12] When she wasn't babysitting the dog, Helen took up gardening—she would grow gorgeous roses—and worked to supplement Ted's meager Army income by writing children's books. Writing under her maiden name of Helen Marion Palmer, Helen regularly produced titles for Disney and Golden Books, including *Donald Duck Sees South America*. "She supported us during the war," Ted said proudly, noting that the only book she'd ever had rejected had to do with the Virgin Mary—that was a bit too touchy for a children's book.[13]

••••

When Geisel arrived at Fort Fox in January 1943, Capra already had been hard at work on the first of what would be seven films in a series called *Why We Fight*. The first of these films, titled *Prelude to War*—examining the conquering of Manchuria by Japan and Ethiopia by Italy—would win the Academy Award for Best Documentary in March, though Capra's name wouldn't appear anywhere on it. None of the films produced by the 834th, in fact, would contain a single creative credit. "You are working for a common cause. Your personal egos and idiosyncrasies are unimportant," Capra told his men. "There will be no personal credit for your work, either on the screen or in the press. The only press notices we are anxious to read are those of American victories!"[14]

Geisel was impressed with Capra from the moment he met him. Capra could look tightly wound—he was short and somewhat bulky, with dark eyebrows, a tight-set mouth, and dark hair slicked back to reveal a widow's peak—but he quickly earned the respect of officers and enlisted men alike. George Marshall thought highly of the prickly director and paid him his highest compliment by referring to him warmly as "that fellow Capra."[15] "The secret of Capra is his patience," said Geisel. "He's always been a good teacher. I never heard him cuss anybody out or embarrass anybody."[16] Geisel wasn't the only one in the 834th devoted to its commanding officer. "The innate quality of Capra's leadership was so implicit that he never had to exert it," said

Paul Horgan, who would later become a Pulitzer Prize–winning historian. "It came from the power of that man's character."[17]

Still, Capra understood that there were men within his division, including Geisel, who were somewhat disappointed to be stationed stateside, away from the action, free to go home each evening as if they were on shore leave. Capra was quick to assure them that what they were doing was vital to the war effort. "Some carping individuals will accuse you of fighting 'The Battle of Hollywood.' Don't argue with them," Capra wrote. "This is a total war fought with every conceivable weapon. Your weapon is film! Your bombs are ideas! Hollywood is a war plant!"[18] Still, military discipline was sometimes tough for the fiercely independent and egotistical Capra. "It was difficult for me to function. I felt very uneasy," Capra admitted.[19] Ted later said that being a good soldier and following orders without question "must have cost Capra a great deal."[20]

From mid-1942 until early 1946, Capra's unit would produce seventeen orientation and propaganda films, each running in length from ten minutes to over an hour. There were also the regular fifteen-minute newsreels, called *Army-Navy Screen Magazine*, to be produced every two weeks for viewing by the troops, as well as the weekly *Staff Film Report*, which was easily one of the most important—and classified—projects Capra would oversee. These invaluable briefing films were compilations of recent war footage, including reconnaissance and other classified materials culled even from enemy films, that was viewed by the president, the joint chiefs of staff, and allied commanders, to provide only slightly delayed details of theaters of combat. Production of these films required sorting through more than 200,000 feet of raw combat footage, then cutting together two or three reels of film quickly, with finished narration—and in some cases, animation—for approval and circulation by military commanders *every week*.

"The work is hard, but fascinating," Geisel wrote for a Dartmouth newsletter. "The Division, as you know, publishes, broadcasts, and makes movies. Everything from *Stars and Stripes*, *Yank*, booklets, news-maps and poster to films of syphilis, malaria, Fascism, and schistosomiasis."[21] While tales of producing films about syphilis would be among Geisel's go-to war stories ("I was in charge of soldiers not getting syphilis. I made movies with a message. The message was, 'Don't do it.'"[22]), he never actually made a syphilis movie. He would, however, become something of a specialist in malaria.

One of Captain Geisel's first assignments was to provide the art for a U.S. Medical Corps booklet that taught soldiers to protect themselves from the malaria-spreading anopheles mosquito. An earlier brochure on the topic—with stilted prose and clinical art—hadn't done the trick. It was little wonder: 37 percent of those serving in the U.S. military in World War II had less than a high school education. A text-heavy, jargon-riddled document probably wasn't going to be understood, if it was read at all.

In stepped Captain Munro Leaf, a public relations consultant to the U.S. Medical Corps, who also happened to be the author of the children's book *The Story of Ferdinand*. Leaf contended that soldiers might be more inclined to read—and more likely to understand—the brochure if it more closely resembled a children's book, with punchier writing and funnier pictures. Leaf, who knew a thing or two about writing prose for kids, offered to compose the new text, writing it out in longhand on a folded mock-up of a brochure titled "This Is Ann"— short for anopheles mosquito. For the illustrations, Leaf thought he knew just who to call.

Creating a mosquito mascot for a malaria campaign was all in a day's work for Geisel. "As an old Flit salesman," he wrote, "I find that I am of occasional use in doing semi-educational propaganda against the mosquito."[23] But it was especially easy to be inspired by Leaf's chatty prose:

This is Ann . . . she drinks blood! Her full name is
Anopheles Mosquito and she's dying to meet you!

Ann moves around at night (a real party gal) and she's
got a thirst. No whiskey, gin, beer or rum coke for
Ann . . . she drinks G.I. blood. She jabs that beak of
hers in like a drill and sucks up the juice . . . then the
poor G.I. is going to feel awful in about eight or
fourteen days . . . because he is going to have
malaria![24]

Geisel drew an appropriately sassy mosquito, beckoning soldiers seductively with one hand on her hip, the other behind her head, wings vibrating. There were cartoons of mosquitoes stinging unsuspecting rear ends, and a malaria-suffering soldier, flat on his back, legs up, radiating steam and stink lines. It was the kind of character work at which Geisel excelled, both charming and disarming, and by all accounts, it made its point—the document would be reprinted multiple times and would appear in newspapers around the United States. But Geisel, in this early assignment for Capra, was unhappy with it. "I did the illustrations, of which I am not overly proud, in my spare time," he explained later. "The booklet is interesting for one main reason: it is, to my knowledge, one of the few booklets assigned by the Chief of Staff and the Adjutant General that is completely goofy and informal in style and content."[25]

Unlike most projects that came out of Capra's unit, Geisel was permitted to sign his name—in this case *Dr. Seuss*—on the "This Is Ann" brochure, making it something of a novelty piece, which may have accounted for its wide circulation outside the military. Still, Capra would maintain that "[e]verybody from top to bottom deserves equal credit for anything we've done."[26] And everybody, from top to bottom, was expected to pitch in on any project, at any time, regardless of their expertise as civilians. While Geisel would continue to be called on from time to time for his talents as illustrator, there was too much work to be done producing the various films. For most of his career as a soldier in the Signal Corps Information and Education Division, Geisel would make movies.

He had a lot to learn—and knew it. "One of the reasons I love Capra," said Geisel, "is that when I arrived at Fort Fox, he gave me the tour, and the last thing he said was 'Here, Captain, are the Moviolas,' I said, 'What is a Moviola?' He looked at me rather suddenly and said, 'You will learn.' The average guy would have thrown me out."[27] For a gadget guru like Ted, the Moviola—an apparatus that permits a film editor to view the film while making manual cuts—was easy enough to grasp and master. But Capra was patient enough and smart enough to teach Geisel and his unit that there was more to filmmaking than just the mechanics; Geisel quickly learned that filmmaking was *storytelling*—and it all began with the writing.

Most of the visuals for the *Why We Fight* films and the *Army-Navy Screen Magazine* were compiled from stock footage—strafing airplanes, tanks rumbling across fields—as well as from the gripping war footage shot weekly by cameramen on the front lines. It was up to Capra's writers to weave the gigantic and regular flow of materials into a coherent, dramatic, and accurate narrative. Because of the nature of the project, there were no true directors for each film, only overseers called project officers. Most films involved the project officer and one or two writers working together on a script, outlining the overall direction of the narrative while simultaneously writing the script for the dramatic voice-over narration. Geisel was learning how to sort through a glut of raw materials, look for the overall story line, then compress both the visuals and the story down into an intelligible script.

Geisel was in awe of Capra's ability to distill a script down to its essence. He would bring Capra his first draft of a script for a training film, then watch with near reverence as Capra slowly went through it with a pencil. "The first thing you have to do in writing is find out if you're saying anything," he told Geisel—and Capra would carefully go through Geisel's script, underlining the places where he had advanced the story. "The rest . . . he left unlined," remembered Geisel. Most of his first drafts would be returned to him with little or no underlining. But Capra "taught me conciseness," said Geisel. "I learned a lot about the juxtaposition of words and visual images."[28] The tight storytelling discipline instilled by Capra would be formative in shaping Geisel's future art.

Geisel's real work for the *Army-Navy Screen Magazine* would begin shortly after his arrival at Fort Fox, when Capra approached him with a concept that Geisel would turn into one of the newsreels' most popular segments. A year earlier, Capra had assigned one of his staff writers with the task of developing a short comedic film called *Hey Soldier!* in which a bumbling private learns the hard way about Army rules and discipline. Capra never made the movie—but as he watched the *Why We Fight* movies in a theater full of enlisted men, Capra noticed that the audience tended to perk up during any animated segments, even if it was just an animated map. Capra revived the *Hey Soldier!* idea, but this time proposed it as a series of animated shorts about a similarly bumbling soldier named Private Snafu—from the military acronym for "Situation Normal: All F**ked Up." Capra thought Geisel, with his crossover experience in design, advertising, and editorial cartooning, would be the ideal man to take charge of the new project.

Because Private Snafu would require actual animators—unlike the live-action films, cartoons couldn't be made from stock footage—Geisel sent the project out for bids from animation studios. Disney and Warner Bros. went head to head for the opportunity, with Warner submitting an aggressive cost per film that significantly undercut Disney's offer. Disney had hampered its bid from the beginning by insisting on ownership of the Snafu character—a condition that Warner did *not* impose—but the loss of Private Snafu was likely a relief to Walt Disney himself, whose studio was already running a deficit on the military films he, too, was producing for the government.

Warner Bros., with its looser animation, loopier sense of humor, and more frantic pacing, was probably the better fit for Geisel anyway. There was plenty of talent among the directors in the stable of Warner Bros. animation—Frank Tashlin, Bob Clampett, Isadore "Friz" Freleng—but Capra was perceptive enough to pair Geisel primarily with a director cut very much from the same comedic cloth: artist, writer, and animator Charles M. "Chuck" Jones. Only thirty years old, Jones had been directing for Warner Bros. for six years, mostly overseeing cartoons featuring Sniffles the Mouse, Porky Pig, and some early iterations of Bugs Bunny and Elmer Fudd. By happenstance, in 1942 Jones had directed *"The Dover Boys at Pimento University" or "The Rivals of Roquefort Hall,"* a spot-on parody of Geisel's beloved Rover Boys novels. As Capra suspected, Chuck Jones and Dr. Seuss would get along just fine.

Together, Geisel and Jones designed the look of Private Snafu, developing the character model sheets with Art Heinemann and another young artist in Capra's unit named Ray Harryhausen, later the groundbreaking stop-motion model animator. "It was a delight to work with him,"[29] Harryhausen said of Geisel, adding that even with all the hands on Snafu's design, "Dr. Seuss . . . was in charge of the Snafu character."[30] While the final version of Snafu soaked up the varying artistic styles of his creative crew, Geisel's influence can still be seen in his basic design: wide eyes with light lashes, car-door ears sticking straight out from his head, and a slightly lopsided grin—all features on Ted's faces since his Oxford notebook.

Geisel would personally write the scripts for the first few installments of *Private Snafu*, setting the tone and establishing the pacing for the thirty or so films that would follow over the next three years—some of which Geisel would oversee, many of which he wouldn't. He was also learning how to storyboard, working with Jones and his animators to sketch out the key moments of stories and sequences, pin them to corkboard, then move them around or add and subtract sections as the story was reworked and revised.

Geisel would work with his staff of "perhaps ten men"[31] to write, design, lay out, and storyboard each six-minute cartoon before sending everything over to Warner Bros. to finish off. "[Chuck Jones's] layout men had to adapt our work," said Maurice Noble, an artist and animator under Geisel's supervision. The director—whether it was Jones, Freleng, Tashlin, or others—and the team at Warner Bros. would complete the animation, dub the voices (most of which were performed by Warner Bros. stalwart Mel Blanc), overlay Carl Stalling's music, and then send the film back to Geisel for release by the Army—at a rate of about two cartoons per month. "It was a very productive small unit," Noble said proudly.[32]

Private Snafu would make his debut in June 1943 in the short cartoon *Private Snafu: Coming!!* On-screen, Snafu's name would be parsed as "Situation Normal: All *Fouled* Up," with the narrator pausing for dramatic effect before refusing to use the expletive. In his first appearance, Snafu is introduced as "the goofiest soldier in the U.S. Army"[33]—patriotic and well intentioned, but inclined to laziness, carelessness with rules and procedures, and shortcuts. But for the purposes of teaching soldiers, those weaknesses were the strengths of the film—for soldiers would learn the value of particular skills or habits by watching Snafu either disregard them or perform them *badly*, often resulting in his imprisonment, his hospitalization, or even his own death. "Snafu gave [Geisel] the chance to write adult humor for adults, or for boys who were being trained to die as men," wrote film critic Richard Corliss. "The series tried to ensure that more of those boys would come home alive."[34]

Geisel's Private Snafu would be frequently aided by Technical Fairy, First Class—a perpetually unshaven guardian angel of sorts, who smoked a cigar and fluttered about wearing only military issue boxers, army boots, and garrison cap. The Technical Fairy would grant Snafu any variety of wishes, all of which go awry and drive home the underlying point of the film. In an early cartoon called *Private Snafu: Gripes*, for instance, the Technical Fairy shows up to answer the undisciplined Snafu's wish that *he* could be in charge of the

Army, granting the request in rhyming verse that could only have come from the pen of Dr. Seuss:

> I heard ya sayin' it: Everything stank!
> That *you'd* run things different if *you* had more rank.
> So as technical fairy, I got a good notion
> To give you a chance, pal—here's a promotion![35]

Naturally, because of Snafu's failure to impose discipline, his unit is completely unprepared when attacked by the Germans, leading the Technical Fairy to admonish him in similar verse:

> No use! They ain't trained! They ain't got no morale!
> Your army's a washout, my fine feathered pal![36]

Because the cartoons were intended to be seen only by servicemen, and not for public release, the government gave Geisel considerable leeway with language, permitting use of the scandalous epithets *hell* and *damn*. Off-color humor was also tolerated, within reason; one of Ted's and Chuck Jones's favorite jokes would appear in the cartoon *The Home Front*, in which Geisel's script described icy conditions as "so cold, it could freeze the nuts off a Jeep." Without missing a beat, the camera pans across a snowbound Jeep, which drops two metal hex nuts onto the ice with an audible clatter.

From the beginning, Geisel also applied Munro Leaf's recommendation that if they really expected young servicemen to pay attention—even to a cartoon—they had to "make it racy."[37] And so the Snafu cartoons feature plenty of shapely women—nurses, WACs, girls back home—in various states of undress. Geisel remembered the problems he'd had with female anatomy in *Seven Lady Godivas* and wisely left the design work to Jones and the Warner animators, who gleefully inserted women who looked as if they had stepped straight out of a pinup calendar by Alberto Vargas. It was all in good fun, but even Jones understood the civilian animators were also taking their patriotic duty seriously. "I tried to make good pictures," said Jones, "and it turns out that some of them did save a few lives, by teaching them through animation."[38]

• • • •

Between scriptwriting, film editing, and conferencing with Capra, the men of the 834th resolutely went through their daily drills and training regimens. Despite swimming and playing handball regularly for the past couple of years, Geisel remained, in the words of Paul Horgan, "hopelessly uncoordinated." "[Ted] tried so earnestly in field drills that it was touching," said Horgan. "He was warm and full of worthy convictions, and patriotic to the limit . . . He was tall, skinny, his hair parted in the middle and falling like some of the birds he drew, and with that great beak of a nose."[39] Even Geisel knew he was not a terrific foot soldier; on the pistol range, he never qualified with his .45—information he likely didn't share with his sharpshooting father—and often joked that if called into battle, he fully intended to "grab [the gun] by the barrel and throw it." He would wear the pistol upside down in his holster for the remainder of the war.[40] Later, Geisel would perform better with an M1, placing fifth among the ninety-three participating members of his division, and qualifying as a marksman.[41]

What downtime the men had—and there wasn't much—was spent drinking in the canteen or playing cards or dice. In a sheaf of unpublished cartoons Geisel drew of life at the 834th, one is of himself leading a visiting colonel around Fort Fox. "And . . . er . . . here, Colonel, are the artists!" says cartoon Ted, pointing to a group of men on their knees, playing dice. The brass must not have minded; a second cartoon shows Ted trying to unsuccessfully pull the same colonel away from the game. To boost morale, Geisel also created the camp's own version of the Academy Awards, handing out statuettes of Private Snafu to award winners. When questioned by Army accountants about the costs of the trophies, Geisel would neither confirm nor deny whether he had buried the expenses among his cost sheets; another of Geisel's cartoons shows him on a witness stand, coolly ignoring a prosecutor's questioning about the hidden costs.[42] In each cartoon, Geisel draws himself with a long pointed nose and round glasses, his hair parted down the middle with a cowlick in the back.

In the evenings, Ted and Helen were doing their best to find some semblance of a social routine in the Hollywood area; it wasn't quite the theater and restaurant scene they'd left behind in New York, but Los Angeles *did* have its own kind of appeal. Sometimes he and Helen would go to the clubs on Sunset, where they once caught a performance by Nat King Cole and his trio. Other evenings, they'd head for the Hollywood Canteen on Cahuenga, where Ted, or any other serviceman, could get in free if he wore his uniform—and might even spot Marlene Dietrich volunteering her time to work as a waitress, or Abbott and Costello busing tables. Lately, too, they'd been attending a racy revue called *Ken Murray's Blackouts*, a burlesque show hosted by comedian Ken Murray at the always-packed El Capitan Theatre on Vine.

As 1943 wound down, Geisel picked up some additional work from the War Finance Division of the Treasury Department doing the art for an international campaign about "the Squander Bug," discouraging profligate spending over the holidays in favor of war bonds. He also oversaw the completion of what would be one of the most Seussian of the Private Snafu cartoons, at least in its overall look and feel. Called *Private Snafu: Rumors*, it opens with more of Geisel's lively verse, bouncing in rhythm reminiscent of *Mulberry Street*:

> 'Twas a bright sunny day with the air fresh and clean.
> Not a rumor was stirring, 'cept in the latrine.[43]

It's while sitting in the latrine that Snafu starts a conversation with another soldier, who makes the flip scatological joke that it's a "nice day for a bombing." Snafu immediately spreads the rumor of an imminent bombing by the Germans—and like the telephone game, the rumor gets larger and wilder as it's passed along. "Now shoot off your face!" demands the narrator as a man's mouth morphs into a cannon. "And baloney is flying all over the place!"

Geisel's design sense was ideal for images of flying baloney, but there are also Seussian-influenced "rumor monsters"—direct descendants of the creatures Geisel had dreamed up to terrorize automobiles in his ads for motor oil—including birds with trumpets for beaks, chattering gas bags, and a horse-faced creature with sleepy eyes and a shock of white hair. The end of the cartoon finds Snafu in a straitjacket, quarantined because of "rumor-itis." It was the animated equivalent of Dr. Seuss's sprawling one-pagers in *Judge* or *Life*.

While Geisel was continuing to serve as the primary producer and project officer for the Private Snafu cartoons, by early 1944 he was leaving more and more of the writing to others, turning frequently to thirty-five-year-old cartoonist P. D. Eastman to write and storyboard the cartoons. Eastman, a former animator for both Disney and Warner, was a fan of Dr. Seuss, and was delighted to have the opportunity to work directly for Geisel. With the writing and storyboarding in the capable hands of Eastman and others, Geisel's duties as project officer mostly required him to run the administrative traps, which included getting all scripts approved and, as needed, cleared by the military to ensure Snafu didn't give away any real military secrets.

While Geisel understood the need to get all scripts sanctioned by headquarters, that didn't make the governmental red tape any easier to tolerate. In another of Geisel's unpublished cartoons depicting army life at Fort Fox, he drew himself standing in an office with his portfolio of scripts and storyboards under one arm, as two officers sword-fight over a particularly problematic page. "Keep it in!" the first officer says as he lunges while the other parries, shrieking, "Take it out!"[44]

Even with multiple eyes on the work, some things nearly got missed. In the 1944 cartoon *Private Snafu: Going Home*, Snafu returns to the States, where he can't resist bragging to friends, family, and strangers about his war service, carelessly revealing the location, missions, and weaknesses of his former unit—with disastrous re-sults when the information gets into the wrong hands. At one point, Snafu mentions a superweapon—"a new flyin' bazooka, with radar control!"—capable of destroying an entire island with one blast. The cartoon was finished and ready for distribution when military intel-ligence suddenly ordered, without explanation, that Geisel shelve the completed film. Not until more than a year later would Geisel realize why: the capabilities of his cartoon superweapon were a little too close to the properties of the atomic bomb, the classified weapons project currently being developed in laboratories in Oak Ridge, Ten-nessee, and Los Alamos, New Mexico. It wouldn't be the last time Geisel would be so prescient about military weaponry.

In early February 1944, Geisel was promoted to the rank of major—and Capra, it seems, was pleased enough with his work heading up the animation unit that he decided Geisel had earned a spot as project officer for a longer film. With the tide of the war in Europe beginning to turn, Capra had been advised to begin putting into production films explaining what would be expected of American soldiers *after* the fighting was over. And so, Capra assigned Geisel to Project 6010X, tentatively titled *Your Job in Germany*, tasked with educating American soldiers on how to responsibly interact with the Germans as a con-quered nation.

Apart from recognizing Geisel's demonstrated skill heading up a project, Capra may also have felt that Ted, as an American of German extraction, was uniquely qualified to take on the subject. Geisel began consulting regularly with the War Department in Washington, D.C., to learn about the United States government's official policies on Germany and the German people, commuting bicoastally in military transport planes nearly every week. "I've done almost enough travel-ing to last me from here on in, having flown half a million missions to the Pentagon building," he told friends at Dartmouth.[45] Sorting through reams of reports, classified documents, photographs, and miles of film, Geisel began working on the script for *Your Job in Ger-many*. "You are up against German history. It isn't good," wrote Geisel solemnly in his script. "The next war. That is why you occupy Germany. To make that next war impossible." Geisel set out to guide viewers through a brief history of Germany and its would-be world conquerors, from Otto von Bismarck to Kaiser Wilhelm to Adolf Hitler. And in no uncertain terms, Geisel's script held the German people responsible for continually propping up one fascist strongman after another. "Practically every German was part of the Nazi network," wrote Geisel.

For Geisel, the larger threat came not from the German people, but from the German youth. "Guard particularly against this group," he warned in his script:

> They know no other system than the one that poisoned
> their minds. They're soaked in it. Trained to win by
> cheating . . . they've heard no free speech, read no free
> press . . . Practically everything you've been trained to
> believe in, they've been trained to hate and destroy.

For Ted, this wasn't hyperbole; in his travels to Germany with Helen several years earlier, he'd seen firsthand the effects of German propaganda on German children, and it had alarmed him. He'd addressed the issue directly in one of his final cartoons for *PM*, showing Uncle Sam discharging a bellows labeled PSYCHOLOGICAL DISARMAMENT OF AXIS YOUTH into the ears of a German child. "We'll have to clean a lot of stuff out before we put peace thoughts in," says Uncle Sam.[46]

While Geisel was a true believer when it came to the skeptical approach to German youth, he was much more dubious about the military's policy of nonfraternization with the German people. Years earlier, Geisel had been moved by the plight of his own relatives in Bavaria. It broke Ted's heart to think the official policy of the United States was to discourage even the smallest of human connection with a conquered people. He thought it was an "impossible and ill-advised" position for the government to take. "I strongly believed in everything that I wrote in this film with the exception of the Non-Fraternization conclusion," he said later, ". . . which I wrote as an officer acting under orders . . . and later worked to get rescinded."[47] For now, though, Geisel wrote it like he meant it. "The German people are *not* our friends," he wrote in his script for *Your Job in Germany*:

> They cannot come back into the civilized fold just by sticking out their hand and saying sorry. Sorry? Not sorry they caused the war, they're only sorry they lost it. That is the hand that *heiled* Hitler. That is the hand that dropped the bombs on defenseless Rotterdam, Brussels, Belgrade . . . That is the hand that killed and crippled American soldiers, sailors and marines. Don't clasp that hand. It's not the kind of hand you clasp in friendship.[48]

Geisel completed his script for *Your Job in Germany* in late spring 1944 and began putting together a rough cut of the movie. For the voice-over duties, Geisel placed a call to the Air Force facility at Hal Roach Studios in Culver City—dubbed "Fort Roach"—where a number of actors were stationed and asked to audition two possible narrators. The officials at Fort Roach sent over two potential voice-over men: Sergeant John Beal—a leading man in smaller films like *The Man Who Found Himself*—and Lieutenant Ronald Reagan, a contract actor with Warner who had memorably played George "The Gipper" Gipp in the 1940 film *Knute Rockne, All American*. Geisel listened carefully as each man read from the script, then dismissed Reagan. "I guess it's one of the few times anyone has said, 'Don't call us, we'll call you' to an incipient President of the United States," Geisel, a lifelong Democrat, said later, with just a hint of pride.[49]

Geisel had a first draft of the script of *Your Job in Germany* completed by June; simultaneously, contractors at the Disney studios were working with Capra to put together a rough cut of the film, and Geisel dutifully submitted paperwork to headquarters to assure them the film was coming in exactly at its budgeted cost of $20,000. Given the sensitivity of the material, the film would need to be approved both by Cabinet-level officials and generals in the field—a process doomed to sluggishness, despite the increasingly critical nature of the project. By late August the Allied liberation of Paris seems to have sped along the approval process, as the War Department okayed Geisel's first script, with some changes— but the commanding generals in the European combat zones were still needed for the film's final approval.

With the help of Academy Award—nominated screenwriter Anthony Veiller, Geisel continued to revise and correct his script. Meanwhile Capra, assisted by Anatole Litvak—a Russian director who'd become an American citizen and proudly enlisted in the U.S. Army— worked quickly to assemble a first cut, completing a ten-minute rough by early November 1944. As the project officer for the film, it was now Geisel's responsibility to get the film approved by the military commanders—which meant he was going to have to personally carry his script and his film cans directly to them in the European combat zones.

For purposes of having the project approved, Geisel was assigned to the Ardennes campaign in the Rhineland, officially serving as a liaison officer for the Information and Education Division in the European theater. On November 11, 1944, Geisel boarded a C-54 Skymaster military transport plane bound for Ireland, with a final destination of Paris. Here Geisel would find the escorts for his trip into the Ardennes Forest: Robert Murphy from the State Department, and Major John Bocttiger, the son-in-law of President Roosevelt, whose name alone Geisel was quite certain would give his mission the heft it needed to ensure every general gave his film their attention.

On November 19, using a Michelin map as their guide, Geisel and his companions traveled by car from Paris through Verdun and into the recently liberated Luxembourg. As Geisel pulled in to Luxembourg City in the middle of a downpour, the sound of "a few distant booms" could be heard from the battlefront, only a few miles to the east. That night, even as fighting continued outside of town, Geisel went to see Marlene Dietrich perform for the troops at a theater in Luxembourg. When it was over, he walked back to his quarters in the middle of a blackout, carefully picking his way down dark, unfamiliar streets.

It was cold and rainy when Geisel and his escorts drove north into the Ardennes Forest on the morning of Monday, November 20. A light dusting of snow covered the roads, where it was quickly stirred and pounded into gray slush by a steady caravan of military vehicles. It was here, deep in the Ardennes, that Geisel was able to track down General Omar Bradley with the First Army and Brigadier General Frank McSherry at the Supreme Headquarters of the Allied Expeditionary Force. Geisel showed his film to the generals in a small church, where "American college football scores were posted over a crucifix"[50] (Ted may have noted without comment that Dartmouth had lost to rival Cornell two days earlier). Bradley and McSherry okayed the film—and with the first of his boxes checked, Geisel continued north toward Veviers, switching to a jeep when his car bogged down in the muddy roads one too many times.

On reaching Veviers, Geisel was both shocked and pleased to find the shell-pocked but newly liberated town in a state of near elation. Hidden stashes of burgundy were broken into by the locals and served to the Americans in what Geisel called their relatively "swank" accommodations.[51] And yet ambulances still rumbled through the town, Geisel noted, with "two pairs of bare feet in each back window"—a reminder of the killing going on just over the horizon. It all made him feel "elated in a depressed sort of way," he later said.[52]

Geisel spent Thanksgiving Day 1944 in the old Dutch city of Maastricht, eating a huge morning meal with American officers—a cheerful experience that was only momentarily marred when Geisel got locked in a bathroom when the doorknob broke off.[53] The contrast between the Dutch people and their American liberators was not lost on Geisel, who noted in a travel journal that "poverty [is] more apparent here. People digging in garbage cans."[54] Later that afternoon, he and his companions finally made it into Germany, arriving in the city of Aachen, the first German town to be liberated by the Allies, who had overtaken the heavily defended city on October 21. Much of the town was in ruins—several medieval churches were damaged or destroyed—but the still-euphoric American occupiers greeted Geisel warmly, offering him his second Thanksgiving meal of the day, a generous serving of "wienerschnitzel, wursts, and wassail."[55]

As Geisel made his way through the city, he was saddened and horrified by the devastation of the war on the German people and the surrounding landscape. Channeling the same haunted war-weariness he'd seen in his own German relatives, Geisel noted his impressions of the battle-scarred city in a stunned, almost staccato manner:

> We go through a typical destroyed house. Broken toy in
> the plaster. In a cupboard with the rain soaking through—
> somebody's hope chest of linens. A doctor's lab. Broken
> bottles + test tubes. An inch of water on the floor. Take
> apart models of a cow + a horse. Chaos.[56]

His sympathies, however, went only so far. Later in the winter, Geisel toured the site of the recently abandoned Natzweiler-Struthof concentration camp in the French Vosges Mountains. As he walked among the abandoned clothing and examined the single crematorium, Geisel found it all almost too terrible to comprehend—surely, he thought, human beings couldn't be *that* cruel to one another. The single crematorium, he insisted, "could never have been used to get rid of bodies of mass-murder victims," while the so-called torture table— where Nazi doctors had carried out cruel human experiments—he was certain *had* to be "a conventional embalming table." It was a nearly unfathomable horror—so much so that Geisel worried it wouldn't be believed. Until the stories were thoroughly investigated and proven to be true—and they would be—Geisel advised that anyone "writing information to troops should be cautioned to steer clear of all German Atrocity Stories unless they have been doubly and triply checked and found *absolutely true* . . . If we overplay one detail and have to retract, our audience will be apt to disbelieve everything." Until that time, he continued, it was already terrible enough "that human beings were actually locked up in them. There is enough horror in that to condemn the Nazi system forever."[57]

In his journal, Geisel also catalogued what he saw as the four most pressing problems that needed to be immediately addressed in Germany to ensure its successful—and nonfascist—reentry on the world's stage. On his list, between "police force" and "coal," he wrote: "Children. Education." After seeing concentration camps and other despicable signs of Nazi cruelty, Geisel remained more concerned than ever about the effect of Nazi propaganda on German children. Left on their own, he worried they might still be inclined toward what he called "the Super Race Disease, the World Conquest Disease."[58] Watching and listening to German children soaked in a fascist doctrine had convinced Geisel that his initial wariness had been correct; instilling the principles of peace was going to be hard work, both now and in the future.

•••

With Robert Murphy's help, Geisel learned that several of the generals whose approval he needed for his film had set up headquarters in a battered castle nearby. Geisel tucked his film cans under his arm and headed for the medieval structure, walking into a war-ravaged venue that was oddly beautiful. "All the water mains were broken and the water was coming down the marble stairs," recalled Geisel. "And there was no electricity; it was lit by candles. We were surrounded by figures in armor holding sixteenth-century banners."[59] It was in this setting that Geisel found the Allied commanders involved in a formal meeting with the newly appointed civilian leaders of the city—"people who claimed they weren't Nazis,"[60] Geisel said somewhat skeptically. The Allied commanders were lined up along one side—Geisel respectfully took his place at the end of the row of officers—while the new city government leaders faced them across the candlelit hall. In a show of respect, the Allied generals crossed the hall, then slowly walked down the length of the German line, shaking hands with each German leader.

The irony of the moment was not lost on Geisel. "[*Your Job in Germany*] was based on the Army's ridiculous nonfraternization policy in Germany," he noted incredulously. "The generals all shook hands with them, and then I—holding these cans of film which said *you should never shake hands with a German*—had to move the can from my right arm to my left arm so I could shake hands."[61]

Geisel would still get all the signatures necessary for the approval of his film, barring one: General George Patton, who allegedly stood up halfway through a showing of the film, growled "Bullshit!" and stalked out of the room.[62] Patton's objections, however, were expected; even General Eisenhower had recently admonished the general to "get off your bloody ass and carry out the denazification program instead of mollycoddling the goddamn Nazis."[63] Ultimately, the film was given the go-ahead by Lieutenant General Walter Bedell Smith, chief of staff for the Supreme Headquarters, who approved the movie on the condition that it not be shown until after V-E Day—whenever that might be. He also ordered that the film be recut with some additional war footage and without some of Geisel's snarky commentary, such as his advice in the film's closing moments to "Just be a good soldier. Leave all the bungling to the State Department."[64]

Situated back in Paris in early December 1944, Geisel made his last edits to the script and shipped it off to Capra to put into final production. Then it was back to Luxembourg, where he was stationed at First Army headquarters. "The Army thought I should see war firsthand, so I'd know what I was writing about, so they sent me to some interesting action here and there,"[65] Geisel said. He had no idea how interesting the action was about to become.

While at First Army headquarters, Geisel ran into Ralph Ingersoll, his former editor at *PM*, who was now serving as a lieutenant colonel with Army intelligence. While neither man recorded exactly what they talked about, Geisel likely mentioned to Ingersoll that during his nearly eight weeks in Europe, he had yet to experience any real fighting. Ingersoll immediately picked up a map and pointed to the Belgian municipality of Bastogne, about forty-five miles to the north. Ingersoll promised Geisel he would be just far enough away from any real danger.[66] Geisel took Ingersoll's map, hailed a driver, and headed for Bastogne.

He arrived in the city only a few hours before the German forces began laying siege to Bastogne, pushing through the Allied lines as part of what would come to be called the Battle of the Bulge—some of the bloodiest days of fighting since D-Day in June 1944. "The thing that probably saved my life was that I got there in the early morning and the Germans didn't arrive until that night," Geisel said later. "I found Bastogne pretty boring and . . . got on the other side of the line and got cut off." Caught in a downpour, Geisel lost his sense of direction and wandered aimlessly before running into a military policeman who had also lost his way. "We learned we were ten miles beyond the German lines," Geisel said.[67]

"Nobody came along and put up a sign saying, 'This is the Battle of the Bulge,'" Geisel said later. "How was I supposed to know? I thought the fact that we didn't seem to be able to find any friendly troops in any direction was just one of the normal occurrences of combat."[68] After three days of hunkering down, they were finally rescued by a British unit clearing out the last of the retreating Germans. "The retreat we beat was accomplished with a speed that will never be beaten," Geisel recalled later.[69]

Safely back in France for the holidays, Geisel spent his Christmas at an officer's holiday party, having gorged himself on peanut butter and salami sandwiches and gotten slightly drunk on lemonade spiked with gin. He would ring in the New Year on the Champs-Élysées, marking the beginning of 1945 by standing pensively in the rain to pay his respects at the Tomb of the Unknown Soldier.

Ten days later, he was back in California at Fort Fox, where the final cut of *Your Job in Germany* was rolling off the spools in the editing room, approved for release once Germany surrendered. Mission accomplished.

• • • •

Frank Capra had a problem. Since mid-1942, he'd been working on draft after draft of a film script aimed at educating American soldiers on their Japanese enemy. With a working title of *Know Your Enemy: Japan*, Capra intended for the film to provide soldiers with a quick history of the Axis nation, its people, its government, and its culture—but the project had derailed quickly, with Capra bickering with one screenwriter after another over exactly how to approach the subject. Capra was trying for a delicate balancing act, making a film that he hoped would be both a clear-eyed history and a hard-hitting condemnation of Japan and the Japanese people. The first script, completed in 1942 by *Angels with Dirty Faces* scribe Warren Duff, had been poked, prodded, picked apart and put back together again by several other writers, including Carl Foreman, who'd later write *High Noon* and *The Bridge on the River Kwai*; *Maltese Falcon* director John Huston; and a young aspiring novelist named Irving Wallace. But Capra was unhappy with everything he'd seen so far; mostly he thought the scripts were too sympathetic toward the Japanese people.

Wallace griped that Capra was too naive to understand the nuances of the war with Japan. "He was totally unsophisticated when it came to political thought," said Wallace. "He came up with a simple foreign policy toward Japan. It added up to this: the only good Jap is a dead Jap."[70] What Wallace didn't realize was that Capra had been *ordered* by the military brass to make that simple policy a central tenet of the film. The real problem, however, was that even the U.S. government wasn't sure what its own policies were regarding Japan. "The central question, which caused the most difficulty, was 'Who in Japan is actually to blame for this war?'" said historian William Blakefield. "[Was it] the Japanese people? The Emperor? A small band of militarists?"[71] Without any real guidance from the military, Capra was flummoxed—and, frankly, a bit exhausted—by it all.

Capra, pleased with the work that had been done on *Your Job in Germany*, asked Geisel in February to assist him on a new draft of *Know Your Enemy: Japan*. The two of them worked together quickly and relatively harmoniously, coming up with a script that walked the very fine line Capra had sought between documentary and propaganda. The new script did a manageable job of concisely summarizing five hundred years of Japanese history and culture, and still managed to have it both ways when it portrayed the Japanese as a war-loving society made up of a peaceful people who had been deceived and betrayed by their leaders. The script was completed in April 1945; a month later, Capra would be gone, honorably discharged from the Army and awarded the Distinguished Service Medal—an honor that so touched the normally unflappable Capra that he vomited in the moments before the medal was pinned to his chest. With Capra gone, it would be up to Geisel to oversee *Know Your Enemy: Japan*'s final approval and release.

At the request of the assistant secretary of war, Geisel added information to the beginning of the film explicitly praising the bravery of the Japanese Americans who fought in the war, and added new footage of American victories in the Pacific as quickly as such footage became available. But the War Department continued to be concerned the film showed "too much sympathy"[72] for the Japanese people. Until the U.S. government could determine and articulate its own position, it was going to bury the film. The film was marked confidential and was endlessly delayed while the War Department continued its foot-dragging.

Victory in Europe officially arrived on Wednesday, May 8, 1945, with the formal surrender of Germany. While Geisel had been ordered in November 1944 not to release *Your Job in Germany* until after V-E day, the film had subsequently been cleared for release on April 13, 1945—the day after the death of Franklin Roosevelt. Victory in Europe, however, didn't mean the war was won; in fact, the war seemed far from over in the Pacific theaters that spring, and Geisel was following with increasing alarm the intelligence he received each week regarding battles in Burma and Okinawa.

"The Germans had folded up, but the Pentagon was concerned about keeping up the fighting morale of our troops until Japan was licked," said Geisel. "At Fort Fox, we decided one way to do this was to scare them about the possible next war."[73] According to Geisel, he had read an article in *The New York Times*—or maybe it was a Buck Rogers comic strip, Geisel could never keep the story straight—that described "how there was enough energy in a glass of water to blow up half the world."[74] Geisel began writing a script in May 1945 describing how to harness that potential energy and use it in a weapon of mass destruction—a weapon that could be launched from a rocket activated by pushing a button a thousand miles away. It was "[all] about the next war being a push-button atomic war," recalled Geisel.[75]

The script landed on the desk of Paul Horgan, who immediately forwarded it to Vannevar Bush, head of the Office of Scientific Research and Development. Bush thought Geisel's "extraordinary projection of the most lethal weapons" sounded a little too much like the highly classified Manhattan Project, which had recently exploded an atomic bomb in the New Mexico desert and was preparing the next one for the military to use on Axis civilians. Vannever ordered Horgan to immediately cancel Geisel's project, and to destroy all storyboards and scripts.

"I called Ted and he was devastated," said Horgan.[76] According to Geisel, Horgan also insisted he burn whatever source it was where he had gotten his information on such a weapon. Geisel later claimed he had burned *The New York Times* in a solemn ceremony. "Then I called Washington," Geisel continued, "and said, 'Mission accomplished, sir. We have burned the *Times*.' 'Well done, Geisel,' I was told, then they went on with the war."[77]

According to Horgan, after he had canceled Geisel's project, Horgan had gone to Europe for six weeks, during which time the United States detonated an atomic bomb over Hiroshima, Japan, on August 6, 1945. "When I returned, my secretary said, 'Major Geisel has been making daily calls from the West Coast,'" said Horgan. "So I called back—and before I could say anything but 'Hi, Ted,' he said, 'I understand everything now. All is forgiven.'"[78] On August 15, due in part to the continued threat of what Geisel had called "a push-button atomic war," Japan announced it was surrendering; the formal surrender would be signed on September 2, 1945. One final casualty was *Know Your Enemy: Japan*, which General Douglas MacArthur himself ordered be permanently shelved "due to change in policy governing occupation of Japan." It would stay in his vaults until 1977.

The war was over. And yet twelve days later, Geisel would be devastated by tragedy.

On Friday, September 14, Ted's sister, Marnie, was in the kitchen in the house on Fairfield, when she mentioned to her daughter, Peggy, now seventeen, that her left arm had gone numb and that she was feeling faint. "But she'd said that for years," recalled Peggy. "She wouldn't see a doctor." Over the past few years, Marnie had grown increasingly angry, paranoid, and withdrawn as she sank deeper and deeper into alcoholism and depression. Lately, she had become convinced that her own family was conspiring against her; Peggy was certain her mother had suffered a complete nervous breakdown. That morning, shortly after announcing that she felt faint, Marnie collapsed in the kitchen and died of a heart attack at age forty-three.

Marnie was buried in Oak Ridge Cemetery in Springfield, close to her mother. Ted would be haunted by his sister's death for the rest of his life. Whether he regretted that he'd fallen out of touch with Marnie as she'd grown more and more despondent—and whether there was a touch of guilt that his self-removal had played some small part in her decline—Ted never said; he would rarely speak of Marnie's death with anyone. Peggy, a freshman at Katharine Gibbs business college in Boston, was invited to live in California with Ted and Helen, an offer Peggy gladly accepted. Perhaps it was Ted's way of atoning for his own benign neglect of Marnie.

Ted's army term of service was ticking slowly toward its end; his days at Fort Fox were now numbered. Late in 1945, Geisel began working on the script for what would be his final project for the Army Signal Corps. With the war now officially over, American soldiers were being asked to occupy Japan—and Geisel, who had laid out how to successfully occupy Germany in *Your Job in Germany*, was now asked to do the same job for Japan. For help with *Our Job in Japan*, Geisel called on his colleague Carl Foreman—who, like Geisel, had also been involved with *Know Your Enemy: Japan*—and this time, unlike *Your Job in Germany*, there would be no loathsome policy of nonfraternization to enforce.

Geisel was convinced that, no matter how bad Japanese atrocities might have been—and in *Our Job in Japan*, he and Foreman called them "so disgusting, so revolting, so obscene that [they] turned the stomach of the entire civilized world"—Geisel thought American fraternization was necessary for the Japanese to become the free and peaceful people they aspired to be. Geisel had come a long way since his "fifth column" cartoon in *PM* questioning the loyalties of Japanese Americans. Furthermore, he also warned American troops against "pushing people around," a progressive directive that could have come straight out of one of Ingersoll's *PM* editorials.

Despite the friendly sentiments—or maybe because of them—*Our Job in Japan* was doomed to suffer the same fate as *Know Your Enemy: Japan*. After its completion in March 1946, General MacArthur asked the Army to pull the film from circulation; in fact, it wouldn't be

released *at all* and was thought lost until it was rediscovered and released as a curiosity in 1982.

The film's fate was of little concern to Geisel anyway; on Tuesday,
January 8, 1946, Major Theodor Seuss Geisel, now forty-one years
old, was awarded the Legion of Merit for "meritorious service in
planning and producing films, particularly those utilizing animated
cartoons for training, informing and enhancing the morale of the
troops."[79] It was an award Geisel would remain particularly proud of
for the rest of his life, always making certain it was included on his
long list of honors and achievements even well into his seventies.

Five days after receiving the Legion of Merit, Geisel was promoted
to the rank of lieutenant colonel.

And then on January 27, Lieutenant Colonel Geisel left active duty
and returned to Helen and their hillside house on Wonder View Drive.
Dr. Seuss was home from the war—and very uncertain about what to
do next.

CHAPTER 8

A GOOD PROFESSION

1946–1949

O n the evening of March 7, 1946, the 18th Academy Awards ceremony was held at Grauman's Chinese Theatre in Hollywood. Inside, the theater was packed with a capacity crowd of 2,100; outside, those without tickets thronged Hollywood Boulevard in what one reporter called the "greatest demonstration of pomp the town has seen since before the war."[1] That evening, the Academy Award for Best Documentary Short Subject went to the film *Hitler Lives?*, a film lifted almost entirely from *Your Job in Germany*. As the winning film's title was announced that night, producer Gordon Hollingshead made his way to the stage to pick up the Oscar. "I didn't get [the Oscar]," Geisel remarked. "The producers did. They don't give Academy Awards for short documentaries to the creative people."[2]

In fact, Geisel wasn't eligible to pick up the Oscar that night *at all*; while *Hitler Lives?* had borrowed heavily from Ted's *Your Job in Germany* documentary for Capra—much of the film used Ted's script *verbatim*—Ted's name appeared nowhere on it. As Geisel later explained it, because *Your Job in Germany* was a government film, it was exempt from normal copyright protection. That made it fair game for director Don Siegel to tweak some of the images and redub most of the narration and for writer Saul Elkins to add some additional exposition. "They took our narrator's voice off and put theirs in and

191

brought it out as *Hitler Lives?*," Geisel said with just a hint of exasperation. "And they got an Academy Award for it."[3]

The Academy Award arrived at a precarious moment in Geisel's career. Since leaving the Army in early 1946, Ted had been somewhat uncertain of his postwar profession. With the filmmaking skills he had honed while working with Capra, Geisel thought he might perhaps quit writing children's books altogether in order to reinvent himself as a film writer, director, or editor—and the Academy Award just won by *Hitler Lives?* did much to make him attractive to more than a few movie studio executives. Shortly after *Hitler Lives?* picked up its award, in fact, Geisel was contacted by Warner Bros. producer Jerry Wald, who offered him a job as a screenwriter and script doctor at a hefty weekly salary of $500—worth about $6,000 today. It was a staggering salary, so it was perhaps little surprise Ted leapt at the offer. Better still, he and Helen could stay in their house on Wonder View Drive, which practically backed onto the Warner Bros. lot, while Ted commuted to the Warner offices.

Wald steered Ted into an office at Warner, its walls lined with cabinets filled with prefabricated jokes that Ted, as a script doctor, could insert into screenplays in need of a quick laugh. Ted's first real assignment, however, was to fix a "problem picture"[4] based on a book Warner had recently acquired: psychiatrist Robert M. Lindner's 1944 *Rebel Without a Cause: The Hypnoanalysis of a Criminal Psychopath.* Lindner's book was more nonfiction than novel, essentially the transcripts of forty-six sessions of hypnotherapy he'd had with a criminal psychopath named Harold—a "maniac" in the language of the day. Whether Warner was looking to create a thriller or sexploitation film based on Lindner's book is unclear—but Wald was unhappy enough with the current condition of the script to ask Geisel to spice things up by incorporating a character named Amy, who, Wald argued, was the most fascinating in the book.

Geisel, who had been reading up on hypnotherapy and had read Lindner's book front to back, was baffled by Wald's demands. Lindner had made very few references to Amy beyond a few sentences,

Geisel said, "in which Harold said, more or less, 'Then I went to the country and met a girl called Amy. Her I never screwed.'"[5] Under pressure from Wald, Geisel dutifully wrote and rewrote, under protest, until he abruptly quit the project—and Warner Bros.—in a pique of disgust. While Warner would test several young actors—including Marlon Brando—using early drafts of the script, the project was indefinitely postponed until 1954, when screenwriter/director Nicholas Ray would try again. Ray's final screenplay, by screenwriter Stewart Stern, would bear little resemblance to Geisel's script—or to Lindner's original book, for that matter. The completed film would also make a movie star out of James Dean.

Shutting the door on Wald and Warner also meant shutting off the $500 in relatively easy money that flowed into the Geisel bank account each week. But Geisel had no regrets. While he'd never been one to adhere to the edict of "follow your bliss," he certainly wasn't inclined to remain in a job that made him creatively and artistically miserable, either. Despite their still-meager returns, Geisel continued to have high hopes for the brat books. "We can live on one hundred dollars a week," he explained to Chuck Jones. "If I could get five thousand dollars a year in royalties, I'd be set up for life!" Jones was unimpressed. "Don't forget that good screenwriters are earning five times that much," he reminded his friend. But Geisel was already moving on. "If I'd wanted to live that way, I'd never have left Warner," he told Jones.[6]

In the meantime, without a brat book in the works or Hollywood calling, Dr. Seuss was still in demand as an adman—and there were still plenty of campaigns to take on for Flit and Essomarine, including another boating brochure called *The Log of the Good Ship*, which Geisel populated with haughty fish and jaunty lobsters.[7] And as it turned out, the Geisels weren't long for their Wonder View address.

Early in the summer of 1946, Ted took a call from Kelvin Vanderlip, the son of Frank Vanderlip, the wealthy banker who had regularly invited the Geisels to dinner parties in his New York home. Frank Vanderlip had died in 1937 but had left behind as part of his enormous estate a beautiful family retreat—which they called Villa Narcissa—built to resemble an old Italian castle in the hills of Palos Verdes, hugging the Pacific coastline. Kelvin wondered if perhaps Ted and Helen wanted to spend the summer at the estate, with its Mediterranean gardens and view of the Pacific Ocean, instead of in landlocked Hollywood, where the only water in sight was a reservoir to the south.

Ted and Helen left almost immediately, making the thirty-five-mile drive south down the Pacific coast and up into the hills of Palos Verdes. From the terraces of Villa Narcissa, Ted could look southwest across an endless vista of colorful hills of palm trees and bougainvillea, out onto the Pacific Ocean, with Catalina Island visible against the far horizon. He told Helen he wanted to live there forever, in weather where he could "walk around outside in my pajamas."[8] Inspired by the landscape, Ted unwound by taking up watercolors, leaning his damp paintings up against the Villa Narcissa's antique chairs to dry. He'd also started kicking around ideas for another children's book, this one about a magical fishing spot, hoping he could somehow bring the lush pastels of his watercolor paintings to the pages of a new hardcover. Random House publisher Bennett Cerf, happy to hear Dr. Seuss was back at work again after nearly seven years, promised Ted he'd see what he could do.

Despite the kerfuffle with Wald at Warner Bros., Ted remained optimistic that a career in film might still provide him with the financial security that the brat books weren't—so when RKO president Peter Rathvon reached out to Geisel in late 1946, he was open to further conversation. And Rathvon, it seems, knew just what to say. For one thing, he clearly understood Ted's annoyance at having his own work poached and repackaged as someone else's film, as Warner had done with *Your Job in Germany*. Rathvon, who had seen a cut of Ted's *Our Job in Japan* before the film was shelved by General MacArthur, was now proposing to turn that film into a full-length documentary—but unlike the suits at Warner Bros., Rathvon wanted Geisel to adapt his own screenplay himself. That would ensure that Geisel received the writing credit he deserved on the final documentary.

This was a savvy play by a savvy executive—little surprise it worked. Geisel agreed to adapt his own script, and—to the extent permitted—oversee the film's production. His only real condition was that Helen be permitted to join him as a credited cowriter, assisting with the research and—as she always did with his children's books—helping him maintain a cohesive narrative. Rathvon willingly consented. This would be one of the last times Ted would get his way on the project.

The Geisels spent most of the early part of 1947 taking apart Ted's script for *Our Job in Japan* and reassembling it into a screenplay they were now calling *Design for Death*. Unlike the knuckle-bruising Ted had given the German people in *Your Job in Germany*, the Geisels' portrayal of the Japanese was mostly sympathetic, depicting them as victims of generations of corrupt government leaders who had perversely wielded the Shinto religion to wage war. Relying on Helen for the background on Japanese history had been a particular boon for Ted, exposing just how badly researched the original *Our Job in Japan* had been. "I had to rely on the State Department for my research [for *Our Job in Japan*]," said Ted, who blamed the poor intelligence "on old men of ninety who had never been to Japan and who thought Shinto was a kind of hockey stick."[9]

Unfortunately, Ted and Helen provided the only steady hands on the wheel of *Design for Death*. Production became a revolving door: Rathvon was dismissed and replaced by producer Sid Rogell, who used the *Design for Death* payroll to employ friends and cronies, including Theron Warth and Richard Fleischer, who would be credited as executive producers for doing little more than moving around paperwork. Rogell wasn't much better creatively, demanding one rewrite after another—by Ted's count, the script was revised thirty-two times. As Ted wrote and rewrote, film editor Elmo Williams patiently assembled and reassembled a rough cut of the film. "Ted and I continued to do the important work," said Williams, who compared his and Ted's creative partnership to that of a writer and an illustrator.[10]

It was a collaboration doomed from the start, due largely to Rogell's dictatorial ways. For one of the film's final shots, Williams suggested to Geisel that they suspend a camera just off the ground and slowly drive through a military cemetery. Both men thought the final shot was artfully done and a profoundly moving summation of the film. "The effect was that you were looking at all of civilization buried in a mass grave," said Williams proudly. "Ted and I felt our message had hit a home run." But Rogell was having none of it, yelling, "What in the hell is that?" during the film's first screening. The scene was cut. "Ted and I were stunned," said Williams.[11]

All in all, it was an experience Ted wanted to forget. "Confidentially, Helen and I are not too well pleased with the job," he confessed to friends at Dartmouth:

> Censorship forced us into straddling lots of issues that should have been met straight on . . . Certain hunks of history are considered too hot to handle. The industry wants to please everyone and offend no one. That's how they make money . . . But don't quote that, or I'll get fired out of Hollywood.[12]

Ted was much happier with his other major project for 1947: *McElligot's Pool*, the book he had promised to Bennett Cerf a year earlier, all about a little boy fishing in a small pool that may or may not open up into a gigantic underwater world of Seussian creatures. For his first book in seven years, Geisel had gone back to his roots in more ways than one—for *McElligot's Pool* not only recalled a fond childhood memory of fishing with his father, but its main character was Marco, the very same little boy who had turned minnows into whales in *And to Think That I Saw It on Mulberry Street*. This time, rather than expanding on a simple horse and wagon, Marco conceives that tiny McElligot's Pool might actually be deeper and larger than anyone imagined, bringing in increasingly larger and more exotic fish from faraway locales.

While the name McElligot smacks of Seussian imagination, Geisel claimed he had lifted the name from a real person: Henry William McElligot, whose name appeared on the safety inspection certificate hanging in every New York City elevator. "I read his name every day for seven years," said Ted, "and it finally came out as a title of a book."[3] For the story, Geisel had stayed with the rhyming verse he'd used in *Mulberry Street*, helping the reader maintain the rhythm through a careful use of italics to indicate stressed words or syllables—a tactic he would deploy more and more.

The art for *McElligot's Pool* is some of Ted's most whimsical and beautiful, drawn with strong black lines with a careful gray wash—and every other full-page spread is in stunning full color, reminiscent of Ted's watercolor paintings. The production department at Random House had delivered on Cerf's promise to make a spectacular-looking book, though at a cost; its $2.50 cover price was significantly higher than many kids' books published at the same time. Surprisingly, Geisel was unhappy with the overall look of it; he thought the book suffered from a "modulation of tones." After publication of *McElligot's Pool*, Geisel would abandon its unique coloring scheme for good, giving the book a look unlike any other book in the Dr. Seuss library before or since.

The reviews were kind—and reviewers were glad to have Dr. Seuss back. "In the seven years since his last book . . . a whole new audience has been born and growing for Dr. Seuss's comic genius," said *The New York Times*, "and with *McElligot's Pool* he snares them, every one."[4] *McElligot's Pool* also earned Dr. Seuss his first Caldecott Honor, awarded by the nation's librarians for exceptional books for children.

Ted warmly dedicated *McElligot's Pool* to his father, reminding T. R. Geisel of the unsuccessful fishing trip he and his son had taken four decades earlier, stopping off at Deegel's fish hatchery on their way home, where they "caught the biggest mess of trout you've ever seen—at $2 a pound."[5] It was a pleasant memory for T.R., who had recently gotten remarried and was making a new life for himself with his wife, Ruth, in the house on Fairfield.

In December 1947, less than a month after the publication of *McElligot's Pool*, RKO premiered *Design for Death* for the sole purpose of ensuring that it would be eligible for the upcoming Academy Awards. A month later, on January 22, 1948, the forty-eight-minute film opened for review. Geisel was nervous; he was unhappy with the way RKO was promoting the film, marketing it with garish posters featuring exploitative tag lines such as *Military Gangsters Dupe Nation into War!* Ted's case of nerves turned out to be well founded; the critics were savage, with the esteemed Bosley Crowther at *The New York Times* railing against *Design for Death* as "a far from sensational factual film . . . Anyone going to see it expecting to be shocked or intrigued by staggering 'revelations' had better think again . . . the weakness with which it is put forth in a mélange of faked and factual pictures and in a ponderous narration does not render it very forceful."[6] It was almost enough to make Geisel regret having his longed-for on-screen writer's credit.

And yet, despite the blistering reviews, *Design for Death* managed to nab a nomination for Best Documentary Feature of 1947, competing with *Journey into Medicine*, a docudrama about treating diphtheria, and *The World Is Rich*, a British study of global starvation. On March 20, 1948, Ted and Helen drove into Los Angeles to attend the 20th Academy Awards ceremony at Shrine Auditorium and sat nervously as nineteen-year-old presenter Shirley Temple read the list of nominees for Best Documentary. Moments later, she announced the winner was *Design for Death*.

Ted was astonished. *Design for Death* producer Sid Rogell leapt onstage to accept the Oscar—and while Ted applauded enthusiastically, film editor Elmo Williams could only seethe that he and Ted were merely "spectators in the audience."[7] But Ted was pleased; while the experience making *Design for Death* hadn't been an enjoyable one, he could now say that a film with his name on it had won an Academy Award. Indeed, he would proudly note the Oscar on his official biography for decades.

• • • •

Despite his Academy Award, Dr. Seuss was done with Hollywood.

In the summer of 1948, after living in the Hollywood area for five years, Ted and Helen packed up the house on Wonder View Drive and headed back to La Jolla. Ted was happy with the home they'd built in the hills of La Jolla—but he had to confess that after spending the summer of 1946 on the seaside terraces of Villa Narcissa, he was aching for an ocean view. He wanted a place "somewhere high up, overlooking everything,"[18] and he and Helen began looking for a new piece of property on which they could build a new home. The Geisels consulted with local architect Tom Shepard, who told them there was no place in La Jolla "overlooking everything" except for an old observation tower high on Mount Soledad, "where the kids go to park."[19]

Ted and Helen drove out to Mount Soledad and trekked up the bushy slopes to the two-story tower, essentially two rooms stacked on top of each other, connected by a flight of stairs. The structure had been erected in the 1920s by area real estate salespeople who used it to point out local landmarks to potential buyers; now it was a neglected make-out spot, covered with graffiti and overgrown with flowering weeds and strewn with trash—Ted opened a supply closet and swore that five thousand beer cans spilled out. But the views were spectacular, with the Pacific visible on three sides, the town of La Jolla stretching away to the ocean eight hundred feet below, the city of San Diego sparkling to the south, and—on a clear day—Mexico visible on the southern horizon.

The Geisels would take it, buying the tower as well as two acres surrounding it, to the surprise and slight distress of local residents, who assumed the tower was publicly owned and therefore off-limits for purchase. Plans were drawn up for a modest two-bedroom, two-bathroom home to be built surrounding the tower, with windows facing the water on all sides. With seed money from Helen's trust fund, construction on their new home began on September 17, 1948—Helen's fiftieth birthday.

The new house wasn't Ted's only major undertaking. Even with his movie career on hold following the completion of *Design for Death*, Ted now had multiple projects on his drawing table. Five days before Helen's birthday came the publication of Ted's second book in less than twelve months, the amiable *Thidwick the Big-Hearted Moose*. Like Horton the elephant before him, Thidwick is taken advantage of because of his own moral forthrightness—in this case, it's his conviction that "a host, above all, must be nice to his guests"—leading a large group of animals to take up residence in his gigantic curling antlers. In the end, as his herd abandons him and a group of hunters closes in, Thidwick literally shrugs off his horns and rejoins his herd. Meanwhile the rude but unfortunate guests find themselves shot by hunters, then stuffed, mounted, and hung over the mantel of the Harvard Club—a bit of grisly comeuppance that Geisel relates with a gleeful, almost horrifying, relish:

> His *old* horns today are
> Where *you* knew they *would* be.
> His guests are still on them,
> All stuffed, as they *should* be.[20]

The final page shows each "guest"—including a bear, a fox, a turtle, a bobcat, and several birds—mounted fully intact, all smiling pleasantly, with an *X* over each eye, the universal cartoon symbol—as every child seems to know intuitively—for *dead*. And yet, in the disarming style of Dr. Seuss, it seemed somehow to be all in good *fun*. Geisel left hand-wringing to the reviewers; he understood exactly what mattered to his young readers: "Thidwick *had* to be reunited with the herd," Geisel said. "If he hadn't been, the book would have been rejected by kids. Because they identify themselves with the moose."

His only real concern about the book's climax seemed to revolve around his decision to have Thidwick's rude guests mounted on the walls of the Harvard Club. This was *not,* as Geisel assured one interviewer, a dig at Dartmouth's Ivy League rival. Rather, it "came out of the exigencies of the problem—I had to end the damn book," explained Ted.

> And I saw the best way to end it would be to put the
>
> animals on some wall somewhere . . . I had recently had
>
> lunch at the Harvard Club, which had about eight million
>
> animals—mostly shot by Teddy Roosevelt—hanging all
>
> over the walls. So it seemed to be a logical place . . . to
>
> have them end up. No animosity to the Harvard Club
>
> at all.[21]

While reviewers tended to overlook the book's ending, Ted's art *did* draw its share of criticism. "Slightly confusing at first glance," wrote one critic, while another thought the drawings were "difficult to see at first."[22] Partly the confusion may have been due to the necessary close-ups of Thidwick's antlers, which practically fill some of the pages. Geisel had also reverted back to his more Spartan use of color, highlighting pages with a careful use of turquoise and rust tones. For readers who remembered the visual excitement of *McElligot's Pool,* it was a bit of a letdown. "There are [no drawings] in full color, which is a pity," wrote an unnamed reviewer in the *Dartmouth Alumni Magazine,* noting that "a certain sparkle and brilliance is missing."[23]

Most often, however, reviewers seemed more inclined to focus on the book's bouncing readability than its art or its dark, somewhat vengeful, ending. "The author's rollicking verse is perfectly suited to this comical tale," enthused the *New York Herald Tribune Weekly Book Review.* "For little children, it is splendid, read-aloud nonsense." Writing in *The New York Times,* Ellen Lewis Buell praised the book's rhyming verses, "which march in double-quick time" and called it "as madly absurd as anything Dr. Seuss has done."[24]

Geisel was relieved at the happy reception for Thidwick. As Ted turned forty-five years old in March of 1949, he, too, was happy and healthy—the California sun was clearly good for him—with a full head of dark hair that still tended to stand on end. Short walks and afternoon swims remained his primary source of recreation; coffee, alcohol, and cigarettes were his only real vices. Long days sitting at the drawing board were starting to take their toll on his eyes, however, and Geisel had begun seeing an ophthalmologist. He would later blame his terrible driving habits on vision problems, though any passenger in the car with him would chalk his erratic driving up to inattentiveness; Geisel loved to talk more than he loved to drive.

••••

In July 1949, Geisel was invited to teach and speak at a ten-day writer's conference at the University of Utah. The invitation had come from Professor Brewster Ghiselin, a scholar and a poet who had founded the conference in 1947 as part of a course he offered called "The Creative Process." As part of the conference, then, Geisel would be one of several writers expected to run writing workshops and give a keynote lecture for all attendees.

Citing his Teddy Roosevelt story, Geisel almost always declined speaking events—but he was intrigued by Ghiselin's offer. First of all, he'd be in good company; besides Ted, Ghiselin had invited the novelist Vladimir Nabokov, best known for his 1947 novel *Bend Sinister* (the controversial *Lolita* was still several years away); novelist Wallace Stegner, already revered for his semi-autobiographical *The Big Rock Candy Mountain*; Martha Foley, editor of the distinguished *Best Short Stories* annual; and poets William Carlos Williams and John Crowe Ransom. But more important, it was the first time he'd ever had an opportunity to really think about what made a good children's story. What did he set out to do with his *own* books? Why did some books sell better than others? What was the writer's responsibility to the reader? Geisel took the assignment seriously, rereading old children's books and stories, reflecting on his own struggles and experience as a writer and artist for children, and handwrote lengthy lecture notes and class exercises. It would turn out to be one of the most important assignments Geisel had ever taken on—a turning point in his career as a writer and artist of children's literature.

Ted and Helen drove to Salt Lake City, and on the day after the Fourth of July in 1949, Ted began his ten-day residency as an instructor and lecturer. In his first class, Ted set out to help his students decide what kind of writers they wanted to be. They could be "torchbearers," he told them, intentionally writing to deliver a moral or message, or they could be "Mrs. Mulvaneys," Ted's most derisive category, reserved for those who wrote kids' books simply for the money, without regard for the content. He hoped, however, they were in a third category of "writers who want to make a profession of writing stories that children will like." But that meant writing "stories they'll like being entertained by. Stories they'll like being educated by."[25]

As he shared his own experiences with the class over the ten days, Geisel urged his students not to be embarrassed about writing for children—to not feel they were "slumming." It was a sentiment he had struggled with in his own work since his earliest days at *Judge*, where he often worried he was "dumb[ing] it down" for the lowest common denominator. It was easy to be slightly defensive about writing for beginning readers—but that was precisely the point of Ted's weeklong workshop: writing for children was actually the *hardest* kind of writing. "One reason it's more difficult," Geisel explained, "[is] because it's easier to fool adults with tricks." Adults, he argued, could be dazzled by "linguistic acrobatics, verbal flights of fancy"—kids not so much. "A child isn't deceived by patter of words," he continued. "His mind is centered on what's going on. He'll see through your words and your style."

Instead, Geisel encouraged his young writers to concentrate on the substance of the story they were telling. "Great style is great artistry," he admitted, "but without a story, great style is *spinach*," discarded by kids in the same way unwanted food is pushed off the dinner plate. Taking a page from Capra, he encouraged his students to carefully go through their stories with a blue pencil and "underline every sentence that advances the plot. None others. If your blue line pattern is irregular, scattered, too far between, you're writing too much spinach," he said. "Get back on your story line . . . You're serving *meat*, not salad."

Pacing also mattered. Kids in 1949—not yet raised on the new invention of television—were devouring exciting, fast-paced comic books by the millions each month; writers of children's books foot-dragged their plots at their own peril. "At the start, when you're setting up your character and situations, you can go like a train starting: CHOO . . . CHOO . . . CHOO," Geisel explained. "But as you go on: *choochoochoochoochoochoo*." He encouraged them to cross out unnecessary words and ideas in their stories, "and stay on that track, going fast and faster."

He also detailed what he saw as a child's "Seven Needs"—a need for security, a need to belong, a need to love and be loved, a need to achieve, a need to know, a need for aesthetic satisfaction, and a need for change—and stressed that not every story needed to cover all seven, "but no juvenile author can ever hope to get to first base unless he can answer *one* of those needs." He urged his class to embrace in particular a child's need to love and be loved. "Too many writers are embarrassed by what they think is a sticky, sloppy emotion," Geisel lectured. "Afraid of tenderness, they take to cleverness. And children find such writing cold. They want affection—and if you don't give it to 'em in your writing, they're going to find it elsewhere." And yet he also cautioned his aspiring writers *not* to stick too closely to templates or algorithms. "[You] can't write by rule," said Geisel. "I can't give you a formula." When writing, he said, "make your own mistakes. Make 'em your own way."

For his class assignments, Geisel asked his students to write several stories over several days—about pieces of wood, or a boy and a worm—writing in verse, if they could, but thinking mainly about story construction. Once their stories were completed, he asked them to critique each other, "from the brutally frank point of view of a child." He'd also devised a series of questions for students to ask themselves while writing their stories—the most crucial of which was probably the one he had written in all capital letters and underlined three times in his notes: "AM I WRITING DOWN TO CHILDREN?"

"Am I doing a namby-pamby 'Climb up on my knee, kiddie-widdies'?" he asked his class rhetorically. "Or am I saying, 'Look here, bub—you and I are citizens in this world together; let's talk about [things] man to man." For Ted—and Dr. Seuss—the answer was always clear: children were to be talked to directly, as absolute equals, with no pandering or condescension. "[Kids] know it if you begin to condescend or write down to them," he explained later. "That's been the trouble with children's books and elementary textbooks for years . . . [and] the kids don't like it. Why should they? The old tellers of fantastic fairy tales, Grimm and Andersen, never talked down to their audiences."[26] It was a way of writing for children that Geisel seemed to realize almost intuitively—and it would set the work of Dr. Seuss apart from the vast bulk of children's books for more than a generation.

Several students asked him what to do when their stories bogged down. "If it's a matter of a word or a phrase, don't stop," said Ted. "Go right on. Fill in the missing word with *dum dum* or *blah blah* or anything at all. If you stop and start searching through the dictionary, you'll get sidetracked." If the plot was beginning to wander or get convoluted, however, Geisel's advice was to stop altogether and consider starting over. "Your trouble probably isn't in the [words in the] paragraph you're working on," he told them.

One of the writers who had likely learned the most from Geisel's classroom lectures was Geisel himself. The lessons he taught his students were the lessons *he* had learned through experience—through trial and error, through writing and rewriting, drawing and redrawing. Thinking about teaching other writers, writing out his lesson plans, had forced him to come to terms with his own creative choices, his own career path. And he had come to understand that what he did was not just hard work, but *meaningful* work. It was work that could change lives—and work that had to be taken seriously. Writing stories that entertained and educated kids, he had finally decided, was a "good profession."

••••

Away from the classroom, Ted, his host, and his fellow lecturers stayed in a sorority house on the University of Utah campus, where they spent most of their evenings around the pool, drinking and swimming. Wallace Stegner remembered Ted as "constantly gay and funny," splashing merrily after Helen in the deep end of the pool, barking like a seal, and affectionately—and very publicly—referring to her by her pet name "Big Boy." Ghiselin recalled Ted as "in fine fettle, energetic, prolific, accommodating, adaptive, always in action—though never ostentatiously."[27]

After one of Ted's first lectures, a Salt Lake City teacher named Libby Childs approached him. She shook his hand and asked if she and her husband could do anything to make his stay in the area more enjoyable. Ted told her that he had always wanted to swim in the Great Salt Lake—he loved the idea that a swimmer could float effortlessly on its surface—and Childs promised that she and her husband, Orlo, a geology professor, would take Ted and Helen to the lake over the weekend.

The Geisels and the Childs spent Sunday, July 10, swimming and floating on the Great Salt Lake, the beginning of what would be a life-long friendship between the families. Ted was astounded by the Childs's three-year-old son Brad, who could recite, word for word, *Thidwick the Big-Hearted Moose* from memory. "I don't write for kids that young," Ted said incredulously. "How does he do it?"[28]

Ted shouldn't have been surprised; the three-year-old was proving one of the points Ted had driven home during his week of lectures. "Rhythmic prose . . . is almost essential in writing for the very young because they don't have much vocabulary," he had told his class. "[They] don't know many words. So you have to convey much of your meaning by sounds and rhythms." Brad could remember and recite *Thidwick* in the same way ancient storytellers could remember and repeat the Iliad or the Odyssey: through a bouncing, rhyming rhythm, and regular repeated phrases. It was a lesson Dr. Seuss wouldn't forget.

••••

Geisel's keynote address, which he had titled "Mrs. Mulvaney and the Billion-Dollar Bunny," was one of the first in the ten-day conference, taking place on the evening of Thursday, July 7. Geisel had announced his lecture as "an illustrated speech," in which he planned to draw on a gigantic chalkboard as he spoke, highlighting his salient points with some appropriately Seussian art. The morning of his talk, Ted let himself into the lecture hall in the University of Utah's physical science building and very lightly drew in the outline of what he intended to draw in chalk on the forty-foot blackboard during his speech. According to Geisel, as he approached the science building on the evening of his lecture, he passed the janitor on his way out. "I just did a very nice thing for you, Doctor," the man happily reported. "That blackboard was filthy. I washed it good and clean." Geisel groaned. "With no guide to draw to," he said later, "I got in trouble in the first five minutes—and soon ran out of blackboard and found myself drawing in the air."

Despite the inauspicious start, Geisel was well prepared for his lecture—the purpose of which, he said, was to "explain, if humanly possible, the state of Juvenile Literature today." And in his opinion, it wasn't good. "I am of the opinion that the *bad* elements in children's books today greatly outweigh the elements that are good," he told his audience. Part of the problem, he explained was that there were too many *Mrs. Mulvaneys* writing books.

As Geisel explained it, Mrs. Mulvaney initially had only the very best of intentions, hoping to write a good book for children. But with no real talent and no real ideas, she casually knocks off a book she *thinks* kids will want to read—a book about a lollipop-carrying rabbit with a "sissy little pink and white bow necktie" called *Bunny, Bunny, Bunny, Bunny, Bunny, Bunny, Bunny*. It was a book kids hated, but which parents loved and snapped up so quickly that Mrs. Mulvaney's publisher demands more and more sequels—one featuring a "cosmic bi-directional Atomic Death Ray"—while her husband begins churning out *Bunny*-related merchandise.

Eventually, librarians—in Geisel's scenario, the arbiters of good taste and quality books for children—demand the Mulvaneys stop "putting silly books into children's hands for every good one a librarian can put there." But Mrs. Mulvaney refuses, "sitting smug and pretty, in her vast and smelly empire," said Geisel scornfully, "turning out stuff that's harmful to children. And harmful to adults, because children become adults." It was this detrimental effect of bad children's literature on literature for grown-ups that was Geisel's larger point:

> I'm bringing Mrs. Mulvaney to your attention, because I believe that she's not only threatening the quality of Juvenile Letters in this country today, but also threatening the quality of Adult Letters in the country tomorrow . . . She is dictating the literary standards that our children are going to follow when their legs grow longer.

Geisel urged parents in the audience to truly think about the reading materials they purchased for their children. "Just try to look at it from the child's point of view," he offered, and encouraged parents—and would-be writers of children's books—to learn from the reading materials kids *liked* to read, training his fire on comic books in particular. Say what one might about the garish four-color super-heroes, vampires, and gangsters, comic book writers and artists knew how to get children excited about reading.

"Writers must also learn from comic book creators that children must be treated as literary equals," said Geisel, driving home the point he'd made to his students about not writing down to children. "They cannot be written down to or preached to."[29] Comic books, Geisel continued, operated under "a very intelligent rule . . . Namely, 'No one will ever read your stuff if you're a bombastic bore.'"

Geisel ended by encouraging good writers to learn the lessons of their competition. There was "a great deal of vigor," for instance, to be found in comic books or well-intentioned but ultimately mindless adventure stories. "If you want to write good books for children, spend a little time studying the bad ones," he said. "I'm not saying ape them . . . I'm saying 'look them over.'" And then, he concluded "bring back some of that vigor. And you'll find that the children will come back with you."

Geisel was proud of the work he'd done for the Utah conference—and when he and Helen returned to La Jolla in mid-July, Ted enthusiastically sent a letter to Louise Bonino at Random House, proposing a book about writing for children, based on his classroom and lecture notes. Bonino sat on the proposal for a bit before skeptically sending it over to editor Saxe Commins for review. On August 9, Ted followed up with a short note, trying to prompt a response. "I've received invitations to give this same talk in half a dozen places from here to Chicago," he told Bonino—likely a bluff, but the radio silence from New York was fraying his nerves. Finally, after another six weeks of silence, Ted could take no more. "Could you please wire . . . today whether you have any interest in lecture notes sent in July?" Ted asked in a telegram. "Am being crowded for decision on this property but will stall if you want this and other children's workshop material developed further."[30]

Bonino, who probably knew she had left Geisel to stew for too long—and who also likely knew Geisel was still bluffing about the demand for his material—wrote back immediately with a kind but firm no. The proposed project had been vetted by Bennett Cerf himself, she assured Geisel, and Cerf had shared her and Saxe Commins's reticence about Dr. Seuss taking on what they viewed as essentially a how-to book. Curiously, they laid some of the blame at the feet of local librarians who might not stock such a book, speculating that they "would feel an author-artist of picture books could hardly qualify as an expert in the entire field of juvenile writing"—a shortsighted and slightly condescending dismissal.

Commins, to his credit, seemed concerned more about scope creep, as well as protecting what he saw as the Dr. Seuss brand—which, in 1949, was based on only seven books. Such an academic project, Commins argued, "would interrupt you in the steady production of your marvelous children's books [and bring] down on your head all kinds of criticism for doing a semi-formal book." He also worried that what Geisel was proposing was akin to a magician explaining how he performed a trick. He was better off, said Commins, by not "explain[ing] method, when there is so much inspired madness in your work."[31]

Geisel was understandably upset. As far as he was concerned, he *was* an expert in the field of juvenile writing, the opinions of the librarians be damned—and to have his own publisher back that outlook hurt him terribly. Geisel responded to Bonino with a tight-lipped letter, pitching a new project instead. "About the next book . . . (if you want a next book)," wrote Geisel darkly, "Would a story about the King's Magicians [from *Bartholomew Cubbins*] be a good thing to do?"[32] Bonino, trying to remain upbeat, encouraged Geisel to write a story using Horton instead. Geisel, dejected, would quite literally go back to the drawing board and start over.

That fall, Ted and Helen moved into their newly completed home in La Jolla, high on a flowery hillside of Mount Soledad. Built in a Spanish style, the red-roofed, pink stucco house—two bedrooms, two bathrooms—wrapped itself around the restored observation tower, where Ted's glass-enclosed office now occupied the tower's top floor, with ocean views on three sides. Helen had stationery printed with their new address—7301 Encelia Drive—but mail would often arrive when addressed only to the affectionate nickname Helen had also bestowed on their new home: the Tower.

It took the locals some time to adjust to the Geisels' presence on the hill. Some evenings, young couples would stride purposefully up Mount Soledad by moonlight, ready for a romantic rendezvous at the old observation tower, only to beat a hasty retreat back to La Jolla, red-faced, when greeted merrily by Geisel at the top of the hill. Geisel also quickly discovered that there was an oceanographer at the Scripps Institution of Oceanography named Hans Suess, PhD—which meant that any mail addressed to "Dr. Seuss" could end up either at the institute or in the mailbox at the Tower. Dr. Seuss and Dr. Suess would meet regularly for years to trade mail.

If there was any disappointment, it was with the studio he'd had prepared in the top room of the Tower. The view was spectacular, but there was no running water in the old part of the building, and the room had a tendency to get chilly in the evenings. So the upstairs studio was converted into a guest room, and Ted relocated to one of the downstairs rooms, with a similarly panoramic view, but with a working fireplace and running water. Here Ted set up his old ink-streaked desk, with the sloping drafting table in the middle, packed with cans and jars jammed with brushes, pencils, pens, and erasers. And always, at Ted's right elbow, was the ever-present ashtray. Everything was good. "I think that La Jolla, at last, will become my basic roosting place,"[33] Ted wrote.

• • • •

Geisel finished out 1949 with another book—he had managed a book per year since 1947—with the publication of a sequel of sorts to *The 500 Hats of Bartholomew Cubbins* called *Bartholomew and the Oobleck*. "I shall never cease to wonder at these figments of your inexhaustible brain," Saxe Commins had written to Geisel admiringly.[34] In this particular case, Geisel had been inspired by a real-life conversation he overheard between two Allied soldiers caught in a rainstorm during the Battle of the Bulge. "Rain, always rain!" complained one soldier. "Why can't we have something different for a change?"[35] Geisel had decided that King Derwin would make a similar wish and inadvertently inflict the gooey, sticky oobleck on the hapless citizens of the Kingdom of Didd.

For Geisel, the most difficult part of the story wasn't the plot or its resolution—the oobleck recedes when the king apologizes for his errant wish—but deciding on the color of the oobleck itself. For months, Geisel had page after page of his book pinned to corkboard on the walls of his office—a habit he had picked up from Capra's storyboarding sessions—and would stare at them, deep in thought, scratching out a word here and there, and puzzling over just what color oobleck was anyway. "[The] problem was to find something unusual . . . but something that wouldn't be weird or unpleasant," he told Louise Bonino. "Pinks are out. They suggest flesh too much. Purples seem morbid."[36] Fortunately, in the same letter, Geisel enclosed a sample of a color he was happy with. "I sort of like this green," he said, and directed the coloring department to match it precisely, and then be sure to print the green on the pages *first*, before reproducing the black line art on top of it.

Bartholomew and the Oobleck was well reviewed and would be Dr. Seuss's second Caldecott Honor book in three years. "Young Dr. Seuss fans will demand many re-readings of this lively, original tale," wrote *The Boston Globe*, "and older Dr. Seuss fans won't mind obliging."[37] "A delight for the youngsters,"[38] declared another reviewer, while the *Chicago Tribune* enthused, "You'll love it."[39]

Ted dedicated *Bartholomew and the Oobleck* to Kelvin Vanderlip, the son of Kelvin and Elin Vanderlip, his hosts at the Villa Narcissa in the summer of 1946. At the end of 1949, as part of his Dartmouth Alumni biographical listing, Ted proudly wrote that "I publish children's books and magazine stories for the offspring of my more fecund class-mates."[40]

What a difference three years had made. In 1946, Geisel had very nearly abandoned children's books in favor of a new career writing and producing films. Now, after teaching the 1949 Utah writer's workshop, he was proud to be Dr. Seuss again, writing and drawing books for children and young readers. More than ever, he was convinced that writing for children was meaningful work that deserved to be taken seriously. "If you really know it," said Geisel, "you can do a lot of good."[41]

It was, indeed, a good profession.

CHAPTER 9

A PERSON'S A PERSON

1950–1954

There were no nerds until Dr. Seuss.

That's not to say there weren't always individuals on the fringes—the awkward, the outcasts, or the single-minded experts in a particular field—but until Dr. Seuss came along, they weren't called *nerds*. Because until Dr. Seuss came along, the word didn't exist *at all*.

In early 1950, Geisel was at work on the first book he would write and complete in the Tower, a rollicking, rhyming romp called *If I Ran the Zoo*. In a story with a structure similar to *Mulberry Street* or *McElligot's Pool*—in which the narrator is inspired by a normally benign setting into dreaming up increasingly bizarre creatures and situations—young Gerald McGrew imagines the changes he'd make if given the opportunity to take over the local zoo. Gerald quickly moves through eight-legged lions and elephant-cats and on to more fantastic animals from remote corners of the globe, like the fluffy Bustard bird, the rhubarb-loving Obsk, and the long-legged insect Thwerll. Eventually he travels to far-off Ka-Troo, from which Gerald brings back

> . . . an It-Kutch . . . a Preep . . . and a Proo
> A Nerkle . . . a Nerd . . . and a Seersucker, too!¹

This was the first time the word *nerd* ever appeared in print. In Geisel's 1950 story, a *nerd* was simply a grouchy-looking creature—essentially the Grinch with muttonchops and (weirdly) wearing a black T-shirt. Within a year, *Newsweek* would be writing about the evolution of regional slang in the United States, noting that *nerd* was slowly taking over for *drip* or *square*.[2] Within a decade, it would be on its way toward entering the vernacular, eventually evolving from a derogatory term to one proudly embraced by—well, *nerds* everywhere.

If I Ran the Zoo was a tour de force of Seussian creatures and Seussian names. Geisel was often asked if it was difficult coming up with names like Joats, Lunks, Chuggs, or the Tufted Mazurka. "I have to say rather disappointingly that it's not hard at all," he explained.[3] "Making up words is the simplest thing in the world. For instance, you draw something and look at it and it's an obsk. There's no doubt about it. It can't be anything else."[4] As for those Seussian animals, the art is some of the most playful of the Dr. Seuss oeuvre, sprawling across the pages in alternating highlights of red and yellow, then red and blue. In the months leading up to the release of *If I Ran the Zoo*, Geisel was repeatedly asked, "Why do you draw animals the way you do?" Geisel's casual explanation would become one of his go-to answers when asked to explain the unexplainable. "Well, I'll tell you," he'd say—then take a slow drag on a cigarette for a dramatic pause and exhale before continuing. "That's the way animals look to me and I just draw them."[5]

That's not to say Geisel still doesn't have some problematic pages. As Gerald dreams of hunting for a Flustard in the land of Zomba-ma-Tant, he describes natives with "eyes at a slant." While the natives resemble bald Chinese men wearing wide sleeves and sandals, it *could* be argued that Geisel is merely drawing residents of the fictional Zomba-ma-Tant—especially as their facial features mirror the giant catlike Flustard they're carrying in a cage on their heads. But Geisel has a similar problem with his pygmies from the island of Yerka—though here, too, he's careful to give them features similar to the Tufted Mazurka they're transporting, with matching tufted hairstyles, circular designs on their stomachs, and skirts that somewhat resemble the plumage of the bird. Still, Geisel couldn't quite shake relying on easy caricatures of exotic people, whether he intended them to be fictional or not.

While it certainly seems as if a book all about a zoo may have been inspired by the days he spent with his father at the Springfield Zoo, Geisel said the idea had been spawned by a conversation he once had with his mother. The book, though, would end up being dedicated not to Nettie Geisel, but to his own godchildren, Toni and Michael Gordon Tackaberry Thompson, the children of New York friends Peggy Conklin and James "Bim" Thompson. Geisel particularly loved the way Michael's name rolled out in what he called a "crazy iambic pentameter." Perhaps inspired by the bounce of Thompson's lively name, *If I Ran the Zoo* contains some of the spryest rhyming verse in any Dr. Seuss book. For instance, as Geisel describes a hunt in the mountains of Zomba-ma-Tant, he tells of trying to catch

> . . . the fine fluffy bird called the Bustard
> Who only eats custard with sauce made of mustard.
> And, also, a very fine beast called the Flustard
> Who only eats mustard with sauce made of custard.[6]

Geisel's verse seems to have similarly inspired reviewers, who took great delight in writing their own assessments of the book in rhyme. "Such a mad lot of animals never could be. You won't want to miss them. Believe me—you'll see!"[7] wrote a reviewer in the *Chicago Tribune*, while in the *Akron Beacon Journal* a similarly well-intentioned critic came up with, "It's flat, funny and bright and the ideas are quite right. Isn't this what you'd do, if you ran a zoo?"[8] Riding rave reviews into Christmas 1950, *If I Ran the Zoo* quickly blew out of its first printing—one of the fastest-selling Dr. Seuss books since *Horton Hatches the Egg*.

The same year would also see Geisel publish several shorter stories in *Redbook*, including a trial run of *If I Ran the Zoo*, several return visits to characters from Mulberry Street with "Marco Comes Late" and "How Officer Pat Saved the Whole Town," and the one-upmanship story "The Big Brag," which would eventually make its way into the 1958 hardcover *Yertle the Turtle and Other Stories*. With these stories, Geisel was practicing some of what he had preached in his Utah workshop, writing stories that were short and punchy, with the rapid pacing of the loathed comic books. "Remember, you're competing with the comic books," Geisel had told his class. "They're terrible, but they're written for twentieth-century kids . . . get out of your rocking chairs. Get into your story *fast* or the children will yawn in your face."[9] Geisel was honing his own storytelling skills, sometimes telling a complete story in just a few verses or with just one or two illustrations.

Other times Geisel didn't illustrate his short stories at all. One story in particular featured a little boy named Gerald McCloy[10] who spoke only in sounds. Geisel shrewdly realized that telling the story effectively meant telling it not on paper, but through the use of sound effects. The story, called *Gerald McBoing-Boing*, would be successfully adapted as an audio story by Capitol Records, narrated by actor Harold Peary—in his over-the-top Great Gildersleeve persona—with Gerald speaking only in sound effects, including a very audible *BOING!* The only artwork Geisel would create for the story appeared on the record's jacket, which featured a little boy in short pants loudly shrieking "*Boing! Boing!*" and startling his dog. It was a charming and innocuous project—and one that would take Geisel on an unexpected career detour, resulting in one undertaking that would win him an Academy Award and another that would sap his creative energy and derail his book-writing progress for nearly three years.

• • • •

In early 1950, Geisel met with an old friend, the artist Phil Eastman, who had served with him in the Signal Corps, where he had assisted on *Private Snafu*. After the war, Eastman had ended up at the nascent

United Productions of America (UPA) animation studio, which was basking in two Academy Award nominations for its Fox and Crow cartoons and had more recently struck gold with the myopic character Mr. Magoo. Geisel was unimpressed with UPA; toward the end of the war, the studio had produced several of the *Private Snafu* cartoons, with less-than-spectacular results. But Eastman promised him that things were different now, boasting that UPA had upped its game and that Warner Bros. or Disney just couldn't compete. "All the cartoons being made [by Warner and others] are obsolete. UPA has a fresh outlook," he told Geisel, and appealed to his friend for some new content. "You must have a story idea for us,"[11] said Eastman. For $500, Geisel sold Eastman and UPA the animation rights to *Gerald McBoing-Boing*.

Geisel handed *Gerald* over outright; perhaps because of his friendship with and trust in Eastman, Geisel never tried to micromanage the project. Even as the animators designed a new look for the character and modified some of the rhyming verses, Geisel was content to merely peer over their shoulders from time to time. In the hands of the UPA crew, the characters in *Gerald McBoing-Boing* would look nothing like Dr. Seuss drawings; the cartoon would instead be animated in the minimalist style that UPA would famously make its norm: little shading or depth of field, minimal backgrounds, and spare with its use of color. Geisel would receive a story credit, along with Eastman and UPA writer Bill Scott. "Don't make fun of [Gerald]," Geisel advised the writers on the pages of the script. "He's a success."[12]

And so, too, was *Gerald McBoing-Boing*. Columbia Pictures, the cartoon's distributor, would premiere the film on November 2, 1950, to make it eligible for the 1950 Academy Awards before officially releasing the cartoon on January 25, 1951. Eastman's assessment of UPA's abilities turned out to be correct; critics were nearly unanimous in their enthusiasm for the cartoon's unique look and sense of humor. "*Gerald* brings beautiful simplicity of background, color, character drawing and movement to the screen," wrote the *Tampa Bay Times*, adding that "[*Gerald McBoing-Boing* had] exploded years of mediocre cartooning."[13] In the *Akron Beacon Journal*, critic Sydney Harris hailed it as "witty and mature—and yet absurdly naïve enough to appeal to children."[14] In March 1951, *Gerald McBoing-Boing* won the Academy Award for Best Animated Short—the third Oscar-winning film based on one of Geisel's scripts in five years.

••••

Helen Geisel wasn't well. Since her bout with polio as a child, Helen had watched her health warily—and now, at age fifty-two, she was always on the lookout for seemingly benign symptoms that could indicate more serious health issues. In early 1951, she was feeling mildly ill; she would get easily tired and was complaining of painful ulcers. Hoping to rest and recover her health, she and Ted retreated to the Tower for the rest of the winter—and with no book on the drawing table in Ted's office at the moment, she and Ted could spend some time enjoying the sunshine and each other's company.

There was other pleasant company at the Tower that spring as well; their niece Peggy had driven across the country in a green Oldsmobile, which was now parked in the Tower's driveway as Peggy looked for work in La Jolla.[15] For a few weeks, Peggy took up residence in the top floor of the Tower, playing canasta late into the evenings with Ted and Helen, casually shopping with them in Tijuana, and spending the days walking with Ted among the flowering bushes on the Mount Soledad hillside. "He was forever pausing beside some little blossom to identify it for me," recalled Peggy, who noted with amusement that Ted identified every colorful bloom as a "California Wildflower."[16]

The Geisels loved having Peggy around. Years earlier, Ted had fondly dubbed her "Peggy the Hoofer" because he was constantly making her run errands; he had even sketched a portrait of her diligently on task with the caption "I run errands for 50 cents." Now at age twenty-three, the young woman referred to Ted and Helen by their first names, though she would playfully call Ted "Uncle Worm" for his aggressive card playing. Peggy would land a job at the Navy Electronics Laboratory in San Diego that spring, where she would shortly meet Navy lieutenant Albert Owens, an electrical engineer. Only a little more than a year later, she and Albert would marry in the Tower as the Geisels stood by proudly, with a well-tanned Ted beaming in a dapper gray suit and striped tie.

Even between hillside walks with Peggy and late night games of canasta, Ted still found time to publish short stories in *Redbook* and other magazines, bringing back one of his most popular heroes for "Horton and the Kwuggerbug," in which the well-intentioned elephant is taken advantage of yet again by another creature who strictly holds him to the credo "a deal's a deal." There was also "The Rabbit, the Bear and Zinniga-Zanniga," all about a rabbit who outsmarts a bear by telling him his head is crooked, and "The Bippolo Seed," a story of wishes gone awry. But there was no major brat book in the works and wouldn't be for some time; Hollywood had turned Geisel's head yet again.

While working with Sid Rogell and RKO on *Design for Death* in 1947 had been a misery, Geisel remained hopeful that his experience there had been the exception, not the rule. So when Columbia Studios, still flush from the success of *Gerald McBoing-Boing*, offered Geisel $35,000—more than $300,000 in today's money—to develop a proposal for a feature-length live-action film, Geisel viewed it as an easy opportunity to revive his aborted career as a screenwriter. He had good reason to be optimistic; whether as the uncredited author of the source material (*Hitler Lives!*), the credited screenwriter (*Design for Death*), or the credited author of the original story (*Gerald McBoing-Boing*), Geisel's last three films had each won an Academy Award—a hot streak in Hollywood few if any screenwriters could match.

Geisel set to work outlining a story about a young boy named Bart Collins—yet another Bartholomew—and his widowed mother, a heroic plumber, and a sinister piano teacher named Dr. Terwilliker. The bulk of the story involved a musical dream sequence full of chases, escapes, and lots of sneaking around, culminating in the conniving Dr. Terwilliker demanding that five hundred of his young pupils, including Bart, play his symphony on a gigantic two-story piano. Geisel titled his movie *The 5,000 Fingers of Dr. T.*, and pitched it to studio executives as a "vicious satire," though what it was satirizing wasn't quite clear. Nevertheless, Columbia was thrilled to have the first full-length live-action feature written by Dr. Seuss, filled with Seussian contraptions and elaborate sets that Geisel was confident studio designers and carpenters could bring vibrantly to life.

On April 27, 1951, Geisel was paired with an up-and-coming thirty-seven-year-old producer named Stanley Kramer, who had so wowed Columbia with the film *Cyrano de Bergerac* that the studio permitted him to open his own production unit within the company. As part of his new contract with Columbia, then, Kramer was committed to producing twenty films over five years, each with a budget of at least $1 million. *The 5,000 Fingers of Dr. T.* would be among his first for the studio.[17]

It seemed an ideal pairing. Like Geisel, Kramer had served in the Signal Corps during the war, eventually attaining a rank of lieutenant; politically, both were progressives, and creatively, each bristled at the idea of ceding control of their work to others. Kramer, too, was a fan of Dr. Seuss, calling *Dr. T.* "one of my favorite properties" and one that he "very much wanted to direct."[18] But Kramer was already at war with Harry Cohn, Columbia's swaggering studio chief, whom Kramer called "vulgar, domineering, semiliterate . . . and some might say malevolent"[19]—and Cohn "wasn't ready"[20] to let Kramer cross over from producing to directing. A frustrated Kramer would shortly leave the studio and slide into the director's chair at his own independent company, eventually helming a number of iconic films, including *Judgment at Nuremberg* and *Guess Who's Coming to Dinner.*

As always, Geisel took his obligations seriously, even renting a house on North Kingsley Drive in Hollywood so he could be readily available for any meetings with Kramer and cowriter Allan Scott as the script progressed. Weekends would still be spent at the Tower—but even here, Geisel was hunched over his desk, handwriting notes, then banging away on the typewriter. Writing a script every two weeks for Capra had taught Geisel how to write a script relatively quickly—but his first draft still came in at a staggering 1,200 pages, as Geisel tried to metaphorically address gigantic issues like world conquest and oppression.[21] By August, he was deep into rewrites, bouncing around ideas with Scott and paring down parts of the script that were too pricey or too difficult to film. Helen watched in mild disappointment as the year dragged on with no vacations, no book on the drawing board, and no real free time together. "This picture is really such a long-time dream of Ted's that whatever we have to give up to do it is really of no importance," she wrote in a lengthy letter to her niece Barbara Bayler.[22]

One of the things Geisel was really giving up was his creative independence. While he had a modicum of control over the script, the majority of the production was completely out of his hands. If Geisel was hoping to have the kind of friendly collaboration with Kramer and Scott on *Dr. T.* that he'd had with Capra and Phil Eastman on *Private Snafu*, he was doomed to disappointment. Decisions were kicked upstairs to be made by committees of faceless executives at Columbia who passed the scripts back with stained pages and cryptic notes. With Kramer forced to cede the director's chair, the task was assigned to Roy Rowland, a competent if uninspired choice—his forte was dramas like *Witness to Murder* and *Scene of the Crime*, not musical fantasies like *Dr. T.* The project became mired in studio stinginess, with budget projections being recalibrated, slashed, reconfigured, then slashed again. Any joy in the project soon evaporated.

Writing slowed to a crawl. By late September, Geisel was still working on the revised second draft, penciling on the red cover of his script the names of twenty songs he was writing. One of the very few pleasures left in the film was that he was being permitted to write the lyrics for the movie's various musical numbers, and Geisel sent his scripts back to Kramer, indicating where in the movie he thought the songs should be inserted. At one point, he spent days fussing over a lyric using the word *Chopin*, trying out the names of several other composers to see if any fit the meter better. "[The songs] are really so lovely that I feel quite optimistic about the whole thing being a success," Helen wrote hopefully. "Maybe we'll make a lot of money. In that case we'll go to Ireland, Japan, South Africa, and Siam."[23] But by November, even Helen was worried that Hollywood had seriously sidetracked Dr. Seuss. While Geisel *had* started a new book called *Scrambled Eggs Super!*, his priorities were elsewhere. "Alas, alas, we have no book this year," Helen told Barbara, "and if this film doesn't hurry up, we're likely not to have one next year, either."[24]

Unfortunately, the film wasn't about to hurry up. Besides writing the script, Geisel had spent the last several months sketching designs for sets, costumes, and characters, hoping to maintain some vestige of control over the look of the film. There were street signs made of gloved hands, ladders climbing up to nowhere, and a terrific drawing of Dr. Terwilliker in his costume for the final concert, with epaulets at his shoulders, a military jacket with medallions, and a "white beaver busby" hat. But budget cuts had slowed the progress of the studio architects, carpenters, and seamstresses charged with making Geisel's designs tangible—and Ted, feeling he was expending too much energy justifying his value to the project, finally decided he'd had enough. Just after New Year's Day 1952, he notified Kramer he was quitting.

Kramer pled with Geisel to stay, telling him the only way the film could be saved was if he remained attached to it. Kramer promised to take Geisel's concerns seriously—the budget would be increased to more than $2 million, making it one of Kramer's most expensive films at Columbia—and Geisel was permitted to submit a final version of the script by the end of January, removing any scenes he considered "vulgar."[25] The final script, credited to Dr. Seuss and Allan Scott, landed on Kramer's desk on January 30. Geisel would never really be happy with it, feeling he had conceded far too much to the whims of Kramer and executives at Columbia.

Rehearsals began in early February, even as sets were still being built across several enormous sound stages, with carpenters working in shifts that kept hammers flying around the clock. Real-life married couple Peter Lind Hayes and Mary Healy ("broken-down, middle-aged nightclub comics," groaned Geisel)[26] arrived to rehearse their dance routines, as did Hans Conried, an accomplished radio actor with a malleable face and distinctive voice who had been tapped to play the dastardly Dr. Terwilliker. "We rehearsed for eight weeks," remembered Conried, "an extravagance that I as a bit player had never known."[27]

Still, production continued to lag as sets remained uncompleted, and Geisel and Allan Scott continued tinkering with the script, arriving on set with their revised final draft on February 25, 1952. Shooting would begin shortly after that, on beautifully finished sets that really did look as if Dr. Seuss drawings had magically popped into the real world. Furniture and windows bulged with Seussian curves and irregular geometry. A gigantic two-story piano wound through Dr. T.'s concert hall, and there were slanted doorways, curving slides, and bending ladders for nine-year-old Tommy Rettig, playing hero Bart Collins, to clamber over and through. Production designer Rudolph Sternad had delivered.

Geisel was on set for most of the filming, standing patiently behind director Roy Rowland, with a well-thumbed script in his hand. Tommy Rettig recalled seeing Geisel lounging in a chair during the long downtime between takes, doodling on the pages of his script. "Mostly he would sit there sketching the next set, or the next scene, showing things to the director and cameraman about how he pictured it," said Rettig. "It was so much fun . . . I mean, just to be able to run up to Dr. Seuss's chair and watch him draw in his script. It was really an outstanding experience."[28]

It was not, however, an outstanding experience for Dr. Seuss. Despite the increased budget, Kramer had still cut some serious corners; for one thing, there weren't the resources to hire five hundred boys—the 5,000 fingers of the title—needed to play the gigantic piano for the finale. "There wasn't enough money to do what should really have been a musical extravaganza,"[29] recalled Kramer, who could only afford to pay for a little more than a hundred boys. Kramer also made the colossal mistake of paying the boys in cash—and one afternoon, as a gigantic thunderstorm raged outside, the bored boys, with their pockets full of money, all filed down to the studio commissary to buy armloads of hot dogs and junk food, then gorged themselves and immediately became sick. "This started a chain reaction causing one after another of the boys to go queasy in the greatest mass upchuck in the history of Hollywood," said Geisel.[30] Even director Roy Rowland, his nerves fraying, had to be taken to the hospital "at the end of his rope," recalled Geisel. "It was the damnedest, nerve-rackingest, screamingest experience of my life."[31]

Geisel was convinced he had a disaster on his hand—he was "discouraged," he said diplomatically, by Kramer's handling of the movie.[32] When filming completed in April 1952, Ted and Helen immediately abandoned their Hollywood apartment and retreated to La Jolla, where Ted dove into work on *Scrambled Eggs Super!*, now woefully behind schedule. "Ted simply has to get his book done and get it to New York," Helen wrote her niece. "It was due in January and if we don't get it there early in June, it will be too late for the Christmas trade."[33]

On Sunday, May 11, Ted drove north to Los Angeles to watch a first cut of *The 5,000 Fingers of Dr. T.* at Stanley Kramer's house. He spent most of the viewing with his head in his hands; the film, Ted thought, was too cynical, with no spontaneity or real dreamlike sense of fantasy. Even the normally upbeat Kramer was depressed. Geisel abandoned La Jolla and *Scrambled Eggs Super!* and returned to Hollywood to spend the next two weeks huddling with Kramer, writer Allan Scott, film editors Al Clark and Harry W. Gerstad, and other studio executives to see if the film could be recut. "Perhaps [Roy] Rowland was not the right director," Kramer offered glumly. "The picture required a tougher man."[34]

Geisel drove back to La Jolla in a dark mood. Arriving at the Tower in the early evening, Geisel stayed up all night, staring out the window into the darkness, fretting over *Dr. T.* and decisions that couldn't be unmade. Partly, too, he was likely worried he'd be blamed for the film's failure—and what that failure might mean for the career he was still hoping to have as a screenwriter. Helen found him still pacing his office in the morning, then handed him a sleeping pill and ordered him to bed. As Ted collapsed with exhaustion in La Jolla, Helen phoned Louise Bonino in New York and told her not to expect *Scrambled Eggs Super!* anytime soon. Several days later, Ted and Helen left for an extended vacation, with *Scrambled Eggs Super!* still untouched on Ted's drawing table. Ted would deliver the book later in the summer, but not in time for the Christmas rush. There would be no new Dr. Seuss book in 1952.

Dr. Seuss would still make an appearance before the end of the year, however, in a remarkable piece written for *The New York Times*. Titled ". . . But for Grown-Ups Laughing Isn't Any Fun," it was the first time Dr. Seuss had ever spoken directly to his readers to explain not only *what* he did but, more important, *why* he did it. Touching on one of the themes he'd explored in his Utah lectures, Geisel first addressed the perceived stigma of writing for children. "Wherever a juvenile writer goes, he is constantly subjected to indignities," Geisel wrote. If he isn't being introduced at a party as the author of "the sweetest, dear, darlingest little whimsies for wee kiddies," his peers are seating him in "the very end seat at the table" at professional gatherings.[35] And yet Geisel informed his readers he was "writing for the so-called Brat Field by choice"[36] and for a very good reason:

> . . . there is something we get when we write for the young that we never can hope to get in writing for you ancients . . . Have you ever stopped to consider what has happened to your sense of humor?[37]

Adults, Geisel argued, had not only lost their sense of humor, but their sense of wonder and their giddy love of nonsense. Children, he maintained, "never let their laughs out on a string,"[38] worrying about what their employers or neighbors or critics might think is funny.

But for grown-ups, laughter had become "conditioned"—and here Geisel for the first time explicitly addressed the issue of laughter at the expense of others:

> This conditioned laughter the grown-ups taught you
>
> depended entirely on *their* conditions. Financial
>
> conditions. Political conditions. Racial, religious and social
>
> conditions. You began to laugh at people your family
>
> feared or despised—people they felt inferior to, or people
>
> they felt better than . . .
>
> In the same way, you were supposed to guffaw when
>
> someone told a story which proved that Swedes are
>
> stupid, Scots are tight, Englishmen are stuffy, and the
>
> Mexicans never wash . . .
>
> Then you learned it was socially advantageous to laugh
>
> at Protestants and/or Catholics.[39]

"Your capacity for healthy, silly, friendly laughter was smothered," Geisel said, admonishing adults everywhere. "You'd really grown up. You'd become adults . . . adults, which is a word that means obsolete children."

Dr. Seuss had drawn a line in the sand, defending not just those who wrote for children, but the children themselves. Geisel had argued in his Mrs. Mulvaney lecture that quality children's books were vital to creating smart young readers who would grow up to become smart adult readers. But here he didn't seem to be arguing that catering to the condition-free laughter of children would translate into condition-free laughter from adults—though if that happened, said Geisel, one should consider oneself lucky.

For the first time, too, Geisel was reproaching adults for their tendency toward laughter at the expense of others—something he'd certainly been guilty of as well. Children, he argued, didn't laugh at race or religion or ethnicity. Children's laughter had no agenda. And so, Geisel was taking a side; if given a choice, he would take the pure, unconditional laughter of children over the stilted, conditional laughter of grown-ups.

In the end, Dr. Seuss wasn't out to save adults; he was here on behalf of children, to help them have the best childhoods they possibly could, celebrating the age when "the one thing you did better than anything else was laugh." Once children grew up, however, that laughter—whether conditioned or not—was someone else's responsibility. "Adults are obsolete children," Geisel would reiterate later, "*and the hell with them.*"[40]

• • • •

In early January 1953, Ted and Helen drove to Los Angeles to attend a preview showing of *The 5,000 Fingers of Dr. T.* Producer Stanley Kramer still had high hopes for the movie, and had convinced Columbia to promote the film aggressively, beginning with a gigantic float in the Macy's Thanksgiving Day Parade,[41] then churning out knickknacks like beanies with the distinctively Seussian yellow hand emerging from the top. Costars Peter Lind Hayes and Mary Healy were dispatched for a promotional junket, singing and dancing their way through ballrooms across the country. As the audience filed into the Los Angeles movie theater that evening, it seemed, for a moment, that *5,000 Fingers* might have overcome the bickering, delays, and mass-vomiting that had plagued its production since almost day one.

Then the lights dimmed and *The 5,000 Fingers of Dr T.* began. It would be, as Ted said later, "the worst evening of my life."[42]

After fifteen minutes, audience members began quietly walking out. Ted sank down into his seat next to Helen, mortified. "At the end, there were only five people left, besides Kramer and our staff," Ted recalled. "It was a disaster. Careers were ruined."[43] It was "as bad as we anticipated," sighed Helen, who could do little to console her husband except talk to him about taking a long vacation far away from everything. "I wish Japan were a little nearer and a little cheaper and we could go there and collect our yen, take hot baths, and begin life anew," said Helen wistfully.[44]

The disastrous preview sent Kramer scrambling back to the editing room to try to salvage the film. Right away, nearly half of the twenty songs Geisel had written were eliminated—a decision that baffled costar Hans Conried, who argued that the movie "might have been an artistic triumph rather than a financial one" if "knowledgeable but inartistic heads of studio" hadn't lost their nerve.[45] Scenes were cut or moved around, while other sequences were entirely rewritten. The cast were called back to the studio for a week of reshooting, but Ted wanted no part of it. He washed his hands of the project entirely and went back home to La Jolla to try to make Helen's dreams of a tour of Japan come true.

While Helen and Ted himself really needed a vacation, there were other reasons he had lately felt compelled to go to Japan. "My conscience got the better of me," Ted admitted later. Perhaps slightly embarrassed by his racist *PM* cartoons and the blatant propaganda of his script for *Design for Death,* Ted may have felt it was finally time for genuine empathy and understanding. He wanted to go to Japan to meet the people, experience the culture, and, perhaps most important to him, talk to Japanese children and their teachers face-to-face. Using his connections at *Life* magazine, Ted managed to finagle a most-expenses-paid trip to Japan, promising to deliver the magazine a piece on Japanese children in the country's postwar American-influenced society—"how the Japanese child's thinking had changed during the [American] occupation," Ted explained.[46]

On Tuesday, March 24, Ted and Helen boarded the ship *President Cleveland* in Los Angeles for the ten-day cruise, bound for Tokyo. On their arrival in Japan, Ted was paired with Kyoto professor Mitsugi Nakamura, dean of Doshisha University in Kyoto, whom Dartmouth classmate Donald Bartlett, now a specialist with American intelligence, had recruited to serve as the Geisels' translator and guide. For nearly three weeks, Ted was swept up by his Japanese publisher and bustled excitedly from one tourist attraction to another, gawking at temples, shaking hands, taking photos, and respectfully bowing to his hosts. The charming Mitsugi interpreted deftly, paying particular attention to syntax to accurately convey Ted's often self-deprecating humor, which could sometimes baffle their literal-minded hosts. The festivities ended with a banquet in a geisha house, prompting Helen to remark that their tour was already "the craziest operation we've ever embarked on."[47]

The Geisels toured schools in Kyoto, Osaka, and Kobe, taking the time at each to talk with teachers and students one-on-one. Ted was immediately impressed "by a people trying to find a voice, and make it known."[48] In each elementary school, he asked students to draw pictures of what they wanted to be when they grew up, anxious to see how peace and American occupation had changed or influenced the answer to such a fundamental childhood question. "If we had given them this assignment ten years ago," one teacher told Ted, "every boy in Japan would have drawn himself as a general."[49] Now, however, the children had different ambitions. "Social concern was the theme that came through," said Ted.[50] "I wish to work against war," wrote one young man, "the thing I hate most," while another charmingly boasted of ending hunger by inventing a machine "to make rice out of the air." One nine-year-old told Ted he wanted to earn a degree and be president of a university, while another drew himself as an astronaut, shaking hands with the king of Mars. Countless others drew themselves as doctors, prompting Ted to wryly comment that if every child who wanted to be a doctor actually became one, there would be one doctor for every seventeen people in Japan.

As much as the responses from the boys fascinated him, Ted was even more encouraged by the drawings he received from girls. Less than a generation earlier, Japanese families made money by renting their daughters to geisha houses. Now Japanese women could vote—

and, as Ted pointed out with a wry smile, they were beginning to use a "startling phrase . . . *'my own.'*"[51] "I want to make my own money in a big office," wrote one girl, drawing herself sitting at a typewriter, while another drew herself as the owner of a beauty shop, writing proudly, "I want to set up and own my own shop." Another drew herself as a scientist, peering into a microscope, saying she had been inspired by Madame Curie. Ted loved it. "Most had visions of themselves working for a better world," he said warmly.[52]

The Geisels returned to Los Angeles in early May on board the *President Wilson* ("we only travel on ships named for Democrats," Helen joked), carrying nearly fifteen thousand children's drawings bundled together in wicker trunks. Ted's article, along with a selection of children's drawings, would appear in *Life* magazine ten months later. Oddly, Ted accused publisher Henry Luce of turning his work into an anti-Japanese screed. "[He] raped the article,"[53] Ted said bitterly, suggesting that the editors at *Life* had been directed to publish only drawings by "the few reactionary kids"[54] or by children who had drawn themselves in traditional Japanese attire.

It was an odd charge; the piece contains few if any "reactionary" drawings. It mostly shows art by children who had chosen more progressive careers, including those by girls who wanted to run their own businesses and boys who wanted to be teachers or astronauts. One boy *did* draw himself wearing a traditional kimono, but he was drawing himself as a rich man, "who has money and time for joy"[55]— the stereotypical equivalent of an American millionaire lounging in a bathrobe or smoking jacket. But whether he was being overly sensitive or not, Ted was furious and vowed he'd never work for *Life* or for Luce again. He also felt he'd let down his Japanese hosts—a slight he was determined to remedy the best way he knew how.

• • • •

Ted and Helen returned from Japan just in time to find *The 5,000 Fingers of Dr. T.* sliding into and quickly out of movie theaters. After its

calamitous January preview, the film had been recut and reconfigured before its final distribution, but Ted would always refuse to
watch the recut version. The film had debuted in San Diego with Dr.
Seuss's name prominently on the marquee—he was a local, after all—
but Ted had been in Japan for opening night and had politely excused
himself from the local premiere by jokingly informing disappointed
San Diegans he was off spending Japanese royalties.

It was probably for the best. Reviews ran the gamut from uninterested to disastrous. "Results are sometimes fascinating, more often
fantastic," wrote *Variety*, trying to see the glass as half full, though it
admitted in the end that, "the material is such that it's hard to keep the
interest from lagging at times."[56] The much-feared Bosley Crowther at
The New York Times was, perhaps predictably, unimpressed, complaining that *Dr. T.* showed "little or no inspiration or real imagination" and
that it was a "ponderously literate affair, pictorially potential but devoid of sense or suspense."[57] Mary Healy and Peter Lind Hayes went on
a charm offensive, gamely suggesting that the film had "passed the
popcorn test,"[58] but Geisel was having none of it. *The 5,000 Fingers of Dr.
T.* was, he said later, the "down period" of his career, an experience so
miserable that he would for years omit the film from his official biography. "I will have nothing more to say until all the participants have
passed away," he said, "including myself."[59]

"[Ted] desperately wanted to be a success in films," said Elin
Vanderlip. "He was so triumphant about the idea of *The 5,000 Fingers*."[60] Idea was one thing; execution was another. "Hollywood is not
suited for me, and I'm not suited for it," Geisel said later.[61] Hollywood
wasn't the easy camaraderie and seat-of-the-pants filmmaking of the
Signal Corps, nor was it passing pages back and forth with Helen as
they mutually rolled their eyes at the clueless antics of Sid Rogell and
his cronies at RKO. Ted preferred working by himself, where the creative decisions were made by him and him alone, and not by a faceless
committee or a sea of executives. The real problem with Hollywood,
he groused, "is that all these people work on things, until even the
author doesn't know what's his and what's not."[62]

And so Dr. Seuss was done with Hollywood—again. "I realized my métier was drawing fish,"[63] said Ted. Late that summer, he set up a meeting with a relatively new professional colleague, Phyllis Jackson, a literary agent with the powerful Music Corporation of America (MCA). The Atlanta-born Jackson was smart and savvy, devoted to her clients, with an intuitive gauge for writers with unique voices. Besides Ted, Jackson represented Beat writer Jack Kerouac—she was presently circulating his manuscript for the novel *On the Road*[64]—and would, over the course of her career, represent a diverse slate of talented authors like Ian Fleming, E. L. Doctorow, and Studs Terkel. Jackson was valued by her clients for her no-holds-barred opinions and frank guidance—both of which, while harsh, were at least brutally honest.

Geisel settled into his seat across from Jackson and went into his prepared spiel. "It's been seven years since I gave up being a soldier," he told Jackson. "Now I'd like to give up movies and advertising and anything that means dueling with vice presidents and committees."[65] What he really wanted to do, he told her, was stay in La Jolla and write children's books full time—all he needed to earn, he assured Jackson, was $5,000 a year. But was such a career even possible?

Jackson considered for a moment, then gave a typically informed answer. After the war, GIs had returned home, gone to college on the GI Bill, gotten jobs, and were now starting families. There was something happening in America, she told him; there was a middle class blossoming in the suburbs, and they were all having kids—a baby boom, as it were. "The children's market is building," Jackson told Geisel, "and you have a reputation."[66] That was true enough; Dr. Seuss *did* have a reputation. But even after nine books, Geisel still wasn't earning enough from them to make a living. What he really needed was a blockbuster—a book that sold hundreds of thousands of copies and was popular enough to send readers looking for his earlier work, which Cerf was determined to keep in print.

Geisel had been pinning his hopes on *Scrambled Eggs Super!*, which Random House published earlier that spring. Dedicated to the Childs family, whom Ted had swum with in the Great Salt Lake, *Scrambled Eggs Super!* is the story of Peter T. Hooper, who decides that regular hens' eggs are too ordinary for his specialty dish, Scrambled Eggs Super-dee-Dooper-dee-Booper, Special de luxe à-la-Peter T. Hooper. In a narrative structure similar to *If I Ran the Zoo*, Peter describes scouring the world for eggs laid by increasingly exotic birds, like the Kwigger, the Stroodel, the Pelf, and the Mount Strookoo Cuckoo. Geisel had written his story in dense—perhaps *too* dense—pages of rhyming verse, with art highlighted by alternating pages of red/blue and red/yellow.

Reviews were generally positive, though never effusive. "Though Seuss-funny, this is not quite as chuckle-rousing as previous works of this ingenius [*sic*] author-artist," wrote the *Philadelphia Inquirer*,[67] while the *Hartford Courant* recognized that the plot was "derived from, and not as good as, *If I Ran the Zoo*."[68] For the most part, however, reviewers seemed glad to have Dr. Seuss back after having had no Dr. Seuss book for nearly three years. In a rollicking review in *The New York Times*, *Pogo* creator Walt Kelly applauded "the fertility rampant in the brain of Dr. Seuss" and cheekily advised parents to "buy the children a television set . . . to divert their attention" while they tiptoed off to the den to have the book all to themselves.[69] One of Geisel's favorite reviews, however, appeared in *Junior Reviewers*, where a seven-year-old critic suggested that "[a]ll ages would like it, from six to forty-four—that's how old my mother is."[70]

Scrambled Eggs Super! wasn't destined to be the blockbuster that Geisel hoped for and needed—but as he left Phyllis Jackson that late summer afternoon, he was more deliberately considering his next book. His last several books had featured some new characters—Thidwick, Peter T. Hooper, Gerald McGrew—and a few old ones, such as Marco and Bartholomew Cubbins. But he hadn't yet revisited the character who stood—or sat, rather—at the center of one of his best-selling books, the character that editor Louise Bonino had urged him to return to time and again, and who hadn't been seen in a Dr. Seuss book in nearly fifteen years: Horton the elephant.

Geisel returned to La Jolla and began writing and sketching, and within a few weeks had the rough outline of a story he was calling *Horton Hears 'Em!*, in which Horton discovers a microscopic civilization of creatures called Whos living in a speck of dust. Geisel was taking particular care with the way the book sounded. *Scrambled Eggs Super!* had been somewhat overwritten, with too many Seussian names and long sentences that could become tongue twisters for parents reading the book aloud. So he and Helen would carefully read the draft pages, crossing out words, substituting others, and reading them out loud to each other for a sense of their sound and ease of readability. For instance, where Ted had written "earsplitting hullabaloo," Helen recommended striking the adjective in favor of a "Seuss onomatopoeic word." Ted came back with "howling mad hullabaloo" instead, which was much better and would stay in the final version.

As always, when he was at work on a book, Ted would sit at his desk all day, sketching, writing, filling trash cans with crumpled art, and wearing pencils to the nub. Other times, when stuck for an idea, he would lean back in his chair, feet up on the desk, and look out the windows at the Pacific or toward the country club far down the hill. "[Working] is rough in a vacation community where everybody's down on the beach or out fishing or playing golf,"[71] said Ted. It was probably why he tended to get more done at night, when it was quieter and the beaches were dark. It was then that Ted got his second wind, sitting at his desk late into the night, drinking one cup of coffee after another and chain-smoking—habits that "drove Helen crazy," said Peggy, "she worried so about them."[72] Ted would finally drag himself to bed around two in the morning, sleep until nine or ten A.M., then head back to the desk again.

Still, Ted wasn't all work and no play. Embracing their new role as permanent residents of La Jolla, the Geisels began hosting small parties, often as entertainment for out-of-town guests like Bennett Cerf or Phyllis Jackson. These were good opportunities for Ted to get away from the drawing board and mingle with friends, many of whom were as colorful—and as colorfully named—as some of Ted's own characters. There was attorney Colonel Sawyer, whose first name really *was* Colonel, as well as lawyer Frank Kockritz and the amiable blowhard Edward Longstreth, a favorite target for Ted's practical jokes. Longstreth was an art collector who claimed to be an expert in abstract art—and Ted, detecting more than a whiff of bluster, couldn't resist boasting that *he* collected the art of "the great Mexican modernist" Escarobus—an entirely fictional painter—and informed the clueless but intrigued Longstreth that he had a few valuable Escarobus paintings for sale. "My god," said Longstreth, "I'd give anything to have an Escarobus!"[73]

And so Ted spent several days painting in what he considered a modern art style—slathering paint onto several canvases, then scraping it off, dragging wet bread across the surface, and rubbing a lead pencil sideways and slantways. "That experience made me suspect that a lot of modern art is malarkey," said Ted. "If I can do it myself, it can't be any good."[74] Ted then delivered one of the barely dry paintings to Longstreth, who gushed over the painting's modernist qualities, paid Ted five hundred dollars, and asked if he had any more to sell. Exasperated—and not quite believing that Longstreth could be fooled this long—Helen finally stepped in to stop the transaction and made Ted return Longstreth's five hundred dollars. "She spoils some of my best gags," Ted lamented.[75]

Despite quashing his pranks, Helen remained Ted's best and most devoted collaborator, keeping him on task, critiquing plot points and poetic scansion, and brewing copious amounts of coffee. The working title of the book had become *Horton Hears a Who!*, a title that reflected Helen's constant advice as Ted revised draft after draft: "[the Whos] are small but important."[76] This was entirely the point. As Ted explained later, the story of Horton and the Whos had been inspired by his trip to Japan the year before. "Japan was just emerging," said Ted, "the people were voting for the first time, running their own lives—and the theme was obvious: 'A person's a person no matter how small.'"[77] It would become the mantra driving Horton's narrative. *Horton Hears a Who!* was Ted offering an open hand of friendship to the Japanese. Through Horton, he was telling them *they mattered* and deserved to be taken care of in a postwar world.

While Geisel had previously written stories that *could* be read as having a message or moral, *Horton Hears a Who!* marked the first time he had *deliberately* written a book with an ethical point of view. But such stories, he thought, inherently came with certain risks. "If you have a burning message that you feel has to be told to children, maybe I guess you have to do it," he had once told his Utah writing class. "But if you're in this group . . . you're not producing juvenile lit[erature]. You're producing propaganda."[78]

In his visits to Germany both before and during World War II, Geisel had seen firsthand the effects of propaganda on children, and its ability to powerfully and immediately shape their morals and worldview. If Dr. Seuss was going to engage in propaganda, Geisel was determined to make certain he was saying something he strongly believed in—and ideally saying it in such a way that readers might not realize they were on the receiving end of a moral or message. "My books don't carry heavy morals," he would say later. "The morals sneak in, as they do in all drama. Every story has got to have a winner, so I happen to make the good guys win."[79]

Still, apart from the obvious message of Horton's humanist mantra, there were other places in *Horton* where readers thought they spotted Geisel's politics and point of view on clear display. Some of Horton's key tormentors, for instance, were a group of monkeys called the Wickersham Brothers, named for the 1931 Wickersham Commission, which had been created by President Hoover in 1929 to study the enforcement of Prohibition laws. Later, after the black-bottomed bird steals Horton's clover holding the speck of dust containing the Whos and drops it in a gigantic field of clover, the Mayor of Whoville describes the wreckage in his town in terms that led some readers to believe that Dr. Seuss was depicting Hiroshima immediately after the detonation of the atomic bomb, leaving behind little but blasted furniture and stopped clocks. Geisel would only quietly raise his eyebrows at such a suggestion, but he did admit to a bit of proselytizing on the importance of voting. "When the little [Who] boy stands up and yells 'Yopp!' and saves the whole place, that's my statement about voting," said Ted. "*Everyone* counts."[80] Geisel would later rightly point out that he knew a thing or two about effective propaganda: not only had he been in advertising—perhaps the ultimate propaganda machine—but his work for the Signal Corps had consisted almost solely of "propaganda and indoctrination films." When Geisel was asked point-blank if he used those "propagandistic skills" in his books, his answer was straightforward and unapologetic: "Of course."[81]

As Thanksgiving neared, *Horton Hears a Who!* was still on Ted's drawing board, with no real ending yet in sight. Ted and Helen had scheduled a Christmas trip to Yosemite to attend the famous Bracebridge Dinner at the Ahwahnee Hotel—but now Helen canceled those plans to give Ted the breathing room he needed to complete *Horton* by early 1954. With his deadline clock ticking, Ted grew sour. "There was tenseness when he was finishing a book," recalled Peggy. "There would be doom and gloom and 'I'm never going to write anything, I've lost it, I just can't do it.' Then suddenly, when something would click, he'd walk out of his studio and the world would be wonderful."[82]

Ted walked out of his studio in late January 1954 with *Horton Hears a Who!*, then tucked it under his arm, flying to New York with Helen to deliver the book personally to Bennett Cerf. They arrived in the middle of an ice storm that gripped the city for more than a week. On their first morning in town, the Geisels taxied over to the Random House offices in the Villard Mansion, a complex of Italianate brownstone mansions at Madison Avenue and 51st Street, and bounded up the stairs to Louise Bonino's office. Bonino looked excitedly through Ted's pages, then called in Cerf and editor Saxe Commins so Ted could read his manuscript to them out loud. Cerf, Commins, and Bonino laughed in all the right places and applauded enthusiastically at the ending—and Ted found he loved having the audience. From now on, Ted would personally deliver his books to Random House and read them aloud. Bonino had started a tradition that would, as the years went on, become a highly anticipated event.

Ted and Helen spent the rest of their week in New York visiting old friends, taking in meetings, and trying their best to enjoy the city that had once been so familiar to them. Ted was still nursing the dream of turning *The Seven Lady Godivas* into a Broadway musical and met with several like-minded funders and producers but left with no real commitments. He would keep trying.

His final obligation, before returning to the warmer climes of La Jolla, was to serve as the host of the NBC telecast called *Excursion*, to be broadcast live on Sunday, January 31. Geisel would lead a discussion about modern art—very much on his mind since the Escarobus prank—and while the show would give the appearance of a spontaneous conversation, Geisel had actually scripted the entire show in advance, filing it away as a "shooting script for TV Ford Foundation telecast attempting to explain something to teenagers of the country about Contemporary Art."[83] Ted made his way up to the NBC studios on the third floor of 30 Rockefeller Center, where he was warmly greeted by the former Dr. T. himself, actor Hans Conried, who was playing the role of "An Intellectual" in Geisel's screenplay, alongside Burgess Meredith, playing "The Average Man."

As part of his discussion on contemporary art, Geisel planned to show how the same animal could be interpreted differently in varying contemporary styles. He would do so by bringing a live horse into the studio, then have six art students from Cooper Union draw or paint the horse in distinctive modern styles. "I know very little about modern art," Geisel told Burgess Meredith's bewildered character. "That's why I'm so interested in this experiment. I not only want *you* to learn something, but I want to learn something myself . . . When a modern artist paints a picture of horse, why doesn't the horse *look* like a horse?"[84]

Since his Escarobus prank, Geisel seemed genuinely interested in figuring out the appeal of contemporary art—as he had remarked at that time, "If I can do it myself, it can't be any good"[85]—and in his view, his first obligation was to take some of the pretense out of it. Thus, Geisel's "Intellectual," played with haughty joy by Conried, gets to spout a lot of Seussian faux intellectual doublespeak as he enthuses about a painting in the modern style:

> You do not feel the spalatinous spiritual significance . . . ?
>
> The paradoxically inverted and unfettered manifestations?
>
> Your eyes do not see the hypnogogic declarations of the
>
> artists' very soul as it struggles in linear combat against
>
> the staccato overtones of an antiquated hypothesis?

But then Geisel takes the air out of Conried's analysis by permitting Meredith to get the last word: "This man is obviously a phony."

Finally, as Geisel circled among the six students painting in various modern styles, he seemed to be explaining his own artistic style and creative decisions as well. Artists weren't necessarily interested in "spittin' images," said the brat-book author who claimed his bizarre animals were an unsuccessful attempt to draw from life; instead, images were processed "in the brain . . . where the artistry takes place." When another artist explained that he was working to capture the "tiredness of the horse," Geisel's response was an insight into his own unique artistic look. "To put over the point strongly, you did two things," Geisel explained. "You threw away the parts of the horse you didn't need; and the parts you needed, you exaggerated."[86] Geisel had never summed up the Seussian style so succinctly.

And yet Ted wrapped things up with disinterest. "I think it's important for everyone out there to know that you young modern artists *can* draw things just exactly like they look . . . if you want to," Ted said. "But if you don't want to . . . that's okay with me." Burgess Meredith's closing statement, as written by Ted, was equally irresolute. "I don't understand *everything* they've told us," said Meredith, "but if we have succeeded in interesting you even a little . . . then perhaps we have done what we started out to do."[87]

• • • •

On March 2, 1954, at home in California, Ted Geisel turned fifty years old. Helen threw a birthday party that grew so loud and raucous that she claimed even their Irish setter had "a complete and permanent hangover" the next morning.[88] Looking back over his last half century, Ted was generally pleased. He and Helen were living a good life in their handpicked location in La Jolla, still enjoyed each other's company after nearly twenty-seven years of marriage, and were well liked in the community. There had been some humps professionally—*The 5,000 Fingers of Dr. T.* would remain an embarrassment for decades and had convinced him to abandon screenwriting for good—but all in all, he was having a respectable, successful career. He was one of the best-known children's authors working, and remained hopeful he was only a book or two away from being able to write children's books full time.

Until then, he was still taking the rare advertising gig—he would shortly be at work on billboards for Holly Sugar—and was continuing to plug away at other side projects he thought had potential, like the *Seven Lady Godivas* musical and a somewhat dirty modern fable he was writing with Kelvin Vanderlip called *Whither California?* that Helen finally scuttled for being "tasteless and not funny."[89] Still, it was all enough to impress his alma mater—and in early spring of 1954, Ted was delighted to learn that Dartmouth planned to bestow an honorary doctorate on him at the college's commencement ceremony in May.

Several weeks before leaving for Dartmouth, Ted and Helen attended a dinner party hosted by their friend, Nikolai Sokoloff, the esteemed Russian musician and conductor who had retired to La Jolla with his wife, Ruth. Helen was active with the Sokoloffs in the La Jolla Music Society, and she and Ruth often hosted fundraising dinners to raise money for a new concert hall at the La Jolla museum, or in this case, to celebrate

the beginning of the summer concert season. At the end of the successful evening, Helen stood to leave, then winced slightly and complained
of pain in her feet and ankles. Another party guest, Dr. Francis M.
Smith, who was a physician at the Scripps Metabolic Clinic, asked Helen
if she wanted him to examine her. But Helen demurred, slightly embarrassed, and refused to let Smith take a closer look, though she conceded
she would let Ted drive them home—a sure sign that Helen was feeling
seriously ill, as Ted's driving was famously terrible.

Ted got them safely home to the Tower, then helped Helen into bed
with a heating pad, which she cranked up to high and draped across
her feet and lower legs. But things were no better by morning, as the
pain had spread up Helen's legs and lower back. The following evening, a distraught Ted parked their car awkwardly in front of the
Scripps Clinic and helped Helen out of the passenger seat. She leaned
heavily on him as he helped her hobble up the short flight of steps and
into the clinic. Things had gotten much worse. The numbness had
spread to her arms, hands, and face, and she was unable to swallow
on her own.

A few days later, Helen Geisel would be completely immobile,
paralyzed from the neck down.

Geisel took great delight in mounting real animal horns on sculpted Seussian animal heads, including this Blue Green Abelard, hanging on the wall of his office. A lifelong cigarette smoker, Geisel regularly tried—and failed—to give up the habit. A frequent effort involved clamping down on a pipe filled with radish or strawberry seeds, which he would water with an eyedropper when he felt the urge to smoke. *John Bryson/The Life Image Collection/Getty Images*

He Studied Under Webster

Geisel's years at Dartmouth's humor magazine, *Jack-O-Lantern*, would be formative in his development as a writer and an artist—and provide some of the fondest memories of his life. Geisel would sign his work with an assortment of names ("Ted Geisel" appears in the 1922 drawing at right, while "T.G." is signed on the 1924 cartoon above) and pseudonyms, eventually arriving at "Seuss"—his own middle name and his mother's maiden name—by 1925. Ted wouldn't sign his work as "Dr. Seuss" until an April 1928 cartoon in *Judge* magazine. *Courtesy of Dartmouth College Library*

jack-o-lantern   25

So This Is Hanover!?

Bennett Cerf, the smart and rakish cofounder of Random House, recognized the brilliance of Dr. Seuss early and wooed Geisel away from his first publisher. Works by Dr. Seuss, along with titles published under Geisel's Beginner Books imprint, would help make Random House one of the most successful publishers in the world. Cerf often remarked that of all the authors published by Random House, Geisel was its "one true genius." *Alex Gotfryd/Corbis via Getty Images*

Geisel was a strident advocate for American preparedness in the months leading up to World War II. In 1941, he stopped working on children's books entirely to focus instead on providing editorial cartoons for New York's progressive *PM* newspaper, as well as artwork supporting the war effort for the U.S. Treasury Department. Geisel's portrayal of Asians and Asian Americans reflected the negative stereotypes typical of the era. *Bettman/ Getty Images*

THE PLEASURE IS ALL OURS!

7 MILLION NEW U.S. TAX-PAYERS

Dr. Seuss

Drawn especially for the Treasury Department's War Tax Program....

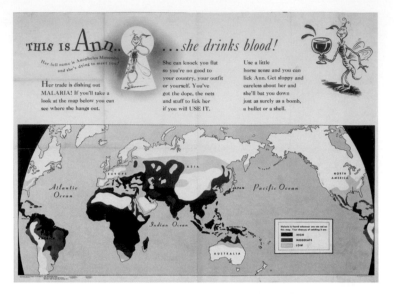

With his background in advertising, Geisel was the ideal artist to illustrate "This Is Ann," a brochure distributed by the U.S. government during World War II to educate soldiers on protecting themselves from mosquito-borne diseases. The brochure was written by Munro Leaf, author of the children's book *The Story of Ferdinand*. *Courtesy of the U.S. Government Printing Office*

As a captain in the U.S. Army Signal Corps, Geisel was tasked by commanding officer Frank Capra with overseeing the development and production of *Private Snafu*. Between 1943 and 1945, the popular animated cartoon series instructed U.S. soldiers on military practices and procedures, usually by showing the comedic and sometimes horrifying consequences of *not* following protocol or instructions. *U.S. Department of Defense/National Archives*

While he would travel the world and see countless exotic locales, Ted's favorite place would always be his studio in La Jolla, with the Pacific coastline visible in the distance. Throughout his life, Geisel would maintain a regular work schedule, sitting at his desk all day, even if stuck for an idea. "For me, success means doing work that you love, regardless of how much you make," said Geisel. "I go into my office almost every day and give it eight hours—though every day isn't productive, of course." *Gene Lester/Getty Images*

In 1955, Geisel was awarded an honorary doctorate from Dartmouth, his beloved alma mater. As he bestowed the honor, Dartmouth president John S. Dickey noted that "behind the fun [in the work of Dr. Seuss], there has been intelligence, kindness, and a feel for humankind." Geisel would forever joke that he could now officially call himself "Doctor Dr. Seuss." *Courtesy of Dartmouth College Library*

Ted and Helen take in the view at the Tower in 1957, around the time of the publication of the blockbuster *The Cat in the Hat*. Because Helen was a talented writer in her own right, Ted valued her strong opinions on rhyme and character and insisted she be granted equal partnership in the fledgling Beginner Books imprint. Because Helen was an active member of the La Jolla and San Diego arts scene, her 1967 suicide stunned the community. *Gene Lester/Getty Images*

Ted signs books for a crowd of enthusiastic children during a visit to Dartmouth in 1958. While Dr. Seuss entertained countless generations of children, the Geisels themselves were unable to have any of their own. He would later develop a close and loving relationship with two stepdaughters, but publicly, his well-rehearsed answer regarding children was: "You have 'em, and I'll entertain 'em!" *Courtesy of Dartmouth College Library*

Protective of his name and reputation, Geisel resisted most efforts to license the Dr. Seuss name for merchandising. One rarity was the plastic model kits of Seussian animals he permitted the Revell company to manufacture, beginning in 1959. Typically, Geisel exerted complete control over the project, even forcing Revell to shut down its production line for ten hours until a problem involving the proper fitting of pieces was resolved. *John Bryson/The Life Images Collection/Getty Images*

Geisel in La Jolla around 1973, with Michael Frith, his editor and art director for the Beginner Books imprint. Frith admired Geisel's commitment to making his books the very best they could be and appreciated that he insisted writers for children treat children like smart and serious readers. "Never for a second did anybody entertain the idea that we were talking down to anybody," said Frith. "The kids were just as smart as we were." *Courtesy of Michael Frith*

Geisel in his Tower office with Audrey around 1969, only a few years into their marriage. Audrey was a different kind of collaborator than Helen, content to support and encourage Ted from the sidelines, though she would advocate for a softer color palate in works like *The Lorax*. It was also Audrey who encouraged Ted to grow a beard. *James L. Amos/Corbis via Getty Images*

While Geisel struggled with vision problems and other health-related issues in his seventies and eighties, his work ethic and creative drive never flagged. *You're Only Old Once!* was Geisel's humorous ode to aging, while his final book, *Oh, the Places You'll Go!*, was regarded by many as a beneficent valedictory. *Bettmann/Getty Images*

CHAPTER 10

A LITERARY STRAITJACKET

1954–1957

Helen's prognosis was devastating—"touch and go," the doctors at San Diego County Hospital told Ted gently.[1] Only hours earlier, Ted had helped Helen through the door of the Scripps Metabolic Clinic, where Dr. Francis Smith—the same physician who had asked to attend to Helen at the Sokoloff party the day before—was brought in to examine her. Helen was weak, barely able to stand, and was having difficulty speaking or even focusing on questions. As Smith continued his examination, Helen grew panicked and hysterical—and Ted, fearing the worst, wasn't much better, growing increasingly more despondent with each passing minute.

Smith quickly dismissed exhaustion as the cause of Helen's condition, but was more cautious in landing on a definitive diagnosis. "Neuritis acute, Landy type?" Smith wrote with some uncertainty, even putting a question mark on his own scrawled diagnosis—then added more conclusively: "Guillain-Barré syndrome," a rare disorder in which the body's immune system attacks its own nerves, resulting in paralysis.[2] Smith brought in neurologist Ralph Barris for a consultation, and Helen was whisked to San Diego County Hospital, less than twenty minutes to the south. By the time Helen arrived in San Diego, she was unable to breathe on her own and was placed in an iron lung, still commonly used in 1954 to treat respiratory problems caused by polio. (The polio vaccine, which was being developed by the Geisels' La Jolla neighbor Jonas Salk, wouldn't be widely available for another year.)

Helen's condition slowly deteriorated until she was entirely paralyzed from the neck down. Incarcerated in the iron lung, where she was only able to see her surroundings reflected in the round mirror mounted over her head, she grew increasingly disoriented and confused, failing to recognize Ted or her doctors, and became convinced she had been imprisoned because she and Ted had lost all their money. Eventually she lost her ability to speak altogether. Distraught, Ted set up a system of mirrors so Helen could see their Irish setter reflected in the overhead mirror, somehow hoping if she saw their dog, she would understand the Geisels weren't despondent. But the outlook remained bleak, and for the first few days Ted refused to return home to the Tower, spending nearly every waking hour at the hospital, running errands for the nurses to keep his mind occupied.

Somehow he remembered to contact Dartmouth to inform them of Helen's illness and apologized that he would be unable to pick up his honorary doctorate. (The college assured him the award could wait until 1955, if he so chose.) It was a wonder Ted was able to function at all; for the past three decades, Helen had taken care of all the details, from the checkbook to the shopping to the mailing of packages. Even as Helen's condition stabilized, Ted remained "frantic and frightened," said Elin Vanderlip. "Helen had always shielded him from the real world."[3] He tried working during the day—he had pages of the alphabet book *On Beyond Zebra!* pinned to the corkboard in his Tower office—but understandably found he couldn't focus and spent his days instead with the Vanderlips at the Villa Narcissa.

Helen's condition began to improve somewhat in late June. She was learning to swallow on her own again—Ted would lower Popsicles into her mouth in encouragement—and could make sounds, though nothing resembling speech. On July 4, she was removed from the iron lung for brief water exercises, and Barris recommended she be moved 130 miles north to the Rehabilitation Center of Santa Monica to begin four months of therapy. Ted was relieved, though cautious in his optimism, writing to editor Louise Bonino that "there is a very good chance that she [Helen] will walk again."[4]

Still not quite certain how to manage, Ted called his niece Peggy Owens, now living with her husband in Virginia, and asked for help moving Helen to Santa Monica. On July 9, as Ted rode in an ambulance with Helen, bound for the rehabilitation clinic, Peggy followed in the Geisels' car, crammed with suitcases, Ted's drawing board and art supplies, and assorted personal items to make Helen's stay at the California Rehabilitation Center more comfortable. Ted, meanwhile, checked into the Ocean Palms Hotel, where he set up an office and spent each morning going through the mail with Peggy, paying bills, and stacking up personal letters to read aloud to Helen.

It was here, in his rooms at the Ocean Palms, that Ted would receive his first copies of *Horton Hears a Who!*, scheduled for publication in August. He wasn't happy with them; under his hyper-discerning eye, the books had been bound in such a way that it looked as if the text was running slightly downhill off each page. "Not griping or complaining, mind you!" he told Bonino. "Just still on my impossible hunt for ultimate ultimates."[5] After this first note, however, Ted would offer few comments; his focus was elsewhere—for Helen had begun to make a rapid recovery.

Throughout July and August, Helen's paralysis began to recede, and the feeling and sensation gradually returned in her neck, chest, arms, and legs. She was still unable to speak or feed herself—she would need physical therapy to learn to use her mouth, teeth, and tongue again—and she couldn't sit up without assistance. However, she could now be moved to a wheelchair and positioned at the clinic's windows, where she could see the lawn outside. As she and Ted sat looking out the window one afternoon, a flash of fur streaked across the grass.

"Ruh . . . ruh . . . ruh-rabbit . . ." Helen said softly.

Ted nearly wept with joy—and Helen's condition would only continue to improve over the next few weeks. The physical therapy was tough—"just about as painful as the disease was," said Ted[6]—but Helen seemed to improve through sheer force of will. "She's a terrific patient and wonderfully cheerful," Ted reported.[7] "Two months ago, the doctors gave her up," he wrote Bonino cheerily. "Today, she can actually do a little bit of walking! Not much, but enough so we know that she's going to get out of here without any crutches."[8]

The news was just as good for *Horton Hears a Who!*, published to rave reviews in August 1954. "Horton the elephant is back in another of those hilarious . . . brews which only Dr. Seuss can compound," wrote the *Chicago Tribune*,[9] while the *Minneapolis Star Tribune* proclaimed, "Dr. Seuss has done it again . . . [*Horton*] is one of the best of the delightfully zany plots presented with a sure Seuss touch . . . don't miss it."[10] Many reviewers, too, seemed to understand and appreciate that Dr. Seuss was intentionally delivering a moral message. "The moral is pointed—but fun,"[11] wrote one reviewer, while another hailed *Horton* as "a rhymed lesson in the protection of minorities and their rights."[12]

Geisel was thrilled with the reception; he had worked perhaps harder on *Horton* to make every word, every drawing count. "I must confess I learned more about writing children's books when I worked in Hollywood than anywhere else," he later told *The Saturday Evening Post*. "For in films, everything is based on coordination between pictures and words."[13] With *Horton*, he probably thought he'd finally coordinated the two as well as he ever had—but once again, while *Horton Hears a Who!* sold well, it wasn't on track to bring in the kind of annual income he had hoped for. And so Geisel would still continue to pick up advertising work, with his largest client being the Holly Sugar company, which was presently featuring Geisel's "All It Needs Is . . ." campaign, showing Seussian giraffes, goats, and children making sour faces as they sampled unsweetened berries, garbage, and juice.

By September, Helen's condition had improved to the point that doctors informed Ted she could return home to La Jolla. However, because Helen was still largely confined to a wheelchair and unable to climb stairs, Ted chose to move her into a friend's guesthouse, just down the hill from the Tower. Helen would now begin a regular series of daily exercises, starting with swimming at seven A.M., followed by walks in wet sand and working with weights to relearn balance and rebuild muscle strength. By October, Ted was writing to Evelyn Shrifte that he was certain Helen would be "almost entirely recuperated from the whole nightmare."[14]

Almost. While Helen would eventually recover from the nightmare, she would forever be plagued by a low-level pain in her legs and feet; she said it always felt as if her shoes were several sizes too small. When doctors recommended that she continue swimming every day as part of her continued therapy, Ted immediately had a swimming pool installed at the Tower. He dubbed it the *Woman's Home Companion* Pool, claiming he'd paid for it using money he'd earned doing work for the magazine—which, while charming and amusing, was also most likely untrue. Such glibness aside, however, Ted had spent the summer and most of the autumn of 1954 giving his loving attention and devotion to Helen during her illness—and to his credit, had been self-aware enough to bring in much-needed assistance from Peggy, even as he largely sidelined his work on *On Beyond Zebra!* Helen later referred to her husband at this time as "part man, part angel."[15]

• • • •

Dick and Jane weren't getting the job done.

In 1954, author John Hersey, winner of the Pulitzer Prize in 1945 for his novel *A Bell for Adano*, decided he'd had enough of *Dick and Jane*, the reading primer familiar to countless generations of school-age children. As chairman of the Citizens' School Study Council of Fairfield, Connecticut, Hersey and his council had spent a year studying their students' academic achievement, with a laser focus on reading and they weren't encouraged by what they'd seen. "Parents have cried in dismay that their children could not read out loud, could not spell, could not write," Hersey reported in an article for *Life* magazine. One of the biggest problems, as he saw it, was with the uninspiring, ineffective *Dick and Jane* reading primers that educators had been putting in the hands of millions of schoolchildren every day since the 1930s. "Children understandably prefer lurid comic books and television shows to insipid, goody-goody school readers," wrote Hersey. "Is not revulsion against namby-pamby school readers perhaps a reason why they like lurid comic books so much?"[16]

In truth, it wasn't just *Dick and Jane*; school readers had always been rather insipid, if well-intended, fare. Up until the early eighteenth century, most children's books didn't bother with teaching reading, but focused instead on religious and moral lessons—stories read *to* children for their ethical well-being, rather than stories that encouraged them to read for themselves. Things began to change in the 1740s, with books like Thomas Boreman's *Gigantick Histories* and T. Cooper's *The Child's New Play-Thing*, which featured alphabets, as well as songs and fables targeted specifically at children.

Then came John Newbery. The first real champion of children's literature, the English printer Newbery published his first children's reader in 1744, an alphabet book with short rhymes called *A Little Pretty Pocket-Book*. Unlike the authors of earlier primers, Newbery thought learning could be entertaining—at least a *little*—and his use of fifty-eight woodcut illustrations over *Little Pretty Pocket-Book*'s ninety pages made the book popular with both children and parents. It would go through twelve printings by 1767. In his lifetime, Newbery would design, produce, market, and sell more than thirty books for children, writing some under his own name and others under names like Abraham Aesop or Tom Telescope. Like Theodor Geisel, John Newbery loved a good pseudonym.

Newbery was one of the first publishers to take children's need for good books seriously; his influence can still be seen today in the medal bearing his name, awarded annually since 1922 by the American Library Association for the year's "most distinguished contribution to American literature for children."[17] And yet, while in his lifetime Newbery would publish spelling, alphabet, and riddle books populated with characters like Willy the lamb or Jouler the dog, he didn't want children having *too* much fun; his books were ultimately meant to produce good and upright citizens. As one eighteenth-century writer tut-tutted, the obligation of children's books was "to restrain a lively imagination."[18]

Children's primers, unfortunately, never got much more exciting—which is partly why Hersey trained his fire on the turgid *Dick and Jane* readers. The brainchild of an Indiana elementary school teacher named Zerna A. Sharp, the *Dick and Jane* primers were a well-meaning effort to encourage children to read by giving them illustrated stories and situations revolving around children just like them. "There's nothing these book children could do that [real children] couldn't remember having done themselves," Sharp insisted. "[*Dick and Jane*] made reading easy for them and encouraged them to read more."[19] Hersey, however, was having none of it, railing against *Dick and Jane* primers for their "insipid illustrations depicting the slicked-up lives of other children."[20] Real children, Hersey contended, wanted nothing to do with Dick and Jane and their lives of quiet desperation.

Dick and Jane didn't rely on phonics to teach reading—a pedagogical choice educators were beginning to decry—but relied instead on the "whole word" or "look-say" approach, in which young readers could learn new words by associating them with accompanying pictures and illustrations. Hersey didn't necessarily object to the look-say pedagogy but argued that if primers were going to rely on pictures to help a child visualize words, it was cruel to subject children to the "uniform, bland, idealized and terribly literal" pictures found in a typical primer. "Why should they not have pictures that widen rather than narrow the associative richness the children give to the words they illustrate?" Hersey asked rhetorically—then answered his own question by suggesting that perhaps what was needed were "drawings like those of the wonderfully imaginative geniuses among children's illustrators: [John] Tenniel, Howard Pyle, 'Dr. Seuss,' [and] Walt Disney."[21]

It's unlikely Ted read Hersey's article in *Life* on its publication in May 1954—but someone else did: William Spaulding, head of the education division for Houghton Mifflin publishing. Spaulding, who in early 1955 was quickly climbing the ranks at Houghton Mifflin—he would be its president within two years—was at heart a crusader who believed children's books *could* be both educational and entertaining. Spaulding also knew that *Dick and Jane* were becoming obsolete— and if Hersey's 1954 *Life* article had been the first sign of the primer's stagnation, author Rudolf Flesch's 1955 criticism of the American education system, *Why Johnny Can't Read*, made *Dick and Jane* not only irrelevant, but practically the enemy, dismissed by Flesch as "horrible, stupid, emasculated, pointless, [and] tasteless."[22]

With both Hersey and Flesch rallying to the cause, then, Spaulding decided the time was right to rethink *Dick and Jane*. And as Hersey had suggested in *Life*, Spaulding thought he should ask Dr. Seuss for help. In early 1955, Spaulding phoned Geisel and invited him to Boston for a conversation. Geisel was glad to take the call—he and Spaulding had run across each other during the war—and happy to meet with Spaulding, who, as the son of a Yale dean of education, was smart and serious about books for children. As he and Geisel began their first conversation in Spaulding's office, it was clear both men understood the importance of writing books that not only helped aspiring young readers learn to read but would also be the kinds of books they *wanted* to read.

The two continued the conversation over dinner and drinks, with Geisel growing more and more animated as he shared with Spaulding his views on the challenges of writing for young readers. Geisel agreed that children's reading primers were terrible—but so, too, were most kids' books. Things hadn't really changed since his 1947 Utah lectures: children's books were still competing for attention with television and comic books—and as far as Geisel could tell, books were losing. Too many books either talked down to children or dealt with mundane, cutesy subjects of little interest to kids—the *Bunny, Bunny, Bunny Books* as Ted always derisively called them. What was really needed, he told Spaulding, was a book aimed at a specific group of young readers—namely, those who had mastered some of the

basics, but remained uninterested in reading. Spaulding got it immediately. "Write me a story that first graders can't put down!" he
demanded excitedly.[23]

But there was a catch. The vocabulary for children's primers was
strictly limited to a certain number of "accepted" words for readers at
each grade level. For first graders, primers were limited to about 300
words; for third graders it was around 1,000, and for sixth graders,
4,000. To write a book for first graders, then, Geisel would be restricted to a word list of 350 words or less—and the preferred number,
Spaulding told him, was closer to 225. Could Geisel write a story first
graders couldn't put down using 225 words or less? Geisel left Boston
without making any promises, but told Spaulding he would take the
word list home and "play with it."[24]

He also told Spaulding he'd need to check with Bennett Cerf, to
see if he could accept an assignment from a rival publisher. The savvy
Cerf signed off on Spaulding's offer, imposing only one real condition: whatever Geisel came up with, Spaulding and Houghton Mifflin
could publish the textbook version that was sold to schools, but Random House would be permitted to publish the trade edition that
would be for sale in bookstores. While he had no way of knowing it at
the time, it would be one of the best deals Cerf ever made.

◆ ◆ ◆ ◆

On Sunday, June 12, 1955, it was pouring rain in Hanover, New Hampshire. Dartmouth's 186th graduation ceremony, scheduled to take
place on the lawn outside the Baker Library, would have to be moved
indoors. Ted and Helen—along with countless academics, honored
guests, and 566 Dartmouth graduates—were funneled into the campus gymnasium, where Ted took his place onstage, alongside the poet
Robert Frost and Congressman Joseph Martin Jr., the minority leader
of the U.S. House of Representatives.[25] Today Dartmouth would at last
bestow on Ted the honorary doctorate he'd postponed since the previous May.

"Creator and fancier of fanciful beasts," began Dartmouth president John S. Dickey as Ted rose proudly and a little nervously. "You have single-handedly stood as St. George between a generation of exhausted parents and the demon dragon of unexhausted children on a rainy day . . . [and] behind the fun, there has been intelligence, kindness, and a feel for humankind," Dickey continued. "You have stood these many years in the academic shadow of your learned friend Dr. Seuss," he added, "and because we are sure the time has come when the good doctor would want you to walk by his side as a full equal—and because your College delights to acknowledge the distinction of a loyal son—Dartmouth confers on you her Doctorate of Humane Letters."[26]

There was thunderous applause as the doctoral hood was draped over Ted's shoulders—and to his likely relief, he wasn't being asked to give a lengthy speech; that honor would fall to Robert Frost, Dartmouth Class of 1896, who received an honorary Doctorate of Laws from Dickey that same rainy morning. Ted would always be proud of the honor; he finally had the doctorate he'd fumbled away during his year at Oxford. He said later that Dickey told him the degree "would make an honest man of me, and no longer would I have to masquerade under a phony doctorate."[27] He would also for the rest of his life announce with a straight face that the honorific meant he could now officially call himself "Dr. Dr. Seuss."

While Dartmouth had honored Ted with a doctorate, that autumn, Ted would honor Helen as only he could: by dedicating a book to her. Published in September 1955, *On Beyond Zebra!* was the first book Ted had completed since Helen's 1954 illness. On the book's dedication page, he had drawn a smiling zebra, eyeing the reader warmly as it walks on its back legs. It carries a sign reading TO HELEN.

On Beyond Zebra! was a Dr. Seuss version of the traditional alphabet book, but "for people who don't stop at Z." It featured Ted at his loopiest, creative best, as he designed and named nineteen new letters of the alphabet, as well as creatures whose names could only be spelled using those letters. There was the letter called *wum*, for instance, needed to spell Wumbus, and one called *flunn*, required to write about the rabbitlike Flunnel.

Filled with the kind of whimsical, anatomically-impossible animals that had been staples of his work since *Judge*—there were hundred-legged cows, whales perched on mountaintops, even a mosquito-like creature that could have buzzed straight out of a Flit advertisement—*On Beyond Zebra!* also gallops along at a breakneck pace, with clever rhymes and some of Dr. Seuss's most energetic verse since *If I Ran the Zoo*:

> And SPAZZ is a letter I use to spell Spazzim
> A beast who belongs to the Nazzim of Bazzim.
> Handy for traveling. That's why he has 'im.[28]

The book was published to nearly universal praise—*delightful* seemed to be the descriptor of choice.[29] "Nobody could possibly have ideas in any way resembling those that occur to this talented man," enthused *The New York Times*, adding that the Seussian letters and creatures in the book were "indescribable, but they are delightful, and it is difficult to imagine how we ever managed without them."[30]

In the *Boston Globe*, a reviewer admitted he enjoyed *On Beyond Zebra!*—"[it] has a quality that all children, grownup ones as well as little ones, can enjoy"—but rakishly accused Dr. Seuss of alphabetical treason. "He's worse than the Russians. They have 36 letters in their alphabet . . . Dr. Seuss wants to add 20 letters to our alphabet," wrote the *Globe*'s reviewer. "Dr. Seuss should stop it; he's going too far. He's subversive."[31] Geisel gleefully agreed. "I'm subversive as hell!" he roared. "I've always had a mistrust of adults," he said later. "And one reason I dropped out of Oxford and the Sorbonne was that I thought they were taking life too damn seriously, concentrating too much on nonessentials."[32]

But it was the essentials, in fact, that were making him miserable at the moment—namely Spaulding's list of acceptable vocabulary words for his reading primer, which he was finding creatively stifling. While Geisel's stories of the agony of cracking the word-list limitations would, perhaps predictably, vary over the years, there's little doubt that he was finding it nearly impossible to find a compelling story buried among the list's 350 words. "All I needed, I figured, was to find a whale of an exciting subject which would make the average six-year-old want to read like crazy," he said later. "[But] none of the old dull stuff: 'Dick has a ball. Dick likes the ball. The ball is red, red, red, red.'"[33] Instead, he was thinking up much more exciting subjects—like climbing Mount Everest, where, he suggested, it could be sixty degrees below zero. It was a "truly exciting" idea, he thought. However, as he scanned the word list, he discovered "you can't use the word 'scaling,' you can't use the word 'peaks,' you can't use 'Everest,' you can't use 'sixty,' and you can't use 'degrees.'"[34]

When stymied, Geisel would kick back in the chair at his desk and chain-smoke for hours as he stared absently out the window at the Pacific, waiting for inspiration. Other times, he would simply doodle, drawing one crazy creature after another to see if anything sparked an idea, or lay down on the sofa in his office and thumb through books and magazines. Copies of *On Beyond Zebra!* were still stacked on the coffee table, and Geisel thought for a moment he might write a story about a queen zebra. "I snuck a look at the word list," he wrote later. "'Queen' and 'zebra' weren't there."[35]

It was, he said, an "impossible and ridiculous" task.[36] But he would keep trying.

• • • •

In their tower up on Mount Soledad, the Geisels—and especially Ted—were considered something of La Jolla luminaries, actively recruited by politicians and community leaders to fill seats on local boards, community groups, councils, and advisory committees. Ted would accept some, refuse others. In 1956, he was persuaded by the Fine Arts Gallery of San Diego to permit them to display some of his original art—an exhibit he was convinced no one would attend until he showed up on opening night and was smothered by more than four hundred children and their parents who cornered him for more than an hour, waving books and scraps of paper for him to autograph.

Ted also agreed to serve as a trustee for the San Diego Fine Arts Museum—the beginning of a long and friendly relationship—and accepted a position as a member of the fledgling town council, which had been created in 1950 to serve as the community's liaison with the city of San Diego on issues related to matters such as zoning, traffic, and pollution. It was a noble endeavor, to be sure, but one that would end up costing him—for in 1956, as the council deliberated whether to outlaw billboards in the La Jolla community, Ted was asked to write and illustrate an appropriately Seussian pamphlet explaining why billboards were eyesores.

Geisel quickly put together an eight-page booklet called *Signs of Civilization!* featuring two competing cavemen, Guss and Zaxx—owners of Guss's Guss-ma-Tuss and Zaxx's Zaxx-ma-Taxx—who make larger and more elaborate carved stone billboards as they strive to promote their businesses and one-up each other. Guss and Zaxx overbuild in a frenzy, uglifying their community and eventually driving down their Stone Age property values, forcing even the dinosaurs to move out. Ted's tale ended with an appeal to his local businessmen's sense of community pride even as it landed on a groaner of a final couplet:

> Which is why our businessmen never shall
> Allow such to happen in La Jolla, Cal.

Unfortunately, Geisel had either forgotten—or didn't care—that two different companies, Holly Sugar and Standard Oil, presently had his art sprawled across billboards in various locations around the country. Standard Oil never blinked, but executives at Holly Sugar were unamused; Geisel's contract with Holly Sugar was terminated, his work replaced by that of artist Bill Tara.

Meanwhile, even as he drew Holly Sugar's fire for his pamphlet for the town council, he was putting the finishing touches on another book he had on his drawing table, *If I Ran the Circus*, the story of a boy named Morris McGurk, who fantasizes about establishing an increasingly larger and more fantastic circus in a vacant lot behind Sneelock's Store. It was intentionally derivative of *If I Ran the Zoo*, but that was entirely the point: Bennett Cerf had asked Geisel for another book with a similar setup, and Ted had obliged, all the way down to the final page, in which the narrator, and the reader, are jolted back to the reality of the untouched vacant lot.

That wasn't to say *If I Ran the Circus* didn't have its charms. While it was heavier on text than some of the more recent Dr. Seuss books— it was perhaps his densest since *Scrambled Eggs Super!*—Geisel made the most of his verses, giving his enjambed lines the cadence of a circus ringmaster or carnival barker:

> When you see what goes on, you'll say no other circus is
> Half the great circus the Circus McGurkus is.[37]

Ted dedicated *If I Ran the Circus* to his father—the second Dr. Seuss book T. R. Geisel would have devoted to him—with the inscription carried across the page on balloons reading, "This book is for my Dad, Big Ted of Springfield, the finest man I'll ever know."[38] There were other little touches of Springfield in the book as well. The names McGurk and Sneelock were taken from a hometown store clerk named John McGurk and a mailman named August Schneelock. "He never forgot anything that he ever saw or did," said Peggy Owens. "It all went into a memory bank and then popped up later on."[39]

Geisel completed *If I Ran the Circus* in time to have it in bookstores by Christmas 1956, where it was quickly snapped up by parents delighted to have the annual Dr. Seuss book to give as gifts. "One wonders how these books can come out year after year with such a high standard of verse, story, and pictures, but they do," mused one reviewer. "We hope that they will continue to do so."[40] Geisel was happy with the book's reception—and yet, even as readers purchased his own book, the overt commercialism and materialism of the Christmas season was beginning to rub him the wrong way. "Frankly, I was annoyed at what was happening at Christmas," he said later.[41] As he stood before the mirror brushing his teeth on the morning of December 26, he caught sight of a face scowling back at him. "It was Seuss!" Geisel exclaimed. "So, I wrote a story . . . to see if I could rediscover something about Christmas that obviously I'd lost."[42]

They were themes Ted had griped publicly about before. As far back as 1924, he'd complained in an issue of *Jacko* that "on Christmas morning, everyone feels disappointed." He'd also written mockingly of commercialism; in a 32-line illustrated poem he'd written for *Redbook* in 1955, Ted told the story of a con man who uses a hyperbolic hard sell to persuade a sunbathing Hoobub to buy a worthless piece of string by convincing him the string is even better than the sun:

> THIS PIECE OF GREEN STRING IS COLOSSAL! IMMENSE!
> AND, TO YOU . . .
> WELL, I'LL SELL IT FOR 98 CENTS![43]

That oily con man's name? The Grinch.

It wasn't the first time Geisel had used the word. In 1953, in *Scrambled Eggs Super!*, one of the birds from which Peter T. Hooper considers pilfering eggs is the "Beagle-Beaked Bald Headed Grinch," a paunchy bird with a perpetual scowl. When the term next appeared in *Redbook* two years later, however, the Grinch looked more catlike, with whiskers and a tuft of fur on the top of his head—and his behavior, while not quite what readers would come to call Grinch-like, at least leaned toward the slightly slippery.

In the days after Christmas 1956, then, Geisel would try to get his complicated feelings on Christmas and commercialism into the character of the Grinch—and for someone who still made a living partly by creating advertising, this was an existential crisis, akin to questioning one's faith. "I did this nasty, anti-Christmas character that was really myself," Ted said later[44]—though the more he doodled the character, the more he thought the Grinch looked "a little like Bennett Cerf."[45]

. . . .

Geisel had been staring at Spaulding's word list for the better part of a year, still looking for something to jump-start his imagination. But the words still weren't coming. Some afternoons, when Helen came into his studio to check on him, she would find Ted lying on the couch, moaning or even thrashing about, as if he were trying to physically force an idea into his head.

Sitting for interviews in early 1956, Ted often casually hinted that he was at work on *three* "supplementary textbooks, for the first, second, and third grades." Most of that was untrue; he was barely at work on *one*. Spaulding would likely have been heartened at the way Ted passionately explained the objective of his textbooks, which was "to make their first experience in reading pleasurable, not difficult."[46] Unfortunately the noble motivation wasn't making the writing any easier. "It took me a year of my getting mad as blazes and throwing the thing across the room," he said later.[47] Stuck, he decided to make another quick pass through the list.

"I finally gave it one more chance," recalled Geisel, "and said, 'If I find two words that rhyme and make sense to me, that's the title.'"[48] But even that approach didn't quite work out as he hoped; a *tall ball* wasn't all that encouraging as the subject for a children's story, and other words that seemed promising for characters, such as *daddy*, didn't rhyme with anything else on the list. "I was forbidden to use any words beyond [the list]," Geisel said in exasperation. "I almost threw the job up."[49]

He went back and read the list one more time, slowly and more deliberately—and then suddenly, there it was: his story in two rhyming one-syllable words.

Cat.

Hat.

"And like a genius," Geisel modestly explained later, "I said, 'That's the name.'"[50]

The Cat in the Hat it would be—so Geisel next went to work trying to figure out what the cat would look like and how he would act. Cats had been appearing in Dr. Seuss cartoons as far back as *Jacko*, though they were usually smaller, more realistic-looking cats, often black, who reacted to events with wide eyes and amused smiles. To turn a cat into a main character, however, Geisel needed one that could walk around on two legs, had hands that could pick things up, and a more expressive face. As Ted doodled and wrote, his cat would be shaped and inspired in part by two other cartoon cats he knew well, and which he had admired since childhood.

The first was the title character from George Herriman's influential comic strip *Krazy Kat*, which ran in newspapers across the country from 1913 until Herriman's death in 1944. Geisel loved the look and feel of the strip—he had praised Herriman's strip for its "beautifully insane sanities"—and Geisel's cat would channel Krazy's physical appearance, all the way down to a red bow tie. Personality-wise, however, Krazy was passive and unsophisticated; for Geisel's cat, he'd look to a more aggressive cartoon feline for inspiration: Felix the Cat, the animated creation of cartoonists Pat Sullivan and Otto Messmer. At one point, Felix had been the most famous animated cartoon character in the world—until pushed aside by Mickey Mouse—and Geisel had even used the pseudonym Felix in the pages of *Jacko* in May 1924. Felix was self-assured and adventurous—though at times awkward or inept—and Geisel's cat would walk and act with a similar swagger and confidence.

As Geisel continued to refine and develop the character over the next few months, the cat began to take on a strong and distinctive personality of his own—so much so that Ted would later feel the need to define, and defend, his cat's highly independent persona. "He is NOT a smart ass," Geisel wrote. "He is NOT loud. He NEVER yells. He NEVER shows off in a bragging manner. He is glib, suave, well-educated."[51]

More than anything, Geisel's cat was a charming and enigmatic force of nature. As Geisel's young narrator (unnamed in the book, though he would later be given the name Conrad) and his sister, Sally, sit inside on a rainy day with nothing to do, the Cat in the Hat suddenly enters their house—he doesn't knock or wait to be invited inside; his presence is marked only by a loud BUMP!—and announces matter-of-factly that he's arrived to provide "lots of good fun that is funny!" But the children's pet fish, standing in for the rule of law as well as parents everywhere, stridently advises the cat to leave, since the children are home alone. "My version of Cotton Mather," Geisel lamented.[52]

"I remember thinking I might be able to dash off *The Cat in the Hat* in two or three weeks," Geisel said later. "Actually, it took over a year." Now that he had a main character, finding things for that character to do within the confines of the word list was like putting his cat in a straitjacket. "*You* try telling a pretty complicated story using less than two hundred and fifty words!" he said with a laugh, then cautioned, "No, don't, unless you're willing to write and rewrite."[53]

And rewrite he did, over and over, with the full support, aid, and encouragement of editor Saxe Commins at Random House. "He was the kind of editor I loved," Geisel said warmly. "He would never tell you anything that you did wrong. He'd make you think, and you'd come around to your own conclusion. He'd spend an hour talking about three or four lines. He made me defend myself, telling me that what I'd said on page 7 should have been on page 3. We had almost abstract discussions of the logical order of a story." Commins, who had edited William Faulkner and Sinclair Lewis, took *The Cat in the Hat* as seriously as he did, say, Faulkner's *A Fable*, which would win the Pulitzer Prize for fiction in 1955. And Commins validated Geisel's firm belief that writing for children was as hard, if not *harder*, than writing for adults. "He helped me realize that a paragraph in a children's book is equal to a chapter in an adult book," said Geisel. "He convinced me that I had as much responsibility to take as much time and work as hard as [writers for adults] did."[54]

As Geisel slowly wrote and rewrote *The Cat in the Hat* throughout much of 1956, he figured out a few tricks to help him work around the limitations of his word list. At times, he would repeat words or phrases, which could not only make rhymes a bit easier, but also gave his verses a distinct and regular rhythm that helped young readers learn words through *look-say* repetition:

> Look at me!
> Look at me!
> Look at me NOW!
> It is fun to have fun
> But you have to know how.

"Kids don't know the words," Geisel explained later. "But we catch them with the rhythm."[55]

At another point in the narrative, Geisel places the cat on top of a ball where he balances various objects—books, cake, a rake, milk in a dish, a cup, a toy ship—which permitted Geisel to cleverly use as many of the words on his list as he could over the span of four pages. "If you drop charm, all you have is a dictionary,"[56] he cautioned, but there was little chance of Geisel's cat being charmless. Catchy rhymes aside, *The Cat in the Hat* features some of Geisel's finest art; there's not a squiggle or line wasted, backgrounds are minimal, and anything mentioned in the text is reflected in the accompanying art—consistent with the "look-say" pedagogy—all the way down to a small toy man standing on the stern of a toy ship balanced on the cat's fingertip. The time Geisel put into drawing and redrawing each page clearly shows.

The cat himself is drawn boldly and confidently—Geisel knew he had created a memorable character—with strong blacks and a minimal use of color, apart from the splash of red on his tie and the stripes on his hat. And he's constantly in motion, carrying the reader from page to page—the book literally becomes a page-turner—with arms and legs bending like rubber hoses, and feet rarely touching the ground; Geisel seemed to always catch him in mid-leap, eyebrows arched, mouth in a wide smile. Even his hat is expressive, bending to reflect the cat's mood or helpfully propping up a cake or a cup. "Ted's animals are the sort you'd like to take home to meet the family," said Helen.[57]

As the book reaches its climax, Geisel has the Cat bring in two of his associates, the rambunctious Thing One and Thing Two—each with a shock of blue hair—who seem id incarnate, flying kites in the house and messily carrying on until even Geisel's child narrator wearies of the antics. As the children's mother comes walking up the sidewalk toward the front door, the kids capture Thing One and Thing Two with a net—and the cat, sensing the fun is over, despondently packs up his wares and leaves . . . until Ted, having fooled the reader with a fake-out ending, suddenly brings the cat back, sitting smartly behind the wheel of a vehicle with mechanical arms that quickly clean up the entire mess. "I always pick up all my playthings," the cat says matter-of-factly, then scoots away—for good, this time— with a coy tip of his hat. "*The Cat in the Hat* is a revolt against authority, but it's ameliorated by the fact that the cat cleans everything up at the end," Geisel said later, sounding only a little disappointed.[58]

Geisel ends the book on a cliffhanger as the children's mother walks into the house—only her leg is visible as she steps inside the door—and asks about their day. Ted leaves the question hanging in the air for his readers to decide:

> Should we tell her about it?
> Now, what SHOULD we do?
> Well . . .
> What would YOU do?
> If your mother asked YOU?[59]

As Geisel bundled up his manuscript to send off to Commins, he knew he had something new and very different in his hands. This was a reading primer that not only had pedagogy—he had dutifully, if painfully, adhered closely to the word list, using fewer than 240 different words[60]—but also personality and punch. With its likable and somewhat subversive main character, galloping verse, and deliberate sense of humor, *The Cat in the Hat* was everything that *Dick and Jane* was not. "I think a youngster likes to read about someone who is bad for a change—then he realizes that he's not the only one who gets into trouble, messes up the house when mother is away," Geisel said in 1960. "The other thing that's new in the *Cat* is humor. Kids respond to a little humor, to a crazy situation instead of that solemn old stuff, 'See my dog, Spot. Run, Spot, run.'"[61]

Proud as he was of it, he was also likely relieved to be done with it. "*The Cat in the Hat* was not my favorite at all," Geisel said later. "It was a reading exercise. And it's painful to write when you can't use any adjectives and few nouns."[62] But Bennett Cerf was delighted with it. Cerf would always maintain that while Random House was home to many brilliant and talented authors, there was only one true genius among them: Theodor Geisel.

••••

With *The Cat in the Hat* off his desk, Ted could return to his other Dr. Seuss book—now called *How the Grinch Stole Christmas!*—whose pages he had pinned up on the corkboard lining several walls of his studio. As he paced the studio, he would slide his hands into his back pockets, palms inward, and lean slightly forward as he slowly walked along the walls, squinting at the pages. At times he might lean in and make a slight adjustment to a drawing; other times he would unpin the entire page and move it to a different spot—or he might crumple it up and throw it away. "All the walls would just be plastered with rough tissue sketchings," remembered Peggy Owens. "Sketches of what the story would be, what the layout would be, with the ideas for texts [and] crossed-out words as he refined over and over again, finding the right cadence and words to use in these stories."[63]

For the most part, writing the Grinch's story had been relatively easy—this was a regular Dr. Seuss book, not a primer, so Geisel wasn't hamstrung by a word list—and he had written much of the book in four quick months. But as he was nearing the climax of the story—the Grinch had finally successfully stolen all the trappings of Christmas from the Whos—Geisel was suddenly unsure how to end it. "The message of the book was that we are merchandising Christmas too much. But I found I could take it into very sloppy morality at the end," Geisel recalled. "I tried Old Testamenty things, New Testamenty things. It was appalling how gooey I was getting."[64]

As always, Helen was a steady head and guiding influence, as well as one of the few people who could challenge Ted's artistic instincts—especially if she thought they were wrong. One afternoon, Ted rushed excitedly out of his studio and into the living room, glasses still pushed up on his forehead, and shoved a handful of pages he'd been revising into Helen's hands. "How do you like this?" he asked her.

Helen scanned the pages, then scowled and shook her head. "No, this isn't it," she told him flatly, and turned the pages toward him to point out one particularly problematic sketch. "You've got the Papa Who too big," she told him. "Now he looks like a bug."

Flummoxed, Ted went on the defensive. "Well, they *are* bugs," he insisted.

But Helen wouldn't hear of it. "They are *not* bugs," she told him sternly. "The Whos are just small people."[65] Ted retreated to his studio to try again.

"I took a month on that last page," Ted said later.[66] "I'm really on the Grinch's side. The Grinch is against the commercialization of Christmas, although he's sort of a mean old so-and-so . . . I just couldn't resolve it because I was cheering for this guy."[67] He still worried about ending the book on a preachy note, until eventually, "I finally decided to cut the moral out and just put a quick ending on it," he explained later.[68] "I showed the Grinch and the Whos together at the table, and made a pun of the Grinch carving the 'roast beast.'"[69] After struggling with what he estimated were "thousands"[70] of overtly religious endings, Ted had gone instead for breaking bread together in the name of universal brotherhood—"without making any statement whatever," he insisted.[71]

As Ted was wrapping up work on *How the Grinch Stole Christmas!*, Helen suffered a minor stroke. Doctors kept her at the Scripps clinic for three days, during which time she lost movement in her right side and suffered from slurred speech. The symptoms would clear relatively quickly and Helen would return home to the Tower to recover. Even as he worked to finish *Grinch*, Ted did his best to tend to Helen as well, but was concerned to find her still "foggy, with lapses of memory . . . and very depressed."[72] The Geisels had planned to take a vacation to Hawaii when *Grinch* was completed, and Ted now saw the trip as a much-needed opportunity to boost Helen's spirits. He was determined to get her there as quickly as possible.

Even still, it took several more weeks for Ted to finish his book, which he dedicated to Peggy's infant son, Theodor "Teddy" Owens, named for his great-uncle. Ted mailed *How The Grinch Stole Christmas!* to Louise Bonino, along with a note reading, "Hope you like it. I'm sorta happy about the drawings."[73] There would be no public reading at the Random House offices with this one; instead, he and Helen left for Hawaii for what had become an essential vacation for both of them.

• • • •

Dr. Seuss had a blockbuster on his hands.

The April 19, 1957, press release from Random House hailed *The Cat in the Hat* as "the biggest event in children's reading for centuries"[74]— and even for Bennett Cerf, who could be inclined to hyperbole in the name of a good story, this was no overstatement. On its release in March 1957, *The Cat in the Hat* was nothing short of a phenomenon. "Hooray for Dr. Seuss!" exclaimed the *Chicago Tribune*[75] as the book blew out of department stores, where clerks could barely keep it in stock. "It became successful almost overnight due to outraged parents who were upset that their kids weren't learning how to read," said Geisel.[76] By some accounts, *The Cat in the Hat* was selling more than a thousand copies *per day*,[77] on its way to selling 250,000 copies by Christmas of 1957, and more than a million copies within three years.

William Spaulding and Houghton Mifflin, however, enjoyed very little of its success. Permitted by Cerf's agreement to sell only the textbook version to schools, Spaulding—who had seen the potential of a popular primer—watched schools respond to *The Cat in the Hat* with a shrug. "There were a lot of *Dick and Jane* devotees, and my book was considered too fresh and irreverent," said Geisel.[78] "The textbook found no acceptance whatsoever in the school system. Just a few hundred were sold here and there. When you try to get rid of *Dick and Jane*, you're in the middle of a revolution."[79]

Parents, however, were more than happy to join Dr. Seuss as fellow revolutionaries. Even if parents didn't necessarily understand the pedagogy, it was easy to see the difference between the staid *Dick and Jane* and the rambunctious *Cat in the Hat*: kids *wanted* to read about the antics of the cat, just as Geisel had hoped. "[First graders] still want to laugh at something that's ridiculous,"[80] insisted Ted, and critics were inclined to agree. "Having only a first-grade mind, I can recommend this as irresistible," wrote an enthusiastic reviewer in the *Los Angeles Times*.[81] John Hersey, whose article in *Life* had rallied Ted into action, thought Dr. Seuss had answered the call perfectly; *The Cat in the Hat*, he said, was a "gift to the art of reading," and proclaimed it "a harum-scarum masterpiece."[82] Similarly, Rudolf Flesch, who had piled onto Hersey's criticism of *Dick and Jane* in *Why Johnny Can't Read*, thought Dr. Seuss had performed nothing short of a miracle. "What exactly is it that makes this stuff [Seuss's work] immortal?" Flesch asked admiringly. "There is something about it. A swing to the language, a deep understanding of the playful mind of a child, an undefinable [*sic*] something that makes Dr. Seuss a genius, pure and simple."[83]

Many critics, too, understood the importance of what Geisel had accomplished by writing an engaging primer. "[Dr. Seuss has] done it again, only differently this time," wrote the *Chicago Tribune*. "[*The Cat in the Hat* is] a book to rejoice seven- and eight-year-olds and make them look with distinct disfavor on the drab adventures of standard primer characters."[84] And for those who appreciated the pedagogy involved, Geisel was praised for working so diligently to keep Dr. Seuss's vocabulary contained to the accepted word list. "Mr. Geisel put on his literary strait jacket [*sic*] with a purpose," wrote *The New York Times* approvingly. "It's a 'reader,' a school book, evidence of an attempt to pep up the pallid stuff too many first graders have been getting during lesson time."[85]

Using less than 250 unique words, Dr. Seuss had harpooned the *Dick and Jane* juggernaut that had dominated reading in elementary school classrooms since 1934. Ellen Goodman, writing in the *Detroit Free Press*, would later call *The Cat in the Hat* a "little volume of absurdity that worked like a karate chop on the weary little world of Dick, Jane and Spot." That was fine by Geisel. "It's the book I'm proudest of," he later said of *The Cat in The Hat*, "because it had something to do with the death of the *Dick and Jane* primers[86] . . . I think I proved to a number of million kids that reading is not a disagreeable task. And without talking about teaching, I think I have helped kids laugh in schools as well as at home. That's about enough, isn't it?"[87]

For most, it certainly *would* have been enough. But 1957 would be an extraordinary year for Ted Geisel and Dr. Seuss—for he would publish not just one bestseller with his name on it, but *two*.

Perhaps appropriately, *How the Grinch Stole Christmas!* made its debut in *Redbook*—the same magazine where an earlier incarnation of the Grinch had made an appearance selling string in 1955. Plugged on the front cover as "a new book-length holiday classic for family reading,"[88] *Grinch* was reproduced in its entirety—and in nearly full color—in the December 1957 issue, which went on sale in October. Several weeks later, on November 24, Random House published the book just in time for Christmas.

Coming in as it did on the coattails of the bestselling *The Cat in the Hat*, most reviews of *How the Grinch Stole Christmas!* seemed to be simply yelps of delight that there was already *another* Dr. Seuss book published—the *Chicago Tribune*'s effusive "Praise be! There's a fine new Dr. Seuss!"[89] was typical—and this one just in time for the holidays. Reviewers tended to simply summarize the plot, then assure parents that they would have no problem giving the *Grinch* to their children because it was, after all, a book by Dr. Seuss—and "no one can talk to children like Dr. Seuss," one reviewer said matter-of-factly.[90]

The first print run for the *Grinch* was 50,000—a large run for a children's book, but Cerf was rightly confident the book would sell quickly. Oddly, there were two other children's Christmas books published in 1957 telling stories of Christmases that were nearly canceled: Ogden Nash's *The Christmas That Almost Wasn't* and Phyllis McGinley's *The Year Without a Santa Claus*. Neither, however, could touch the *Grinch*; within days of its publication, it was clear Dr. Seuss had created an iconic Christmas classic.

While Geisel had struggled to make the ending to his story as nonreligious as possible, he was amused to find parents, critics, and religious leaders hail the book for its moral and ethical point of view. "Ministers are reading a lot of religion into it," Geisel said, practically rolling his eyes. "Ha! You can fill a vessel up with whatever you want to."[91] He often joked that he was being called the greatest moralizer since Elsie Dinsmore—a stridently moral character in a series of stridently moral books published in the late nineteenth century—but agreed that there was probably a lesson or two that could be learned in the pages of *How the Grinch Stole Christmas!* "Children have a strong ethical sense anyway," he said. "They want to see virtue rewarded and arrogance or meanness punished . . . If the Grinch steals Christmas . . . he has to bring it back in the end."[92]

But beyond the obvious right-versus-wrong morality of returning something that had been stolen, the real moral message behind *How the Grinch Stole Christmas!* could probably be found in its stance on the commercialization of Christmas—and more broadly, on the misplaced desire to equate happiness at the holidays with the acquisition of material things. If, as he said, Geisel had truly written the Grinch's story to "see if I could rediscover something about Christmas that obviously I'd lost," then he'd perhaps found it in one of *Grinch*'s most memorable tercets:

> Then the *Grinch* thought of something he hadn't before.
> Maybe *Christmas*, he thought . . . *doesn't come from a store.*
> Maybe *Christmas*, perhaps . . . means a little bit more![93]

The Grinch and Geisel appear to have had a mutual epiphany about the holiday; it was no wonder Ted confessed to be "kind of rooting" for the Grinch and even felt slightly protective of him.[94] Later, when two little boys from Ridgefield, New Jersey, named David and Bob Grinch wrote to Dr. Seuss complaining that they were picked on every Christmas because of their last name, Geisel immediately wrote back defending the Grinch. "I disagree with your friends who 'harass' you," Ted responded. "Can't they understand that the Grinch in my story is the Hero of Christmas? Sure . . . he starts out as a villain, but it's not how you start out that counts. It's what you are at the finish."[95]

Asked later which of his two superstar characters he'd rather have as a dinner guest, Ted didn't hesitate in his answer. "Kids like [the Cat in the Hat] because he's against law and order. The fact that he cleans up at the end is just an easy out; he really prefers a mess. So I wouldn't like to have him here—I'd rather visit him in *his* house," said Geisel. "[But] the Grinch? Personally, I like him."[96]

At age fifty-three, Geisel finally had his blockbuster. In 1957 alone, *The Cat in the Hat*, with a cover price of $1.95, earned more than $2 million in sales—a pace exceeded only by the year's bestselling novel, Grace Metalious's scandalous *Peyton Place*.[97] As Ted's agent, Phyllis Jackson, had predicted over their lunch several years earlier, all it took was one big book; the spectacular success of *The Cat in Hat* would be the rising tide that floated all other previously published Dr. Seuss books. *Horton Hatches the Egg*, for example, which had struggled to sell 5,801 copies in 1940, would sell 27,463 copies in 1958—and then go on to sell 200,000 more over just the next few years.

While Dr. Seuss had been something of a brand name before—after all, he had published thirteen books between 1937 and 1956—the two books published in 1957 would catapult Dr. Seuss from the status of merely beloved writer to that of national icon. Fan mail poured into the Random House offices so fast that the mailroom stopped counting individual letters and weighed the daily influx instead, eventually reporting that Dr. Seuss had received 9,267 pounds of mail for the year. Random House would forward any letters from teachers, librarians, or sick children to the Geisels in La Jolla, where Helen would personally answer every letter and sign them, charmingly, as "Mrs. Dr. Seuss."

Most of the mail, however, remained with Random House, where it was responded to with a copy of a signed form letter Ted had written and drawn, thanking the letter writer and explaining that Dr. Seuss's mail delivery was slow because he lived on a mountaintop where mail could only be delivered by a Seussian beast called a Budget, pulling a cart driven by a Nudget. Most young correspondents were delighted just to receive a response, though a few regular writers grew impatient with the repeated response. "I want a letter from you," insisted one young fan, "but not from the Budget and Nudget again."[98] Ted would eventually create several different signed form responses, hoping to soothe any hurt feelings.

More and more now, Geisel found himself being asked to make appearances at bookstores or being pressed for his autograph. There were also regular requests for interviews, and Geisel was surprised to find there was enough interest in him to make him the subject of a lengthy article in *The Saturday Evening Post*—the very same magazine where he'd seen his first professional work published three decades earlier. Such pieces could usually make Geisel sound impish and whimsical, the perfect caricature of what readers expected of a children's author. "The mind of Ted Geisel is so fanciful that he has never been able to completely subdue it," gushed the *Post* piece; there would be little or no mention of Dr. Seuss's regular drinking habits—dinner was still almost always preceded by cocktails—though Geisel's chain smoking would usually be mentioned as a matter of course. Lately Ted had been trying to break the habit by sucking on a pipe stuffed with radish or strawberry seeds; when he felt the urge to smoke, he would water the seeds with an eyedropper. Eventually the seeds would sprout and Geisel would return to cigarettes again. He would get a great deal of mileage out of having himself photographed clamping down on a pipe with a sprout growing out of it.

Bennett Cerf wasn't the only one impressed by *The Cat in the Hat*; so, too, was his wife, Phyllis, a dynamic and talented former actress, newspaper writer, and advertising executive.[99] One evening Phyllis came to her husband with an unconventional idea; she had been talking about *The Cat in the Hat* with Louise Bonino and both had come to appreciate that Geisel had created something new and entirely unique by writing an entertaining children's primer. Phyllis suggested to her husband that Random House set up an imprint dedicated solely to publishing other children's books just like it—books with a deliberate pedagogy, but also fun and entertaining so that kids would actually *want* to read them.

Cerf was intrigued. While the publisher's own tastes ran toward more traditional adult fare—"Ted and *Babar* were the only children's books that Bennett wasn't condescending about," said one Random House editor[100]—the numbers couldn't be ignored. With the sales of *Cat in the Hat* and the entire Dr. Seuss library exploding, Random House had suddenly found itself positioned as the largest publisher of juvenile books in the United States. It was an idea worth pursuing—and it didn't hurt that Bennett Cerf adored Ted Geisel.

Sometime in late 1957, then, during one of Ted's regular trips to New York, Phyllis invited him to lunch at the upscale Quo Vadis restaurant on East 63rd Street. Over French food and fine wine, Phyllis explained to Ted that *Cat in the Hat* had opened up an enormous creative opportunity and a potentially lucrative market for quality children's readers. She proposed creating a new imprint inside Random House—she and Bennett had already decided it would be called Beginner Books—that would use the list of approved vocabulary words, but would also ideally do what *The Cat in the Hat* had done so well: straddle the line between pedagogy and pleasure. Further, she envisioned launching the new imprint with four or five books, leading to ongoing regular releases every year. Cerf was committed, she told Ted, but the entire initiative depended on one thing: the involvement of Dr. Seuss. Phyllis promised him he could be president of the new imprint. All he had to do was say yes.

Geisel *was* interested. Phyllis Cerf had teed the question up perfectly, appealing to both his ego and his sense of obligation to producing quality books for children. "Writing for adults doesn't really interest me anymore," he would say later. "I think I've found the form in writing for kids, with which I can say everything I have to say a little more distinctly than if I had to put it in adult prose."[101] As the head of an imprint, Geisel would have the opportunity to recruit and select writers and illustrators, and put them to work under his own rigorous standards to produce a line of books that he hoped would encourage better reading habits for an entire generation.

If Phyllis wanted him, there were two conditions he wanted met. First, he wanted the ability to continue to produce Dr. Seuss books that weren't under the Beginner Books imprint or its limitations—that meant that while *The Cat in the Hat* would bear the Beginner Books imprint, a book like *How the Grinch Stole Christmas!* wouldn't. Second, he wanted Helen to join the effort as an equal partner and editor—a move Ted had proposed largely to ensure that he could outvote Phyllis two to one on any matters that required consensus. As the meal ended, Ted and Phyllis shook hands. They had a deal.

It was the beginning of a productive and unbearably terrible relationship.

PART III

OH, THE THINKS YOU CAN THINK UP IF ONLY YOU TRY

CHAPTER 11

BEGINNER BOOKS

1958–1960

'd say that the most useful of [my] books is *The Cat in the Hat*," Geisel told *The New York Times* in 1962. "That had a different purpose—to help reading—and it goes back to my old ambition to be an educator."[1] Such noble ambitions aside, there was no denying that *The Cat in the Hat* was also a publishing powerhouse—and the savvy Phyllis Cerf had cannily seen that there was money to be made in producing reading primers that children actually *wanted* to read.

Geisel had responded to Phyllis's offer to go into business together with excited skepticism. The deal had been sealed on a conditional handshake that would permit him to continue to produce his own books independently of their new venture, and—perhaps more critically—brought in Helen as a full partner, giving him, in the event of a conflict, a potential tie-breaking vote. Phyllis—who knew her new Beginner Books imprint needed Dr. Seuss more than it needed her—willingly signed off on Geisel's conditions; as far as she could tell, both she and Geisel had high demands, high expectations, and mutually big plans for their new imprint. Disagreements, she thought, would be minimal.

"We want to publish books that take up where textbooks leave off," Phyllis excitedly told *Publishers Weekly* as she and Ted officially launched Beginner Books in June 1958.[2] Their bold new idea—an entire line of accessible primers!—was met with some skepticism from teachers and parents alike. *The Cat in the Hat* was one thing. Could Beginner Books continue to produce similarly fun, easy-to-read books year after year, even with the steady hand of Dr. Seuss at the helm? It remained to be seen—and even Dr. Seuss himself wasn't certain. "When we started Beginner Books we had no idea what we were doing," Geisel admitted later. "It was *really* an 'empty' mind."[3]

The first order of business, then, was to formally establish the imprint as an independent corporation, with Ted serving as president, Phyllis as its chief executive, and Helen as an equal but untitled partner. While Random House would serve as the distributor for all Beginner Books, the imprint remained otherwise free from oversight or influence of its publisher—or at least *mostly*. Random House would still provide the initial loan of $200,000 that Beginner Books needed to start recruiting, and then paying for, the stable of writers and artists that would be needed to produce a steady stream of books. The money would also be used to fund a hundred shares of Beginner Books stock, valued at thirty dollars per share, to be divided among the partners.

All Beginner Books would go through the imprint's editorial board, comprised solely of Ted, Helen, and Phyllis, with mostly Phyllis and Ted empowered to decide what got published and what didn't. As president, as well as the only one of the three partners with a bestseller to his name, Ted tended to believe his editorial opinion mattered the most—and Ted *did* have strong views on the creative philosophy of Beginner Books that would come to define their look and feel.

As always, he dismissed the "*Bunny Bunny* books . . . sugar plums, treacle, whimsy."[4] Kids of the late 1950s, Ted explained in *The New York Times*, had been brought up on television, where they could visit exciting places like the Old West or outer space with the twist of a dial. "Practically every book that [a child] is able to read is far beneath his intellectual capacity," Geisel wrote sadly. "At age six, [a child] has seen more of life than his great-grandfather had seen when he died at the age of 90."[5] The biggest sin a Beginner Book author could commit, then, was that of condescending to children. "Most people who write children's books try to write for the child," said Ted. "I write for myself. Anyone who fills a page with, 'Run, John, run. See, Mary, see,' is insulting the intelligence of the youngster. I wouldn't treat a kid that way!"[6]

Phyllis Cerf, for the most part, seemed happy to acquiesce to Ted's philosophic views of the imprint. The real strength of Beginner Books, she thought, was in their pedagogic rigor—that is, how closely they adhered to the approved word list. And Phyllis took the word list *very* seriously, poring through countless reading primers to compile a list of words that showed up on *every* list. Eventually, Beginner Books would provide its authors with an alphabetical listing of 361 accepted words—"words which appear in the leading first grade textbooks, and which young readers have learned by sight"—and authors were encouraged to tell their stories using 200 unique words or less. Authors were given other explicit restrictions as well:

> No "ed," "ing," or "er" endings except those specifically listed can be used in a Beginner Book. Plurals <u>are</u> allowed, if they can be made by adding only an "s." Only the listed contractions can be used. NO POSSESSIVES ARE ALLOWED.[7]

Included within the list of 361 words were 74 words marked with an asterisk—words like *another*, *maybe*, and *surprised*—which were words that did *not* appear in every primer Phyllis had consulted. Authors were advised to use these words only "with care and in strong context." Finally, Beginner Books authors were permitted to use up to twenty "emergency words"—words that didn't appear on the list at all and had to be "absolutely necessary to the story," like names for characters.

Ted knew from experience that the word list could be a challenge. "The writer gets his first ghastly shock when he learns about a diabolical little thing known as 'The List,'" Ted wrote. "School book publishing houses all have little lists. Lists of words that kids can be expected to read, at various states in their progress through the elementary grades."[8] While Ted had sweated the use of the word list while working on *Cat in the Hat*, he was now publicly assuring would-be authors that it had all come naturally to him, "because I had a 17-year career as an advertising copy writer in which I used only four words."[9]

The Beginner Books editorial team threw a wide net in its search for authors to write and illustrate their five debut titles, to be published concurrently—and with great fanfare—in the autumn of 1958. Ted approached his old Dartmouth pal Mike McClintock—the former Vanguard editor whose chance encounter with Ted in 1937 led to the publication of *And to Think That I Saw It on Mulberry Street*—as well as P. D. Eastman, who had helped bring *Gerald McBoing-Boing* to UPA but hadn't yet written a children's book. Phyllis recruited several established children's authors, including Marion Holland, who had written books for Knopf like *Billy Had a System*, and who was also a strict grammarian—just the sort of pedant Phyllis admired.

And of course it was a given that the imprint would also kick off with a brand-new book by Dr. Seuss. While he was never expressly told to do so, the unspoken expectation was that, with *The Cat in the Hat* still selling 2,500 copies a week nearly a year after its publication, Ted would write a sequel to his bestseller. And so Ted had grudgingly started work on *The Cat in the Hat Comes Back*, with the Cat returning to cause more chaos on a winter day, creating a pink bathtub ring that transfers from one surface to another until it ends up tinting the snow. It wasn't one of Ted's more remarkable efforts, but for the moment, he was more interested in his role as president of Beginner Books than his role as an author.

Already Phyllis Cerf wasn't making things easy for him. "She is a woman who loves combat," remembered Phyllis's son Christopher, "and Ted was so much the other way."[10] Right away she and Ted bickered over P. D. Eastman's rookie effort, an innocuous book called *Sam and the Firefly*. It was bad enough that Eastman had used the word *firefly*, which wasn't on the word list—but both *fire* and *fly* were, so it might be argued that *firefly* could scrape by on a technicality. Ted's real heart-burn, however, was with Sam, who was an *owl*—a word that *also* wasn't on the word list, but Eastman had cleverly opted to simply write around it, referring to his main character only as Sam, and never as an owl. But for Ted, this created an unresolvable conflict between the text and the artwork: it wasn't right, he argued, to have a drawing of an owl without ever identifying it to readers by that term—especially when it was the main character. "It's not easy to write Beginner Books," Ted explained patiently, "and we have trouble finding people who can write and illustrate them to the satisfaction of the editors."[11]

Phyllis *was* satisfied with Eastman's book and was pushing for its acceptance and publication. But with Helen in Ted's corner, the Geisels could overrule Phyllis—just as Ted had intended. "Ted and I don't think [the books] are awful good, but they're as good as we can make them," Helen said.[12] Frustrated, Phyllis eventually pulled rank on the Geisels and pled Eastman's case to a respected third party, senior Random House editor Donald Klopfer, who all but ordered the Geisels to accept *Sam and the Firefly* and call a truce with Phyllis. "There is no question about whether we should publish [the book]," Klopfer wrote Helen in late 1958:

> This has developed into a moral question . . . [Beginner
> Books has] given our word [to Eastman] and to me this is
> inviolable . . . You use the words "honest,"
> "straightforward" and "integrity" in your letter. God knows
> that must apply to the people who are running it or it
> won't percolate down to the books themselves. Helen, I
> beg of you . . . agree—even though you hate the book.[13]

Chastised, the Geisels and Phyllis would enter into an uneasy dé-tente and Eastman's book would become one of the first five titles published by Beginner Books in late 1958—along with Ted's *The Cat in the Hat Comes Back*, McClintock's *A Fly Went By*, Holland's *A Big Ball of String*, and Benjamin Elkin and Katherine Evans's *The Big Jump and Other Stories*.

It was not a harmonious start for the new partners. Publicly, however, Ted was all smiles, diligently promoting the new imprint and writing a thoughtful piece for *Book Chat* magazine equating literacy with civic responsibility. Good books made for good citizens, he explained—and he and the Beginner Books team were doing their best to give young readers "stuff that is more interesting to read."[14] Reviewers tended to agree that the first five Beginner Books were doing just that. "Parents whose children are just beginning to read can hardly go wrong with any of them," wrote one enthusiastic critic.[15] While *The Cat in the Hat Comes Back* tended to draw the most attention and praise, critics also acknowledged the general quality of the other four titles, each "with varying appeal, but all excellent for beginners."[16]

That included *Sam and the Firefly*.

• • • •

When Ted wasn't serving as president of Beginner Books, he could still be Dr. Seuss, writing and drawing his own books, independent of the Beginner Books imprint. Ted would come to call these his "Big Books," due mainly to their physical size—about 11 by 8 inches, compared to the Beginner Books, which were roughly 9 by 7 inches—which permitted him to really cover the page with art from one edge of the page to the other. Better yet, he was also free of the restrictions of the Beginner Books word list—though the project he had pinned to his corkboard in the early weeks of 1958 would cause him headaches for the use of a single, controversial word: *burp*.

Yertle the Turtle began strictly as a doodling exercise—a common enough way for Ted to try to spawn an idea. "[My books] always start as a doodle," he said later. "I may doodle a couple of animals; if they bite each other, it's going to be a good book."[17] In this particular case, the animals didn't bite; they simply stacked one on top of another, as

Ted drew one turtle—and he was never sure why he had started with a turtle—then drew another and another until he had a stack of them. As he had done years earlier, when he had Horton the elephant up in a tree, he had to determine what the story now was—who was the turtle at the top?

Channeling the language of his days at *PM*, Geisel decided the top turtle must be "a little domineering guy who pushes people around"[18]— and then suddenly realized the domineering turtle *had* to be Adolf Hitler. "I couldn't draw Hitler as a turtle," Geisel said later, though for a moment, he considered drawing Yertle with the familiar Hitler mustache before deciding "it was gilding the lily a bit."[19] Instead, "I drew him as King What-ever-his-name-was, King of the Pond. He wanted to be king as far as he could see," explained Geisel. "So he kept piling them up. He conquered Central Europe and France, and there it was. Then I had this great pileup, and I said, 'How do you get rid of this impostor?'"[20]

It was a question Geisel couldn't answer for some time. Typically, he paced his office, absently smoking one cigarette after another, or threw himself down on the couch, one arm across his face, covering his eyes, as he moaned his way through his predicament. "I think writing is the worst job that anyone ever got into," Helen wrote sympathetically.[21] But Ted had found his ending. What brought down despots? Ted decided it was "the voice of the people." More specifically, "I said, 'Well, I'll just simply have the guy on the bottom burp.'"[22] Never was the precarious foundation on which fascists build made so successfully literal than when Mack, the turtle at the bottom of the turtle pile, burped loudly, sending the stack of turtles tumbling and plunging Yertle the Turtle into the mud.

It was an elegant, albeit controversial, conclusion. "I used the word *burp*, and nobody had ever burped before in the pages of a children's book," said Ted. "It took a decision from the president of the publishing house before my vulgar turtle was permitted to do so."[23] The Hitler metaphor, however, went unquestioned.

Yertle the Turtle was published in April 1958—around the time Ted,

Helen, and Phyllis Cerf were starting their hunt for Beginner Books authors—and landed in bookstores matter-of-factly, with excited announcements of its arrival but few real reviews. It was the third Dr. Seuss book in two years; for most, that was enough. The book would go on to be one of the best-loved and most-talked-about Dr. Seuss books—a relief to Ted, who knew he was taking a chance by writing a book with an explicit message. While readers had long been reading morals into his previous books—the Grinch was a favorite to pick through—Ted usually insisted they were reading too much into things. "There is a moral inherent in any damn thing you write that has a dramatic point," he argued pointedly. "People change places, and with any resolution of conflict or narrative motion, a moral is implied." But that wasn't the case with Yertle, who was "a deliberate parable of the life of Hitler."[24]

While most readers were thrilled to watch the tyrannical Yertle get his comeuppance at the end, there were some who later puzzled over Dr. Seuss's final couplet:

> And the turtles, of course . . . all the turtles are free
> As turtles and, maybe, all creatures should be.[25]

In an interview, Geisel was asked why his concluding line used the equivocal *maybe* instead of the more definitive *surely*. "I qualified that in order to avoid sounding too didactic or like a preacher on a platform," Ted explained. "And I wanted *other* persons, like yourself, to say 'surely' in their minds instead of my having to say it."[26]

Geisel had dedicated *Yertle the Turtle* to the families of two of his oldest and dearest friends: his Dartmouth classmate Donald Bartlett, and Joseph Sagmaster, who had formally introduced Helen to Ted at Oxford. Perhaps because of his newly prominent role as a leading advocate for children's literacy, Ted was feeling particularly in awe of Bartlett, one of Dartmouth's most respected educators. "I stack you up on the top of my list as one of the greatest successes I have ever known," Geisel wrote to his old friend. "You are tops among the few dedicated people who are doing the most important, most under-paid goddamn necessary job in the world. You are doing what I didn't have guts enough to do, because I took the easier path. A much much easier path than you have taken."[27]

Bartlett, with perhaps an equal reverence for Geisel, generously offered to host the Geisels in Hanover in the late summer of 1958. It was partly a thank-you for the dedication in *Yertle the Turtle,* but Bartlett had other motives as well: Geisel had recently promised his alma mater he would donate his original manuscripts to the college in his will—and maybe, he hinted, a little bit more—and Dartmouth was eager to show its appreciation. The Geisels made the trip to Hanover, and Ted trekked over to meet Bartlett on the Dartmouth campus, where he was stunned to find the faculty had arranged to have him greeted by reception committee, which included nearly a hundred children dressed as Dr. Seuss characters. After being serenaded by the costumed children, Ted was led to an old convertible Packard Phaeton and slowly driven around the campus, where he was swarmed by even larger crowds of children, who pressed scraps of paper and copies of *The Cat in the Hat* and *Yertle the Turtle* into his hands to be autographed.

Ted was furious about all the fuss and grumbled to Bartlett that he was reconsidering his promise to donate his manuscripts. He eventually cooled down—"Dartmouth will always be number one for me," he said[28]—and insisted that he had only been joking. "They don't come any better than Ted," said Bartlett later, sounding slightly relieved. "He has a wonderful sense of humor and is always fun to be with."[29] In the end, however, most of Geisel's original manuscripts would be donated to the University of California at San Diego, much closer to La Jolla.

Regardless of Geisel's discomfort at being paraded around campus, however, there was no denying that crowds of fans were becoming inevitable—and in late 1958, with *Yertle the Turtle* selling strongly and Beginner Books picking up steam, Bennett Cerf made the decision to pair

Geisel with a savvy new sales and marketing manager, a freckled thirty-four-year-old named Robert Bernstein. Bernstein had started his career running errands at rival publisher Simon & Schuster, and as he slowly made his way up in the corporate structure, he discovered he had a knack for the marketing of children's books and authors. During his twelve years with Simon & Schuster, Bernstein had worked diligently with *Eloise* creator Kay Thompson on marketing and securing her subsidiary rights—earning the eternal gratitude of Ms. Thompson, who continued to retain Bernstein's services even after he was hired away by Bennett Cerf.

Now in his first months as a sales manager for Random House, Bernstein was itching to get his hands on Dr. Seuss. Bernstein was immediately smitten with Geisel, finding him "charming, modest, and funny," and explained that he wanted to apply to Dr. Seuss the same strategy he'd brought to *Eloise*: promotion, promotion, promotion. "I told [Ted] that we could really increase his sales if children got to know Dr. Seuss," recalled Bernstein, who suggested sending Geisel on a book tour of some of the major midwestern and northeastern booksellers, most of which were large department stores. "Author tours weren't really a commonplace thing," said Bernstein, "but I thought the publicity we could generate through word of mouth would be more valuable than any advertising we could do."[30]

And so Bernstein had arranged for Geisel to visit ten cities, stretching from Boston to Minneapolis, where he would sit for press conferences and lunches, meet with store managers and librarians, and sign books for crowds that seemed to only grow larger as he moved from city to city. At Marshall Field & Company in Chicago, the line snaked through most of the department store, requiring five ushers to keep things organized and moving. In Detroit—where Geisel arrived by helicopter, to the delight of shrieking children—the Northland branch of Hudson's department store had to stay open an extra two hours to accommodate the crowds, while the central branch was so mobbed during Geisel's signing that his table was eventually moved from the cramped book section to the larger cafeteria. In

Cleveland, Higbee's department store required tickets for Geisel's appearance, and were stunned when all five hundred tickets immediately sold out. On the day of Geisel's signing, the line of ticket holders stretched out the door, with patrons standing in the rain for more than an hour just for the opportunity to shake the hand of Dr. Seuss.[31]

Despite his distaste for crowds or public appearances, Geisel found he enjoyed meeting with his readers, who came in all ages, colors, and sizes. Ted took special care to spend a few moments with each child as he or she approached his table, and objected when one store began removing from the autograph line any children who hadn't purchased a book for him to sign; Ted made it a policy of signing almost *anything* a child put in front of him, whether it was a book, an index card, or a crumpled piece of paper. Still, being Dr. Seuss came with its hazards; at one store, a woman carrying a two-year-old on her shoulder—with "his fist in his mouth," recalled Geisel—sidled over to his table and told her son to remove his hand from his mouth to shake hands with Dr. Seuss. "And he did," said Geisel, shuddering only slightly at the memory.[32] But "meeting all those kids was wonderful," he said later.[33]

He also liked Bob Bernstein, who shared his affinity for practical jokes. During a signing in Chicago, Geisel found himself shadowed by a local entertainer dressed in Native American attire and called Chief White Cloud, who prowled the lines of autograph seekers, chatted up parents, and then signed his own name in copies of *Yertle the Turtle* or *The Cat in the Hat*. At Geisel's request, Bernstein shooed away the interloper—but a few days later, at a stop in Minneapolis, Bernstein sneakily scrawled *Chief White Cloud* on the title page of a few books. When Ted saw the signature, he roared with laughter. "Bob!" he shouted to Bernstein. "The damned Indian has followed us all the way to Minneapolis!"[34]

It was Bernstein, too, who badgered Geisel into permitting his characters to be licensed for marketing—a creative decision that had made Kay Thompson a very rich woman. While Geisel had allowed some very limited marketing of his creations in the past, like the mounted Seuss animal heads, these were the exceptions, not the rule—and Geisel had been largely in control of the products anyway. But Bernstein could practically smell the money to be made in an officially sanctioned line of Dr. Seuss merchandise. "Once started, a property develops like a snowball rolling down a mountain," Bernstein wrote in a memo to Donald Klopfer. "I've worked myself into an absolute frenzy thinking about merchandising Dr. Seuss."[35]

Dr. Seuss was skeptical, but Bernstein was persuasive—and in 1958, the Revell company was permitted to produce a series of small, colorful plastic Seussian animals with removable arms, heads, legs, and other body parts that could be assembled and reassembled in nearly infinite ways. Revell, known for their plastic model kits, was thrilled to have a licensed Dr. Seuss product, but at a cost: namely, Geisel insisted on being involved in nearly every step of the process, even providing the sculpted molds that Revell's engineers would use to cast the figures. "I would sculpt them, and the engineer would work them, and I would resculpt them, and the engineer would change them, and I would resculpt them and so on," said Geisel.[36] Figures were reworked constantly so they could stand on their own when assembled. "None of my animals have joints and none of them balance,"[37] Geisel sighed. As the plastic figures moved through production, Geisel would hover over the engineers as they worked at the Revell factory in Venice, California—the same factory that made plastic parts for Convair aircraft—and look for any imperfections. At one point, he confessed to "causing a hullaballoo over the animals not fitting," thus forcing Revell to shut down their production line for ten hours until the problem was resolved.[38]

The fuss, however, seemed worth it. "The hottest items we have for pure enthusiasm," announced Revell—and Geisel had to admit he loved playing with the plastic figures, even permitting Revell to photograph him pulling them apart and reassembling them, one eyebrow cocked approvingly at the camera. The toys went on sale in September 1959 and quickly became one of Revell's bestselling products. Bernstein had been right: people wanted Dr. Seuss toys.

Bennett Cerf, too, could come up with his own savvy marketing initiatives. A witty raconteur, Cerf had become something of a household name with his regular appearances on the CBS-TV quiz show *What's My Line?* Cerf had run a charm offensive with executives at CBS and secured Geisel an appearance on the show *To Tell the Truth*, where celebrity panelists tried to decide which of three gentlemen before them was the real Dr. Seuss. Only one panelist, the entertainment reporter Hy Gardner, chose Geisel—even though "he doesn't look like a cartoonist," said Gardner—with most of the panelists voting for a grinning gentleman named Burton Browne, who turned out to be the founder of a series of gentleman's nightclubs.

For the most part, though, Cerf stayed out of the way, preferring to cheer Geisel on with encouraging notes and to count the money Random House was making as the distributor for Beginner Books. In March of 1959, he enthusiastically reported to Geisel that after only eight months, sales of Beginner Books were exploding. "The net result is simply amazing," Cerf wrote, "and I doubt whether anything like it has ever been pulled off in the whole damn publishing business heretofore."[39] He also asked Geisel for one of the Revell model kits—"so that I can play with it myself!"—and told Ted and Helen he was setting aside "a whole office here for Beginner Books, but don't want to do anything definite until you both get here and can approve it in person."[40]

Ted definitely approved—surprising, since the space had been conceived by Phyllis, who had envisioned the area as a whimsical attic taking up most of the sixth floor. A false floor had been constructed to elevate the entire Beginner Books suite to halfway to the ceiling, accessible by a short flight of carpeted stairs. This had the effect of pushing the Beginner Books offices up under the eaves of the sixth floor, giving their headquarters the look and feel of a clubhouse for grown-ups. Ted loved it, decorating desks with silly nameplates for nonexistent staff—there was one for Dr. Valerie Vowel, Director of Consonants—and making signs with colorful arrows pointing the way for visitors the moment they stepped off the elevator. One sign read *etaoinshrdlu*—an in-joke among publishers, as it was the lettering sequence linotype typesetters used to fill blank lines—while at the foot of the stairs leading to the office door was an arrow-shaped sign reading, "This way to Dr. Schmierkase,"[41] the name of a fictional editor Ted had created solely to take the blame for rejecting manuscripts.[42]

The West Coast headquarters for Beginner Books wasn't nearly as quirky; it was mostly just Helen's office, which had been built into one section of the garage at the Tower. Framed and hanging on one wall was a needlepoint given to her by Phyllis Cerf of the Cat in the Hat, on which Phyllis herself had embroidered THIS CAT STARTED A PUBLISHING HOUSE. NO OTHER CAT CAN MAKE THIS CLAIM. While Helen was content to let Ted—or at least, Dr. Seuss—remain the public face of Beginner Books, she, too, was actively involved in the recruitment of authors and editing of their books. And like Ted, she, too, was squabbling with Phyllis.

For Helen, the contentious book was *You Will Go to the Moon* by Mae and Ira Freeman, who had written several children's science books for Random House, like *Fun with Astronomy*. Helen found the Freemans' main character to be "lunkheaded," and argued that they had depicted the moon as "a dusty, rather disappointing locale." Phyllis, as she had done during her dispute with Ted over *Sam and the Firefly*, opted to pull rank on Helen and consulted first with noted chemist and Nobel laureate Harold Urey—who confirmed that the moon was, indeed, dusty and disappointing—then went straight to Bennett Cerf and demanded he order Helen to accept the Freemans' book. Helen grudgingly accepted *You Will Go to the Moon*, but the Ted-Helen-Phyllis relationship would continue to erode. Bennett Cerf, meanwhile, with his head spinning, pled with the Beginner Books team to stop recruiting from his roster of Random House authors. (That prohibition, however, didn't apply to Cerf himself, who would have several books published under the Beginner Books imprint, including *Bennett Cerf's Book of Laughs* and *Bennett Cerf's Book of Animal Riddles*.)

Cerf's ban on poaching Random House talent also didn't discourage Ted from going after one of Cerf's breakout authors, Truman

Capote, whose novella *Breakfast at Tiffany's* had been a sensation on its publication in 1958. Unfortunately, Capote had delivered a disappointing first draft, and Ted didn't have the nerve to deliver the bad news, leaving the task to Phyllis, who "had to tell Truman that Ted didn't feel it publishable."[43] Years later, Ted was happy to let the story of Capote's rejected children's book transform into something of an urban legend that concluded with *Ted* firing Capote, instead of Phyllis.

Author selection aside, Ted was continuing to lay down a strict set of rules for authors to follow, usually having to do with the relationship between the text and the art. There could only be one drawing per page, for instance, and the illustration could *not* show anything that wasn't included in the text—and to the extent possible, illustrations should contain as many of the items mentioned in the accompanying text. Some authors grumbled that Ted was trying to turn each book into a Dr. Seuss book—but Ted really believed he had done enough time in the trenches to know what worked best. "If a book pleases me, it has a chance of pleasing children," he explained.[44] "I changed the rules, based on my belief that a child could learn any amount of words if fed them slowly, and if the books were amply illustrated. We began to concentrate our efforts on linking the artwork with the text."[45]

Ted also continued to rail against any authors who he thought were writing down to children ("They see right through you," he warned would-be authors)[46] or—worse—tried to write the kind of book they thought kids were *supposed* to read, which usually resulted in Ted dismissing their manuscript as one of the dreaded *Bunny Bunny* books. He was also a stickler about ensuring stories had an internal consistency. "Children are tough critics," said Ted. "You can't kid kids. They have a relentless sense of logic."[47] His own approach, he said, was to stick to what he called "logical insanity." "If I start with a two-headed animal, I must never waver from that concept," he explained. "There must be two hats in the closet, two toothbrushes in the bathroom, and two sets of spectacles on the night table."[48]

The logical insanity seemed to be working; by mid-1959, Beginner Books, with first printings of more than 60,000 each, was becoming one of the most profitable lines at Random House, surging past even the distinguished Modern Library imprint. "Whoopee! We're in the black after four months!" wrote Helen after learning of their profits.[49] Ted's own "Big Books," too, were selling so briskly that they earned him $200,000 in 1959—about $1.7 million today—easily outpacing the earnings of most bestselling novelists of the time. Ted's latest book, *Happy Birthday to You!*, released in November that year, would continue the string of Seussian successes, blowing through its print run of 100,000 copies in only a few weeks.

Happy Birthday to You! was a beautifully produced book, with each page painted in rich, full color—his first full-color book since *McElligot's Pool*. Following the flight of the Birthday Bird in the Land of Katroo as it guides a child through all-day birthday festivities, *Happy Birthday to You!* was also a celebration of one's own uniqueness, containing what would become one of Dr. Seuss's most inspiring and oft-quoted couplets:

> Today you are you! That is truer than true!
> There is no one alive who is you-er than you![50]

Ted had dedicated the book to "my good friends, The Children of San Diego County." And he *was* genuinely fond of the children in his neighborhood, even if at times he found them slightly exasperating. The Geisels' doorbell at the Tower was regularly rung by young fans who had made the trek up Mount Soledad to say hello to Dr. Seuss, often waking him up on mornings when he was trying to sleep late. He also worried that once he staggered downstairs, children who expected Dr. Seuss to "be wearing a hat" and baggy clown pants would be disappointed by the bleary-eyed, slightly disheveled, but otherwise normal-looking man who answered the door.[51]

It wasn't only children who knocked on the front door of the Tower.

Summertime, in particular, brought tourists—"white trash," muttered Helen[52]—some harmless, who merely came to gawk, but also a fair share of what Helen called "the crackpots, would-be authors, PTA's, and visiting friends of sub-cousins, aunts-in-law."[53] And for those who saw Dr. Seuss as their Patron Saint of Literacy, the Tower became something of a mecca for well-intended librarians and reading teachers. "It sometimes seems to me that half the teachers and librarians in America come to La Jolla for their holidays," said Ted.[54]

Interruptions notwithstanding, however, Ted and Helen loved their lives at the Tower. The home seemed to be in a constant state of improvement now, as new rooms were added—it would eventually be expanded to nine rooms, including a huge mirrored dining room—and all completed in an elegant Spanish style, with a pink stucco exterior and a rust-red tiled roof. There were outdoor pavilions and shady sitting areas dotted with flowering bushes and trees, and Ted and Helen still enjoyed having morning coffee and evening cocktails as they sat by the swimming pool, where Helen still swam for therapy most mornings.

While Ted loved gardening, his real passion was *rock* gardening, hunting for interesting rocks on the hillside, then positioning them dramatically around the yard, lining paths or making borders around the succulents he had planted in the rich California soil. "That's what I do," said Ted. "I have a rock garden. And then I get tired of looking at the rocks in one arrangement, and so I move them."[55] The showcase of his collection, however, was the fossilized dinosaur footprint his father had given him decades ago, and which he had hauled from New York and now had displayed prominently in his garden. "Ted has no extravagances," said Helen. "I can't think of anything he likes except cigarettes and rocks."[56]

One probably needed to define *extravagances*, however. Even a mostly clear-eyed profile of Ted and Helen in *The New Yorker*—written by one of the magazine's most distinguished contributors, E. J. Kahn—tried to explain with a mostly straight face how the Geisels lived in "relative austerity" by noting that they "have only one car, only one maid—part-time, at that—and only one swimming pool."[57] Still, Ted ended up enjoying the four days he had spent being interviewed by Kahn and was relatively pleased with the lengthy profile—at least at first. Typically, he would later complain that the piece had been "butchered . . . They took out all the funny stuff."[58]

At age fifty-five, Ted was as trim as ever; he still looked good in a suit, though his preferred attire for lounging around the house was comfortable trousers and colorful shirts. His hair—always messy, and still parted in the middle—had grown streaked with gray, and the lines at the corners of his eyes were more pronounced, due in no small part to his habit of squinting over his pages as he drew and colored them. While he still relied on glasses to correct his sight, he often could be found hunched over his desk with his glasses pushed up just above his eyebrows, looking like another set of eyes on his forehead. Helen, meanwhile, who would turn sixty-one that fall, seemed mostly recovered from her earlier hospitalizations. Only a very slight slur in her speech gave any indication she had ever had a stroke, for she remained mentally as sharp as ever.

And yet even as a full partner in Beginner Books—with her own books to edit and her own authors to recruit—Helen remained deferential to Ted, still managing his finances and correspondence, and still checking on him during the days to see if his coffee needed refilling or if he was ready to break for cocktails at six. While Helen maintained her own work schedule, it was clearly Ted's whose mattered the most—as far as Helen was concerned, Ted was working *two* jobs, one as president of Beginner Books and the other as Dr. Seuss. While one visiting journalist from Dartmouth called them "virtually inseparable,"[59] Helen thought they often seemed perpetually out of sync. There were times, she admitted, when "it is quite difficult for me . . . because the very time I make no plans seems to be the times he wants to go out, and when I have a lot of people coming, he wants to work."[60]

At the moment, Ted's work schedule was more demanding than

usual as he worked to complete his next Beginner Book, *One Fish Two Fish Red Fish Blue Fish*. Every day, including weekends, Ted would get out of bed a little after nine, to be at his desk in the studio no later than ten. And there he would stay all day, seated at the desk in a high-backed swivel chair, even if no ideas were coming. He insisted on quiet while he worked—there would be no records, no radio, no background noise of any kind—but would permit himself short breaks to swim, move around the rocks in his rock garden, or take a walk. And as usual, when stuck, he would doodle aimlessly—still using the same drawing board he'd been using since he had set up shop in his father's office in 1927—or would lie down on the sofa by the fireplace, where he would read mystery novels or biographies.

He thought his best ideas came "on toward midnight" when he was "a bit tired,"[61] though it helped, too, that neither the phone nor the doorbell rang at that time of night. He often said he would start a book "with a situation or a conflict and then write myself into an impossible position so there is no way of ending," and then work his way toward *finding* the ending ("people who think about endings first come up with inferior products," he groused).[62] In the case of *One Fish Two Fish*, Ted had sweated over his word count for months, and thought he at last had a finished book pinned to the corkboard of his office—but then couldn't stop messing with it. Helen assured him the book was a winner, maintaining that he should leave it alone. "Now, if I can just keep Ted from fussing with it and telling me that it is no good," she wrote to Bennett Cerf with just a touch of impatience. "He gets me to the point where I don't know what is or what isn't, or was or wasn't, or could be or would be or should be."[63]

Ted had reason to be anxious about *One Fish Two Fish Red Fish Blue Fish*. The book was an experiment of sorts—he was calling it a pre–Beginner Book—"a book based on an educational theory I have, but one that unfortunately I can't define," he said rather unhelpfully. His unnamed theory was that children would learn to recognize familiar words if the corresponding illustrations were placed as close to the words as possible—and thus, on the opening page of *One Fish Two Fish*

Red Fish Blue Fish, he had placed the text as close as he could to each of the named fish.

Geisel was inconsistent in the execution of his own proximity theory as the book went on, at times dismissing the practice altogether in favor of increasingly sillier and tongue-twistier rhymes—but Geisel thought the rhymes, too, helped children learn to read. "Rhyming more or less makes kids pronounce words correctly," he insisted. "For instance, if a youngster is sounding out the words, what a help when 'sing' is related to 'ying' and 'thing.'"[64] What Ted was doing with rhyme was actually closer in practice to the teaching of phonics, which had fallen out of favor with many educators, who still preferred the "look-say" approach to reading embraced by *The Cat in the Hat*. Lately, however, schools were beginning to pivot to a balance of both phonics *and* the look-say method, teaching reading by both the sight and the sound of the words. Without quite meaning to, Dr. Seuss had put himself at the forefront of the ever-evolving—and ever-contentious—efforts to improve student literacy.

It was yet another thing for Ted and Phyllis to fight about. *One Fish Two Fish Red Fish Blue Fish* was a prototype of sorts for what Ted and Phyllis were informally calling "Beginning Beginner Books," with an even *more* restrictive word list aimed at very early readers with limited vocabularies. "When we began Beginner Books, we found that *The Cat in the Hat* was at that time hard for first graders to read," Ted recalled.[65] And so Phyllis had pared the word list down from 361 to 182 very simple vocabulary words. *One Fish Two Fish* didn't rely on the new word list—the word *fish* wasn't even on it—but Ted was determined to put his theories about word proximity and rhyme to work in *One Fish Two Fish* and any other Beginning Beginner Books. Phyllis, however, remained a stickler about the word list.

Christopher Cerf remembered hearing his mother and the Geisels argue about the placement of three words on a page. "Helen sided with Ted much more than not, but she was an independent thinker and sometimes took my mother's side," said Christopher. "Ted was incredibly rigorous about getting the books the way he wanted. [Phyllis] was incredibly brilliant about the discipline of vocabularies and the reading skills, stuff that became boring to Ted."[66] The arguing tested even the patience of the normally benevolent Bennett Cerf, who recalled bolting from the Thanksgiving dinner table in 1959, as Ted and Phyllis continued their increasingly louder argument over the main course.

Days after the fractious Thanksgiving dinner, Ted and Helen hand-delivered *One Fish Two Fish Red Fish Blue Fish* to the Random House offices, where Ted once again read the book aloud to the editorial staff. He also brought with him the nubs of several well-worn crayons, which he pressed into the hands of production manager Ray Freiman, then loitered over Freiman's shoulder until he matched the colors perfectly. Satisfied, the Geisels left New York for a monthlong vacation in Spain—but Ted fretted that in his absence, Phyllis might try to wrest control of Beginner Books away from him by rallying their authors to her side.

• • • •

The Geisels returned from Spain in time to ring in 1960 at the Tower. For much of late 1959, even as he was finishing up *One Fish Two Fish*, Ted had been agonizing over another book pinned to his wall—a book he had taken on as the result of a friendly bet with Bennett Cerf himself. As the new year began, then, Ted was slowly feeling his way around with a narrative, trying to meet Cerf's challenge head-on.

Cerf knew Ted had struggled for nearly a year with *The Cat in the Hat*, trying to overcome the limitations of its restricted vocabulary. And, of course, now Beginner Books was preparing to launch a new line of books using an even more restricted word list of 182 words. Cerf understood that sticking with even 182 unique words was tough—but now the publisher issued a very specific challenge to Ted: could he write a book using only *fifty* unique words or fewer? It seemed impossible—and Cerf bet Ted fifty dollars he couldn't do it.

Ted would rise to meet Cerf's challenge—and it was probably not entirely a coincidence that the central plot point of the resulting book was all about convincing someone to do something he didn't really want to do.

Green Eggs and Ham would be its own kind of misery for Ted to write, requiring him to create complicated charts, checklists, and multiple word counts as he struggled to keep track of exactly which and how many words he was using. He also imposed an additional restriction on himself by limiting his vocabulary to one-syllable words, with the exception of *anywhere*, which was composed of two short words early readers would know.

The Tower office was a mess as Ted toiled over *Green Eggs and Ham*, discarding typewritten pages directly into the fireplace or letting half-drawn pages simply fall to the floor—or at times angrily crumpling them up and launching them toward the trash can, which he usually missed. He would stare at his typewritten pages over and over again, reading them aloud to check the scansion, crossing out words or syllables that disrupted the rhyme. Then he would pace the floor for a while, scanning his word list, and suddenly bang away furiously on his typewriter, rewriting the entire page again. Rhyming, too, was particularly tough with a fifty-word list. "The agony is terrific at times, and the attrition is horrible," said Ted. "If you're doing it in quatrains and get to the end of four lines and can't make it work, then it's like unraveling a sock. You take some of your best stuff and throw it away."[67] Sometimes when Ted was out of his office, Helen would retrieve some of the abandoned pages and place them back on his desk to see if they might meet with his approval on a second look. They usually didn't.

Ted worked on *Green Eggs and Ham* until early spring 1960, when he was finally ready to take the book to Random House for its unveiling. Helen was a bit uneasy about it—"If you do not like [the book]," she wrote nervously to Louise Bonino in March, "we will return to our swimming pool on the [next] plane."[68]

Ted was generally a nervous wreck on the days before he was due to leave La Jolla for New York to deliver a manuscript. He would carefully spread his completed pages out on the floor of the living room, then get down on his hands and knees and slowly crawl across the floor, staring at every drawing and agonizing over every word choice. At times, he would call on his neighbor from just down the hill, a spry seventy-five-year-old retired railroad executive named Bert L. Hupp, to ask for a second opinion. Hupp, too, would get down on his knees to stare at the pages, but wisely offered little more than moral support. Suitably bolstered, Ted would send Hupp on his way, then pack up his pages and spend the rest of the night staring out the windows in his office, unable to sleep.

For the debut of *Green Eggs and Ham,* Bonino initially invited Random House staff to gather in her office at eleven on April 19, 1960. But Bennett Cerf was going to be out of the office that day and canceled the in-house reading in favor of a small dinner party—to the likely relief of some Random House employees, who enjoyed the readings, but sometimes groused about "the tensions [Dr. Seuss] leaves in his meticulous wake."[69] Indeed, all office operations would come to a halt during Ted's readings; even the Random House switchboard operators usually showed up, jamming into Bonino's office and leaving ringing phones unanswered.

This time, as Cerf had asked, Ted read *Green Eggs and Ham* aloud at the dinner party, where it was met with enthusiastic applause. As was typical, however, Ted was worried the audience hadn't laughed hard enough in certain places and went back to his hotel room that evening to fuss over his pages, debating whether he needed to rewrite them. He would also micromanage the production department, injecting himself into decisions about paper quality and overall color palettes. "From a genius, you tolerate a little bit more," one Random House employee commented.[70] But for Ted, no decision was ever truly final. After *The Cat in the Hat Comes Back* had sold more than 100,000 copies, Ted informed Cerf that a single line on the book's cover was too dark and asked that a new jacket be printed. Cerf could only do as Ted asked.

"You don't tell Joe DiMaggio how to hit the ball," he said.[71]

• • • •

Nineteen sixty would be another blockbuster year for Dr. Seuss, with the publication of two enormously successful books: *One Fish Two Fish Red Fish Blue Fish* in April and *Green Eggs and Ham* in August.

As Geisel had hoped, many critics recognized *One Fish Two Fish* as successfully balancing the "look-say" and phonics pedagogies, and it had been released "with the advance endorsement of some top educational consultants who praise its use of rhymes to teach both the sound and the recognition of words."[72] The *Dartmouth Alumni Magazine*—which had made a point of reviewing every Dr. Seuss book since *Mulberry Street*—noted that its regular rhythm and repeated words and sounds encouraged young readers as well. "Repetition, at any level, is a basic method of teaching," wrote the Dartmouth reviewer. "Dr. Seuss applies this with such skill that it is not obvious or boring."[73]

The New York Times appreciated that Dr. Seuss had come up with yet another highly entertaining reading primer, "[s]imple enough in vocabulary to encourage the pre-schooler . . . if he can just stop laughing long enough to take advantage of the opportunity."[74] And in the same vein as *The Cat in the Hat*, Geisel had created yet another crossover hit that appealed to both children *and* their parents, with one reviewer noting that "[*One Fish Two Fish*] should improve the children's physical condition, too, since they will probably have to forcefully wrest this latest book from the hands of their hysterical parents."[75]

But *One Fish Two Fish Red Fish Blue Fish* was a minnow when compared with the whale that was *Green Eggs and Ham*—still the bestselling Dr. Seuss book of all time, with total sales over sixty years still climbing well past eight million copies. The story of Sam-I-Am, trying to convince someone to eat green eggs and ham, would be analyzed for hidden meanings and metaphors—but for Geisel, it was only ever about one thing. "The only meaning was that Bennett Cerf, my publisher, bet me fifty bucks I couldn't write a book using only fifty words," he said. "I did it to show I could."[76] He would also claim, only slightly in jest, that Cerf had never paid him the fifty dollars.

"The good doctor has scored another triumph," proclaimed *The New York Times*.[77] The fact that Dr. Seuss had told the story of *Green Eggs and Ham* using only fifty unique words was reported in nearly every review of the book with breathless awe.[78] "The biggest news is . . . a good—and frequently hilarious—story is told in from 50 to 100 different words," wrote the *Chicago Tribune*.[79] The *Dartmouth Alumni Magazine* could only agree that "[i]n spite of the vocabulary limitation, Dr. Seuss gets surprising variety into his arrangements, and the swing of the verse is catchy."[80] (Dartmouth students would later joke that the title referred to the breakfast served in the cafeteria of his alma mater.) Perhaps one of the most thoughtful—and prescient— reviews came from the *Poughkeepsie Journal*. "A vocabulary of only fifty words," wrote the *Journal* reviewer, "but they will be long remembered."[81]

For the rest of his life, Geisel would find himself served plates full of green eggs and ham at book signings and social events hosted by well-meaning friends. "Deplorable stuff," he said later. "The worst time was on a yacht in six-foot seas."[82] *Green Eggs and Ham* would prove to be a sales juggernaut whose popularity carried all other Dr. Seuss books along with it. By 1960, in fact, nearly three million copies of Dr. Seuss books had been sold, with the money coming in so deep and so fast that Geisel eventually asked that any royalties beyond $5,000— that magic annual salary he had spoken with agent Phyllis Jackson about—be deferred and invested in mutual funds to reduce his rapidly growing annual tax bill.

Beginner Books as a whole were selling well, too. In addition to the two Dr. Seuss books published in 1960, there was also Benjamin Elkin and Leonard Shortall's *The King's Wish and Other Stories* and

Robert Lopshire's *Put Me in the Zoo*. Both sold respectably, though *Business Week* warned that "[s]ome librarians and store buyers say the Beginner Books trade on Dr. Seuss' reputation and not all are up to his quality."[83] That certainly couldn't be said of what would become one of Beginner Books's most beloved titles, P. D. Eastman's *Are You My Mother?* in which Eastman had managed to tell his story using just under a hundred unique words.

There was clearly big money to be made in writing for children. "It is a good business," Geisel said later. "It turned good after World War II . . . everybody got out of the Army under the [GI] Bill and got married and proceeded to have seven or eight kids. That built the market."[84] Following Random House's lead—or at least inspired by the success of *The Cat in the Hat*—other publishers were now establishing their own labels for children's books, most notably the I Can Read imprint at Harper & Row, which was publishing the successful *Little Bear* series by Else Holmelund Minarik and illustrator Maurice Sendak.

Practically the only publisher not making any money off the new glut of children's books was poor William Spaulding at Houghton Mifflin, who'd come up with the idea of entertaining reading primers in the first place. Spaulding had watched in frustration as Bennett Cerf's trade edition of *The Cat in the Hat* far surpassed the sales of Houghton Mifflin's textbook edition—and then saw the same thing happen with the textbook editions of *The Cat in the Hat Comes Back* and *Yertle the Turtle*. Spaulding eventually threw up his hands and sold the textbook rights for the titles back to Cerf, who quietly shelved them at Geisel's request. Geisel wanted only "a supplementary reader that can be read for fun. I don't want teachers assigning pupils to read two pages of it a night."[85]

But Geisel also thought there was more to it than merely money. "I think something much bigger has happened," he wrote at the time. "I think that writers have finally realized that children's reading and children's thinking are the rock-bottom base upon which the future of this country will rise. Or not rise."[86] For Geisel, writing for children was part patriotism, part moral calling. "In these days of tension and confusion, writers are beginning to realize that books for children have a greater potential for good, or evil, than any other form of literature on earth," he wrote. "The proportion of fine books versus junk is growing steadily. And the children are eagerly welcoming the good writers who talk not down to them as kiddies, but talk to them clearly and honestly as equals."[87]

Still, Beginner Books were selling briskly enough in their first printings—even a slow-selling title would move an impressive 30,000 copies—that by April 1960, the imprint was now earning more than a million dollars annually for Random House. "Beginner Books was getting so big, it was becoming embarrassing," said Bennett Cerf.[88] While he had been content to let the Geisels and Phyllis oversee the imprint through its start-up phase, Beginner Books now had his attention. The imprint had quickly become a viable and very profitable commodity—and one Bennett Cerf now wanted entirely under the Random House roof, especially as he was mulling over recommendations to sell the company at some point in the not-too-distant future.

The savvy Cerf decided to make a deal with the Beginner Books team using the best leverage he had. In October 1959, Cerf had taken Random House public, with individual shares valued at $11.75.[89] Now, in August of 1960, after consulting with the Random House board, Cerf was prepared to swap the 100 shares of Beginner Books stock for 25,000 shares of Random House stock, now valued at around $32 per share. All total, Cerf had just laid an $800,000 offer on the table.[90]

Ted and Phyllis initially balked, mostly for tax reasons—but the proposition was too good *not* to consider seriously. The three partners would eventually accept Cerf's offer, though—perhaps predictably—not without causing further hard feelings between the Geisels and Phyllis. While the exact terms of the agreement would never be made public, those who knew Ted—and Bennett Cerf—were certain that the publisher had further sweetened the deal for Ted, providing the Geisels with additional financial incentives, profit sharing, or stock options that Cerf didn't make available to his own wife. "We bought Beginner Books from the three of them for a pretty penny," Bennett

Cerf reported several years later. "Phyllis is still yapping that we cheated her, but actually the three of them were very happy."[91] That was typical Cerf overstatement; the deal had served only to widen the cracks in what was now a rapidly fracturing partnership.

••••

When they weren't playing businesspeople, Ted and Helen seemed, according to one journalist, "an uncommonly close and devoted couple."[92] When Helen informed Ted in 1960 that she wanted to write her own Beginner Book based on "Gustav the Goldfish"—Ted's story of an ever-growing goldfish he had drawn for *Redbook* in 1950—he wrote her a charming "Dear Spouse" letter granting her permission to adapt the work. "You have the right to use any of the situations or any of the words from the original story that your little heart desires," he wrote. "You must, however, comply with all necessary steps in protecting my original copyright. . . . Very truly yours, and I hope you will have dinner with me tonight and many nights following."[93]

While Helen was more actively involved in social and community events, she could still successfully persuade Ted to join her in causes they mutually supported, such as raising funds for the foundation the Geisels had established to support the new children's wing at the San Diego Fine Arts Museum. Ted was actively involved in helping the museum conceptualize exhibits; in 1955, he had written a proposal for a potential Dr. Seuss museum, where every exhibit would be marked with signs reading D̲O̲ TOUCH. He envisioned having a printing press where kids could print their own books, or an exhibit on Venetian windows where children could learn to blow their own glass. He was hoping to bring similarly exciting, though hopefully safer, exhibits to the San Diego Fine Arts Museum.

He would attend, though rarely enjoy, the countless cocktail parties and receptions mandated by such fundraisers, where small talk and forced grins were the coin of the realm. He was "funny, intelligent, a bit shy," recalled one La Jolla acquaintance—but such gatherings were agony for someone who still blanched at public speaking. "He would go to cocktail parties, and he would talk to you if you were there," remembered one friend. "He would stand quietly in a corner, in his bow tie, and not make a big deal about approaching you. But if you approached him, he was a friendly and interesting conversationalist."[94]

Mostly, though, Ted stood in receiving lines, a cocktail in his left hand as he shook hands with his right, thanking patrons for donations. In 1960, during a reception celebrating the staff of the Scripps Clinic, Ted stood patiently shaking hands and making small talk when he was introduced to a married couple who had only recently moved to the area: Dr. E. Grey Dimond, founder and head of the Institute for Cardiopulmonary Diseases at the Scripps Clinic in La Jolla, and his wife, Audrey, a former nurse who was now volunteering in local cancer wards.

"As we went through the line, I noticed that when we got to Dr. Seuss, the inflection of the person introducing us was slightly different," recalled Audrey. "I thought, 'Well, it's for some reason.' Being my facetious best, I said, 'Dr. Seuss, you must have a very interesting specialty.'" Then, drawing attention to Ted's hawkish nose, she asked, "The right or the left nostril?"

Ted was caught flat-footed. "I remember him looking at me kind of startled and making no response," said Audrey. "Of course, in no time at all, Helen and Ted became our very good friends, and we did things as a foursome. My husband was very taken with Ted."[95]

And Ted was very taken with Audrey.

CHAPTER 12

THE WORK

1961–1963

tan and Jan Berenstain were big fans of Dr. Seuss.

The laid-back, low-key married Berenstains—both thirty-eight years old in 1961—had been successful cartoonists since the early 1950s, with their accessible, family-oriented work appearing regularly in magazines like *Collier's* and *McCall's*, and in lighthearted parenting guides like *The Berenstains' Baby Book*. The Berenstains were initially familiar with Dr. Seuss's work as an adman, admiring his campaigns for Flit and Esso. Things would change, however, following the birth of their sons Leo and Michael—more specifically, beginning in December 1952, when four-year-old Leo asked for *McElligot's Pool* as a Christmas gift. Reading the book was "a delight and a revelation," the Berenstains later wrote. "It was rollicking, irreverent, and robust, and it was *funny*."[1] But it also, they admitted later, "scratched at an old itch" of theirs to write books for children.[2]

Nine years later, between magazine work and greeting card jobs, the Berenstains had at last written and illustrated their first real children's book, featuring a family of bears based loosely on themselves—the first time they'd ever used bears in their storytelling. Titled *Freddy Bear's Spanking*, the Berenstains' book told in rhymed verse the story of a misbehaving little bear who tried to talk his way out of a spanking by proposing one alternative punishment after another. Their agent read through the pages, liked what he saw, and put them in touch with Phyllis Cerf—who also saw the potential in the talented couple and put them under contract with Beginner Books. The Berenstains were signed. Their book had been submitted. Now all that remained was to see Dr. Seuss himself, who now made frequent trips to New York to meet personally with Beginner Book authors.

The Berenstains were excited and slightly nervous as they exited the elevator on Random House's sixth floor and headed for the stairs of the quirky clubhouse headquarters of Beginner Books. Geisel was already at the top of the steps waiting for them, in a bright red bow tie, with his glasses pushed up onto his forehead.

"Hi, Berenstains!" he called out. "Come on up!"[3]

As the couple walked into the main suite, they found the pages of their book pinned up on the corkboard walls of Geisel's office. Ted, Helen, and Phyllis Cerf greeted the Berenstains warmly. Then Geisel immediately started asking pointed questions about the "internal workings" of the bears. "We need to know more about them," said Geisel. "What are they about? Why do they live in a tree? What does Papa do for a living? What kind of pipe tobacco does he smoke?"[4] ("There was no way Papa Bear was going to smoke," grumbled Stan Berenstain.)[5] Geisel didn't necessarily want the Berenstains to include all that information in the story, but he wanted them to have an absolutely clear grasp of their characters and their world—that "logical insanity" that made Dr. Seuss books so oddly coherent. "It was slowly dawning on us that Ted took these little seventy-two-page, limited vocabulary, easy-to-read books just as seriously as if he were editing the Great American Novel," the Berenstains said later.[6]

Geisel walked the Berenstains slowly around the room to look at their pages. "There's a hell of a lot wrong with it," he told them, pointing out places where he thought their story was too long or complicated. "Think short sentences," Geisel instructed them as he picked apart their plot, telling them it had a good beginning and ending, but no real middle. And nothing, it seemed, was too small or unimportant. Even the length of the lines of text mattered; lines had to *look* good on the page, and to the extent possible, be of similar length. But when Phyllis tried to helpfully suggest the Berenstains not write their story in rhymed verse, Geisel interjected. "Their rhyme *does* work," he insisted. "I like their rhyme. It's got get-up-and-go. It just needs to be simplified and cleaned up a little."[7]

At the end of the meeting, Helen unpinned the Berenstains' pages and handed them back in an envelope. "Berenstains, I can't tell you how happy I am to be working with you," Ted told them as he shook their hands. "I just know we're going to get a wonderful book."[8]

The Berenstains left feeling "spent, drained, and exhausted, but also exhilarated, excited, and challenged." As the Berenstains would discover, those emotional extremes would be typical of their thirty-year relationship with Ted Geisel. "Like the Cat [in the Hat], he could be charming, courtly, congenial, and delightful to be with," wrote the Berenstains years later. "Also like the Cat, he could be demanding, dismissive, and downright difficult."[9]

After leaving their first meeting with Geisel, the Berenstains boarded a train to take them back home to Pennsylvania. As they sat in a stunned silence, Jan quietly asked, "I wonder what Ted thinks of us?"

"You know," said Stan, "I don't think he thinks about us at all. I think all he thinks about is the work."

That realization would be the key to their productive relationship. "That's what Ted was about: *the work*," wrote the Berenstains. "Every aspect of it: the title, the endpapers, the title page, the meter . . . He could spot a faulty iamb in your pentameter from a mile away."[10] His criticism, while often harsh, "was pretty much on target."[11] For the next several months, the Berenstains would rewrite and revise their story, consulting with Geisel in person in New York or mailing bulky packages back and forth between their home in suburban Elkins Park, Pennsylvania, and the Tower in La Jolla. "The process became progressively manic," said the Berenstains—and Geisel, who tended to veer toward over-the-top action scenes, encouraged the Berenstains to come up with increasingly wilder scenarios until finally both Helen and Phyllis decided Ted had gone too far. "This is getting crazy," Helen told her husband firmly. "You're turning this into a Dr. Seuss book. That's not what Stan and Jan do."[12]

"Some of the air went out of [Ted's] tires," said the Berenstains—but Geisel conceded the point. The Berenstains chose instead to focus on one story element that had remained intact through every rewrite—a hunt for a beehive—and turn that into their main plot instead. "The fever had broken," wrote the Berenstains with palpable relief. And so it had—at least for now.

Meanwhile, Geisel still had his own books to work on. In 1961, the pages pinned to the corkboard of his office in the Tower were for the collection *The Sneetches and Other Stories*, a reworking of a very brief single-paneled cartoon he had drawn for *Redbook* in 1953. *The Sneetches* was a not-so-subtle statement on discrimination, with Star-Belly Sneetches declaring their superiority to Plain-Belly Sneetches and refusing to socialize with them on the Sneetch beaches. There was likely an element of his own childhood trauma informing the story—memories of being shunned for the arbitrary offense of being German American during World War I—but more recently, Geisel had been shocked by the undercurrent of anti-Semitism that seemed to be slowly infiltrating his own community. He was stunned to learn, for example, that the Real Estate Brokers' Association of La Jolla refused to rent or sell to Jewish families. And lately, one of his neighbors casually informed him that the La Jolla Beach and Tennis Club had an unspoken policy of not accepting Jewish members. "All it did was really confuse Ted," said his friend Judith Morgan, "because that wasn't who he was or the way he was thinking."[13]

And yet Geisel knew he was walking a fine line. As he had with *Grinch*, he didn't want to be seen as overtly preachy or deliberately moral—that would violate one of his cardinal rules of writing for kids. Making matters worse, a recent visitor to the Tower who had seen the pages pinned up in his study thought the book actually *promoted* anti-Semitism or prejudice—an assessment that sent Geisel spiraling into depression. When Bob Bernstein made the trip from Random House to check on Geisel's progress with the book, he found him in a funk. "I've decided to abandon this book," he informed Bernstein. "Someone I respect told me it was anti-Semitic."[14] A flabbergasted Bernstein told Geisel not to be rattled by "one stupid comment."[15] "His relief when I told him this was nonsense was overwhelming," Bernstein said later. "I always found it hard to believe that this amazing man had self-doubt for even a moment."[16]

Still, Geisel was going to sweat over every single line, discarding pages that went nowhere or moving them around on the wall. Other times, there might be a scrap of a good idea that didn't seem to fit his story—but rather than throw those pages away, Geisel would put them in what he called his "bone pile," usually just a drawer filled with discarded and half-realized ideas. "I dig into it occasionally and start working some of the material over again," he explained later. "Some of it can be expanded into a book, other material is shortened to a story."[17]

In the case of *The Sneetches and Other Stories*, he was taking several previously published brief magazine pieces and expanding them into a collection of slightly longer stories, which included not only "The Sneetches" but also "The Zaks," (renamed as "The Zax"), a 1954 tale of two stubborn creatures who refuse to change direction. *The Sneetches* would also contain two other short stories, "Too Many Daves," a three-pager about Mrs. McCave who named all twenty-three of her children Dave, and "What Was I Scared Of?" which contained what Geisel later said was one of his favorite characters, an empty—and misunderstood—pair of pants with a personality of its own. "I think there's more life in the pair of green pants with no one inside them than a good many of the other [characters]," he said.[18]

Ted and Helen delivered *The Sneetches and Other Stories* to Random House in early 1961, then stayed in the Hotel Madison for six weeks to wait out renovations at the Tower, which was being expanded and remodeled. Helen made good use of the time away, as she was finishing up *A Fish out of Water*, her adaptation of Ted's short story "Gustav the Goldfish," with illustrations by P. D. Eastman. Ted, too, was doodling around ideas for another Big Book, this one about sleeping and snoring.

The Tower would be renovated just in time for a visit from Geisel's father—"ramrod-straight, silver-haired"[19] T. R. Geisel—who had flown west from Massachusetts in a snit. Only a year earlier, in June 1960, the eighty-one-year-old T.R. had been feted in his hometown as the city's oldest employee, having served the Springfield Parks system for fifty-one years, with "no plans to retire."[20] Now, a year later, he was refusing to take a physical exam to determine whether he was still fit to carry out his duties, and the stubborn T.R.—feeling pressure from his fellow commissioners—abruptly resigned and jetted off to La Jolla, to spend some time with Ted, Helen, and Peggy Owens, quietly stewing and licking his wounds. Ted could only shrug in silent sympathy; stubbornness was a well-known trait of the Geisel men.

The Sneetches and Other Stories was published by Random House in August 1961 and was another immediate triumph. Printed using shades of yellow, red, and green, *Sneetches* contained some of Geisel's loosest art and most daring uses of color. "What Was I Scared Of?" features every page soaked in blue-green, while "The Zax" takes place almost entirely against a desert of bright yellow. "Dr. Seuss hits the bullseye again," read one typical review,[21] while most also picked up on the message of the story, even as Geisel continued to deflect questions or assumptions about its moral. "Adults and children build their own moral into my books," he protested. "You can't really preach to youngsters, but in any creative writing you are trying to communicate some ideas."[22] Ted's protestations aside, *The Sneetches* remains Dr. Seuss's unambiguous statement on bigotry and racism—a reminder that we're all the same on the inside, regardless of outward appearances, presented to children in terms even the most jaded grown-ups could understand. While the younger Dr. Seuss could sometimes be insensitive when it came to matters of race, the fifty-seven-year-old Ted Geisel was making it clear that Dr. Seuss had evolved.

While "Big Books" like *The Sneetches and Other Stories* sold well, the Beginner Books were where Geisel was making his real money—the recent renovation of the Tower had been paid for largely with earnings from the imprint.

At the same time, Grolier's children's book club announced an exclusive deal with Random House to sell Beginner Books through direct market sales. Initially, Grolier had proposed to carry books published by Beginner Books and rival publisher Harper, but Phyllis Cerf had rejected that offer, on the grounds that she didn't want "anyone else's children's books riding on ours."[23] Grolier, eyeing a regular line of Dr. Seuss books, wisely agreed to Phyllis's terms, and would begin offering Beginner Books by mail order in 1963—and the money would continue to come pouring in. The Geisels often joked that they would have to refer any financial questions to their lawyers, Grimalkin, Drouberhannus, Knalbner and Fepp—a fictional law firm with a suitably Seussian name.

Lately, too, Geisel had taken to "rescuing" faltering or rejected manuscripts, completely reworking them into something new—or, if a manuscript couldn't be salvaged, Ted might tinker with one of his own abandoned manuscripts in the bone pile and turn it into a Beginner Book. "There are millions of figures—drawings, kids, clothes—which haunt me, because I can't seem to do anything about them, dozens of ideas which have never jelled," he said later. "Sometimes I can take chunks and drop them in somewhere, but the rest just float around waiting."[24] That had been the case with the Beginner Book *Ten Apples Up On Top!*, published in March 1961, with art by Roy McKie and a script by Geisel, but credited to one of Ted's oldest pseudonyms: Theo. LeSieg.

That October, Ted and Helen traveled to Europe to discuss the possibility of bringing Beginner Books to the United Kingdom. Geisel had hoped to include the Soviet Union in their trip, but to his disappointment, Bennett Cerf was unable to pull the right diplomatic strings. "The idea of Moscow with two feet of snow on the ground didn't appeal to us," Ted said dismissively.[25] Instead, he and Helen spent most of their time in England, visiting classrooms of enthusiastic six-year-olds who shrieked with delight when Geisel jokingly informed them that Christopher Columbus was his uncle.

But despite his fans among the six-year-olds, the British were decidedly lukewarm on Dr. Seuss. *The Cat in the Hat* had already been rejected by British publishers for being "too vulgar for words" and many of his other titles puzzled the English as being too informal or too full of Americanisms. Still, UK publisher Billy Collins was optimistic, noting that Dr. Seuss books seemed to sell better among adults who were learning to read, and were being used inside prisons to encourage literacy in inmates. "An illiterate old convict would object to being handed a children's book," said publicist Michael Hyde, "but he'll settle in with Dr. Seuss."[26]

Before wrapping up their English adventure, Ted and Helen visited Oxford, nostalgically dropping by the sites where they had met and fallen in love four decades earlier—including the boardinghouse where Helen had lived, with the bathroom window that wouldn't close. Nearly forty years later, the window was still open.

••••

While travel normally invigorated Geisel, he was feeling the stress of presiding over Beginner Books. The creative and editorial feuds with Phyllis Cerf over issues large and small—ranging from word lists to the selection of writers and artists to the final approval of manuscripts—were continuing, though Helen had successfully inserted herself between the two of them well enough to keep the flare-ups to a minimum. Helen had also managed to keep Ted distracted from business during much of the holidays, throwing an enormous Christmas party at the Tower for forty-six guests, where Ted paraded one partygoer after another into his studio to help him set up and play with the gigantic electric train set Helen had given him as a Christmas gift.

By New Year's Day 1962, however, he was feeling the pressure of completing his most recent Big Book—tentatively called *The Sleep*

Book, and now in its third rewrite. After nearly a year of writing, drawing, erasing, and crumpling up page after page, he was still having a hard time landing on the narrative. Pounding hard on his Smith Corona typewriter, Geisel banged out the line:

> Sleep's better than butter . . . I'd rather (be sleeping/have
>
> sleep) than—

It petered out, a false start. Next, he filled pages with a few test rhymes:

> They are snoring in throats, boats, goats, notes,
>
> thousands of throats . . . The sweet sounding notes of
>
> goats snoring in boats.[27]

That was enough to spark an idea—of a yawn that gets passed from one creature to another—and Geisel would continue with that plotline as he carried the pages with him to New York in April, where he met with the Cerfs to discuss an editorial change to Beginner Books that he was certain Phyllis would hate: the word list. "I hope we will expand [the list]," said Geisel as he floated the idea in the newspapers, and claimed an advisory board of teachers were supporting his efforts to widen the vocabulary list."[28] While that may have been true, the real impetus behind increasing the number of permissible words was Dr. Seuss himself, who had always found the word list creatively oppressive. But Phyllis wouldn't budge. "She was coeditor," said Bennett Cerf. "It soon developed that Phyllis was getting stronger and stronger and more opinionated as she waxed more successful."[29]

Geisel would remain in New York for several weeks, working on *The Sleep Book* in his hotel room, filling an ashtray with one stubbed-out cigarette after another or, when stuck, sprawling out on the bed to read Ian Fleming's James Bond novel *Live and Let Die*. He completed his book late in April and delivered it to Random House where, as usual, he read it aloud in Cerf's office. Lately, too, Geisel had set a policy of *not* signing a contract for any of his Big Books until the day the book was delivered. "He didn't believe that authors should be paid for their work until the book had actually sold," explained one of his later editors.[30] It was likely, too, part of his effort to keep his annual tax burden down. Grimalkin, Drouberhannus, Knalbner and Fepp would approve.

With the book delivered, Ted and Helen headed briefly for Las Vegas—"ugly" was Helen's blunt assessment[31]—then spent part of June with the Cerfs at their vacation house in Mount Kisco, New York. Ted brought with him a few manuscripts he was considering for publication in the coming year—including books by P. D. Eastman and Roy McKie—which provided yet another opportunity for him and Phyllis to argue. "They began fighting with each other over every book," Bennett Cerf recalled. "Phyllis is a perfectionist. So is Ted. Neither would compromise . . . When [the Geisels] flew east, they would come up to Mount Kisco for the weekend; and I'd just clear out because they would argue all day over a page because they cared so desperately."[32]

One book they could both agree on, however, was the Berenstains' debut book, *The Big Honey Hunt*, which would be published that fall to enthusiastic reviews. Prior to its release, the Geisels had summoned the Berenstains to New York for a leisurely lunch at the Park Lane Hotel to discuss the couple's follow-up book. Ted ordered a Bullshot— a heady elixir of beef bouillon and vodka—and Helen ordered white wine, while the Berenstains, who admitted they usually felt like rubes in the big city, ordered Gibsons—martinis served with a small onion instead of an olive, "to demonstrate our sophistication."[33] Over dessert, the Berenstains enthusiastically pitched another Beginner Book featuring their bear family, but Geisel immediately quashed the idea, arguing there were too many books on the market with bears in them. "A series would be a millstone around your necks," he contended—a curious argument coming from the artist who, as a young man, had regularly pitched one series after another to editors at *Liberty* and *The New Yorker*.

The Berenstains were "shocked, stunned, catatonic,"[34] but went back to Pennsylvania to regroup and eventually submitted to Geisel a new story featuring a clueless penguin at the South Pole. When the Berenstains returned to New York after the successful release of *The Big Honey Hunt*, they found the pages of their penguin story already pinned to the walls of Geisel's Beginner Books office—but as he reviewed the pages with them, Ted seemed suddenly struck by a new idea: *The Big Honey Hunt,* said Geisel, was such a big hit that the Berenstains should probably think about dropping the penguin story and following up instead with another book featuring their bears.

Jan Berenstain never blinked. "Yeah, sure," she replied without a hint of exasperation. "I think we could do that."[35]

The Berenstains would follow *The Big Honey Hunt* with the equally successful *The Bike Lesson* in 1964—and were shocked when they saw the bright magenta cover announcing that their new book was *Another Adventure of the Berenstain Bears*. "We didn't quite get it," the Berenstains admitted—but Geisel, ever the advertising man, explained that he was turning them into their own brand. "You know, your bears are a vaudeville troupe, like Murgatroyd's Mules and Dugan's Dogs," he told them.[36] And rather than continuing to credit them as "Stanley and Janice Berenstain"—a bit of a mouthful—Geisel had shortened their credit on *The Bike Lesson* to "Stan and Jan Berenstain." "Hey, that's what you call each other," he told them. "Besides, it rhymes."[37]

Autumn of 1962 would also see the publication of the Big Book that Geisel had been working on for more than a year, *Dr. Seuss's Sleep Book*. It would be the first of his books to incorporate the name *Dr. Seuss* as part of the title, a clear indication of the growing value of the Dr. Seuss brand. Geisel had turned his initial single plot note—that of a yawn spreading from creature to creature—into a magnum opus of sleeping animals of every size and shape, who snore, talk, walk, dream, roll hoops, and carry candles in their sleep. The *Sleep Book* is crammed with some of the wildest creatures Geisel would ever create, like a Collapsible Frink, the Curious Crandalls, a Chippendale Mupp, and the Foona-Lagoona Baboona. Inevitably, Geisel would be asked how he came up with such unusual creatures. "I have a special dictionary which gives me most of them," he told *Life* magazine coyly, "and I just look up the spellings."[38]

It had been twenty-five years since the first Dr. Seuss book had been published in 1937—an anniversary that didn't go unnoticed, despite Geisel's best efforts to keep his head down. As part of the anniversary, his books were publicly rediscussed, reexamined, and reappreciated, which sent sales of nearly every Dr. Seuss book soaring during 1962. Even Vanguard, which still owned the rights to *Mulberry Street* and *Bartholomew Cubbins*, rode the coattails of Dr. Seuss's twenty-fifth anniversary, with *Mulberry Street* finally selling more than 100,000 total copies after twenty-five years in print. Geisel also saw his own life story told and retold in quickly written newspaper tributes, with several mistakenly reporting that he had taken the pen name of Dr. Seuss because he had studied medicine at Oxford. "No matter what I say, all these clippings keep repeating the same old lies," said Geisel, "which unfortunately I usually started."[39]

Still, the anniversary gave him another opportunity to pontificate earnestly about the importance of good books for children and, more crucial, the responsibility of children's authors to take their jobs seriously. "I think that writers of children's books should work themselves harder than they do," Geisel told *Publishers Weekly.* "They should be sure that everything is right. Too many of them just turn in their first drafts."[40] He continued to blanch at the suggestion that all it took to write a book for children was a bit of imagination and a dash of good intentions; writing a kids' book, he argued, was precision work. "To get a sixty-page book, I may easily write a thousand pages before I'm satisfied," said Geisel. "The story has to develop clearly and logically with a valid problem and a valid solution. The characters, no matter how weird, have to be vivid and believable and consistent. Then I have to get illustrations that fit the text and don't destroy the mood. The whole effect has to be just right."[41]

Helen, who understood Ted better than most, thought she knew exactly how and why Dr. Seuss did what he did. "[Ted is] a man who isn't happy while he's working on a book," said Helen, "and even less happy when he isn't."[42]

• • • •

Nineteen sixty-three would be both a productive and a tumultuous year for Geisel and Beginner Books. Following the publication of *Dr. Seuss's Sleep Book* in late 1962, Geisel would sideline his Big Books for the next three years to focus exclusively on Beginner Books, starting with *Hop on Pop* and *Dr. Seuss's ABC*, both of which would be published within six months of each other in 1963.

Geisel snuck a bit of bawdiness into an early draft of *Hop on Pop*, just to see, he said, "if Bennett is reading my stuff":[43]

> When I read, I am smart.
> I always cut whole words apart.
> Con Stan Tin O Ple, Tim Buk Too
> Con Tra Cep Tive, Kan Ga Roo.[44]

While it was likely editor Louise Bonino who caught the offending phrase, it was Bennett Cerf who made the call to the Tower to tell Geisel in mock serious tones, "You can't put words like *contraceptive* in a kid's reader."[45] Cerf had passed the test; the quatrain with the offending word would be entirely rewritten.

Mostly, however, Geisel was growing increasingly tired of the restrictive word list. While he'd never discard it altogether, his own word list was becoming more flexible, and he was more inclined to break some of his own rules about so-called emergency words. In *Hop on Pop*, for example, Geisel used both *sister* and *brother*—neither of which were on the list—and rhymed the word *night*, which *was* on the list, with *fight*, which wasn't. But part of the purpose of *Hop on Pop* was to familiarize new readers with words through a combination of phonics and "a new visual method of showing sounds and letter patterns"[46]—a pedagogy similar to the "proximity" approach Geisel hadn't quite been able to pull off in books like *One Fish Two Fish Red Fish Blue Fish*. To this end, then, *Hop on Pop* used inch-tall text for its key words, and aligned *night* and *fight*, for instance, in such a way that young readers could easily see that the two words were made using the *-ight* sound.

Most reviewers immediately recognized that *Hop on Pop* was a new kind of Dr. Seuss book—and with its large type, it certainly didn't *look* like any of the other books. One of the punchier reviews, and one that likely delighted Geisel, not only praised his book, but also took a shot at the kind of turgid reading primers he loathed. "*Hop on Pop* has a 'controlled' vocabulary but it is bright and amusing, with Seuss' wacky creatures," wrote the *Indianapolis Star*, "whereas 'Run, Sally, run,' etc. is practically an insult to a child's intelligence."[47] Geisel couldn't have asked for a better review if he'd written it himself.

Geisel's other Beginner Book for 1963 was *Dr. Seuss's ABC*. Geisel may have seen the book partly as his opportunity to finally complete an alphabet book, since the one he'd illustrated more than two decades earlier had failed to sell and then had mysteriously gone missing in the mail. And once again, just as he'd done with *Hop on Pop*, Geisel couldn't resist checking to see if Cerf and his editing team were paying attention, inserting as his entry for the letter X the following four lines:

> Big X
> Little x
> X . . . x . . . X
> Someday, kiddies, you will learn about sex![48]

Once again, the editorial team was paying attention, and Geisel submitted a rewritten entry for X.

Geisel's contempt for the word list was on open display in *Dr. Seuss's ABC*—perhaps a deliberate thumb in the eye of Phyllis Cerf—as Dr. Seuss rolled out a menagerie of animals found nowhere on the word list, including *alligator, camel, kangaroo,* and *ostrich.* For perhaps the first time in a Dr. Seuss book, Geisel had intentionally populated his pages with real animals—yaks, hens, goats, foxes—as he made his way through the alphabet, giving young readers familiar-looking animals to match with the appropriate letters of the alphabet. Ted's ability to draw recognizable animals was the subject of some debate in the Geisel household. "If I draw what I think a kangaroo looks like, that seems to turn out all right. But if I go to the zoo and look at a real kangaroo and try to figure out what his legs do, it comes out all wrong,"[49] said Ted. "Even now, none of my animals are really animals. They're all people, sort of."[50] Helen, however, was more to the point. "Ted never studied art or anatomy," she told *The Saturday Evening Post.* "He puts the joints where he thinks they should be."[51]

Both *Hop on Pop* and *Dr. Seuss's ABC* had a fan in the novelist and short-story writer Shirley Jackson, whose short story "The Lottery" had rocked readers and literary critics alike on its publication in 1948. Jackson, who had recently written her first children's book, *9 Magic Wishes,* took to the newspapers to share her enthusiasm for the seemingly effortless skills of Dr. Seuss. "I've lost count of how many books Dr. Seuss has written, but I do know that his books are one of the rare bright spots in children's literature today," she wrote. "*Dr. Seuss's ABC* along with *Hop on Pop* will give young readers a head start on reading for the sheer joy of it, which is no small accomplishment."[52]

Beginner Books was publishing plenty of other quality children's books, too—1963 would see the release of Helen's latest, the photo book *Do You Know What I'm Going to Do Next Saturday?* as well as Alice Low's *Summer*—but the imprint had become synonymous with the name of Dr. Seuss. Even Geisel's distinctive color and design sense were beginning to be felt across the imprint, sometimes confusing readers who picked up a book with Seussian lettering on the cover only to discover it wasn't an actual Dr. Seuss book. Clearly, Beginner Books was Geisel's imprint—and Ted wasn't going to let Phyllis forget it. The relationship between Ted Geisel and Phyllis Cerf was nearing a critical mass.

The phone calls between Geisel and Cerf had become louder and more heated. "[Phyllis and Ted] simply could not work together because Ted has to have his own way," said Bennett Cerf. "He was out in California and they would talk for an hour on long distance and Phyllis would usually end up in tears because neither would give in. They would fight over a single word for three hours. I used to go crazy listening."[53] Helen, in an effort to arbitrate, encouraged her husband to extract himself from Beginner Books and let her handle the editorial duties while he went back to just being Dr. Seuss. But Ted refused to let anything go. He was convinced Phyllis was trying to outmaneuver him with Bennett Cerf, and even canceled another long vacation with Helen in order to keep an eye on Phyllis. Finally, an exasperated Bennett Cerf brought in Bob Bernstein to mediate the dispute, telling him in frustrated tones that he had "better do something."

"Bob Bernstein was not supportive of me," Phyllis said later. "His role was to keep Ted happy. He didn't need to keep me happy."[54] The relationship was so irreparably damaged that even the normally cool Bernstein got dragged into the fray, arguing furiously with Phyllis even as he tried to keep Ted at arm's length. It was all too much. For the good of Beginner Books, Bernstein recommended to Bennett Cerf that Phyllis be dismissed entirely from the imprint.

Cerf, bracing himself for what would surely be a long evening, exhaled slowly. He was going to sign off on firing his own wife in order to keep Geisel happy. "Do whatever you have to," he told Bernstein, "but don't talk to me about it."[55]

"It ended up with Phyllis absolutely furious [and] cutting off their friendship," said art director Michael Frith, who would mark his first day at Random House by walking right into the middle of the Geisel/ Cerf feud.[56] Phyllis, however, wasn't going to go away entirely. Almost immediately, she would start another imprint at Random House, this one aimed at slightly older readers, called Step-Up Books—and it was unclear whether the title of the new imprint was meant as a veiled *screw you* to Ted Geisel. Over the next decade, Step-Up Books, with Phyllis as its president, would publish more than thirty books, including nature books like *Birds Do the Strangest Things* and biographies of notable Americans, like *Meet Abraham Lincoln*, lusciously illustrated by Jack Davis. There would be none written or illustrated by Dr. Seuss.

Later, Phyllis tried to view their falling-out pragmatically. "It wasn't really Ted," said Phyllis. "It was his maleness of not wanting to be bossed by all women. He had an agent [Phyllis Jackson], he had a partner [Phyllis Cerf], he had a wife—you know, he was surrounded by women telling him what to do. And he really was the genius—none of us were. But I think that we all guided him to where he needed to go."[57] That was likely true—but when this factor was combined with Geisel's inherent tendency to believe his opinion mattered the most, it made a genuine partnership nearly impossible. Bennett Cerf, who knew and understood Ted well, later admitted he thought the partnership had likely been doomed from the very start. "Ted is not used to being crossed," said Cerf.[58]

CHAPTER 13

STINK. STANK. STUNK.

1963–1967

Phyllis Cerf was out.

And when Jan Berenstain heard the news from Ted, she made what she called "the Eisenhower face"—the downturned mouth and skeptical sideways eyes a photographer had caught on General Eisenhower when he learned President Truman had relieved General MacArthur of duty. The Berenstains loved working with Geisel, but they also knew Phyllis had been their constant advocate and defender, gently but persistently nudging Geisel to let the Berenstains pursue their gentler, family-friendly stories, rather than writing the wackier, more outrageous books Ted tended to prefer. "You guys'll be working directly with me from now on," Geisel told the Berenstains.[1] Jan wasn't so sure—but then Ted informed her that he had a big idea for a brand-new kind of children's book, and he "definitely" wanted the Berenstains in on it.

Geisel's new project was an imprint called Bright and Early Books, "for younger and younger readers." It was a concept he and Phyllis had been kicking around for some time before her dismissal, based on feedback from educators and parents who loved Beginner Books but wanted books that could be read by new readers who might not have the vocabulary skills needed for a Beginner Book, even with its limited word list. "I realized that there was a level below Beginner Books," said Geisel, "so we began making things simpler and simpler." *Hop on*

Pop and *Dr. Seuss's ABC* had each been a dry run for the imprint, phonics-focused books with large, easy-to-read print—and based on the success of those books, Ted was right to believe that the new imprint could be "even bigger than Beginner Books."[2]

Geisel wanted a new look and feel for Bright and Early Books, starting with a lower page count—twenty-six pages versus the sixty-four for Beginner Books—which also meant faster-paced stories or narratives. There would be a word list, certainly, probably similar to the abbreviated one Geisel had relied on for *Green Eggs and Ham*—but Ted naturally wasn't going to be quite the stickler for the list that Phyllis had been. The point was simply to make each word work in perfect sync with illustrations—and if a word like *clown* wasn't actually on the word list, that was okay; it could be used so long as it was adjacent to a drawing that was unmistakably a clown.

The Berenstains were intrigued by the idea and promised to come back to Geisel with a story outline (Ted's only condition: *no bears this time*). Meanwhile, Geisel, too, would start doodling around, understanding full well that when he launched the Bright and Early Books imprint, it would be expected to have at least one, if not two, Dr. Seuss books to offer.

Apart from the new imprint, there were other big changes at Random House; for one thing, Ted's reliable editor Louise Bonino was ailing, and had stepped aside from her editorial responsibilities, which were then assumed by juvenile editor Walter Retan. Bob Bernstein had also designated his own personal assistant, Anne Marcovecchio, as the Geisels' personal handler, funneling all correspondence, requests, and anything requiring Ted's attention through her—and then routing all responses back out through her again. Similarly, back in La Jolla, the Geisels had hired twenty-five-year-old Julie Olfe to manage the stacks of mail that flooded into the Tower every week. This put two much-needed gatekeepers between Geisel and potential Beginner Books authors, sparing Ted the need to reject manuscripts personally. With Marcovecchio and Olfe on hand to break the bad news to would-be authors, Ted could finally retire Outgo Schmierkase as well as Grimalkin, Drouberhannus, Knalbner and Fepp.

There was also Michael Frith, the funny and talented young art director who had been friends with the Cerfs' oldest son, Christopher, at Harvard, where they'd worked together at *Harvard Lampoon.* Frith had arrived in the middle of the Geisel/Cerf blowup, and on one of his first days at Random House, he'd been warned by a still-smarting Phyllis Cerf to never speak with the Geisels. "If you see Ted or Helen in the elevator, don't even say 'hello' to them," she told Frith. "You're not allowed to talk to them."[3] And yet Frith would manage to successfully straddle the battle lines, becoming a trusted colleague both to Phyllis at Step-Up Books and to Ted at Beginner Books, where he would fill the role vacated by Cerf and serve as the imprint's editor in chief. Geisel, of course, would remain as president—and now the final arbiter of everything.

Unshackled from Phyllis, Geisel began recruiting Beginner Books authors from among his friends in La Jolla—a practice Phyllis had vetoed earlier, reminding him that his neighbors "weren't professional writers."[4] But Ted was optimistic that all it took was a little training, coaching, and careful editing—at least among his friends who had some experience writing technical or scientific papers. Fred Phleger, for instance, was a professor at the Scripps Institution of Oceanography whose major published work was *Ecology and Distribution of Recent Foraminifera.* Under Geisel's guidance, Phleger would author a number of moderately successful Beginner Books, including the ecologically themed *The Whales Go By* and *You Will Live Under the Sea.*

In the thirty years since Ted and Helen had first selected La Jolla as their home, the community had quickly grown into one of the wealthiest in California—and the Geisels, despite their general modesty, fit right in. At a time when the average annual income in the United States hovered around $4,400, Ted was earning more than $200,000, about $1.6 million today. Although he still tried to live within the self-imposed limits of a $5,000 annual salary, he could always withdraw against his royalties when needed—a luxury that had allowed the Geisels to easily renovate the Tower and travel widely.

The newly established University of California at San Diego (UCSD), too, had made La Jolla an even more desirable place to live—and Geisel thought the presence of the university had improved more than just property values. One of the most active advocates for the establishment of the university in the area was the noted climate change scientist Roger Revelle, who made it clear to the community that the anti-Semitic housing policies of the local La Jolla Real Estate Brokers' Association did not make for the kind of environment in which to establish a university. Local leaders, he said, would have to "make up their minds whether they wanted a university or an anti-Semitic covenant. You couldn't have both."[5]

More inclusive heads had prevailed, and since 1960, UCSD had been attracting residents who were intellectual and socially progressive—and Geisel, who often felt like the only Democrat in a sea of conservative Republicans, welcomed the company. At dinner parties, he would often get a laugh by telling the story of trying to register as a Democrat in La Jolla and having the registrar ask him if he was joking. "During a political campaign, my La Jolla friends all try to convert me," he said later, "but on election day I manage to be out of town."[6] Eventually, his Mount Soledad neighborhood would be populated by multiple Nobel Prize winners—"and that makes for some pretty stimulating get-togethers," said Ted.[7]

Such get-togethers, however, still fell under Helen's jurisdiction. Of the two of them, Helen was still the more social, as well as an active member of the La Jolla community, serving on boards and committees, recalled neighbors, "with a determination of an army general when it came to a favorite cause."[8] Besides assuming oversight of the Seuss Foundation, Helen was also active with the La Jolla Museum—she would be elected its president in 1966—and served as secretary of the advisory board at Scripps Memorial Hospital. Ted, meanwhile, would quickly lose interest in foundations and boards, attending only a smattering of meetings before deciding community advocacy turned the gears of change too slowly. "This isn't going anywhere," he would say in frustration, and wheel out of the room. "He wanted the results," said Judith Morgan, whose husband, Neil, had served with Geisel on several boards. "It had to be worth that two hours away from his desk, because he loved that room. It was his life."[9]

When he wasn't sitting at the desk in that room, Geisel could be found more and more standing at an easel, dabbing at gigantic ink and watercolor paintings. Lately, too, he had begun to work in the new medium of oil paint, producing paintings with titles like *Plethora of Cats*, *Venetian Cat Singing Oh Solo Meow*, and *I Dreamed I Was a Doorman at the Hotel del Coronado*—"serious examples of Seuss art,"[10] he said with mock solemnity, though he admitted that "some people say I should throw out the paintings and keep the titles."[11] For painting, too, he still generally preferred working after midnight, when he had put aside his latest book and could paint at the canvas quietly—though, as Helen groaned, never neatly. "Paint seems to land on everything from chairs to tables to sofa covers to his own hair," she said.[12]

Invitations to receptions at the Tower or to Helen's annual Christmas party were some of the most coveted in the region. "A cocktail party is something you invite people to that you don't like well enough to invite to dinner," Ted joked—but the Geisels also hosted a sit-down dinner at least once a week, with nearly thirty invited guests. "[Helen] had her way of disciplining time for social things and giving parties," Judith Morgan remarked later. "I think she believed, truly, it was good for Ted to stop work for a while—and he might not have done it [otherwise]." As a couple, they were good hosts, playing to each other's strengths as they worked a room or presided over a large dinner table conversation. "Helen was the social one," remembered Morgan. "She was outgoing, [though not] in the outburst way Ted was. He would burst out and everything would be terribly funny, and then he'd withdraw, and she would carry on."[13]

While old Army buddies like Meredith Willson—whose latest musical *The Unsinkable Molly Brown* had just been made into a film for MGM—and polio pioneer Jonas Salk could sometimes be found at the

Geisel dinner table, Ted and Helen were spending more and more time with Grey and Audrey Dimond. Ted liked Grey, a dashing figure who looked as if he had stepped out of a Hollywood medical drama. "Grey was really a handsome rogue," said Morgan, "certainly kind of suave."[4] Prior to relocating to La Jolla, Dr. Dimond had served in the U.S. Army Medical Corps and then as the head of the Department of Medicine at the University of Kansas Medical Center. But under the intimidating job titles and serious demeanor was a droll sense of humor that Ted appreciated, and the two of them enjoyed teasing each other "like fraternity mates," Morgan recalled.[5]

But Ted was even more taken with Audrey, who could be unabashedly silly and never minded being the center of attention. Born in Chicago and raised in New York City, Audrey had been the child of a broken marriage and had been raised by a single mother; she was determined that her own two daughters would *not* share a similar fate. From a young age, she thought she had her future "all figured." After graduating from Indiana University with a nursing degree, "I would marry a doctor," explained Audrey later. "I would have two children. They would both be girls. They would take care of me. And they would not be alone as I was with my mother. That was it." So far she had followed her own plan to the letter, as she and Grey lived with their two daughters, Lark and Leagrey, near the base of Mount Soledad on the quaintly named Ludington Lane. "Then life just came along," Audrey added, "and changed everything."[6]

The Dimonds would often pick up the Geisels and drive them to parties together—a wise decision, given Ted's driving—where Ted and Audrey would amuse themselves braiding the fringe on their hostess's expensive draperies, or Ted would watch with obvious glee as Audrey joined a rambunctious group gathered around the piano, where she would whistle along loudly instead of singing. Other times, they would all spend their evenings at the Tower, cocktails in hand, talking late into the night. Ted had even let the Dimonds into his studio to examine the early drafts of a book he had pinned to the corkboard—the Beginner Book *Fox in Socks*—and was delighted when Audrey recited every tongue twister in the book quickly and without a single mistake. "Audrey was always bubbly and merry and he loved that," recalled Judith Morgan.[17]

Helen could sense a change in the group dynamic, even if she couldn't yet pinpoint exactly what it was. "I don't know how it happened," she told Morgan, "but suddenly we four have to go everywhere together."[18]

What had happened was that Ted and Audrey were in love.

• • • •

Geisel spent much of 1964 working on two books he hoped to have completed by early 1965: the Beginner Book *Fox in Socks* and the Big Book *I Had Trouble in Getting to Solla Sollew*. The name Solla Sollew, like many Seussian names, had been inspired by a real person, in this case the president of La Jolla Federal Savings and Loan Association, and friend of the Geisels, named Sibley Sellew. Ted had struggled with the book, which featured one of his wordiest and most complicated story lines as it followed his narrator on a journey to the City of Solla Sollew, "where they *never* have troubles! At least, very few."[19] The Geisels spent several weeks in Australia, giving Ted an opportunity to clear his head and Helen the chance to have Ted's undivided attention, free from the Dimonds, for perhaps the first time in months. Geisel loved Australia and would always be impressed with how literate the Australians were. "Ted should be put on the Chamber of Commerce for Australia," joked Helen. "He tells everyone he would get there in a minute to start life again if he were twenty years younger."[20]

Geisel's peace of mind would fade the moment he returned to his desk in La Jolla and to *Solla Sollew*, eventually becoming so distraught that he exhausted even Helen's seemingly infinite patience. "About two weeks before the completion of every book, he seems to go into a tailspin," Helen wrote to Anne Marcovecchio with slight exasperation. "[He] decides that nothing in the book is any good, that he can't possibly finish it, and . . . I have a great job to do in keeping everything from falling in the scrap basket. I'm at my wit's end trying not to be rude."[21] To her frustration, her own health had begun to decline again, and she feared she was beginning to go blind.

Ted would deliver *I Had Trouble in Getting to Solla Sollew* in April 1965. The staff at Random House gathered excitedly to listen to Ted read it aloud in Cerf's office, "suitably the grandest in that very grand building," remembered Michael Frith. "High-ceilinged, wood paneled . . . it looked by then like a classic, old-line men's club library, [with] his large desk in front of the tall windows looking out on Madison Avenue with St. Patrick's Cathedral across the street." Ted would carefully read each page, holding up the drawings as he did so. "They were, of course, as integral to the experience as the text," said Frith warmly.[22]

Despite his year of reworking and revising, Geisel was still unhappy with *Solla Sollew*, calling it "not one of my more successful books."[23] Parents tended to enjoy it more than younger readers, perhaps appreciating its more complex plot and what seemed like a constant stream of new characters on every page. "I have a secret following among adults, but they have to read me when no one is looking," said Ted.[24]

But if *Solla Sollew* failed to find the kind of crossover appeal typical of most Dr. Seuss books, that certainly couldn't be said of the Beginner Book Geisel delivered that same year, the rocking and rollicking *Fox in Socks*. "Take it slowly, this book is dangerous!" joked Geisel[25]— and the cover copy actually *dared* kids to "READ ALOUD to find out just how smart your tongue is."[26] With a come-on like that, it was little wonder the book would become one of the bestselling and best-loved Dr. Seuss books, with sales surpassing three million copies by the end of the twentieth century. Most readers, however, paid scant attention to Ted's dedication page, which proclaimed the book was for his neighbors "Mitzi Long and Audrey Dimond of the Mt. Soledad Lingual Laboratories." Ted and Audrey's devotion was there in plain sight, if one knew where to look.

Geisel would make another appearance as Theo. LeSieg that summer, writing the Beginner Book *I Wish That I Had Duck Feet*, with art by Barney Tobey. The LeSieg books were still the recovery room for manuscripts Ted felt he had to rescue and rehabilitate—sometimes with hard feelings. While the worst thing Geisel could tell an artist was that something in his or her work "made my teeth hurt," for a writer, it was learning that a submitted manuscript had been deemed so unusable that it would be completely rethought, rewritten, and reassembled, often Frankenstein-style, and published under the LeSieg pseudonym. Geisel, in fact, had had a falling-out with Mike McClintock over a Beginner Book at some point—an experience that left such a bad taste in Ted's mouth that when McClintock died suddenly in 1967, Ted refused to donate to a memorial service for the man who had given him his first big break in publishing in 1937.[27]

Helen, too, was working hard on Beginner Books—"toiling busily away," she said, while at the same time "tiptoeing around the house so as not to disturb" Ted.[28] For some time, they had slept in separate bedrooms—mostly an accommodation to Ted's late hours, so he could retire to bed at two in the morning without disturbing Helen—but lately it seemed each was being particularly mindful of staying out of the way of the other.

Bennett Cerf, meanwhile, was actively wooing a suitor of his own: the Radio Corporation of America (RCA), which he hoped would purchase Random House for his asking price of nearly $40 million. Despite Cerf's ambitions, it was an odd transaction. "Large corporations like RCA and IBM were buying up publishers in the 1960s because they thought the computer would be primarily a teaching tool," explained Bob Bernstein. "The thinking was that educational publishers would provide the software for the hardware owned by these corporations."[29] Oddly, however, RCA couldn't have cared less about Beginner Books as a potential educational publisher; its executives instead were more excited about the textbook publisher L. W. Singer that Random House had recently acquired at a fire sale price. RCA would make the deal official in early 1966, and Bennett Cerf would slide over to a seat on the RCA board of directors, while Bob Bernstein would take over as Cerf's handpicked successor. For Geisel, who also owned stock in Random House, it was both a profitable and happy transaction: he had gone from working for Cerf, who admired him, to Bernstein, who adored him.

It was a benevolent, beneficent, and significantly wealthier Cerf who showed up in San Diego that February to attend, at Ted's request, a Dr. Seuss–themed charity ball benefitting the San Diego Children's Hospital. Ted and Helen, both fighting the flu, attended as guests of honor, with Ted in a tux and Helen looking elegant in a white dress with pearls and gloves. More than a thousand guests danced among gigantic cutouts of Dr. Seuss characters, with Seuss animals serving as centerpieces, hanging from the balconies and chandeliers, and marching across the front of the menu, which featured items like "roast beast *au jus Seuss*."[30] Cerf made a brief but rousing speech in which he remarked that "when a country stops laughing at itself, it's in trouble," and only slightly scuttled his goodwill by endorsing Democrat Tom Braden in his ultimately unsuccessful bid for governor of California.[31]

One of Ted's original oil paintings, an abstract titled *Chase in the Forest*, was auctioned off for $2,800, though the winner was not one of its most persistent bidders: Phyllis Cerf. But the one item nearly everyone wanted to take home that evening was the program Ted had designed for the event, filled with Seussian characters climbing around ads purchased by local businesses, and "so clever that no one would want to give one up."[32] One of those local businesses with a large ad in the program was Marvin K. Brown Cadillac—a name Geisel would file away and use, in only somewhat modified form, several years later.

• • • •

Only days before the charity ball, Geisel received a note from an old friend who wanted to discuss adapting a Dr. Seuss book into an animated cartoon. It wasn't the first time such an entreaty had been made. "Everybody wanted to make a series," said Geisel, but he was skeptical; most television producers, he said, wanted to "bat 'em out fast and use up my whole life's work in a year."[33] But this plea was different from the others. It came from someone Ted knew and respected—someone he'd worked with on *Private Snafu* cartoons during the war, and who knew exactly what he was doing. "Maybe you don't think I can draw your character," said the note, under which was a nearly perfect rendering of the Cat in the Hat to prove otherwise.[34] And underneath that was the author's crabbed signature: Chuck Jones.

Jones, now fifty-four, had recently been let go from Warner Bros., after more than thirty years of turning out one iconic cartoon for the studio after another. Now he was in charge of MGM Animation, where he was revamping the shopworn *Tom and Jerry* series. Knowing Geisel as he did—and well aware of his penchant for perfection—Jones knew it was going to be a tough sell and decided to take on the task in person. "Unsurprisingly, Dr. Seuss was not eager to have more of his books made into film," Jones said later.[35] Jones drove from Los Angeles to La Jolla, and as he came up the winding road leading to the Tower at the top of the mountain, Ted was standing at the end of their long driveway to greet him. Jones, who hadn't seen Geisel since 1946, thought his old friend looked "not very different. He didn't change a lot."[36]

Geisel's initial strategy was simply to stonewall Jones. "He had planned that we'd talk about old times," Jones recalled, "and then I'd go home." But Jones was persuasive. "I told him it was time to put Dr. Seuss on television,"[37] said Jones, who was as passionate and as meticulous about animation as Geisel was about writing children's books. Like Geisel, Jones had put serious thought into what did and didn't work in his craft, and had even developed a series of hard rules he expected his designers and animators to follow, like "All living creatures, fictional or not, have anatomy."[38] Ted could respect that kind of discipline. The more Jones talked, the more excited Helen became about the project—and with both Jones and Helen now enthusiastically double-teaming him, Ted finally wore down. "I decided that if I was going to go on TV, I'd better do it before I'm 70," he said later.[39]

The only real question was which book Jones would adapt. "It was early enough in the year that we could get it done for Christmas," said Jones, "so it had to be the *Grinch*."⁴⁰ Geisel was fine with that—but on the condition that he would be permitted to serve as a producer of the film alongside Jones, so he could keep a close eye on as much of the production as possible. The two shook hands and Jones left satisfied. "I climbed the mountain to meet this wonderful hermit and persuaded him to allow the Grinch off the hill,"⁴¹ said Jones, then immediately went to work on the character designs and storyboards he would need to sell the show to a sponsor. Geisel, meanwhile, called on agent Phyllis Jackson to have her draw up the contracts between him and Jones, then notified Bob Bernstein of the deal. To Geisel's surprise, Bernstein, who rarely saw a marketing opportunity he didn't like, was hesitant, asking Ted over and over again to make sure he was comfortable with Jones. Even Jackson's heart wasn't quite in it, though she diligently drew up a low four-figure agreement between Geisel and Jones.

It took two months to storyboard the *Grinch*. Geisel and Jones worked together closely, with Jones making regular trips to the Tower to consult with Geisel over the Grinch's design, and Geisel shuttling over to Jones's offices at MGM to help develop the storyboards. For the most part, the two were in sync, picking up without missing a beat the collaborative rapport they'd developed two decades ago working on *Private Snafu*. The only real disagreements had to do with the design of the Grinch. Color was the first issue to be resolved; in the book, the Grinch had been uncolored, with only his eyes a burning red color. After much discussion, Geisel agreed the Grinch could be green—which, Jones later confessed, matched the color of every rental car he had driven around La Jolla that summer.⁴²

Color decisions aside, bringing any character from the page of a book to an animated cartoon required some serious thought. On the TV screen, the Grinch couldn't just be a series of poses, as he was on the page; Geisel and Jones had to really think about how he moved and how he walked and sat and frowned. The two passed drawings back and forth for some time until Jones—exercising a rare veto authority—approved the final design. "Ted was very patient with me.

He felt that my Grinch looked more like *me* than his Grinch," said Jones. "Well, something had to give, so we ended up with a sort of mélange of all the Grinches."[43]

With the storyboards complete, Jones began the thankless task of carting his boards around town to meet with potential sponsors, displaying the storyboards on an easel as he enthusiastically acted out scenes before rooms full of skeptical candy company executives. For a while, Geisel tagged along to watch, but Jones, who "kept seeing his poor face" as they were rejected by one executive after another, finally told him to stop attending the pitch sessions.[44] Jones remembered approaching twenty-six uninterested sponsors, including Nestlé and Kellogg's, before finally finding a home for the Grinch with the Foundation for Commercial Banks. Jones could barely contain his amusement at the irony. "You have to be kidding!" Jones wrote later. "The bankers bought a story in which the Grinch says, 'Maybe Christmas doesn't come from a store'??!! Well, bless their banker hearts!"[45]

With their backing secured, Geisel, Jones, and the crew at MGM ramped up production immediately and intensely. Geisel had made it clear from the start that he didn't want *Grinch* to look "mass-produced," with the assembly-line animation typical of most television cartoons. Jones assured him that there would be no scrimping on the production; whereas an average episode of the prime-time cartoon *The Flintstones* might use 2,000 individual drawings in thirty minutes—about three drawings per foot of film—Jones promised that *How the Grinch Stole Christmas!* would utilize 25,000 in thirty minutes, or fifteen drawings per foot. Jones also vowed there would be no hastily assembled cut-and-paste backgrounds, and called in an ace: his former colleague from Warner Bros., the designer and background artist Maurice Noble, whose panoramas had given Road Runner cartoons their magisterial sense of desert space, and ambitious cartoons like *What's Opera, Doc?* their epic feel.

Noble admitted to being somewhat starstruck during his first meeting with Geisel. "I was an admirer of Ted Geisel," he said, "but I *loved* Dr. Seuss."[46] As with Jones, he and Geisel would also often go round and round, arguing over the look of Noble's backgrounds. Noble tried to explain that part of his job was to expand on the limited backgrounds Geisel had provided in the original book—the backgrounds had to extend well beyond what was on the page and had to flow logically into each other from scene to scene. "You have to enrich the design," explained Noble, "you've got to give it more schmaltz, and this is where I'd run into difficulty with Ted," he recalled. "But you don't argue too long with God."[47] Noble would eventually produce more than 250 backgrounds for *Grinch*, more than twice the amount used in the typical thirty-minute cartoon.

While Jones intended to stay as faithful as possible to Geisel's original story, Jones had timed the book as taking about twelve minutes to read out loud. That meant the pace of the story would have to be stretched to fill a full running time of twenty-four minutes. Neither Jones nor Geisel wanted the story to feel artificially padded, so Jones suggested they could spend some time using the character of Max, the Grinch's put-upon dog, as "both observer and victim, at one with the audience." Geisel, who already loved the character, enthusiastically agreed, saying Max was "Everydog—all love and limpness and loyalty."[48]

The remaining time would be filled with songs, and here Geisel was delighted to take on the task himself—he hadn't written lyrics since *Dr. T.* in 1950—writing songs for the Christmas-loving Whos and the Christmas-hating Grinch. Sometimes writing by hand, sometimes typing them out neatly, Geisel filled page after page with snippets of lyrics, clever turns of phrase, and—more often than not—lots of long blank lines to fill in later, when he could think of a good rhyme.

The songs for the Whos had been the easier ones, mainly because Geisel could make up what Jones called "Seussian Latin" to fit his rhyme schemes.[49] Initially, Geisel had written a long Christmas concert, in which the Whos conversed with each other in their own language: "Qwee kon who bah. Multrew Fultrow! Fultrow Multrow!" Geisel had eventually abandoned that idea as overly complicated, and focused instead on an opening Christmas carol called "Welcome

Christmas," combining both English and Seussian Latin. Ted started off writing "Dah Who Deeno!" then crossed it out in favor of "Noo Who Frobus!"[50] After a bit more fussing, he would finally arrive at "Fahoofores, Dahoodores" as the refrain.[51] "[It] seems to have as much authenticity as 'Adeste Fideles' to those untutored in Latin," said Jones encouragingly.[52]

It was the Grinch's song, however, that Geisel intended to be the showstopper, coming at the moment the Grinch actually steals Christmas, oozing around Whoville to poach their gifts and decorations. "You're a grizzly, ghastly goon," Geisel wrote at the top of one page, then played around with a few rhymes, finally circling "dried up prune." But then, after writing "You brush your teeth with turpentine," he scribbled the entire page out darkly, a false start. Starting again at the top of another page, he typed "You're the king of all that rots," then listed several possible rhymes down the right-hand side of the page: *Knots. Tots. Spots. Pots. Lots. Tangled up in kinky knots.* Once more, the entire page would be crossed out.[53]

Other times, he would write out couplets—some of which rhymed, some of which didn't—to see if anything amused him enough to remain intact through draft after draft. While the rhyming couplet "Mr. Grinch . . . We don't adore you, / Mr. Grinch, we ABHOR you," would be discarded, he was delighted with the nonsensical—and nonrhyming—"You nauseate me, Mister Grinch. / With a nauseous supernaus." Whatever it meant, Geisel liked it; it would stay. Meanwhile, on yet another page, he struggled to find the closing lines to follow an opening couplet he liked, inserting long blanks to be filled in later:

> You're a foul one, Mr. Grinch
>
> Oh, you really are a punk.
>
> You're as _____ as a_____
>
> You're as _____ as a _____

Again on the right-hand side, still trying out words, Geisel had written *contempt* and *contemptible*, neither of which he was happy with. This page, too, would finally be abandoned, with the exception of three words Ted had written in, almost as an afterthought, to rhyme with *punk*, and which he would use memorably in the final song: *stink stank stunk*.[54]

Ted eventually completed the Grinch's song, "You're a Mean One, Mr. Grinch," a tour de force of over-the-top gross-out images—a bad banana with a greasy black peel, a dead tomato with moldy purple spots, a sauerkraut and toadstool sandwich—that made the Grinch seem even *more* deliciously nasty than he had in the book. With the addition of the Grinch's song, the animated feature suddenly transcended its source material, giving the cartoon its own unique place in the Dr. Seuss oeuvre, beyond that of a mere adaptation.

Geisel worked on the songs with Albert Hague, who wrote the music, then passed them off to Eugene Poddany, who orchestrated the songs and conducted a thirty-four-piece orchestra and twelve-voice chorus. In his notes for the Grinch's song, Geisel had written that he wanted it sung in a "very low, hoarse gravelly basso." Jones had already hired seventy-eight-year-old horror movie icon Boris Karloff as the narrator and to provide the speaking voice of the Grinch, a decision Geisel supported. But the singing would be assigned to a voice actor Jones had called in to perform several other background voices for the cartoon: Thurl Ravenscroft, a rangy fifty-two-year-old with the basso voice Geisel wanted. "[Chuck Jones] handed me the song sheet and we made it in about three takes," said Ravenscroft.[55] Both Geisel and Jones sat in on the recording sessions. Photos taken that afternoon show Jones in a tweed coat and bow tie, with a slightly impish smile on his face, while Geisel listens intently, in a dark bow tie and jacket. After Ravenscroft finished singing, the crew gathered in the control room to listen to the playback.

"I liked what I heard," said Geisel as Jones queued up the tape.

As the song started again, Jones turned to Ravenscroft with a wry smile. "Thurl, what do you think?"

"If you're happy, I'm happy," said Ravenscroft diplomatically.

"Well," said Geisel, "we think it's perfect."[56]

The only remaining point of contention was the story's ending. Geisel knew how he wanted the last scene to play out; in his copy of the *Grinch* script, he had circled the Grinch's great epiphany—"Maybe Christmas, he thought, doesn't come from the store . . ."—and had written "*slow delivery, as if dawn is breaking.*"[57] Geisel wanted the final moments to be deliberately paced—he had worked hard when writing the book in 1957 to make it as non-preachy as possible, and didn't want the cartoon going for an easy, saccharine, Technicolor Christmas ending. It was Noble who came up with an elegant solution, by having the Whos join hands and "create" a star as "a manifestation of their love and joy," said Noble. "The star then moved up and joined with the Grinch, and he was transformed."[58] Perfect.

Nearly everyone involved loved the final product. "Everything seemed to come together beautifully," said Noble.[59] Although Phyllis Jackson and Bob Bernstein were still uncertain—Noble, with some hyperbole, recalled that "Dr. Seuss's agents screamed and yelled"— Geisel was standing by the project, convinced that he and Jones had something special on their hands. Jones, too, would always regard the *Grinch* with considerable pride. "How could anyone—how could I—not love the Grinch?"[60]

As the December airdate neared, Jones negotiated a deal with the CBS network, which paid $315,000 for the rights to air *How the Grinch Stole Christmas!* in 1966 and 1967. TV critics snickered, convinced CBS had paid far too much for a cartoon that would surely be forgotten and shelved, never to be seen again. Jones joked that on a per-minute basis, the twenty-four-minute *Grinch* had cost the network more than rival ABC had recently paid to show the two-hour-and-forty-minute Oscar winner *The Bridge on the River Kwai*. All they could do now was wait.

How the Grinch Stole Christmas! aired on CBS on the evening of Sunday, December 18, 1966—and for a moment, it appeared the skeptics might have been right. "Fell a trifle short of expectation," sniffed the feared TV critic Jack Gould of *The New York Times*. "It may just be that the Grinch is a creation that should be left undisturbed on the printed page."[61] On the West Coast, Hal Humphrey, writing for the *Los Angeles Times*, tended to agree, calling it "a disappointment . . . It is my opinion that the book was better than this expensive half-hour color TV adaptation proved to be."[62] But their voices, it soon became clear, were in the minority. Most critics, like most viewers, *loved* the *Grinch*. Cynthia Lowry, writing for the widely circulated Associated Press, directly refuted the assessments of Gould and Humphrey, enthusing that the story had "lost nothing and even gained its transition from the printed page to television."[63] The *Indianapolis News* called it "beautiful," the *Orlando Sentinel* found it "whimsical and tuneful," while the *Philadelphia Inquirer* hailed it simply as "classic."[64] Closer to home, Donald Freeman, writing in the *San Diego Union*, thought it "a triumph of major proportions."[65] *How the Grinch Stole Christmas!* would become a beloved and perennial holiday classic, rivaled only, perhaps, by Charles Schulz's *A Charlie Brown Christmas*.

That Christmas, Geisel's La Jolla neighbors embraced the Grinch as their very own; volunteers at the La Jolla Museum decorated the building to look like the pre-Grinched Whoville. Meanwhile, up at the Tower, Helen's annual Christmas Eve party—now one of the most desirable invitations of the season—had swollen to a guest list of sixty-five. Next year's party, she vowed, would be even larger and grander.

• • • •

It was hard for Ted and Audrey to be alone together. While Geisel could walk down the streets of New York and not be recognized as Dr. Seuss, he was easily recognized in La Jolla, so sneaking around their town with Audrey—who was also a prominent member of the community—was going to be out of the question. "I cannot imagine anyone having ever seen them coming out of a hotel or whatever," said Judith Morgan, though that didn't stop tongues from wagging.[66] For the most part, then, they would have to take what they could get at parties or other social events, huddling together off to one side of the room, or engaged in chatter over a chicken dinner at one of the countless La Jolla fundraisers or charity events. While some friends had their suspicions—"it wasn't the best-kept secret," said Morgan[67]—Ted and Audrey managed to keep their relationship low-key enough that the Geisels and the Dimonds continued to socialize, making it appear from the outside, at least, that both couples were still blissfully happy.

Still, the cracks were starting to show. On the evening of Friday, March 24, 1967, a San Diego police officer in the Mission Bay region pulled Geisel over after witnessing him changing lanes three times. Geisel was questioned briefly, then arrested and booked at city jail. Here he was given a sobriety test, in which his blood alcohol level registered at .13, just under the so-called indisputably impaired level of .15.[68] He was released and the embarrassing incident blew over without much notice or damage to his reputation, beyond a few newspaper headlines that tittered, "Dr. Seuss Was Soused?"[69] But the episode stirred a flurry of gossip and speculation about Geisel's mental state, as well as unanswered questions about what a notoriously bad driver was doing driving by himself—if he truly *was* by himself—in San Diego in the first place.

Still basking in the success of *Grinch*, Geisel and Jones had immediately negotiated a deal to follow up with an adaptation of *Horton Hears a Who!* Phyllis Jackson, no longer skeptical of Jones and MGM, wanted Geisel to hold out for more money than he had taken for selling the rights to *Grinch*, but Ted waved her off. He didn't care about or need the money; at this point, he just wanted to write the songs.

His most recent book, in fact, *The Cat in the Hat Songbook*, was made up entirely of songs, with Ted's lyrics scored for guitar and piano by Eugene Poddany, who'd orchestrated the music for *Grinch*. If *Grinch* and *5,000 Fingers of Dr. T.* had proven anything, it was that Geisel was capable of writing catchy songs, with fun-to-sing lyrics and catchy hooks—and Ted was rightly very proud of the songbook. But parents, it seemed, didn't want songbooks from Dr. Seuss; they wanted funny stories, with bouncy rhymes they could sing without picking out a melody on a guitar. As a result, *The Cat in the Hat Songbook* bombed on its publication, and Bernstein quietly permitted the book to go out of print—the only Dr. Seuss book, along with *Seven Lady Godivas,* consigned to such a fate during Ted's lifetime. Even as the book sank from sight, many had silently noted that Geisel had dedicated the book to Audrey's daughters, *Lark and Lea of Ludington Lane.* He was continuing to openly show Audrey his devotion wherever he could.

Most of the summer of 1967 was spent working with Jones on *Horton Hears a Who!* "What Jane Goodall is to baboons and Dian Fossey to gorillas Dr. Seuss is to the mind and heart of the male elephant,"[70] said Jones. Geisel had taken his songwriting duties seriously, scribbling rough notes in blue pen and red pencil all over the back of Beginner Books stationery. Lyrics were also scribbled on the back of pieces of cardboard, yellow paper—anything he could find.

He was also using a hardcover copy of *Horton* as his working script for the cartoon, marking passages with paper clips, rewriting some sections, and scribbling notes in the margins. Unlike *Grinch, Horton* wouldn't be a word-for-word adaptation; Geisel agreed to rework some of the book's verses to give Horton more dialogue in the cartoon, and chose to flesh out the character of the astronomer at the expense of mayor, who had carried much of the plot in the book. Ted was also responsible for crafting the new "slingshot ending," in which the astronomer catches a speck of dust as a little voice cries out "HELP!" "Oh no!" says the astronomer as the screen irises in on him. *Fin.*

For Jones's part, he was working hard to sand some of the rough edges off characters in the original book that he thought were too mean or too scary—and there were lots of them. One of Jones's writers, a recent film school graduate named Nick Iuppa, recommended in a memo that Ted give a new name to the eagle who carries away the clover, suggesting that while Vladikoff—the eagle's name in the book—was acceptable, "[it] should be preceded by a name so un-Russian that the content is humorous." Just below Iuppa's suggestion,

Ted had written *Whizzer MacWoff* in large print, a name that would stick.[71] Still, the characters in *Horton Hears a Who!* remain some of the most unlikable and most malicious in the Dr. Seuss menagerie—and even Jones, with his whimsical, wide-eyed sense of design, couldn't seem to make them any more endearing. *Horton* would air in September to generally positive reviews—"Another gem," was a typical response[72]—but would never reach the level of adoration attained by the Grinch.

In August, Bernstein and his wife came out to La Jolla to visit the Geisels. It was an opportunity for Bernstein to get a peek at the latest project Ted had pinned to the corkboard in his studio—at this time, it was *The Foot Book*, one of the first titles in the new Bright and Early Books imprint, which Ted was hoping to finally launch in 1968. "He would rush me to the studio and show me the pages, still mounted on the cork wall," said Bernstein excitedly. "He would then read them to me and then anxiously ask what I thought. This can be an uncomfortable moment with some authors, but I looked forward to it with Ted—his work always thrilled me."[73]

The mood at the Geisel household, however, left Bernstein concerned. Ted was grumbling that he was finding it difficult to work in the Tower and that he was "considering leasing a studio" somewhere in town. Bernstein thought Ted seemed "strangely down and jumpy," and wondered if perhaps the Geisels' marriage was in trouble. Editor Walter Retan also sensed trouble during his visit to the Tower that summer. "They had so much in common, but they were driving each other crazy," said Retan. "Helen wasn't well, and she probably depressed Ted. She had been very, very good for him, but I could not say she was good for him at that time."[74]

On September 23, 1967, Helen turned sixty-nine years old. Shortly thereafter, perhaps in an effort to reset their relationship, Ted and Helen left for an extended vacation in Colorado. Helen loved the remoteness of the Rocky Mountains and marveled at how they could drive for hours and rarely see another car. She and Ted stayed for three nights at the Garden of the Gods Club near Colorado Springs, then drove to Golden for a long stay with Orlo and Libby Childs, who had served as Ted's tour guide in Utah in 1947 and to whom he had dedicated *Scrambled Eggs Super!* in 1953. Libby remembered Helen as being "in such high spirits," with none of the indicators of the Geisels' souring relationship that had so concerned Bernstein and Retan.[75]

The Geisels returned to La Jolla in mid-October, and by the afternoon of Sunday the fifteenth were sailing with friends around Point Loma in San Diego. Photos show Helen in a turquoise bandanna and sunglasses, with a white sweater over a dress, and pearls around her neck, looking reserved, but impeccably dressed, as usual, even on the water. Six days later, they attended a dinner party at the sprawling Rancho Santa Fe estate of Luba and Duke Johnston—one of Ted's favorite prankster cronies. Duke thought Helen seemed "strangely low" that night, and as the Geisels prepared to leave that evening, Duke wrapped Helen in a bear hug. Helen seemed taken aback. "You don't know how I needed that!" she told Duke.[76]

The following evening, Helen retired to her bedroom around eleven. Ted was still working in his studio, fussing with *The Foot Book*, and would remain there until two in the morning, when he finally headed to bed in his own room. The following morning—Monday, October 23—the Geisels' housekeeper, Alberta Shaw, arrived at the Tower around ten to begin her usual shift. She found the house locked and quiet; while it wasn't unusual to find Ted still in bed when she arrived, Helen would usually have been up for several hours, working in her office or having coffee out by the pool. Alberta let herself into the house, where she found the door to Helen's bedroom closed. She quietly opened it and went inside.

Helen was still in bed. On her nightstand was a half-empty bottle of sodium pentobarbital tablets, and a handwritten note.

CHAPTER 14

I INTEND TO GO ON DOING JUST WHAT I DO

1967–1971

Julie Olfe, the Geisels' reliable secretary, pulled into the long driveway at the Tower around lunchtime. Olfe, now nearing thirty, was pregnant with her first child and had recently informed Helen that she wanted to retire from her duties to devote more time to family—a decision Helen supported, and had thus put Olfe to work on a final task of cleaning out old files and sorting correspondence to clear the way for a new secretary.

As Olfe approached the Tower on the afternoon of October 23, ready to dig back into the Geisel files, she could tell something unusual had happened. For one thing, there were several cars in the driveway—odd in itself, as guests were usually discouraged during the daytime hours when Ted was working. Then as Olfe approached the front door, she heard the gardener say in a hushed voice "something about Mrs. Geisel."[1] Olfe let herself in and found Ted in the living room, "grim-faced, with eight or ten friends in a loose circle around him."[2] Finally, Grey Dimond stepped over to Olfe to quietly break the terrible news: Helen Geisel was dead at age sixty-nine.

Before going to bed the night before, she had downed a handful of barbiturates—the bottle was still on the nightstand—then penned a final note, which she placed neatly on the bedside table:

Dear Ted,

> What has happened to us?
>
> I don't know.
>
> I feel myself in a spiral, going down down down, into a black hole from which there is no escape, no brightness. And loud in my ears from every side I hear, "failure, failure, failure . . ."
>
> I love you so much . . . I am too old and enmeshed in everything you do and are, that I cannot conceive of life without you . . . My going will leave quite a rumor but you can say I was overworked and overwrought. Your reputation with your friends and fans will not be harmed . . . Sometimes, think of the fun we had thru the years . . . [3]

She had signed it with the name of the fictional law firm to whom she and Ted often threatened to refer problematic clients—a final private joke, and a last reminder of the fun she and Ted had had through the years.

Ted was stunned and visibly rattled. "I didn't know whether to kill myself, burn the house down, or just go away and get lost,"[4] he said later. Informed of the news in Los Angeles, Peggy Owens sped to the Tower and arrived late in the afternoon to find the living room still filled with people, still talking in hushed tones, but no one daring to use the word *suicide*. Peggy cleared out the house and spent the next few days sitting with her uncle, talking late into the evenings. Only then would Ted permit the word to be said aloud: "I guess you know it was suicide," he told Peggy.[5]

As word of Helen's death spread beyond La Jolla—the carefully crafted statement Ted issued to the media kept Helen's cause of death intentionally vague—condolences and reminiscences flooded into the Tower. Bennett Cerf, who had learned of Helen's death in *The New York Times,* remembered her as "one of the most wonderful women I've met in my whole life . . . We regarded Helen—as a worker, a creator—[as] the most unselfish person we've ever known."[6] Al Perkins, one of Helen's favorite Beginner Books authors, wrote fondly that, "I am sure she will be mourned by thousands . . . who knew her, or knew of her not as Ted's helpmate, but as a brilliant writer, editor, and critic in her own right."[7]

Sometimes kindness came from unexpected places. One afternoon Geisel opened the front door in response to furious knocking, only to find two little boys gaping up at him. Finally one managed to ask, "Are you the man that wrote about the Grinch stealing Christmas?" Ted, expecting a request for an autograph, promised them that he was. "We just wanted to tell you we're sorry your wife died," said the boys, then turned and ran back down the mountainside.[8]

On November 9, the La Jolla Museum, where Helen had recently served as president, held a memorial service in her honor and announced that its reference library would be renamed the Helen Palmer Geisel Library. Ted, still shaken, attended the service with Peggy Owens and with Grey and Audrey Dimond. "It was a hard winter for him," said Julie Olfe, who had decided to remain at her post as Ted's secretary. "It was terrible. He was not happy in those days."[9]

Partly he was becoming more and more aware of both the sideways glances and the furious gossip swirling round about him and Audrey—chatter that had only grown louder in the weeks since Helen's suicide. Even among friends there was hushed speculation about what had driven Helen to take her own life. The word *affair* was whispered. Had Helen learned of Ted's relationship with Audrey? And now that Helen was gone, would Ted and Audrey drop any pretense and publicly begin a relationship?

Neighbor Stanley Willis thought Helen had surely known of the affair all along. "She was always cheerful, right up to the time she began to realize someone was moving into . . . what shall I call it? . . . her marital territory?"[10] said Willis. Friend and journalist Judith Morgan, who was tasked with writing Helen's obituary for the *San Diego Union*, thought Helen had long suspected Ted and Audrey's relationship, but had only recently had her suspicions cruelly confirmed. "My first thought was, 'Someone told her,'" said Morgan, "[with] 'someone' being Ted or Audrey."[11]

Ted attended Helen's memorial service in the company of the

Dimonds. If he felt even partly to blame for Helen's death, he never said. There would be no self-reflection in public or confessions in private journals; that simply wasn't Ted's way. Meanwhile, Audrey seemed to believe her relationship with Ted had been inevitable from practically the moment they met. "He fell in love," she said later. "I have to feel that in the big picture, it was meant to happen."[12]

Within six months, Geisel would put an end to at least some of the speculation—and further divide the La Jolla social community. In the spring of 1968, with contractors ready to begin another renovation and remodeling of the Tower, Geisel informed the crew that there had been a change of plans. The neutral colors he and Helen had selected in 1967 were to be discarded, he said, in favor of a bolder and brighter palette. When the architect came to consult with Geisel to confirm the new designs, he discovered Audrey was living at the Tower, happily selecting the new colors and overseeing the remodeling.

Only weeks earlier, in fact, Audrey had informed Grey Dimond that "something was lacking" in their marriage, and that she would be moving to Reno long enough to meet the residency requirements necessary for a quick divorce. Dimond was stunned but had presence of mind enough to drolly ask that she not get into any car if Geisel, a notoriously bad driver, was behind the wheel. "I don't want any wife of mine marrying a man who drives the way Ted does," he told her.[13]

Geisel, too, would sardonically inform one acquaintance that, "My best friend is being divorced and I'm going to Reno to comfort his wife."[14] The news of the pending nuptials sent Ted and Audrey's social circles into yet another maelstrom of gossip and controversy. Longtime friends squared off into separate camps, either approving or disapproving of the relationship. "[It caused] a rather large ripple in the community of La Jolla," said Audrey.[15]

Writing to Donald Bartlett in late May 1968, Geisel assured his old friend that "I have not flipped my lid":

> . . . let me put it out, flat on the line, without any comment or
> begging for understanding.

On the 21st of June, Audrey Dimond is going to Reno to divorce Grey Dimond . . . Audrey and I are going to be married about the first week in August. I am acquiring two daughters, ages nine and fourteen. I am rebuilding the house to take care of the influx. I am 64 years old. I am marrying a woman eighteen years younger . . . This is not a sudden nutty decision . . . This is an inevitable, inescapable conclusion to five years of four people's frustration. All I can ask you is to try to believe in me.[16]

Later, Audrey would muse that "it would've been nice if we'd met and married earlier."[17] Now, however, "the feeling was that at his age, you grab for the gusto," she said. "You don't wait. You don't think you have much time."[18]

On June 21, 1968, as renovations began at the Tower in La Jolla, Geisel and Audrey Dimond checked into the Ponderosa Hotel in Reno, taking a room in the charmless midtown hotel where the two of them would remain for six baking-hot weeks. Since both of them had only a passing interest in gambling, there wasn't much to do. Some days Ted would review the manuscript pages of a Bright and Early Book he had brought with him, Al Perkins's *The Hand Book*—later to be retitled *Hand, Hand, Fingers, Thumb*—writing Perkins pithy letters encouraging him to make the book "more exciting."[19] Other times, he would meet with attorney Frank Kockritz to take care of all the necessary legal paper work to finalize Audrey's divorce and make arrangements for marriage.

At 5:00 P.M. on Monday, August 5, 1968—six weeks and three days after their arrival in Reno—Ted and Audrey were married at the Washoe County Courthouse by a justice of the peace, with no one else in attendance. Ted was sixty-four years old; Audrey would turn forty-seven later in August. The Geisels would honeymoon for two days at South Lake Tahoe before returning to La Jolla. Duke and Luba Johnston, who had been with Helen the night before her death, hosted a dinner party for the newlyweds, but the community—"full of broken glass," as Audrey put it—would remain divided on the Geisels for some time.[20]

While marriage to Audrey also meant an instant family of two young daughters—Lark was fourteen, Leagrey nine—Ted found the concept of parenting daunting. "It slicks his hair back," Audrey told one journalist cheekily,[21] but the truth was less amusing, as Audrey sent her daughters away to live with their father, who had relocated to Washington, D.C. "They wouldn't have been happy with Ted, and Ted wouldn't have been happy with them," Audrey said later. "Ted's a hard man to break down, but this is who he was. He lived his whole life without children and he was very happy without children." As far as her decision to relinquish custody of her daughters, Audrey admitted she had "never been very maternal. There were too many other things I wanted to do. My life with him was what I wanted my life to be."[22]

In time, Ted and his stepdaughters would become friends, and then learn to adore and eventually love each other. He and the dark-haired Leagrey—who he jokingly called "Leagroo"—would tease each other mercilessly, hurling such savage insults at each other over breakfast that Audrey would leave the table, slightly terrified. Lark, meanwhile, was her sister's opposite, blond and willowy, with an artistic streak. When Lark graduated from boarding school in Arizona in 1972, Ted, bursting with pride, presented her with an oil painting of a bird with long blond hair wearing a cap and gown. And both daughters remembered the joy in receiving the funny notes or drawings that seemed to show up everywhere. "You saw him at his desk making these things," recalled Leagrey. "He would drop little notes on your bed or put them in your coat pocket. Everybody has memories of their pop and their mom. Those are your memories if Ted was your step-pop."[23]

The disapproval of some of his La Jolla neighbors didn't necessarily bother Geisel all that much. He was far more concerned about how Audrey would be accepted where it really mattered: at Random House, where Helen had been as much a part of the Dr. Seuss and Beginner Books empire as Ted. While Audrey wouldn't be formally involved with Beginner Books, it mattered to Ted that the staff at Random House liked her. Ted was relieved to find the Random House crew was generally charmed by Audrey, who could easily chat up nearly anyone. Anne Marcovecchio—now Anne Johnson—signed off on the new Mrs. Geisel by declaring that Audrey "gave [Ted] new vitality and kept him alive longer."[24] Most also noted with some amusement that Audrey already had Ted dressing better, abandoning his neutral tones and staid suits or slacks for brightly colored pants and plaid jackets.

At Beginner Books, Helen's death had left Ted as the last man standing in what had originally been a three-way partnership. While Ted was trying to shoulder some of Helen's workload, Bernstein was moving around staff to try to get Ted both the editorial and managerial support he needed, especially with the Bright and Early Books imprint nearing its debut in the autumn of 1968. Anne Johnson had been promoted to vice president of Beginner Books, while Michael Frith was assigned the role of editor in chief—with Ted, of course, remaining as the final arbiter on everything.

Though the two had been thrown together by Bernstein, Geisel found he enjoyed working with the twenty-seven-year-old Frith. They shared a similar sense of humor—both had worked at their college humor magazines and both, said Frith, had "this absolutely mutual delight in . . . loving absurd verse."[25] Frith was also a talented writer and artist who had illustrated several Step-Up Books for Phyllis Cerf, and he and Geisel had a mutual respect for the power of words and images working harmoniously to educate and entertain. There was also just the slightest hint of father-son in their relationship—each could find each other exasperating—and Frith thought it was no coincidence that Geisel and his own father were not only the same age but had even been at Oxford at the same time, where neither one of them had done much studying.

As Geisel prepared to launch the first four titles in the Bright and Early Books imprint that autumn, Frith found that much of his job required acting as mediator—and emollient—between Geisel and his stable of talent. "Ted wasn't easy to work with," said Frith. "He had very little patience for . . . a lot of the people with whom he worked because Ted knew better. Whatever was going on, they couldn't be as good, and as smart, and as inventive, and as good a designer, and all those things as Dr. Seuss—and where Dr. Seuss is concerned," added Frith, "I have no argument."[26] Moreover, Geisel didn't believe in managing his writers and artists so much as he believed they needed to be *corralled*. Ted's style, explained Frith, was "you've got to . . . I won't say *crush* them, but you really have to sit on them, step on them, make sure they do it exactly your way, or it won't be what it could be."[27] As Julie Olfe put it, "In his head, he had such definite ideas about books he wanted others to do, but they could not carry out ideas that he could not express."[28]

Whether he had crushed them or not, the corralling seemed to have paid off, as Bright and Early Books would debut in October 1968 with four strong and memorable titles. As expected, a Dr. Seuss book was among them, *The Foot Book*, Geisel's spry study in opposites ("Wet foot / Dry foot / Low foot / High foot"), but so, too, was a LeSieg title, *The Eye Book*, featuring art by Roy McKie. The reliable Al Perkins had provided *The Ear Book*, with illustrations by Henry Payne, and the ever-dependable Berenstains rounded out the four with their bubbly *Inside Outside Upside Down*—and once again, despite Geisel's initial admonition, their book featured the Berenstain Bears. They were simply too good *not* to use at this point.

Reviews of the new Bright and Early Books were positive, often fulsome, and usually focused mostly on *The Foot Book*. "With an extremely limited vocabulary, Dr. Seuss as usual, manufactures a masterpiece," a reviewer for the *Cincinnati Enquirer* wrote enthusiastically.[29] "A new book by Dr. Seuss is always an occasion for celebration," said another critic, who hailed *The Foot Book* as a "witty and rhythmic romp with hilarious illustrations."[30] Geisel was relieved; his new imprint was a success—so successful, in fact, that over the next five years, he would write more books for the new Bright and Early imprint than he would for Beginner Books or his own "Big Books."

And yet, in December, following the success of Bright and Early Books, came hardship, both professional and personal. At the urging of Bob Bernstein, Geisel agreed to appear on *The Dick Cavett Show*, a relatively new talk show, hosted by the droll but always engaged Cavett, a former writer for *The Tonight Show*. It was one of Dr. Seuss's first major national television interviews—and Geisel, understandably nervous, spent several days putting together a series of prepared questions for Cavett, writing them on one numbered note card after another and then memorizing his own pre-written responses. On December 5, with a thunderstorm raging outside Cavett's ABC studio, Geisel waited in the wings for more than an hour—he was the final guest, following director Jules Dassin, singer Mitch Miller, and critic Rex Reed—but his nerves were fraying, especially as the power began to flicker off and on inside the studio. Once he took his seat next to Cavett, however, he was dumbfounded when the host casually began asking the prepared questions out of order. Ted sat speechless, unable to recall any of his answers. "I laid the most colossal bomb," he said later, and vowed that *The Dick Cavett Show* would be his final television appearance.[31] Bernstein, to his credit, wisely concurred, conceding that Dr. Seuss was not an act made for television.

Then, four days later, on December 9, 1968, Ted's father, Theodor Robert Geisel, died at a nursing home in Agawam, Massachusetts, at the age of eighty-nine. Ted and Audrey had visited T.R. in August to move him into the nursing home—but Ted had a larger agenda in mind: he wanted his father to meet and approve of Audrey. To Ted's delight, his father had given the marriage his blessing, even as he forcefully resisted his relocation to the rest home in Agawam, stubborn to the very end.

• • • •

Geisel spent the last part of 1968 and early 1969 in a courtroom, fighting for his creative rights against an unexpected adversary: *Liberty* magazine. While the periodical had ceased publication in 1950, Broadway producer Lorraine Lester had purchased all 17,000 copyrights owned by the magazine, in search of potential merchandising. Looking through magazines from 1932, Lester found the ideal materials in a few of the Dr. Seuss cartoons of the era and had partnered with Cincinnati manufacturer Poynter Products to produce a series of cheap and badly made plastic figures based on some of Dr. Seuss's whimsical creatures. "My reaction was very black," said Geisel, with some understatement, and he immediately took Lester to court.[32]

The outcome was discouraging, and would be a lesson to other artists, at Geisel's considerable expense. In a sixty-three-page ruling, Judge William B. Herlands determined that Geisel had signed a contract giving to *Liberty* "all rights," which, Herlands added, could even include "skywriting on Mars."[33] The suit had cost Geisel nearly $100,000 in attorney's fees—and made him only more determined to ensure he retained all subsidiary rights on his work and rigidly controlled any merchandising. Frith recalled with considerable glee how Geisel would become "one of the most despised people in the toy industry" for his refusal to permit most Dr. Seuss merchandise.[34]

For now, Geisel would exert absolute control over the one product he could: his books. With neither Phyllis nor Helen to impose a strict adherence to the word list, Ted was determined to abandon the approved vocabulary altogether. Lately, he had become convinced that a limited vocabulary list was "insulting" to children anyway—that they could absorb a far greater number of words than those on any word list. "We just try to say what we have to say simply and concisely," he told *The New York Times*. "If we're successful in this," he joked, "we'll do prenatal books."[35] Instead, Geisel was all about the way the material was presented, striving for synchronicity between words and pictures.

The Big Books, however, were an entirely different matter. While Geisel always worked hard to achieve the ideal relationship of verse to illustration, the Big Books were his opportunity to really stretch out. "They were Ted kind of freewheeling," said Frith. "He was able to become much more silly and Seussy with the Big Books."[36]

That was certainly the case with the newest Dr. Seuss book for 1969, *I Can Lick 30 Tigers Today!* a collection of three stories, two of which featured the Cat in the Hat's son—or was it the Cat as a kitten? Geisel had illustrated this one in a style different from any of his previous books, using gouache and a brush, and a bright palette of colors, instead of the more typical pen and ink with flat colors. The lead story—in which the little cat, wearing a familiar hat and gloves and bow tie, struts and boasts of his ability to beat up thirty tigers— was Ted's brightly colored love letter to Audrey. The book was even dedicated to her, his none-too-subtle way of letting her know that she made *him* feel he really *could* take on thirty tigers.

While Audrey wasn't the kind of creative partner that Helen had been, Ted found her presence exciting and inspiring. "Sometimes he would bounce into the room in great excitement and say, 'Something's happening!'" said Audrey. "I learned never to ask what it was because his answer was always the same: 'I can't tell you until it's all together.'"[37] He was careful, however, never to ask her opinion directly. "If she says something is bad, it can destroy me for three days," Ted admitted.[38] And when everything finally did come together, "Audrey has to listen to revision after revision," said Ted. "She's my mainstay."[39]

And yet there were still days when Geisel sat at his desk for hours with the pages blank, the pens scattered on the desk, untouched. Lately, when lost for a word, he had begun filling in curse words to complete his rhymes—not to check if his editors were reading his work, as he had done with *Dr. Seuss's ABC*, but simply for his own amusement. "I'll come back and clean it up later, but my original manuscripts are some of the most pornographic things you've seen in your life," said Geisel. Still, there were times when Geisel couldn't resist teasing Bernstein. In March 1969, two months after Random House published Philip Roth's groundbreaking and *very* sexually explicit novel *Portnoy's Complaint*, Geisel sent Bernstein a two-page proposal for a children's book with a similarly pornographic theme, then refused to answer Bernstein's frantic phone calls for a few days. "If there was a title, it was so dirty I wouldn't tell you," Geisel told an interviewer later. "[Bernstein] was going crazy trying to figure out how to break the news that it wouldn't be a good children's book."[40] Geisel left Bernstein dangling for a week, then called to let him off the hook. "He'd caught on by that time anyway," said Geisel.[41]

In September 1969, Geisel published *My Book About Me*—with words by Dr. Seuss and art by Roy McKie—a different kind of Beginner Book in which young readers were encouraged to write and draw directly on the pages as they filled in their name and address, counted the number of forks in their home, collected autographs from a policeman, and answered yes-or-no questions about their hobbies. Geisel liked the format so much he would use it again a year later for *I Can Draw It Myself*, encouraging young artists to draw stars on the bellies of Sneetches and horns on the heads of goats. Ted proudly called the books "a revolt against coloring books."[42]

As *My Book About Me* went to press, Ted and Audrey flew to Hawaii for the first stop on a planned seven-week trip around the world—their first long trip as a married couple. Typically, Ted spent much of his travel time kicking around ideas for a book; this time he was considering a Dr. Seuss travel guide and could be found writing and drawing silly comments on menus, in the pages of his guidebook, even on his visa. Visiting the temple of Angkor Wat in Cambodia, for instance, Ted was suddenly inspired to describe "rice-stuffed-rice," while the busy shopfronts of the streets of Tehran moved him to write a Seussian observation on his hotel stationery: "All barber chairs in Sleefa face in the direction of Sloofa, birthplace of Ali Hoofa, patron saint of the scissors." As the Geisels made their way around Paris in October, Ted used stationery from the Ritz to scrawl a bit of political commentary. "It is absolutely forbidden to give gratuities to kings," he wrote. "All other people, animals, or inanimate objects may be tipped, or else."[43] By the time the Geisels wrapped up their trip at Brown's Hotel in the Mayfair district of London, Ted had compiled a sheaf of notes, sketches, and observations . . . all of which would go into the bone pile when he returned to the Tower in La Jolla in November, filed away as unusable.

The bone pile could still be a source of inspiration, though Geisel had come to dread the inevitable question, *Where do you get your ideas?*—to his disappointment, it would be the first question Jacqueline Onassis would ask when he met her in 1971. Over the years, Geisel

would have a number of prepared answers ready for just such a scenario; lately his favorite was "I get them in a little town near Zyb-
liknov, where I spend an occasional weekend."[44] But there were times
when ideas *did* come in from explainable though unexpected places.
Such was the case with what would be one of Geisel's most quoted—
and most controversial—Dr. Seuss books, the ecologically minded
The Lorax.

The Lorax was written in anger—"one of the few things I ever set out
to do that was straight propaganda,"[45] he said later—spawned as Geisel
stood at the windows of his studio looking out at the San Diego coastline, where residential development and cookie-cutter condominiums
were slowly encroaching on the pristine hillsides. "Everything God
took years to put there, they are tearing down in a week-and-a-half," he
said later.[46] Geisel wasn't the only one concerned; environmental ac-
tivism was on the rise in the United States, especially in Southern
California. In early 1969, an oil well just off the coast of Santa Barbara
had blown out, killing countless dolphins, sea lions, fish, and water-
fowl and staining the picturesque coastline. A year later, in April 1970,
the United States would formally celebrate its first Earth Day, marking
a new commitment to and support for environmental policies. Geisel,
too, was determined to say something about saving the environment—
but it was harder than he thought, especially if he didn't want it to turn
into "a preachment."[47] "The ecology books I'd read were dull," he said
later. "But I couldn't get started on [*The Lorax*]—I had notes, but I was
stuck on it for nine months."[48]

Struggling with writer's block and out of ideas, Ted took Audrey
for a safari trip in Kenya in 1970, hoping to clear his head. For the
Geisels, their safari consisted mostly of swimming, reading, and
drinking at the Mount Kenya Safari Club—but it ended up being inspiration enough. "I hadn't thought of the Lorax for three weeks," Ted
said later.[49] "Then I happened to be in Kenya at a swimming pool, and
I was watching a herd of elephants cross a hill. Why that released me,
I don't know—but all of a sudden, all my notes assembled mentally."[50]
The only paper within reach was a small notepad, and Ted spent the

next ninety minutes filling page after page with the Lorax's story. "[I] wrote the whole book that afternoon on a laundry pad," he explained later, still slightly amazed.[51] "I've looked at elephants ever since, but it has never happened again."[52]

Back in La Jolla several weeks later, Geisel was clear enough on the story, but was now struggling with the look of the main character. At first he sketched the Lorax as a small gopher-like creature, but soon discarded that design and started over again. In another version, he was mechanized, like a robot. "That didn't work," said Geisel flatly. "He was big at one point. I did the obvious thing of making him green, shrinking him, growing him." Finally he arrived at a squat orange creature, with sleepy eyes and a drooping mustache. That was it. "I looked at him, and he looked like a Lorax," said Geisel.[53]

Nearly five decades later, anthropologists at Dartmouth would claim they had discovered in Africa Geisel's inspiration for the design of the Lorax. By scanning photos of African monkeys and the Lorax into a facial recognition program, they determined the Lorax most closely resembled the glowering, orange-faced patas monkey. Geisel would likely have dismissed such a suggestion; he had drawn the Lorax the way he had "because that's what he was."[54] And while some saw in the Lorax's beloved Truffula Trees the foreign greenery of the plains of the Serengeti, La Jolla residents were fairly certain they resembled the wind-blown trees on the hills surrounding the Tower.

Audrey, too, would be involved in the overall look of *The Lorax*, advising her husband on the book's color palette, encouraging him to bring in more colors "women can relate to," such as purple, mauve, and "evening shades," as opposed to Ted's usual bold colors. "Before that, I'd just popped in a color here, suggested one there," said Audrey. "*The Lorax* was my first sustained effort."[55]

The Lorax is one of Geisel's most beautiful and complex narratives, with a rapidly moving plot told mostly in dramatic flashback. An unnamed young boy, standing in for the reader, walks through a polluted landscape to the Street of the Lifted Lorax and entreats the world-weary Once-ler—who is never fully seen—to tell the story of the long-departed Lorax. The Once-ler explains how he had come to the region when it was pristine and perfect, and began cutting down the beautiful Truffula Trees to use their tufts to manufacture Thneeds. At once, the Lorax had appeared to speak for the trees—"for the trees have no tongues"—and to explain to the Once-ler that the loss of any Truffula Trees also meant the fuzzy Bar-ba-loots had fewer Truffula fruits to eat and less shade in which to play. For their own good, then, the Lorax had sent the Bar-ba-loots away. But with an eye on future profits, the Once-ler shrugged off the warnings of the Lorax, and continued cutting down more and more trees and building larger and larger factories in which to manufacture Thneeds.

Eventually the Lorax informed the Once-ler that the air and the water had become so polluted by the Thneed factories that he had sent away the Swomee-Swans and the Humming-Fish as well. But the Once-ler had lost his patience with the Lorax, and screamed at him for harping about responsibility to the ecosystem:

> Well, I have my rights, sir, and I'm telling *you*
> I intend to go on doing just what I do!

At that moment, the Once-ler's company chopped down the very last Truffula Tree, exhausting all the natural resources of the region. Lacking trees to manufacture Thneeds, the factories closed, all the Once-ler's employees departed, and the Lorax disappeared forever through a hole in the smog, leaving behind a small pile of rocks engraved with one word: UNLESS. And at this moment, Geisel jolts the narrative back the present to leave the reader with the underlying message of *The Lorax*, in what would become one of Dr. Seuss's most-quoted quatrains:

> "UNLESS someone like you
> cares a whole awful lot,
> nothing is going to get better.
> It's not."

At this, the regretful Once-ler throws down the last remaining Truffula seed and encourages his young listener—and the reader—to take better care of the trees in the future:

> "Grow a forest. Protect it from axes that hack.
> Then the Lorax
> and all of his friends
> may come back."

Typically, Geisel had fretted over his ending, finally deciding that his readers deserved an upbeat, if enigmatic, ending. "A child identifies with the hero, and it is a personal tragedy to him when things don't come out all right," he said.[56]

• • • •

Even as Geisel was finishing up the tale of the Lorax, he was commuting regularly to Los Angeles to consult with animators David DePatie and Friz Freleng, who had finally convinced Ted—after his two animated specials with Chuck Jones at the now-defunct MGM animation studio—to give DePatie-Freleng Enterprises a chance to bring Dr. Seuss's creations to the television screen. Geisel hadn't agreed without a bit of grumbling, however. "First I have to pick one of my books to be animated, and there's always a long discussion about that," he groused. "Then I have to revise my characters—for some reason, in animation, the rounder the figure the better."[57]

The first book DePatie-Freleng would adapt was the one they'd wanted to get their hands on all along: *The Cat in the Hat*. Despite his public moaning, Geisel had been delighted to work on the project—he was always happy to write song lyrics—and DePatie recalled the working relationship with Geisel as both productive and pleasant. "He was a very hands-on guy," said DePatie. "He lived down in La Jolla and he would fly over here. During the course of the production it wasn't unusual to see him once a week. He was very instrumental in the creation of the series. Friz [Freleng] and I had a very good rapport with him."[58] The singer/satirist Allan Sherman, tapped to provide the Cat's voice, also loved working with Geisel, in whom he found a kindred spirit who delighted in wordplay. "Dr. Seuss and I are both crazy about words," said Sherman. "There we were in the studio . . . two grown men, debating whether one of [the Cat's] words should be poopoodler or poobledly-poobler."[59]

The animated version of *The Cat in the Hat* aired on CBS on March 5, 1971, right at the time *The Lorax* was going into production at Random House. There had been a moment of panic in the weeks leading up to its showing when a major earthquake rocked the San Fernando Valley at the very time the only print of the animated special was being processed in a Los Angeles photo laboratory. "All morning I kept calling out there and I couldn't reach anybody," said Geisel. "I didn't know what had happened to it."[60] Fortunately, the print had already left the lab and was on its way to the network.

Written by Geisel, *The Cat in the Hat* cartoon expanded on the plot of the book—he would even reveal the name of the scolding goldfish as Karlos K. Krinklebine—and contained a number of clever songs, including one featuring the words *cat* and *hat* in various foreign languages. Warmly reviewed by critics, the special would be rebroadcast regularly over the next two decades, and would cement the relationship between Geisel and DePatie-Freleng, who would work together on six more Dr. Seuss specials over the next nine years. And they'd already decided on which Dr. Seuss book they would adapt next: *The Lorax*, still six months from publication, but which was already being anticipated as a very different kind of Dr. Seuss book.

As advance copies of *The Lorax* circulated—and word spread that Dr. Seuss had taken on an ecological agenda—Geisel was trying warily to manage expectations. "It well may be an adult book," he said guardedly. "The children will let us know. But maybe the way to get the message to the parents is through a children's book."[61] An advance copy had also made its way into the hands of former president Lyndon B. Johnson, who thought the book's message was consistent with the conservation initiatives he and the First Lady had pursued during his administration. "I know my grandchildren will enjoy [*The Lorax*]," Johnson wrote to Geisel, "but not more than we will."[62] Inspired, Lady Bird Johnson had written to express her admiration for the book and asked Geisel if he would consider donating the original manuscript of *The Lorax* to the Lyndon B. Johnson Presidential Library. Geisel agreed and made the trip to Austin for the official opening of the library on May 22, 1971. While Dr. Seuss was one among three thousand invited guests in Austin that afternoon, the former president made a point of writing to Geisel to assure him that had anyone taken a popularity poll in Austin that weekend, "you would have won it hands down."[63]

The Lorax arrived in bookstores in late September of 1971—and Geisel tried to head off any controversy by sitting patiently for one interview after another, answering the same old questions ("Where do you get your ideas?") and giving the same old answers. Geisel still looked good at age sixty-seven, though the bags under his eyes were deeper now, and his hair had gone from black streaked with silver to silver streaked with black. The bow tie was still there, too, but, reflecting Audrey's influence, it was now likely in a bolder pattern or an offbeat color. As he stubbed out cigarettes in an ashtray, Geisel admitted that he worried the pro-environment stance of *The Lorax* might cost him some readers. "It insinuates that there might be something wrong with Big Business," he said.[64]

The backlash Geisel anticipated never really happened—or at least not to the degree he initially feared. While some reviewers were put off by even the very idea of a Dr. Seuss book with an explicit agenda—conveniently forgetting the obvious messaging in *Yertle the Turtle* or *The Sneetches*—most were content to simply acknowledge that the book had an ecological slant and then move on. Some communities actively embraced its conservation message—a reviewer in Jackson Hole, Wyoming, saw her own community reflected in the Lorax's story, as the "last bastion of beauty that has not been ruined by pollution"[65]—while others savaged what they perceived as purely an anti-logging agenda. The book would be removed from shelves in at least one logging community—"Our kids are being brainwashed!" complained one critic[66]—and would find itself on several banned books lists over the years. Geisel was sympathetic, at least to a point, but encouraged critics to read the book carefully. "The Lorax doesn't say lumbering is immoral," he pointed out later. "I live in a house made of wood and write books printed on paper. It's a book about going easy on what we've got. It's anti-pollution, anti-greed."[67]

Over time, Geisel would come to regard *The Lorax* as his personal favorite of all his books. "In *The Lorax,* I was out to attack what I think are evil things and let the chips fall where they might," he said later.[68] "But it was not a great seller. And I knew it wouldn't be."[69] Still, he was confident that its message had been received and that he had made a difference; indeed, the book would gain traction and sell more and more strongly over time—especially as new readers came to understand and appreciate its underlying ideas.

"I'm naive enough to believe that society will be changed by examination of ideas through books and the press," Geisel said, "and that information can prove to be greater than the dissemination of stupidity."[70]

CHAPTER 15

YOU'LL MISS THE BEST THINGS IF YOU KEEP YOUR EYES SHUT

1971–1978

Ted rarely visited Random House anymore. Partly, some of the magic was gone; in 1969, the rapidly growing company—now a corporation—had abandoned the old school elegance of its headquarters at the Villard Mansion to take over fourteen floors of a forty-story Manhattan skyscraper at Third Avenue and 50th Street. "Of course we all hate to leave," said Phyllis Cerf, but admitted to *The New York Times* that she was looking forward to leaving the quirky offices of Step-Up Books under the eaves of the Villard Mansion attic, and moving into a place where they could "stand up without bumping our heads."[1]

Worse, Bennett Cerf was gone, too. On August 27, 1971, the rakish raconteur, who had done perhaps more than anyone to bring the world the brilliance of Dr. Seuss, died in his sleep at his Mount Kisco house. He was only seventy-three. Cerf's funeral service, in the chapel of his beloved alma mater, Columbia University, was, appropriately, the social event of the season, with luminaries like Frank Sinatra, Truman Capote, Ginger Rogers, and Philip Roth in attendance. Geisel had been unable to attend the service[2]—fortunately, he'd spoken with Cerf on the telephone as the publisher lay in a hospital room several weeks earlier—but he surely smiled in agreement as he read the eulogy by *What's My Line?* host John Daly, who called Cerf "a glorious amalgam of pragmatist and leprechaun."[3]

This all made Geisel less inclined to deliver his books in person and read them aloud in the Random House offices; from here on, he would do so only intermittently. He was also less motivated to do Beginner Books business in the new but charmless Random House headquarters. So, more often than not, the mountain would be brought to Muhammad, with Michael Frith or Walter Retan making regular trips from New York to La Jolla to discuss any of Geisel's latest books—whether it was a Beginner Book, a Bright and Early Book, or one of his own Big Books. Here in sunny La Jolla, the young men would take up temporary residence in the new guest wing at the Tower, and Audrey took great delight in awakening her guests each morning by loudly whistling "Reveille" over the Tower's intercom system.

The two young editors had very different relationships with Geisel. Of the two, Retan was the more reticent, recalling that he would quietly offer suggestions while "sort of holding my breath." Geisel would usually bristle, then make exaggerated chomping noises on a cigarette before finally grumbling, "I was afraid you'd say that."[4] More often than not, however, he made Retan's recommended change.

Frith, however, could give as good as he got, trading jokes, keeping up with Geisel swig for swig as they drank from a bottle of vodka, or making a game of calling out the code numbers of the Random House color charts. When progress on a book bogged down, Geisel might suddenly say, "Time for a thinking cap!" and pull one his countless hats from the corner closet—"two grown men in stupid hats trying to come up with the right word for a book that had only fifty words in it at most," said Frith.[5]

The Beginner Books were Frith's favorite to work on. While Geisel had grown to loathe the word list, Frith actually enjoyed the discipline of sticking to a restricted vocabulary. "The whole idea of Beginner Books was so unbelievably tightly designed and regulated, and every aspect of every word examined and reexamined a trillion times," said Frith. "To me, it's like writing a sonnet. A sonnet isn't a sonnet unless there are that number of lines, that number of beats in that particular form. And that's what makes it work."[6]

Eventually, Geisel came to trust Frith's artistic instincts implicitly—at least when it came to the LeSieg books. For these, Frith would often storyboard each book, typing the text directly onto Ted's mock-ups—"so I could see just where everything fell," explained Frith, "and properly coordinate the words and pictures"[7]—before sending the book off to Geisel's handpicked illustrator. "By the time I would hand a book over to a writer and/or illustrator, it was laid out right down to the last square inch of white space," said Frith, "[showing] what goes where, where the text goes, exactly how the text would read."[8]

Frith's skills as a writer and artist would even help prompt a long-distance collaborative with Ted, the rhythmic *Because a Little Bug Went Ka-hoo!* For months, the two of them mailed sketches and draft text back and forth between La Jolla and New York—"pinned to the corkboard walls in our respective offices," noted Frith—and eventually settled on Frith's suggestion to begin the book with a simple poetic rhythm that builds to a rollicking climax. "It just kind of worked," Frith said modestly. To celebrate his only joint effort with Frith, Geisel wanted to create a unique nom de plume, and the two quickly arrived at the name *Rosetta Stone*—"a pleasant little amusement," recalled Frith, "and a nice nod, for those who got it, to the goals of Beginner Books, breaking down the mysteries of written language."[9] Highball glasses of vodka tonics would be clinked together in celebration.

Frith, too, appreciated Geisel's fundamental respect for the intelligence of his readers. "Never for a second did anybody entertain the idea that we were talking down to anybody," said Frith. "The kids were just as smart as we were. They just hadn't been exposed to the world as much. And we had to do the very, very best we knew how to do."[10] Still, there were many times Geisel's Beginner Books authors didn't or couldn't maintain the high standards he expected, severely testing his patience and forcing him to limit the imprint to four books a year so he could spend more time with each. "I know that I'm not going to get more than four good ones," said Geisel. "I take my four authors and my four illustrators and push them and push them and push them.["11] As Frith notes, "we really had to beat up on them to get things kind of to the quality that you wanted."[12]

Still, there were some Beginner Books authors Geisel reliably returned to again and again. Apart from the dependable Berenstains, one of Geisel's favorite illustrators—especially for LeSieg books—was fifty-year-old Roy McKie, who was not only a great artist but also *fast*. "[Roy] was never late for a deadline, always working all night, all weekend," remembered his wife, June.[13] A former commercial artist, McKie loved receiving the latest LeSieg scripts and didn't mind if they had arrived already laid out with rough pencils. He *liked* the way Geisel thought about the relationship between text and image, and trusted Geisel without question.

"I believed in him completely," said McKie.[14]

• • • •

The animated version of *The Lorax* premiered on CBS on Valentine's Day 1972 to considerable buzz and decent reviews, but unimpressive ratings. "Have you an ax to grind?" snickered one critic. "Be careful when you try it on TV."[15] Still, it was artfully enough done that it would receive the Critics Award at the International Animated Cartoon Festival, and the Geisels and the Frelengs would travel together to Zagreb to proudly accept the award.

The Lorax was a success, too, as a piece of propaganda. The Keep America Beautiful campaign would present Geisel with a special award for his environmental improvement efforts.[16] A decade later, the United Nations would distribute the book in several languages to reinforce a conservation message globally, and the environmental group Global Tomorrow Coalition would seek permission to name its highest award after the Lorax—a request Geisel granted. (He wouldn't always be so generous when he felt his message was being misconstrued or misappropriated. When Horton's humanist mantra, "A person's a person, no matter how small!" showed up on the letterhead of a pro-life organization, Geisel's attorneys slapped the organization with a cease-and-desist order.)

Most of the mail that flowed out of the Tower, however, was what Geisel called Cat Notes. Geisel had reams of stationery printed with a large image of the Cat in the Hat taking up the left-hand side of the page. Geisel would write notes in the blank space next to the Cat, sometimes drawing a word bubble coming from the Cat's mouth in which he'd write a thank-you, other times filling the space with cartoons or funny observations, all handwritten in his distinctive print. Incoming mail was still sorted and managed by the Geisels' secretary—and in 1973, the steadfast Julie Olfe stepped down and the position was passed to a young woman named Claudia Prescott, whom Ted would quickly come to adore. Prescott would be particularly adept at making up fanciful but believable excuses for Ted to use to decline the glut of invitations that flooded into the Tower every week. She was so good at this that Ted would dub her Claudia the Prevaricator.

When Peggy's teenage son Ted—whom Geisel had dedicated *Grinch* to in 1957—was put into a full body cast for nine months following spinal fusion surgery for scoliosis, Ted kept him entertained with a steady stream of drawings, cartoons, notes, and envelopes full of stamps, coins, and postcards. Bob Bernstein, too, was on the receiving end of endless Cat Notes; one of his favorites had come from Geisel after Bernstein mentioned that his young son asked how fertilizer companies got manure into bags. Geisel sent him a cartoon with a wide-eyed cow holding a canvas bag and asking a farmer skeptically, "In a *bag*???"[17]

Even Audrey would receive Cat Notes and letters, especially around holidays like Valentine's Day or their anniversary, where Ted would leave her love letters rather than have to express his feelings verbally. "He couldn't say 'I love you'—he was too private," said Audrey, "—but he could write it."[18] For events like her birthday, St. Patrick's Day, or Halloween, he would give her homemade cartoons, which, Audrey said, were "mature, sophisticated, not always entirely to my liking, but always howlingly funny."[19]

While Ted and Audrey's relationship had fractured their La Jolla social group, over time they had settled into a new social circle, welcoming in politicians and friends like polio pioneer Jonas Salk and his wife, the artist Françoise Gilot, who had lived just down the hill for ages, and who would become one of Ted's favorite confidants and beer-drinking buddies. Audrey would never be quite the hostess Helen had been—part of being a good hostess required knowing how to fade into the background, which was never Audrey's particular forte. But she was trying. She collected cookbooks and hired her own housekeeper, and there would be regular dinner parties at the Tower again. Audrey's strength as a hostess was her good taste and eye for details: the dinner table would be set with crystal and silver, the dining room chairs featured carved medallions with Seussian creatures on them, and the ceiling was covered with Schumacher damask. Under Audrey's management, every party was an *event*, with personalized place cards, neatly folded napkins, unique appetizers, and after-dinner aperitifs.

Ted wasn't big on all the trappings, but he loved watching Audrey flit from guest to guest, laughing at everyone's jokes and being very much the center of attention. Ted's own stories at parties seemed to be getting longer, but he always seemed to stick the landing on a well-timed punch line. Ted often regarded himself as a wry observer of La Jolla society; indeed, among the large paintings in his studio was a series he had dubbed *La Jolla Birdwomen*, winkingly portraying some of La Jolla's socialites as Seussian birds with garish plumage and gigantic feathered hats.

Geisel would be a whirl of activity for the next few years—as Frith had noted, he seemed perpetually in motion—completing four Bright and Early Books and one Big Book, and overseeing two more animated specials between 1972 and 1974. It was no wonder there were times when Geisel couldn't remember which age group he was writing for.

"In those earlier and regular-sized books I'm writing for people; in the smaller-sized Beginner Books I'm still writing for people, but I go over them and simplify so that a kid has a chance to handle the vocabulary," he said. "But basically, I've long since stopped worrying about what exact ages the books are for—I just put them out."[20]

Fortunately, the 1972 Bright and Early Book *Marvin K. Mooney Will You Please Go Now!*—about a defiant little creature in footed pajamas who refuses to go to bed—had come to Geisel relatively quickly. The name had been borrowed from the local Cadillac dealer and had been inspired, at least in part, by guests who lingered a little too long at the Geisels' Thursday-night dinner parties. And with an unapologetic use of words like *broomstick* and *bureau*, Geisel had clearly scuttled the approved vocabulary list for good.

Marvin K. Mooney would pick up greater significance two years later, during the height of President Richard Nixon's Watergate scandal, when Geisel happened to run into the political humorist Art Buchwald during a visit to the San Diego Zoo. In July 1974, Buchwald sent Geisel a copy of his book *I Never Danced at the White House*, "along with a rather snide remark that I was incapable of writing anything political," Geisel added.[21] Rising to the challenge, Geisel picked up a copy of *Marvin K. Mooney Will You Please Go Now!*, replaced every mention of Marvin K. Mooney with the name Richard M. Nixon, and shipped the book back to Buchwald.

Buchwald loved it—and on July 30, 1974, in his syndicated column running in several hundred newspapers, Buchwald ran the entirety of *Richard M. Nixon Will You Please Go Now!* and encouraged his readers to "read it aloud," especially as they reached the closing lines:

> Richard M. Nixon!
> Will you please GO NOW!
> I said GO and GO I meant . . .
> The time had come.
> SO . . .
> Richard WENT.[22]

Nine days later, Nixon resigned. "My finest hour!" Geisel joked to a reporter, then added in mock innocence, "But of course children's books writers are apolitical. They never smoke or drink, either."[23] (Meanwhile several cigarette butts smoldered in the ashtray.) Writing to Buchwald, however, Geisel took an enthusiastic victory lap. "We sure got him, didn't we?" he said. "We should have collaborated sooner."[24]

One of Geisel's more unusual Bright and Early Books, *The Shape of Me and Other Stuff* would appear in the summer of 1973. Inspired by photographs of Inuit stone-cut silhouettes of hunters and whales, Geisel created a book in which readers were encouraged to study and identify people, animals, and things by their silhouettes alone—a beautiful book that looked like no other in the Dr. Seuss oeuvre. More traditional, however, was Geisel's other book from that year, the Big Book *Did I Ever Tell You How Lucky You Are?*, Geisel's reminder that no matter how bad a day you might think you're having, there's always someone who has it worse than you do. He had struggled somewhat with the verse—*Did I Ever Tell You How Lucky You Are?* was perhaps his most densely written book since *Scrambled Eggs Super!*—and Audrey soon got used to watching him "jump up and start chain-smoking and walking around the house, all but tearing his hair out—and in the middle of the night yet," she said. "He gets so impossible, I've pushed him in the pool."[25] Geisel would ultimately dedicate the book to one of the people in his life who constantly reminded him of how lucky he was: his agent, who he teasingly called "Phyllis the Jackson."

There would be two more Bright and Early Books in 1974, starting with *A Great Day for Up!*, a rarity in the Dr. Seuss catalog, in that it would be the only book featuring text credited to Dr. Seuss with illustrations by another artist, in this case the English cartoonist Quentin Blake.[26] "He loved Quentin Blake's stuff," says Michael Frith, "which thrilled me, because of course I think Blake is such a genius."[27] Then in November came *There's a Wocket in My Pocket!*, a rhyming book filled with some of Geisel's most uproarious nonsense names (there was a *zable* on a table, and a *nooth grush* on a toothbrush). One particular creature took its name from a serendipitous typo on the part of secretary Claudia Prescott, who couldn't read Geisel's writing on his handwritten manuscript and transcribed a U as a V, turning an *Uug under the rug* into a *Vug*. Geisel liked it better and left it in the final manuscript.

A Great Day for Up! and *There's a Wocket in My Pocket!* marked a major turning point for Geisel in that after their publication he decided to significantly scale back the amount of time he spent overseeing Beginner Books. Not that he would be stepping *down*, but he had decided to cede to Walter Retan much more editorial control over the two imprints. Retan frankly thought the decision was overdue. "Ted really should have allowed someone else to do more editing earlier," said Retan. "He didn't mean to, but he almost choked off that series."[28] Meanwhile, Michael Frith had also decided that *A Great Day for Up!* would be his last book with Geisel, and had announced his departure from Random House to accept a position working as creative director for Muppet creator Jim Henson.

Geisel had no regrets about his decision. Overseeing the two imprints had finally become too exhausting, with too many authors needing to be hounded, too many manuscripts needing to be reworked. Partly, too, his fatigue had to do with age. In 1974, Geisel would turn seventy years old. While he was in good health—he really did look like a man ten years younger—decades of eyestrain were taking their toll, as would become all too obvious during Ted's seventieth birthday celebration in Las Vegas. One evening as Ted and his friend Duke Johnston lounged at the Hilton Hotel, a fleet of scantily clad women came roaring past them on Harley-Davidson motorcycles. When an amused Johnston asked Geisel what he thought of the women, Geisel was confused; he'd been able to see only the motorcycles. "I realized I was getting blind," he said flatly.[29]

For the moment, the deterioration in his vision primarily affected his ability to distinguish colors, though Geisel knew the Random House art department's color charts well enough to remember exactly which colors to assign to his art as he completed his first Beginner Book in five years, *Oh, the Thinks You Can Think!* Geisel was trying to do something a bit different with the book, calling it a "cabbages-and-kings job, in which I decided I would like to shock the child: lead him a certain way, get him into a plot, and then take it away from him on the next page and move him to another land or another completely different set of ideas."[30] Unfortunately, the book felt like a structureless unveiling of Seussian names and creatures—though it does contain what is likely one of Geisel's most frightening images, the mysterious, shadowy Jibboo, waving from the end of a dark street—and the *Southern Literary Journal* sadly dismissed the book as "mediocre." *The New York Times Book Review* gently agreed with the *Journal's* assessment but was always willing to give Dr. Seuss the benefit of the doubt, suggesting he still deserved a Nobel Prize. "Think of the influence he has had on the human race!" gushed the *Times*. "And all of it good!"[31]

While eye surgery had eventually reset Geisel's color sense—Audrey recalled him riding in the car on the way home from the hospital, raving about how brightly colored everything now appeared—things suddenly became more serious in early 1975, when Ted casually mentioned to Audrey that he was having a hard time focusing on his pen lines—"everything is squiggly," he told her, indicating a sure sign of glaucoma.[32] Ted immediately began seeing eye doctor David Worthen at the University of California San Diego School of Medicine, the beginning of three long years of surgeries to treat glaucoma and remove cataracts that had developed in both eyes.

As Ted lay in a hospital bed in June 1975, recovering from one of his first surgeries, Audrey suggested he grow a beard, insisting that his face would simply look better with one. "His head was mine. I created the beard," Audrey explained later. "He had a nose that was looking for that beard all his life."[33] Ted shrugged and agreed, joking that growing a beard seemed to be the only thing he was permitted to do in the confined boredom of his hospital room. Geisel would leave the hospital with his beard coming in gray. It would be a defining feature for the rest of his life.

That same month, the Geisels made the trip to Hanover to attend the fiftieth anniversary of Ted's graduation from Dartmouth. Ted refused to make any speeches or have any fuss made about his attendance; he was there to stand with the men of the Class of '25, nothing more. And yet it was hard for his alma mater and his classmates not to show their excitement. There was an exhibition of his art on display at the Dartmouth Library, and during a breakfast with his old friend Donald Bartlett, the retired professor became so worked up he accidentally ordered a martini with his breakfast. Ted could only encourage his old friend to drink up.

During Geisel's stay in Hanover, the dean of libraries, Edward Connery Lathem, convinced Ted to sit for a lengthy recorded interview, hoping Geisel might be inspired by the recordings to begin writing his memoirs. But Geisel blanched at the very idea of it; he insisted he was far too busy to write about himself. With Geisel's permission, Lathem would use their interviews as the basis for a profile of Dr. Seuss in the *Dartmouth Alumni Magazine*—but while Geisel liked the piece, he still refused to be persuaded by Lathem's further entreaties for a memoir. "[My story] would become a source of irritation to the reader in a 200-page volume," Geisel moaned. "Who could possibly care about all these details?"[34]

••••

Dr. Seuss could rock.

Even into his seventies, Dr. Seuss could be surprisingly hip. In 1975, CBS aired *The Hoober-Bloob Highway*, another of his collaborations with DePatie-Freleng, but unusual in that it wasn't based on a Dr. Seuss book. Instead, Geisel had written an original teleplay in which Mr. Hoober-Bloob, from a location high above the Earth, gives yet-to-be-born children the opportunity to decide if they want to live as humans on the planet below. With songs by Geisel and composer Dean Elliott, Geisel was proudly referring to *The Hoober-Bloob Highway* as a rock musical in the same vein as *Jesus Christ Superstar* or *Godspell*. He had enjoyed the experience so much, in fact, that he told the *Los Angeles Times* he was even considering writing a ballet or a full-blown rock opera for Broadway. "About what? I don't know," he confessed. "That's why I haven't done it. But I've done so much lyric writing in putting the television things together that I'd like to do an opera."[35] He'd even come to change his views on television, which he once considered the greatest threat to children's literacy. "Television is the biggest, the most exciting medium there is," he said. "I just want to live long enough to do something terrific on TV."[36]

Still, he understood that television remained reading's primary competitor, vying for the time and attention of elementary school students everywhere, every day. Even with the recent efforts on public television to teach children the alphabet on *Sesame Street* or phonics on *The Electric Company*, Geisel remained convinced those shows, no matter how well intended, were no substitute for the power of reading an actual book. "I want to . . . give kids the opportunity to have books if they are excited about them and want them. They should be allowed to find the joys of reading," said Geisel.[37] He also called out parents who put children down in front of the television set instead of reading to them. "Kids who have no interest in books are usually from slob parents who themselves had no interest in books," said Geisel. "The trouble is, the hour parents used to spend reading to their kids is now spent drinking martinis which, let's face it, is more fun."[38]

Audrey, who loved hearing Ted talk excitedly about reading, encouraged her husband to do more book signings and tours to bring his positive message to the masses. More important, she also thought it was good for Dr. Seuss to leave the Tower every once in a while. "Lately it seems as though Ted's really quite happy to sit on his little mountain and produce," said Audrey. "But every once in a while, he feels he has got to come down and touch hands again. He's a very humble person and always seems amazed on these trips that there's anybody out there."[39]

As it turned out, there were *plenty* of people out there, eager to see, touch, and talk with Dr. Seuss. Fans would stand in line for hours for a chance to get his autograph—and more and more, the fans standing in line were adults in their thirties or forties who had grown up on his books and were now waiting in line with children of their own. And even at age seventy-two, Geisel still had stamina. At most appearances, he would generally announce that he would be signing for an hour—but then after the hour was up, he would stay to sign books for everyone who had been in line, usually spending two or three additional hours to make sure everyone in line got an autograph and quick hello.

Watching as hundreds of children eagerly pressed around Dr. Seuss as he signed books, reporters were apt to keep asking Geisel the same question over and over again: *Do you like children?* Geisel had a careful reply. "I like children in the same way that I like people," he said. "There are some stinkers among children as well as among adults. I like or dislike them as individuals."[40] Ted smiled at nearly every child— he rarely lost his patience even as children huddled around him, leaning on the table, breathing in his face, fingers in their noses, many of them clutching well-loved books. Conversation was kept to a minimum; he might quietly say, "Thank you," or ask, "Is this your book?" "I don't talk with them a lot," Geisel admitted. "I prefer to look into their eyes, personal contact, you know. I can tell what they're thinking."[41]

While countless parents had sent children to their rooms with a Dr. Seuss book to keep them busy, there were times fans took his reputation as a great babysitter a bit too literally. Once on an airplane, a stewardess asked Geisel if she could put an upset little girl in the seat next to him to see if perhaps Dr. Seuss could "calm her down by telling her some stories." Geisel gamely did his best, telling her to be good and talking to her quietly—and meanwhile "wishing that the plane would make an emergency landing."[42] Still, he understood why kids tended to gravitate toward him. "My books don't insult their intelligence. Maybe it's because I'm on their level. When I dropped out of Oxford, I decided to be a child, so it's not some condescending adult writing."[43]

By Random House's own count, it had sold more than sixty-five million Dr. Seuss books by 1976—nearly eight million of which were copies of *The Cat in the Hat*.[44] When editor Walter Retan warmly reminded him that Bennett Cerf had once declared Dr. Seuss to be Random House's one true genius, Geisel was typically dismissive. "If I were a genius, why do I have to sweat so hard at my work?" he mused.

"I know my stuff always looks like it was rattled off in twenty-three seconds, but every word is a struggle and every sentence is like the pangs of birth."[45] He still continued to work at his desk eight hours a day, seven days a week. "If I didn't, I would become a bum," he told the *Rocky Mountain News*.[46] Standing at the window of his studio with one journalist, Geisel gestured at the beach below. "Those are some of my retired friends down there, but retirement's not for me!" he said. "For me, success means doing work that you love, regardless of how much you make. I go into my office almost every day and give it eight hours—though every day isn't productive, of course."[47] If nothing was happening, it was back to the couch and the growing pile of books on the coffee table—mostly "history or some classy junk."[48] At the end of the day, it was cocktails with Audrey, or he would swim, poke around in his rock garden, "or yell out to [neighbor] Jonas [Salk], and we'll go and drink beer and have a good time."[49]

Some days, however, he was visited by Dr. Worthen from the UCSD eye clinic, who would sit in with Geisel in his Tower studio for more than hour, applying eye drops as part of the treatment for his eye problems as Geisel relaxed on the couch. In 1976, he had gone through another surgery, part of the ongoing effort to remove the cataracts that had resulted in what he called a "dulling brownout" in his field of vision.[50] While Geisel's eyes were now improving, he was still having a hard time focusing on small details—an inconvenience that had affected the way he had completed his latest book, *The Cat's Quizzer*. Subtitled *Are You Smarter Than the Cat in the Hat?*, the book was largely a collection of brainteasers, puzzles, and trivia questions—and with his eye problems, Geisel had been forced to draw his pages at a larger size, with thicker lines, and then had the Random House production department reduce each page for publication.

While his eye for fine detail might have been compromised, his sense of color was as keen as ever—and *The Cat's Quizzer*, with a jumble of bright colors on each page, required careful work by Random House's design department to precisely match Geisel's mandated hues. As the Geisels packed and prepared to leave for an extended visit to Australia and New Zealand in the late spring of 1976, Audrey jokingly remarked that they were probably wise to leave the country while the art department was still working on *The Cat's Quizzer.* "So many colors," she said, shaking her head in mock regret. "So much on every page."[51]

While Dr. Seuss was still something of a head-scratcher to readers in the United Kingdom, Geisel's UK publisher, Billy Collins, who also negotiated Ted's Australian deals, had found a strong fan base among readers in Australia and New Zealand. The sales numbers, in fact, were particularly impressive: in a region with a population of a little more than 13 million, Australians had purchased nearly 1.5 million Dr. Seuss books.[52] Collins casually wondered if Dr. Seuss might want to make a trip halfway around the world to meet some of his most enthusiastic fans. Geisel—who had fallen in love with the place during his 1964 visit—didn't need to be asked twice.

Given the strong sales numbers down under, it was little wonder Geisel was greeted as a rock star almost the moment he landed at New Zealand's Auckland Airport on April 26. His arrival was announced on the front pages of most newspapers, with banner headlines like "Dr. Seuss Drops In" and "What's Up Doc?"[53] His photograph was everywhere. On the front page of the Wellington, New Zealand, *Dominion,* he was having a drink with their winner of the Esther Glen Medal, presented for outstanding children's literature. In an Auckland paper, he was shown with his arm draped around a young lady dressed as the Cat in the Hat, grinning happily as he clutched his Air New Zealand bag. In another, he was standing outside a bookstore wearing a gigantic bow tie, with Audrey beside him, showing genuine interest in a group of people dressed as Seussian animals.

The Geisels were whisked across the region in high style, galloping through Sydney, Melbourne, Brisbane, and Adelaide, and feted wherever they went. At the Hotel Wairakei in Taupo, he found the restaurant menu featured fresh trout à la Dr. Seuss. At several locations, he found himself presenting awards—usually bicycles—to young readers who had submitted essays explaining why they loved Dr. Seuss, and signing autographs for long lines of children. There were countless photos with cutouts of his characters, and with fans—usually young women—dressed as the Cat in the Hat. And always, at the end of each day, was a scheduled happy hour.[54]

Both Ted and Audrey found themselves sitting for countless interviews during their two weeks, and each of them—perhaps feeling they were half a planet away from home, where no one would ever read what they said—provided remarkably frank answers. Audrey in particular opened up to the New Zealand *Evening Post,* talking about her hatred of plastic surgery and her interests in psychology—she was particularly interested in Transcendental Meditation, ESP, "all that pop psych that's comin' down the pike," she said—and sharing her daily exercise regimen, though she complained that "when you're traveling, you can feel the flab beginning to develop."[55]

Ted, it seemed, couldn't eat breakfast without having a journalist at his elbow, asking questions with a tape recorder running. But Ted didn't seem to mind. He had charmed his interviewers right from the start, when a Southland journalist asked if it was okay if reporters referred to him as Dr. Seuss instead of Ted Geisel. "I would be offended it you call me anything else!" he responded happily.[56] With a cigarette constantly burning, Ted talked at length about literacy, sounding genuinely alarmed about reading competency in the United States—especially when compared with Australia, which he called "the most literate country I have ever visited . . . Everyone [here] reads anything they can get their hands on."[57] He fretted that in the United States, "the situation is getting worse all the time—20 percent of college freshmen take remedial reading[58] . . . Some graduates can't even make out a laundry list," he said.[59]

"Right now in the United States we have a nation of people who don't read much," he continued. "My revolution is to try to supplant the *Dick and Jane* or Janet and John thing. Children don't want to read about hitting a ball with a stick."[60] While he was thrilled to have played a part in the demise of the *Dick and Jane* readers, he tried to remain modest about his own contributions to children's literature. "I look at the world through the wrong end of my telescope, clean it up a little, put it down with some of my silly cartoons, and hope that children find reading books can be interesting and fun."[61]

On Saturday, May 22, the Geisels left Sydney on a Qantas flight bound for Honolulu, on their way back to San Diego. Ted was genuinely sad to leave what he called the "readingest" country in the world.[62]

He'd have little time to ruminate on his Australian experience. Geisel returned to the Tower in time to work with the La Jolla Museum of Contemporary Art on a seven-week exhibition called "Who Is Dr. Seuss?" Ted carefully selected artwork hanging on the walls around his own home, handing over not just paintings but also a few of his old taxidermy heads as well, including a Mulberry Street unicorn. In the blank spaces on the Tower walls, Ted helpfully posted drawings of a cat holding a sign reading, "A masterpiece is missing from this spot."[63]

The museum exhibit opened in time for the 1976 holiday season. Geisel was noticeably grumpy at the opening—his eyes were bothering him again—but the crowds were large and enthusiastic. And despite some grumbling from critics that Dr. Seuss's work would *never* be worthy of being called contemporary art, museum director Sebastian Adler, who helped arrange the exhibit, defended the show—and Geisel—passionately, calling him "beyond category."

"He's not just an illustrator, not just a painter, not just a cartoonist, though he is all of those things. He simply stands alone," said Adler. "Ted Geisel is one of the most important artists in this country."[64]

••••

In March 1977, Geisel's longtime agent, Phyllis Jackson, died of a heart attack at her home in New York at age sixty-nine. Geisel was devastated. Jackson—concisely eulogized as "tough, but a lady"[65]—had been looking out for him for nearly three decades. Ted sat quietly in his Tower studio for three days, unable to work, mourning Jackson with a grief so profound it frightened Audrey. Trying to cope in his own way, Geisel handwrote a short verse he called "How Long Is Long?," which he dedicated to Jackson "with all my love." "So Long is forever," he noted sorrowfully. "I guess I won't be seein' ya."[66]

There would be no Dr. Seuss book in 1977; following a second operation for his cataracts, Geisel was again having trouble discerning colors. "I've slowed down," he admitted. "It was impossible for me to mix a palette—I didn't know which colors were which. With my cataract, I had two color schemes—red became orange, blue became slightly greenish. My left eye was like Whistler, and the right one was like Picasso, seeing things straight and clear in primitive colors."[67] He was still due for one more surgery to remove the cataract in his other eye—"they claim I'll be as good as Picasso," he joked[68]—but until then, he was having to relearn and readjust his sense of color.

While illustration was out of the question—at least for the moment—Ted could still write, and in spring of 1977, he had been asked to deliver a commencement speech for Lake Forest College in Chicago. Geisel had initially accepted the invitation from the college with the understanding that he was simply receiving an honorary degree; only later had he been informed that he was expected to speak. Geisel was annoyed—"I talk *with* people, not *to* people," he grumbled to Lake Forest president Eugene Hotchkiss[69]—but eventually conceded. He was determined, then, to keep his remarks short, preparing a short poem—which he was still fussing with on the morning of the speech—called "My Uncle Terwilliger on the Art of Eating Popovers." In it, Ted related how his uncle was always very careful to eat only the solid part of each popover, and spit out any air. It was advice worth listening to, he told a rapt audience, as he encouraged them to follow his Uncle Terwilliger's example:

> As you partake the world's bill of fare,
> That's darned good advice to follow.
> Do a lot of spitting out the hot air.
> And be careful what you swallow.

The audience erupted in whoops and cheers; Dr. Seuss was a

radical. The students in the audience, who'd been raised on his books, suspected it, but now they were sure of it. Geisel later joked that the students had cheered only because his speech had been short.

More and more now, college students who'd been raised on his work as children were taking it even more seriously as graduate students and academics. Geisel was amused to find his books being vivisected and reinterpreted as scholars analyzed even books like *Green Eggs and Ham* for deeper or hidden meanings. Geisel was particularly taken with the writing of scholar and essayist Selma G. Lanes, whose 1971 book of essays *Down the Rabbit Hole* contained an entire chapter devoted to his work. Lanes was a fan, but her adoration was expressed in such academic doublespeak ("Dr. Seuss in his books . . . can be said to provide his young disciples with a literary release not so far removed from orgasm"[70]) that Geisel could barely keep a straight face. He would very kindly write her a note applauding her analysis, even as he teased her for not allowing her "voluminous research to bog down the spirit of your writing."[71]

Still, Geisel could remember his own days as a graduate student— when he'd been challenged to scrutinize the life and works of Jonathan Swift—and understood that overblown academic analysis of his own work was probably inevitable and, as far as he was concerned, almost always amusing, if misinformed. "The people who are working for their doctorates do the most amazing things," he mused to the *Los Angeles Times*. "For example, they'll take a book of mine that has only one color in it and talk about my great color sensitivity . . . and why I chose that color—when the fact is that Bennett Cerf called me up one morning and said, 'We're having a bit of a financial problem, so cut down your colors.'"[72] Joan Knight, who served briefly as his secretary, remembered receiving fan mail from "readers treating him like a philosopher, trying to interpret what he wrote, trying to get him to say he was preaching some unsaid message, but he never would. All he wanted was for people to read."[73]

After a year without a new Dr. Seuss book, Geisel would finally be back at the drawing board to prepare a book for release in 1978. His eyesight was mostly restored. To his relief, his color sense was as sharp as ever, though his line work could still be a little shaky and uncertain. While there were times he'd labored at his desk, doodling "hundreds of characters"[74] in search of an idea, for this particular book, he knew exactly what he wanted to write about—the two things that were on his mind the most at the moment: literacy and eyesight.

The Beginner Book *I Can Read with My Eyes Shut!* would be a celebration of the joys of reading, with the Cat in the Hat and his son guiding the reader from the delight in picking out colors with one eye shut—inspired, no doubt, by Geisel's real-life situation—and the thrill of reading long words like *Mississippi* and *Hallelujah!* to the excitement of learning how to do new things from reading books.

> The more that you read,
> The more things you will know.
> The more that you learn,
> The more places you'll go.[75]

It was clear he was having fun again. "I write for myself, and for the pleasure of saying, 'Audrey, don't you think this is funny?'" Geisel told *The Christian Science Monitor.* That didn't mean it wasn't still hard work—"two sentences in a children's book is the equivalent of two chapters in an adult book," he said ruefully.[76]

Geisel had shortened his work hours slightly, spending six hours a day in the office instead of the usual eight. As always, the well-worn stuffed dog Theophrastus sat propped up near the desk, silently watching over Geisel as he sketched, then traced over the drawings in black ink and filled them in with colored pencil. His day could still be interrupted by phone calls—often Retan wanting to consult on Beginner Books—and Geisel would lean back in his chair, one foot against his desk, as he took the call, exhaling endless streams of cigarette smoke toward the ceiling "to ease the embarrassment of talking to someone," he said sheepishly.[77] As he shipped the final manuscript off to Random House—a parcel that included detailed instructions for the production department, with every color clearly labeled and numbered—he inserted one last page, this one dedicating the book to his hardworking ophthalmologist, "David Worthen, E.G." ("Eye Guy")."

With *I Can Read with My Eyes Shut!* quickly blowing through its first printing, Geisel did the best he could to keep up with the countless requests for interviews and the frequent demands for his time and attention. Bob Bernstein, always looking for opportunities to put his favorite author in front of large and enthusiastic crowds, encouraged Geisel to accept an invitation to speak at the American Booksellers Association's (ABA) annual meeting in Atlanta, where he would be sharing the bill with two fellow writers who were also big Dr. Seuss fans, Maurice Sendak and Judy Blume.

Ever since his successful "Uncle Terwilliger" speech at Lake Forest College, Geisel had wisely opted not to give lengthy prepared remarks, but rather to compose a few short, Seussian lines appropriate for the occasion. His speech before the ABA, then, would set the crowd roaring as he poetically explained:

> As everyone present undoubtedly knows . . .
> Due to a prenatal defect in my nose . . .
> (Which seems to get worse the longer it grows)
> I am completely incapable of speaking in prose. . .[78]

That same year would see him standing at a podium before a hometown audience at UCSD's Revelle College, the campus's academically rigorous liberal arts college. For the occasion, Geisel composed what he called a "Small Epic Poem (Size 2¾ B)," which mostly made fun of the fact that he had traveled less than five miles to be there for the lofty occasion:

> I've been brought here this morning
> At the enormous expense
> Of precisely one dollar and fifty-five cents

—plus 19 cents more if you add on the tip
To the driver who drove on this hazardous trip . . . [79]

But it was the final quatrain that brought the 360 graduates to their feet:

I wish you good luck
And a hasta luego
From U.C. La Jolla
. . . I mean San Diego.

Dr. Seuss was seemingly everywhere that autumn—it didn't hurt that a lengthy profile written for *The Christian Science Monitor* had been reprinted in countless newspapers throughout the year—and Geisel found himself applauded by crowds as he entered a room. In Detroit, he served as the grand marshal for the city's Thanksgiving Day parade. He won an Emmy for *Halloween Is Grinch Night*—another of his collaborations with DePatie-Freleng—and scarcely seemed to mind that his name had been mispronounced as *Geezul*. Jed Mattes, who had taken over as his agent after the death of Phyllis Jackson, thought Ted was slightly embarrassed by all the fuss. "He had a lot of distrust and wariness in any efforts to make him an icon," said Mattes.[80]

But really, it was out of his hands at this point. Over the objections of Theodor Seuss Geisel, Dr. Seuss was becoming an icon.

CHAPTER 16

A FEW YEARS LONGER

1979–1984

O n March 2, 1979, Ted Geisel turned seventy-five years old.

In La Jolla, he was feted with an early birthday celebration thrown by forty friends who presented him with a pair of handmade Cat in the Hat cuff links made of pure gold. Geisel dashed off his thank-you notes, then headed for Las Vegas to celebrate with Audrey, figuring "nobody will look for a children's book author in Las Vegas."[1] Random House, noting that it had now sold more than eighty million Dr. Seuss books, marked the occasion by declaring May 1979 to be Dr. Seuss Month, which only made sales of Dr. Seuss books spike again.

The benchmark birthday would also be marked by a lengthy and widely circulated interview with *Washington Post* writer Cynthia Gorney. For the first time, Geisel eschewed his usual pat answers for a more thoughtful conversation about writing for children ("a child can understand anything that is read to him if the writer takes care to state it clearly and simply enough") and what he saw as the everyday absurdities in growing older. "It's getting awful, because I meet old, old people, who can scarcely walk, and they say, 'I was brought up on your books,'" said Geisel. "It's an awful shock."[2] For the first time, too, he was careful not to be photographed while smoking.

Random House president Bob Bernstein, always working a good

marketing angle, again tried to persuade the enigmatic Geisel to consider writing his memoirs. Now several years removed from the Edward Connery Lathem interviews, Geisel was interested enough in the idea again to begin working what he called his "Non-Autobiography," which he wrote out as a long interview with himself. But once again, he would get no further than a small stack of handwritten pages before abandoning the idea of a memoir.

Birthday wishes poured into Random House from all around the world, some enclosing handmade toys and sculptures, homemade versions of oobleck, even a wrapped package of green eggs and ham. Most were answered with one of three different form letters, two of which were signed by Dr. Seuss, the other by the Cat in the Hat, who also received his fair share of mail.[3] Some of the more thoughtful letters were passed on to La Jolla to be personally answered by Geisel, who would respond with genuine warmth. One aspiring young author excitedly told Dr. Seuss he'd waited in line for his autograph twice, and eagerly asked if there was a "strategy" for writing books for children. "Always remember when you're writing that you're not writing for kids—you're writing for people," Geisel advised, then added cheerily, "I'd never stand in line to get MY autograph twice. But I'm very flattered that YOU did so. And I'll stand in line for you when you write that book of yours."[4]

Fans also still made their way to the Tower on a daily basis, mostly children who learned that Dr. Seuss lived at the house at the top of Mount Soledad and just wanted to say hello or happy birthday. Audrey did her best to keep unwanted callers away from Ted, patiently speaking with them at the front door and gently letting young visitors know that Dr. Seuss was either away or too busy to come see them personally. Most left happy, though one persistent young man asked if he could use the bathroom and then waited for Dr. Seuss to show up.[5] Ted was so touched by the outpouring of interest in and love for Dr. Seuss on his seventy-fifth birthday that he assured Audrey that he intended "to stay alive a few years longer."[6]

Even at seventy-five, Geisel seemed determined to work as hard as he could, telling one journalist that he tried to have "a couple of books" and an animated television special in the works at all times. "When I hit a snag on one," he explained, "I go on to another."[7] At the moment, he was preparing for publication in autumn the Beginner Book of "terrible tongue twisters," *Oh Say Can You Say?* "I had to do a book to use the title," confessed Geisel,[8] but he was pleased with the tongue twisters he'd written, which he thought were even harder than those he'd composed for *Fox in Socks* fifteen years earlier. "I suddenly came to the conclusion that we were making it too easy for kids," he said. The tongue twisters in *Oh Say Can You Say?* were meant for families to read aloud in what he called "competitive reading."[9] He was particularly proud of one he titled "Merry Christmas Mush":

> One year we had a Christmas brunch
> With Merry Christmas mush to munch.
> But I don't think you'd care for such,
> We didn't like to munch mush much.[10]

"[It] can't be done after three martinis," he said proudly. "It's a two-martini tongue twister."[11]

His eyes were finally recovering after multiple surgeries, so Geisel's line work was steadier, though there would never again be the kind of variation in line thickness that had distinguished his earlier style. And now that he could better differentiate hues, he was again as picky as ever about colors, staring for hours at the Random House color chart to try to find the one that most closely matched the colored pencils he'd used on his original pages. He was usually disappointed—at one point he simply attached a note to a manuscript page and asked the Random House art department to come up with a "more parroty" green.[12] Grace Clark, who oversaw the art department for children's books at the time, always knew the latest Dr. Seuss book would be a challenge. "His color sense is the most sophisticated I've ever run into," said Clark,[13] even as she proudly noted that her department had never let Dr. Seuss down. Geisel would dedicate *Oh Say Can You Say?* to his youngest stepdaughter, Leagrey, who he had dubbed "Lee Groo, the Enunciator" due to her ability to read his tongue twisters aloud perfectly—just as her mother had with *Fox in Socks*.

The only thing, really, that kept Geisel from his desk for any length of time in 1979 was *Pontoffel Pock, Where Are You?*, another original musical cartoon produced with DePatie-Freleng. As always, Geisel had whizzed back and forth between La Jolla and Los Angeles to consult with the animators on what turned out to be an interesting, if sometimes complicated, story in which a failed pickle packer is granted a magical piano to whisk him anywhere in the world. The cartoon debuted on CBS in May to decent critical acclaim but less-than-enthusiastic fan response—and even after repeated showings over the next few years, *Pontoffel Pock* would remain a novelty in the Dr. Seuss cartoon catalogue. "I knew it wasn't a good title,"[14] Ted mused, but he'd already moved on to his next project for DePatie-Freleng, a new story featuring two of his best-known characters. "I'm experimenting to see how *The Cat in the Hat* will play against the *Grinch*," he mused to the *Los Angeles Times*. "I think it will."[15]

• • • •

Geisel was still happiest working at his desk—and couldn't imagine doing anything else. "People of my age are all retiring, which is something I would never want for myself," Geisel told *The Saturday Evening Post*.[16] But despite his drive and willpower and his continued busy schedule, he was slowing down. After publication of *Oh Say Can You Say?* in 1979, there wouldn't be another Dr. Seuss book published for three years; and while he was still writing for Beginner Books, *Oh Say Can You Say?* would be the last in the imprint to feature his art. Geisel still believed in his studio time, but more and more now he could be found sitting on his sofa calmly reading through the latest biographies, histories, and crime novels—paperbacks, never hardcovers—going through them so quickly that there were times Audrey couldn't replace them with new ones fast enough.

Under Audrey's eye, the Tower had been in an almost constant state of renovation and redecoration for the last decade. Sizing up the Tower for an article in *Architectural Digest*, writer Sam Burchell called it "ever-evolving," a description Audrey could only agree with.[17] "It just grew, Seusslike," she said of their maze of quirky rooms.[18] In the living room was a fountain, while the dining room—the busiest room in the house—was lined with mirrors to make the room feel even more gigantic. Out by the swimming pool, petunias seemed perpetually in bloom.

While there was a sign at the Tower's front door warning visitors to BEWARE OF THE CAT, there were actually no real cats in the Geisel household. Instead, there was a miniature Yorkshire terrier named Sam—short for Samantha, not Sam-I-Am—a dog so shaggy that guests often joked she looked the same at both ends. "I've been accused of having drawn [her]," said Ted.[19] In the garage was another of Ted's babies, a gray Cadillac Seville with a California license plate reading GRINCH—and to Ted's shock, the plate had been unavailable the first time he'd applied for it, having been scooped up by a Dr. Seuss fan who had placed it on an RV. Eventually, the plate holder moved to Iowa, freeing up GRINCH for the Geisels—and the RV owner, mortified, wrote an apologetic note to Dr. Seuss for having held on to the plate for so long.[20]

For decades, Geisel had dreamed of staging a Broadway musical or ballet based on his works—he would casually mention it in nearly every interview—and had resisted entreaties from other playwrights who wanted to adapt his work to the stage. As far as Geisel was concerned, the only one who would be adapting Dr. Seuss for the stage would be Dr. Seuss himself. That would change, however, when Geisel was approached by the Children's Theater Company of Minneapolis about a musical adaptation of *The 500 Hats of Bartholomew Cubbins*. Geisel had been so impressed with the company's 1977 production of *The Little Match Girl* that he had quickly agreed to let director John

Clark Donahue take on *Bartholomew Cubbins*—but cautioned Donahue not to stray too far from the source material or to add any characters.

It was advice that Donahue's handpicked scribe, John Lewin, promptly dismissed, turning in a rambling libretto with an unfamiliar introduction and several new characters. Geisel torpedoed Lewin's script and asked Donahue to try again. This time Donahue brought in twenty-nine-year-old Timothy Mason to quickly write not only a new script, but also compose several songs. Instead of adding new characters, Mason simply fleshed out existing ones, giving more depth and backstory to minor characters like the Executioner to advance the plot. Donahue submitted Mason's script to Geisel, then waited nervously for the other shoe to fall. It never happened. "Tell that Mason not to worry," Geisel told Donahue. "It's damn funny. Damn funny."[21] Ted was particularly effusive about Mason's lyrics—always one of Geisel's favorite parts of any production—and gave Mason his highest compliment: "You are writing very good Seuss."[22]

Geisel was in the audience for the 8:00 P.M. preview performance at the Children's Theater on April 17, 1980, and then again at the premiere the following evening. Backstage, as he signed autographs for the cast, Geisel was beaming. "I am more than happy," he said, and judged the evening "very exciting."[23] Theater critics agreed, calling *Cubbins* "extraordinary" and "a fine effort by all concerned."[24] *Bartholomew Cubbins* would be the only stage adaptation of a Dr. Seuss book during Geisel's lifetime; Mason, after his success with *Cubbins*, would write the songs for the 1994 musical *How the Grinch Stole Christmas!* After playing in Minneapolis and San Diego, it would make its debut on Broadway in 2006, where it would play to sold-out crowds.

• • • •

Dr. Seuss continued to sell well into the millions of books each year. Teachers adored him, as he gave them books they could put into the hands of even the most stubborn readers. Parents revered him, giving them something they felt good about their children reading when they finally pried them away from the television. And kids? Kids were *crazy* for him. He gave them books of their very own that spoke directly *to* them, and not down to them. In newspaper and magazine pieces, Geisel was frequently referred to as "the good Dr. Seuss," or "the beloved Dr. Seuss." And yet for all the success and the adulation, there was still one thing Dr. Seuss didn't have that Geisel truly wanted for him: critical acclaim.

While Ted liked to say publicly that awards didn't matter, in truth, he longed to be recognized as an artist and as a major force in literature.[25] To the layman, children's books looked easy—pleasing pictures accompanying easily knocked-off rhyming verse. But Ted knew better. "It's hard. I'm a bleeder and I sweat at it," he confessed. "As I've said before: the 'creative process' consists for me of two things: time and sweat."[26] And yet while librarians loved Dr. Seuss, none of his books had received the prestigious Caldecott Award from the American Library Association (ALA)—though he'd come close twice—nor had he received its Newbery Medal, the highest award in children's literature.

Charlotte Leonard, a librarian at the Dayton and Montgomery County library in Ohio, was determined to have her organization acknowledge the contributions of Dr. Seuss somehow—especially as there were some places in the country where his books were practically keeping local libraries in business. "Books by Dr. Seuss are replaced over and over again because they circulate so much," Leonard wrote to the ALA. "Dr. Seuss is one name the children and parents know; he is a household word."[27] While there was some pushback inside the organization—one librarian said disparagingly that "many critics find his artwork too sadistic, his nonsense and fantasy too extreme"[28]—Leonard was convincing enough that the ALA finally announced it had selected Dr. Seuss to receive its Laura Ingalls Wilder Award, an award given every five years "for recognition of distinguished books published in the United States, which have over a period of years made a substantial and lasting contribution to literature for children."[29] It wasn't the Newbery Award, but it was something—and Geisel was delighted to learn he'd received it.

Geisel—wearing an patch over one eye following yet another surgery—traveled to New York with Audrey in late June of 1980 to pick up the award. True to form, he'd prepared a bit of rhyming verse for his acceptance speech, giving a generous tip of the hat to Miss Bodanker, his boyhood librarian in Springfield, as well as to Mr. Strathmore, the supplier of "the paper that I ink up," and to Mr. Smirnoff, who "furnishes the vodka that occasionally I drink up."[30] Ted concluded his speech to enthusiastic applause. The Laura Ingalls Wilder Award would be the only award he would ever receive from the ALA.

Dartmouth College, however, would continue to honor its favorite son. In 1981, student organizers of the Winter Carnival overwhelmingly supported adopting "Hanover Hears a Who" as the theme for that year's winter celebration. The campus green would be filled with gigantic snow sculptures of Dr. Seuss characters, including a two-story Cat in the Hat. Geisel was unable to attend but sent along his thanks. "I'm very flattered. And delighted," he told the *Dartmouth Review*. "I feel very honored and wish that I could be up there with them and cavort with them in the snow."[31]

That winter, Geisel was still working slowly on his first Big Book in nearly a decade, *Hunches in Bunches*. "It is a psychological study of what goes on in a kid's head when he can't make up his mind," Geisel said. "He follows many hunches at once." And so, Geisel had drawn his interpretation of what different kinds of "literal Hunches" might look like, sketching a Real Tough Hunch on roller skates or a Sour Hunch in a striped costume, all in vibrant colors and traipsing across some of Geisel's most twisted, Seussian landscapes. "It's more modern in treatment and illustration," Geisel explained.[32]

Geisel's work habits hadn't changed much, with one exception: he had stopped smoking—or at least he was *trying*. Concerned for her husband's health, Audrey had encouraged Ted to give up his cigarettes—a promise, it seemed, he could keep for only a day or so at a time; while he vowed to Audrey that he had quit, she soon caught him sneaking outside to smoke in the evenings. And so Audrey had taken to hiding his cigarettes, or rationing them out to him one at a time so she could keep track of how much he was smoking. But it was hard for Ted. His addiction was part of his creative process; when stuck on a manuscript, he found his hands fumbling for cigarettes that were no longer there. His solution was to circumvent Audrey entirely, asking his assistant to pick up a pack or two on her way to the Tower each afternoon. Audrey eventually figured out that bit of subterfuge and put a stop to it.

It seemed the more Audrey thwarted Ted's efforts, the more determined he was to keep smoking, coming up with one ridiculous plan after another for sneaking cigarettes. Audrey once caught him strolling too casually through a restaurant, picking up and pocketing discarded or half-smoked butts. When she admonished him, Ted went to Plan B, asking friends to leave cigarettes in his car. For a while he had even gone back to his old trick of putting radish seeds in a pipe and watering them when he wanted a cigarette, but the urge to smoke would eventually become too strong, and he'd start begging friends to smuggle cigarettes into the Tower. When Duke Johnston refused to do so, Ted was visibly upset. "I thought you were my friend," he sulked. "That's the point," Johnston shot back. "I *am*."[33] Still, Ted sometimes felt as if Audrey and their friends were ganging up on him. At one of the Geisels' large dinner parties in September, Audrey had NO SMOKING printed on small cards, to be put in front of each place setting. Ted set his on fire.

Ted awoke the morning after the dinner party complaining of heartburn—and then again the following day. Audrey decided to have him examined by a doctor, who discovered that Ted had suffered a very minor heart attack. His directive to Geisel: no more coffee—and no more smoking. Ted's agent, Jed Mattes, often remarked that Audrey had kept Geisel "alive and lively."[34] That was probably true—and when it came to breaking his smoking habit, she may have literally saved his life.

Geisel completed work on *Hunches in Bunches* in early 1982 and made the trip to New York to deliver and read the manuscript to Random House in person—an increasingly rare occurrence since Random House's 1969 relocation—and where the editorial musical chairs continued. Walter Retan was out as editor in chief for juvenile books, replaced by the level-headed Janet Schulman, while the art department had been put in the hands of a talented new art director, thirty-year-old Cathy Goldsmith. The first time Goldsmith met Geisel, she could barely speak. "[Dr. Seuss] wasn't God to me, but he was close," said Goldsmith. "I had no idea what to call him. You couldn't call him Dr. Seuss, and I didn't hear anybody refer to him as Mr. Geisel. You didn't call your parents' friend by a first name, and certainly no one as important and famous as he was." Geisel, towering over the barely five foot Goldsmith and sensing her shyness, leaned over her and said quietly, "If you don't call me Ted, I'm going to call you *Little You!*"[35] Geisel ended up having a genuine affection for Goldsmith—never more evident than when he handed over *Hunches in Bunches* for her to read aloud so he could watch the reaction in the room.

On its publication in the fall of 1982, *Hunches in Bunches* suffered through some mixed reviews. "The rhythm [of the rhyme] . . . is rough in places," went one typical review, "other Seuss stories are much better."[36] But Ted was happy with it. He knew it looked and read a bit different from some of his other books—and that had been intentional. "After you've done fifty books, you want a little change," he said. "It isn't that I'm bored. But you get into a rut."[37]

More successful was *The Grinch Grinches the Cat in the Hat*, the animated special Geisel produced with DePatie-Freleng—now under the umbrella of Marvel Productions—featuring Dr. Seuss's two best-known mischief-makers. Geisel had suspected the two characters might play off each other well, and he'd been right—though in the end, the Cat gets the better of the Grinch, thwarting the Grinch's reality-bending plans by reminding him of how much his mother loves him. The cartoon would win Geisel and DePatie-Freleng an Emmy for Outstanding Animated Program of 1982—and Geisel would

win an additional Emmy for the songs he had written with Joe Raposo, his partner on both *Pontoffel Pock* and *Halloween Is Grinch Night*.

• • • •

In December 1982, the San Diego Museum of Art opened an exhibit
featuring the work of one of the most popular children's authors of
the last twenty years—a writer who had "never presumed to write for
children" and who was constantly trying to stage ballets and write
operas based on his work.[38]

The author was Maurice Sendak—and on the evening of Thursday,
December 9, he and Geisel had agreed to be interviewed together in
an open forum in Copley Auditorium at Balboa Park in San Diego.
Each was a great fan of the other. "I've never appeared in tandem with
anyone else. I would do it with no one else," remarked Sendak.[39] For
his part, Geisel had loved *Where the Wild Things Are* from the moment
it was published in 1963, sensing in Sendak a kindred spirit. "Sendak
has the courage not to be influenced by editors," Geisel said later.
"Everybody said his book *Where the Wild Things Are* would drive kids
crazy, and they love it."[40]

Though twenty-four years separated them—Geisel was seventy-
eight, Sendak fifty-four—their views on writing for children were
remarkably similar. "We write for people," said Geisel as Sendak
nodded enthusiastically. "We have never presumed to write for children," Sendak said. "We do very different work, but what I see as
similar is an honesty in [our] work," continued Sendak. "Geisel is a
real human being at work, and you can see that in what he writes.
There are so few of my colleagues that I feel that respect for." Still,
their different styles, and different approaches to storytelling, could
be seen in the way each responded to the audience. Sendak, in a dark
suit and tie, was more animated, answering questions directly.
Geisel, meanwhile, in a light suit and a floppy bow tie, preferred a
folksier approach, telling stories, giving some of his well-rehearsed
answers, and providing what for many would be the most memorable

line of the night: "Reality is there, but we look at it through the wrong end of the telescope."[41]

At the end of the evening, Geisel shook Sendak's hand warmly. Their time together, he told the younger man, had been "sort of a sentimental journey."

••••

In early 1983, Ted Geisel signed the biggest merchandising deal of his career, and wasn't entirely sure what he was getting out of it except more work and more headaches. Coleco—manufacturer of the popular Cabbage Patch Kids and the ColecoVision video game system—struck a ten-year deal with Geisel, laying down $10 million to market Dr. Seuss plush toys and video games. Despite the lucrative offer, Geisel nearly balked, grumbling, "I don't know that I want to spend the last several years of my life doing this."[42] But he signed the deal anyway, on the condition that he be given final approval on all products, even the computer games that so baffled him—why would anyone want to assemble a puzzle on a computer screen when they could do a real puzzle?

Samples of stuffed toys—the Cat in the Hat, the Grinch, the Lorax, even Thidwick—would soon begin making their way to the Tower for Geisel's approval. Ted threw them into the swimming pool in dramatic disgust. "When you go to three dimensions, there will always be something wrong," he groused to agent Jed Mattes.[43] With Geisel's stern guidance, Coleco would eventually begin producing a respectable line of plush stuffed animals and computer games—but he would tire of babysitting Coleco's designers, and by 1987, Geisel would ask Mattes to negotiate an exit from the contract, forfeiting millions of dollars for peace of mind. Coleco, already hemorrhaging money from the same implosion of the video game market that would bring down the juggernaut Atari, would file for bankruptcy a year later.

The day after signing the Coleco agreement, Geisel went in for a routine dental checkup and was stunned to learn the dentist had found small cancerous lesions at the base of his tongue—a horrific consequence of Geisel's sixty years of chain smoking. Geisel's doctor recommended surgery to remove the affected section of his tongue, but Ted rejected that particular recommendation—he didn't want his speech to be permanently affected—and sought another opinion from doctors at the University of California Medical Center in San Francisco.

In San Francisco, doctors confirmed the initial diagnosis, but recommended a less invasive treatment comprised of radiation, followed by an iridium transplant at the base of his tongue to kill any remaining cancer cells. But Geisel once again rebuffed the proposed treatment, telling doctors he didn't want his hair and beard falling out from the radiation. After consulting with Audrey, Ted offered a compromise: he'd agree to let doctors excise the cancer—without removing part of his tongue—and then have the iridium implant inserted near the site of the lesions. On Valentine's Day 1983, Geisel underwent the surgery, followed by five days of recovery in the hospital. He told no one about his cancer or his treatment or even his trip to San Francisco.

Geisel was back in La Jolla by early March, still in visible pain; the iridium affected the circulation in his jaw, causing some of his teeth to loosen. And yet on Friday, March 4, Ted managed to accompany Audrey to a black-tie party hosted by Queen Elizabeth and Prince Philip on board the Royal Yacht *Britannia* to celebrate the thirty-first wedding anniversary of President Ronald and Nancy Reagan. Several weeks later, with his jaw still smarting, he attended a reception at the Hotel del Coronado honoring his old friend and commanding officer Frank Capra, whose film work was being featured at the newly christened San Diego Museum of Photographic Arts.

When asked—as he almost inevitably was—where he received his most useful training as an artist, Geisel would always reply, "In the Army, working with Frank Capra."[44] It was Capra who had helped him understand the need for tight pacing and concise storytelling and—most important—the wonderfully useful skill of storyboarding. Geisel approached Capra and the two of them spoke together quietly, trading war stories, then posed for photographs—Ted, in his suit and bow tie, with his left arm draped warmly around Capra's shoulders. Even forty years after they had served together, it was clear each still understood his place: Capra, in a loud-checked suit, beams widely, while Geisel, with his head slightly bowed, shows just a hint of a respectful smile, as if awaiting Capra's "At ease, soldier."

In May came the release of Jonathan Cott's acclaimed history and analysis of children's literature, *Pipers at the Gates of Dawn*—named for a chapter in Kenneth Grahame's *The Wind in the Willows*—featuring essays and interviews with prominent children's authors, including Maurice Sendak, Mary Poppins creator P. L. Travers, and Dr. Seuss. Geisel had sat with Cott for an extended interview session at the Tower, giving lengthy and thoughtful answers to Cott's questions and observations—and giving many readers their first real public look into the mind of Dr. Seuss and his creative process:

> The difficult thing about writing in verse for kids is that you can write yourself into a box. If you can't get a proper rhyme for a quatrain, you not only have to throw that quatrain out, but you also have to unravel the sock way back, probably about ten pages or so . . . And you also have to remember that in a children's book a paragraph is like a chapter in an adult book, and a sentence is like a paragraph.[45]

When pressed, Geisel could speak the language of academics—he could still recite Goethe's *The Erl-King* in its original German, a novelty rattling around in his brain since his days at Oxford. At one point, Cott described the thirteen rules of composing verse for children outlined by Russian children's poet Korney Chukovsky in his 1925 book *From Two to Five*. As Cott reached rule 10, declaring that "the predominant rhythm [must] be that of the *trochee*," Ted nodded in agreement. "That could be true in Russian," he told Cott. "It could come out of the way the Russian language sounds. In most of my work, I use anapests. But in any case, I think the subject matter is more important than what meter you use."[46] What he hadn't told Cott at the time was that the subject matter for his next book was going to be his most important, and most serious, yet.

Nuclear war.

• • • •

Dr. Seuss was looking for a crazy reason to go to war. In the Seussian universe, what was a cause worth fighting over? There had been conflicts in his books before, of course—after all, Bartholomew Cubbins had been unable to remove his hat, earning the wrath of the king—and Geisel had even portrayed something like the cold war between the United States and the Soviet Union, when a North-going Zax had encountered a South-going Zax and each refused to change direction to accommodate the other.

Not that reasons for war in the real world were any less outrageous; in 1983, the threat of nuclear war seemed very real indeed. Both the United States and the Soviet Union were ramping up their nuclear capabilities and investing heavily in weapons. President Reagan was proposing the Strategic Defense Initiative (SDI), a space-based weapon to knock any nuclear missiles on the way to the United States out of the skies. In September of 1983, the Soviet Union shot down a Korean Air Lines flight that encroached Soviet airspace, killing 269 people, including a U.S. congressman. Both nations held their breath, fearing retaliation. On November 20, 1983, ABC showed what such retaliation might look like, broadcasting the made-for-television movie *The Day After*, about life in the United States following a nuclear strike. The entire world was on edge about the possibility of nuclear annihilation—which was exactly the reason Geisel wanted to say something about it.

After thinking about it for weeks, Geisel decided to tell the story of the Zooks and the Yooks, who disagree over whether to eat their bread butter side up or butter side down. Geisel informed editor Janet Schulman that he was working on a story he called *The Butter Battle Book*, but told her little else. "All he would tell me . . . was that it was about some people who ate their bread butter side up, and some others who ate their bread butter side down," said Schulman. "I had no idea that it was a book about nuclear disarmament until he brought it all finished to New York."[47]

With a fundamental disagreement over which side of the bread to butter driving the plot, *The Butter Battle Book* tells the story of nuclear proliferation, with the Yooks and Zooks patrolling a border wall separating them with increasingly larger and more dangerous weapons. Geisel even parodied Reagan's SDI proposal with the Zooks' invention of a Jigger-Rock Snatchem, which has the ability to catch rocks slung over the wall by the Yooks' dreaded Triple-Sling Jigger and fling them right back. Each side taunts the other—the Yooks stage a military-style parade with Right-Side-Up Song Girls—until eventually both sides simultaneously develop the Bitsy Big-Boy Boomeroo, capable of blowing either side into "small smithereens." As each side stares down the other and threatens to drop their ultimate weapon, Geisel ends the book on a terrifying cliffhanger:

> "Grandpa!" I shouted. "Be careful! Oh, gee!
> Who's going to drop it?
> Will you . . . ? Or will *he* . . . ?"
> "Be patient," said Grandpa. "We'll see.
> We will see . . ."[48]

Geisel knew he was doing something important with *The Butter Battle Book*, telling Teddy Owens it was "the best book I've ever written."[49] He was feeling very much like the cockeyed crusader he'd been during his time at *PM* in the early days of World War II—and yet his idealism was tinged with realism. "If I'd have to say we should arm or not, I'd say we arm," Geisel said later. "But if we arm toward nuclear climax, we're finished. Before, when I was fighting against Hitler, we were dealing with human will which could accomplish miracles . . . Today, no amount of spirit or belief can win a war of this sort . . . Critics may say the book is too simplistic. I think it has to be simplistic. I think this problem would be solvable if we made it more simplistic. The damn thing has got to stop. How it stops, I don't know."[50]

Geisel personally delivered *The Butter Battle Book* to Random House in October 1983. The response was muted and slightly confused. Geisel sensed the editorial bewilderment immediately. "I have no idea if this is an adult book for children or a children's book for adults," he told his production team. Even Ted's cover, showing a Right-Side-Up Song Girl carrying a butter-side-up banner, came under scrutiny, with art director Cathy Goldsmith recommending something "more confrontational," that might give readers a better idea of the themes being addressed inside.[51] But Geisel clearly didn't like that idea, and the conversation became more heated as the morning wore on. Finally marketing executive Jerry Harrison suggested Goldsmith put together a mock-up of an alternate cover for Geisel to consider. Ted told her he would take her cover back to La Jolla and think it over. Goldsmith knew immediately that Geisel's original cover would stay. "If you were his friend, he couldn't look you in the eye and say he didn't like something," said Goldsmith.[52]

The title, too, came under scrutiny, particularly from the marketing and sales teams, where there was concern that *The Butter Battle Book* was too vague and gave no indication of what the story was about. Bob Bernstein gently encouraged Geisel to change the title to *The Yooks and the Zooks*—a title that stuck long enough to show up in an early press release announcing the book. Ted was furious, and Audrey took it on herself to call Bernstein personally to explain how much Ted was committed to his original title. The title was changed back to *The Butter Battle Book*.

Random House's jitters continued through the editing process— usually the part of the process where Geisel's word was beyond reproach. And yet Janet Schulman gently pointed out that while the opening pages of *The Butter Battle Book* appeared to be told in flashback—with the grandfather telling the tale of the weapons buildup to his grandson—it concluded in the present tense, with the grandfather running to the wall and threatening to drop the Bitsy Big-Boy Boomeroo. Again, Geisel refused to budge. "I see what you're saying," he told her, "but I'm not going to change it. The grandfather is just a device."[53] Schulman wisely let it go. "When you're dealing with a genius and he won't change, you don't change," she said.[54]

Schulman also sent an early proof of the book to Maurice Sendak, asking for his opinion and perhaps a blurb Random House could use in its promotional materials. Sendak sent back a rollicking endorsement in no time. "Surprisingly, wonderfully, the case for total disarmament has been brilliantly made by our acknowledged master of nonsense, Dr. Seuss," wrote Sendak. "Only a genius of the ridiculous could possibly deal with the cosmic and lethal madness of the nuclear arms race . . . [Dr. Seuss] has done the world a service."[55] And yet, the Random House sales department worried that Sendak's politically tinged endorsement might discourage families with a conservative bent from buying the book. Bernstein called Geisel to let him know of the marketing department's concern—and Ted, with a gusty sigh, agreed to keep Sendak's message out of the marketing materials. But he resented the suggestion that *The Butter Battle Book* was a negative statement about the military. "I'm not anti-military," he insisted, "I'm just anti-crazy."[56]

• • • •

The cancer had spread. On December 16, 1983, Geisel underwent surgery for a radical neck dissection and deep biopsy to thwart the cancer that had moved into one of his lymph nodes. The surgery was invasive and painful and would require a lengthy postoperative stay at Scripps, forcing him to miss his own Christmas party at the Tower. For the next two months, he would exist in a fog of pain and heavy medication. Doctors had tried to persuade him to recover in a hyperbaric oxygen chamber that would make his wounds heal faster, but

Geisel had refused. The confined space made him feel too much like he was being buried alive.

Geisel would feel sufficiently recovered to travel to New York to celebrate the publication of *The Butter Battle Book* on March 2, 1984—Dr. Seuss's eightieth birthday. Geisel gamely attended a birthday party thrown by Random House at the New York Public Library, with more than two hundred guests in attendance, then slid into a limousine that shuttled him over to a more intimate formal party at the 21 Club—the very same place Ted had been wooed away from Vanguard and over to Random House by Bennett Cerf in 1938. This time, however, Geisel was feted by the new owners of Random House, Donald and Samuel I. Newhouse Jr., whose family company had just acquired the publishing firm from RCA for $70 million.

Among the fifty-nine guests in attendance were old friends and colleagues like Maurice Sendak, the Berenstains, and Joe Raposo—but Ted, as usual, seemed embarrassed by all the fuss, and could only loosen up after downing a few vodka martinis. One by one, guests stood and toasted his health, usually delivering a few rhyming couplets in their best imitation of Dr. Seuss. Geisel raised his glass respectfully to each.

Dr. Seuss's eightieth birthday—just like his seventy-fifth—was cause for celebration around the country, and congratulatory letters and telegrams streamed into Random House. Everyone, it seemed, was trying to "do Dr. Seuss," toasting him in mostly bad but well-intended rhyming verse. Senator Daniel Patrick Moynihan acknowledged the occasion with a Seussian speech on the floor of the U.S. Senate, though Congressman Ed Boland—who represented Geisel's hometown of Springfield in the House of Representatives—played it straight. Perhaps the most accurate Seussian parody came from New York mayor Ed Koch, who even managed to work the latest Dr. Seuss book into his celebratory letter:

> All is calm at City Hall.
> Toward peace we've made great strides.

The secret is really very simple:
We butter our bread on both sides.[57]

While Dr. Seuss may have been adored without question, some critics weren't so sure they felt the same way about *The Butter Battle Book*. *The New York Times* bluntly called it "bleak" and disparaged it as "an arms control polemic that has no happy ending"[58]—failing to realize that the enigmatic ending had been precisely Geisel's intention. *The New Republic*, too, seemed to miss the point entirely, maintaining that there were real-life issues that mattered far more than which side of the bread one buttered. A blasé review in *Kirkus* yawned that "all this seems, however well-intended, a little out-of-date, even a little out-of-keeping."[59]

There was even some hate mail from parents who accused Dr. Seuss of intentionally scaring children, admonishing Geisel for not providing them with a happy ending. "I was tempted to give it a happy ending," admitted Geisel, "but then I would have gotten into dishonesty." The ending in the book, he said, was "the situation as it is."[60] But newspaper columnist Ellen Goodman publicly took Geisel to task for that decision, arguing that while the ending might have been honest, "what children need from the good doctor, from all adults, is a dose of hope."[61]

Geisel, predictably, refused to explain himself. "Since this is the hottest topic in the world, if kids are at all intelligent and read anything, of course they're facing it," he said.[62] He was proud he wasn't talking down to kids about tough issues—and he was perfectly willing to put his fate in their hands. "One thing I think is great is that kids are discussing problems in a way they didn't when I was a kid. So I am leaving it up to them to write the happy ending for me. Adults haven't been able to do it so far."[63]

And yet despite the controversy—or maybe because of it—*The Butter Battle Book* would race to the top of both the juvenile and adult fiction bestseller lists, elbowing its way into position alongside books by Stephen King and Robert Ludlum. "It's not a book that should be ignored," wrote a reviewer for Gannett News, who compared the eighty-year-old Dr. Seuss to "a prizefighter in his prime."[64] Bob Bernstein would forever rate *The Butter Battle Book* as Geisel's finest hour, while Cathy Goldsmith hailed it as "a statement from an elder statesman."[65] While frequently banned for its perceived politics, *The Butter Battle Book* would come to be embraced and appreciated for its allegorical brilliance in the nerve-racking years that would define the end of the Cold War. While he was unable to promise that everything would be okay, Dr. Seuss had nonetheless held his readers' hands tightly through a frightening, formative experience. For most readers, that was more than enough.

Back in La Jolla in early April, with *The Butter Battle Book* making its way up the bestseller list, Geisel was considering subjects for his next book—and wondering, at times, whether at eighty years old, he even had another book in him at all. He was still dabbing at paintings—though usually only after midnight—and found himself on the couch in his office reading more "history or some classy junk"[66] one morning when the telephone on his desk jangled loudly. It was a reporter from the Associated Press, calling to ask Geisel if he had heard the news.

Dr. Seuss had just won the Pulitzer Prize.

CHAPTER 17

OFF AND AWAY

1984–1991

r. Seuss could hardly believe the news. When a reporter from the Associated Press called to notify him
that he'd won the Pulitzer Prize, Geisel was nearly
speechless. "The damnedest thing," he said over and
over.[1] The award, a special citation, hadn't been bestowed on any particular Dr. Seuss book, but rather in recognition of
his entire body of work, and "for his contribution over nearly half a
century to the education and enjoyment of America's children and
their parents."[2]

Geisel could only shake his head in awe. "That's amazing. All I can
say is I'm highly gratified and surprised,"[3] he said, then added, "I
think it's amazing that it came at all."[4] While plenty of other writers
won Pulitzer Prizes in 1984—notably William Kennedy for his novel
Ironweed and David Mamet for his play *Glengarry Glen Ross*—it was
usually Dr. Seuss's name that appeared in the headline and his photo
that appeared alongside the story. Everyone, it seemed, knew he'd
won the prize, and for a few weeks "all hell broke loose"[5] as the phone
rang constantly with congratulations from friends and requests from
journalists for interviews. Cards and letters piled up in his office.
Michael Frith sent a telegram with an intentional groaner of a rhyme
he knew Geisel would appreciate:

Had I but paid more attention in schoolitzer,
I could've come up with a good rhyme for Pulitzer.[6]

Geisel admitted he liked "some" of the fuss, but groused that all
the attention had made things "rather unprivate" for him.[7] Mostly, he
was pleased that he could explain to any skeptics that "all my books
are a war against illiteracy,"[8] and repeatedly joked that he should have
received a Pulitzer when he was an actual journalist at *PM*.

Ted and Audrey celebrated the honor at a dinner with friends,
where the wine flowed freely during laughter and conversation. But
such dinners out were getting rarer; Ted preferred eating dinner on
TV trays with Audrey in the living room—though rarely with the television on—to going out to restaurants down the hill in La Jolla or San
Diego. Most evenings out tended to end with Ted, eyes rolled skyward, hovering near the exit waiting as Audrey flitted from table to
table, saying one long goodbye after another.

Lately, Geisel's life had become a series of one waiting room after
another. Between trips to the UCSD Medical Center at San Francisco
and the Scripps Clinic closer to home, Geisel complained that he was
"fed up with a social life consisting entirely of doctors."[9] He called his
illness "a series of everything," requiring endless tests, endless poking and prodding, and endless rounds of paperwork. "When I discovered I was spending more time in hospital vestibules than I was at
my drawing board, appearing before various doctors and taking
various tests, I began drawing what was happening, or what I thought
was happening, which I did just to amuse myself."[10] And suddenly
Geisel found himself working on his next Dr. Seuss book.

While Ted wanted nothing more than to sit and work at his drawing table, Audrey encouraged him to accept an invitation to receive
one more honorary degree, this time from Princeton University. In
June 1985, as Geisel stepped forward on a New Jersey stage to be
hooded by president William Bowen, all 1,500 graduates rose to their
feet for a lengthy standing ovation, shouting in unison, "I am Sam!

Sam I am!" Ted was visibly moved as the degree was conferred—"He shows [children] the way to the adult world," said speaker John Coburn, "as he shows adults the way to the child"[11]—and gave the briefest of remarks. "It was a very sound decision to honor somebody who writes children's books," Geisel told the crowd. "They usually live without honor."[12] As he sat down, a light drizzle of rain began to fall.

••••

Back at the Tower, Geisel was slowly pinning up the pages of the manuscript that would take up most of his time in 1985, the satirical paean to aging, *You're Only Old Once!* More and more of his personal experiences and frustrations with doctors and hospitals were showing up in the book. In the waiting room in San Francisco, Ted had sat next to a fish tank containing a sad-looking fish named Norval that Ted couldn't resist putting into the book as a recurring character. His unpleasant and expensive memories of his first cancer treatment—in which doctors had proposed several unacceptable treatments and *still* socked Ted with a $75,000 bill—would also make it into the book, as his main character peered through a complicated contraption at an eye chart that read, HAVE YOU ANY IDEA HOW MUCH MONEY THESE TESTS ARE COSTING YOU?

Complaints about costs aside, *You're Only Old Once!* was Ted's protestation against needless procedures and what he often saw as a disregard for the concerns of patients—like himself—who didn't want to be forced into entering frightening-looking machines. Geisel's book would be filled with odd and scary contraptions—beds of nails, a Diet-Devising Computerized Sniffer called a Wuff-Whiffer—as well as doctors who asked endless rounds of useless questions before finally shuffling patients off to billing. "I don't think he was an easy patient," said Peggy Owens sympathetically.[13] One could hardly blame him. Ted loved to tell a story about the time he was being rolled into the operating room on a gurney, and "the guy who was wheeling me in . . . brought a book out just before we got to the swinging doors and asked for an autograph," said Ted, laughing. "He probably figured it would be the last I ever gave. I was very flattered, but I wanted to sock him."[4]

For the first time, Geisel was writing specifically for the "obsolete children" among his readers. "Is this a children's book?" he asked rhetorically. "Well . . . not immediately. You buy a copy for your child now and you give it to them for their 70th birthday."[5] While the book would be full of appropriately Seussian contraptions with Seussian names, there would be no imaginary creatures; and with the exception of Norval the fish, Geisel had populated his book entirely with humans—something he hadn't done since *Bartholomew and the Oobleck*. The main character, in fact, was based on a real person: P. D. Eastman, one of Geisel's favorite Beginner Books authors, whose *Are You My Mother?* and *Go, Dog. Go!* were nearly as popular as the titles by Dr. Seuss. "That character is Phil [Eastman], because Phil was going through a lot of medical problems at that time," said Michael Frith.[6] The character even looked like Eastman, bald with a brush mustache. Unfortunately, Eastman would never see his alter ego in print; he would die in January 1986 at age seventy-six, six weeks before the publication of *You're Only Old Once!*

As Geisel was completing *You're Only Old Once!* in late 1985, he had two visitors to the Tower. One was Bob Bernstein, who tried to make it to La Jolla at least once a year to pay his respects to the closest thing Random House had to a living icon. Bernstein always loved seeing what Geisel had pinned to the walls of his studio. "He would wait for my opinion, actually nervous about what he had produced," said Bernstein. "When I expressed my complete delight, which was so easy to do, he would still challenge me to be sure I wasn't just being kind."[7] The book was mostly finished now, and Ted was working from photocopies of his finished line art, carefully coloring them with his colored pencils. From there, he would then find the corresponding color on the Random House color chart and write the color's chart number directly onto the photocopy, with an arrow pointing to the precise area to be filled. From a distance, it looked like a complicated math problem. "People think you can just sit down and write a children's book in an afternoon," he said, then waved a hand at the sheaf of colored and labeled pages, "but look at all this!"[8]

The other visitor was Geisel's neighbor Joe Hibben, a trustee of the La Jolla Museum of Contemporary Art, who asked Ted if he had any interest in working on a Dr. Seuss retrospective. While Hibben's own museum had declined to host such a project, he had found an eager supporter in Steven Brezzo at the San Diego Museum of Art, which had presented exhibits on pop culture figures and artists like Jim Henson, and was eager to accommodate a Dr. Seuss show. Geisel agreed, on the condition that he be permitted to work closely with curator Mary Stofflet to determine what went into the exhibit and what didn't. While Geisel understood that the exhibit would showcase much of the art from his books, he also wanted to feature some of his paintings—a request Brezzo was happy to accommodate, eventually taking three watercolors, three oil paintings, and two ink and crayon drawings Ted had personally selected for the exhibit.

As for materials Ted *didn't* want included, he prohibited any mention of his abandoned *Seven Lady Godivas* musical, and asked that there be no displays of merchandise from the Revell and Coleco deals. "He was concerned [the exhibit] would become a Disneyesque celebration of fluff and frivolity," said Brezzo. "You could see his jaw set when we started making selections. He knew this would be his retrospective, and like any artist, he dreaded what it might say about his life."[9] Privately, too, Hibben worried about Geisel's health and urged Brezzo to try to have the exhibit ready by May 1986—a staggeringly short six months to prepare a major exhibit.

Geisel spent the early months of 1986 ferrying *You're Only Old Once!* through production and marketing at Random House. To his surprise, the book had started something of a turf war. Because the book was aimed at older readers, not his usual audience, Random House's Adult Trade Division wanted to oversee its production and marketing, instead of the Juvenile Division. But Ted cringed at the very suggestion.

Janet Schulman, Cathy Goldsmith, and their staffs were the only ones he trusted with his work; they knew his style and his quirks—and after all, he argued, it was *still* a Dr. Seuss book. He would eventually agree to a compromise, with the Juvenile Division managing the production of the book, while allowing the Adult Trade Division to oversee its marketing.

Perhaps fittingly, *You're Only Old Once!*—subtitled "A Book for Obsolete Children"—would be published on Geisel's eighty-second birthday. On its first page, he had dedicated the book to his fellow Members of the Dartmouth Class of 1925, of which there were approximately 200 left of the original 500 or so graduates.[20] To Ted's amusement, Random House had cleverly marketed the book as "Dr. Seuss's first book for grown-ups! (the grown-upper, the better)" and for "Ages 95 down."[21] "I can now go among the grown-up people and say, 'I'm a grown-up author!'" he joked.[22]

Just as he had on the release of *The Butter Battle Book*, Ted celebrated both his birthday and his new book with a party hosted by Random House at the New York Public Library. He had spent three hours earlier that morning signing more than 1,300 books at a local bookstore, but arrived looking happy and well pressed in a gray three-piece suit with a paisley bow tie. Random House had kept the party small—there were less than a hundred guests in attendance, including some Dartmouth alumni—and Geisel seemed to appreciate the intimacy of the event, casually sipping white wine as he chatted with old friends. When finally pressed to make some impromptu remarks, he reminded guests of the similar party two years earlier. "At that time, I called you all together to help abolish nuclear weapons," he said. "Now we have a new goal—to abolish old age! Our lobby is having a hell of a time getting it by the White House."[23]

Critics were slightly confused by the very idea of a Dr. Seuss book for grown-ups. Reviewing the book in *The New York Times*, fifty-seven-year-old cartoonist Edward Sorel found "something amiss in the blithe assumption that the sort of rhymes which delight a four-year-old (or an adult reading to a four-year-old) will still entertain when read alone through bifocals," but admitted the book was "not my cup of Geritol."[24]

But readers, like always, came to Dr. Seuss without question. *You're Only Old Once!* quickly sold out of its first print run of 200,000, which sent it soaring to the number one spot on the *New York Times* adult nonfiction bestseller list. While the book was marketed to adults, Geisel met plenty of young fans at book signings who also loved the book for its funny illustrations, even if they didn't always understand all the health and hospital references. "I tried to take the books away from them, but it didn't work," he told *The Washington Post* playfully.[25] With both obsolete and non-obsolete children eagerly buying the book, *You're Only Old Once!* would sell a million copies in less than a year. Geisel joked that with his new, significantly older fan base came new responsibilities. "The book is wrecking my social life because prior to this, the only places that I was ever invited to go were to have cocoa in kindergarten," he said. "Now I'm getting invited every day to have martinis in old folks' homes."[26]

Geisel was trying hard to be comfortable with his advanced—and advancing—age. He was still relatively fit, carrying only 150 pounds on his six-foot frame, with a full head of silver hair and a neatly trimmed matching beard. Compensating for his erratic vision problems required him to wear large eyeglasses with thick frames, which only made him look even more studious, and very much in line with what journalists expected Dr. Seuss to look like. He still spent some mornings answering mail, usually sending out short, pithy Cat Notes, and often joked that he had been writing in verse so long that even short notes or letters came out in rhyme. "It's becoming a normal method of expression," he said.[27] He was also trying to keep up with the latest technology—he had even made a reference to video games in *Hunches in Bunches*—but he would never embrace the new word processors, faxes, or even an answering machine. His only real high-tech equipment was a photocopier he would sometimes use to reduce the size of a drawing. He wouldn't even write with an electric typewriter, preferring his old reliable Smith Corona.

There were days he was feeling every one of his eighty-two years. His neck and jaw were sore, and his eyes still bothered him, but with a steady regimen of daily medication—he was taking eight pills every day—he felt he had most of his ailments under control. When a concerned reporter asked what his specific health problems were, Geisel refused to elaborate. "It's not out of modesty," he explained, "but if I began listing what I had that was wrong, I would get fan mail from everybody in the United States who had the same thing wrong and I would go absolutely nuts trying to answer it all." The main malady, he explained, was mostly just "old age."[28]

••••

On May 17, 1986—almost exactly six months after pitching the idea to Geisel—the Dr. Seuss retrospective opened at the San Diego Museum of Art. Officially titled "Dr. Seuss: From Then to Now," the exhibit featured more than three hundred items—taken from the Tower and plumbed from the archives at UCLA—representing the entirety of Dr. Seuss's career. The morning before, Geisel had slowly walked through the exhibit by himself, stopping to look at old cartoons from *Jack-O-Lantern*, *Liberty*, and *PM*—all lovingly displayed under glass—advertisements for Flit, paintings, animation cels, and rough drafts and mock-ups from nearly every book, all the way up to *You're Only Old Once!* and including the little-seen *The Seven Lady Godivas*. Large banners hung from the ceiling, bearing words of wisdom from Dr. Seuss, including one reading, "Dr. Seuss's advice to all young, starting artists: Don't start your career when a Great Depression is also starting." Outside, a twenty-two-foot Cat in the Hat peered down at guests over the roof of the museum. It was an elegant exhibit and a fine tribute to his long career. Geisel told everyone he thought it was "terrific."[29]

Unfortunately, the first critical review was devastating. "This simply is not an art exhibition," said critic Robert Pincus in the *San Diego Union* disparagingly. "The chief function of an art museum is to show art."[30] That one hurt—and it was from his hometown newspaper, no less. Despite all of his success—even despite a Pulitzer Prize—Geisel still believed his work wasn't being taken seriously. He badly wanted to be regarded as a Great Artist, on the same level as Picasso, and not as a novelty act, relegated to the realm of children's artists or entertainers—as he would often derisively remark, he wasn't Walt Disney. Still hanging on the wall of Geisel's studio was one of his father's target-shooting bull's-eyes, put there, he said, "to remind me of perfection."[31] He would never feel he had achieved such a state, largely because criticism from highbrows like Pincus devastated him. He scarcely realized that, in the long run, their opinions mattered little when it came to his artistic legacy.

Yet while the critics yawned, the public thronged. Nearly every morning, museum staff found crowds of excited fans waiting outside the building for the doors to open. By the end of the exhibit's ten-week run, more than 250,000 visitors had streamed through the museum's doors—the kind of crowd most museum curators could only dream of. It was inevitable, then, that the exhibit would be sent on tour—and Geisel would try to go with it as it made its way through Pittsburgh, New York, Baltimore, and New Orleans. He was particularly excited about seeing the exhibit on display at the New York Public Library and was upset to learn it wouldn't be featured in the main library gallery—a display of medieval manuscripts was already there—but would instead be shuffled upstairs to a third-floor corridor. Geisel canceled his plans to attend.

In late spring, Geisel planned to travel to Connecticut to accept an honorary degree from the University of Hartford, a scheduled appearance that had not gone unnoticed by Richard Neal, the savvy thirty-seven-year-old mayor of Springfield, Massachusetts, who noted that Hartford, Connecticut, was less than thirty miles away. Geisel's hometown was in the midst of celebrating the 350th anniversary of its founding, and Mayor Neal thought a visit by its most famous living son would be a highlight of the monthlong festivities. Months before his Hartford visit, then, Ted had found the Tower swamped with mail bearing a Springfield postmark, most of it from schoolchildren asking Dr. Seuss to visit—including a letter from eight-year-old Joel Senez, whose family now occupied 74 Fairfield Street. It was all too much for Geisel to resist—and with Springfield only a half-hour drive from Hartford, Ted promised he'd come home in May.

On Sunday, May 18, 1986, Geisel received his ninth honorary doctorate from an American university as he was hooded at the University of Hartford in front of 1,800 whooping students. At age eighty-four, Geisel gave very few speeches and simply bowed respectfully to the crowd and sat down. "That's part of the deal I make when I come to these things," he told the *Hartford Courant* later. "I like coming and talking to young people who have to solve problems I don't have to worry about solving anymore."[32]

Two days later, Dr. Seuss was on Mulberry Street.

On a day filled with official receptions, lunch and dinner with Springfield's leaders, and endless crowds of excited children, Geisel requested that there be no formal interviews or any scheduled book signings or appearances; he simply wanted to enjoy his hometown— the one he'd left nearly sixty years ago. "I'm very sentimental about Springfield," he admitted.[33] Ted and Audrey were driven around town in an antique bus, with Mayor Neal helpfully pointing out key landmarks and major changes in the cityscape. There was a short stop at Sumner Avenue School—where children dressed like Bartholomew Cubbins or the Cat in the Hat filed out onto the front lawn, cheering excitedly as Ted waved from the bus—and then a brief visit to Geisel's childhood home at 74 Fairfield Street. "I just stopped by to make sure you're taking proper care of the house," Geisel said merrily as he shook hands with its current owner, Ron Senez. For a while, he sat in his old bedroom with Senez's two young sons, pointing out places where he had poked holes in the plaster, and left them with a tantalizing story, claiming there was a mural of "a lot of crazy animals"[34] that was now covered by their bedroom wallpaper.[35]

As the bus slowly turned off of Maple and onto Mulberry Street, Ted could see it lined with hundreds of schoolchildren and teachers, cheering loudly and waving a long banner reading *And to Think That I Saw Him on Mulberry Street!* Audrey nudged her husband. "Give them a good wave, darling,"[36] she said gently—but to her surprise, Ted asked the bus driver to stop. Geisel stepped out of the bus and onto the sidewalk, looking dapper in his checked gray suit and paisley tie, and the crowd excitedly roared its approval and pressed forward slightly—and suddenly, Dr. Seuss was being mobbed like a rock star. Small hands reached out to touch him as he walked past, and he reached back, trying to shake as many as he could. As Ted waved goodbye, hundreds of voices shouted in unison the final line of *Green Eggs and Ham*: "Thank you! Thank you, Sam-I-Am!" Ted boarded the bus, choking back tears. "Wow," he said quietly.

As the sun began to go down, Mayor Neal took Ted to Forest Park—one of the many parks Geisel's father had overseen in his half-century as park superintendent—and presented him with an item that had recently been discovered thirty feet up a tree: a rusted iron sign reading GEISEL GROVE, the picnic park created by Ted's father a lifetime ago. Before Geisel left, a librarian shook his hand warmly. "Thank you for being so good to the kids," she said.[37]

•••

Ted was still trying to keep to his regular work schedule, diligently going into his studio every day, but it was clear he was slowing down. Breakfast was still around nine-thirty, though health problems had forced him to stop eating eggs and switch to cold cereal or oatmeal. "He rants and rails at the change," noted Audrey, "but man does not live by cholesterol alone, although he sometimes dies by it."[38] After breakfast, he would head for the familiar desk, with a short break for lunch. The cork walls were still lined with drafts of books in various stages of development, the drawing table covered with sketches of unusual characters or half-finished typewritten manuscripts. He was still trying to work on three or four books at a time. "They'll fight with each other until finally two of them win and I'll finish those," he explained. "The others will go back into the files for a while and then come out eventually."[39]

Some days, Audrey caught him in what she called "a state of flux," kicked back in his chair, with a vacant stare. Ted explained that he was merely "puzzling my puzzler," as he thought through troublesome plot points or difficult rhymes while staring at the Pacific coastline beyond his studio windows. "I can't imagine Ted being productive without that view, and the way his seat knocks back and his feet go up—and [then] he gets a thought and slaps forward," said Audrey. "That is all part of his creativity."[40] The only interruptions Geisel permitted were telephone calls from Random House; at the moment, he was working with Schulman on the final touches of a Beginner Book called *I Am NOT Going to Get Up Today!*, which he'd written, but had been too tired to illustrate, handing those duties over to artist James Stevenson.

By 5:30 P.M., he would be done for the day and would exit his studio, loudly announcing, "I have now left the office, now hear this!" Then he and Audrey would have cocktails—lately his preferred beverage was a vodka tonic—and watch the evening news together. While Ted preferred to stay at home most evenings, Audrey could still persuade him to accompany her to dinner parties or charity events from time to time, telling him it helped him "stay rounded." And if Ted groused that he was feeling old and tired, she would dismiss him playfully, telling him that going out in the evenings kept his mind young. "After the children's hour, the crazy little kid grows up, and he's a crazy grown-up," Audrey said warmly. "[Ted's] mind just keeps flipping out . . . getting kind of crazier all the time."[41]

Ted was still a good dinner guest, though he did more listening than talking these days, especially when it came to politics. "I stay out of politics," he said flatly, "because if I begin thinking too much about politics, I'll probably . . . drop writing children's books and become a political cartoonist again."[42] While he liked Reagan personally, Ted's own politics were still fiercely liberal, and he couldn't bear listening to anyone defending the president's brand of fiscal or social conservatism. Rather than argue, however, he would simply sit back and stew, one eyebrow slightly cocked—"the twinkle went out," as Judith Morgan put it.[43]

He also found himself getting bored easily and looking for other things to do. At a charity gala at the high-end Neiman Marcus department store in San Diego, Ted disappeared for hours. When Audrey finally found him, he was sitting in the women's shoe department, happily switching all the prices around. At that moment, he informed Audrey he was done attending charity balls and galas.

As Christmas of 1986 approached, Ted found he was having problems hearing and grudgingly began wearing a hearing aid. His hand-drawn Christmas card to Audrey showed the Cat in the Hat with a matching hearing aid, with the caption "Damn it all, Audrey, I heard you! You said, 'Nerry Jistmas!' And so do I."[44] He had also developed gout, and was—understandably—feeling suitably grouchy enough that he refused an invitation to serve as the honorary chairman of the Holiday Bowl football game in San Diego. Typically, however, Audrey talked him into reconsidering—and on December 30, Ted found himself in the traditional red jacket, waving dutifully during the parade, and watching the game from a comfortable private box. Despite his initial misgivings, he was all smiles afterward. "I'm delighted to have been chosen," he told the *San Diego Union*. "I was completely surprised—my athletic prowess has never been terrific."[45]

Still, his mood continued to sour as his health continued to decline. Everything, it seemed, was a problem. In early 1987, Geisel went in for root canal surgery and developed a major infection, which led to further deterioration of his already fragile jawbone. More rounds of poking and prodding followed, but Ted was tiring of doctors—and they were tiring of him, too. Ted was such a notoriously grumpy patient that

Audrey even caught one physician trying to sneak out a back door rather than have to diagnose Dr. Seuss. Through it all, Ted refused to have surgery on his aching jaw. He would eventually be put on a medication cocktail heavy on antibiotics to fight his infection.

Nineteen eighty-seven would mark a major anniversary in Dr. Seuss's career, as it was not only the thirtieth anniversary of the publication of *The Cat in the Hat*, but the fiftieth anniversary of his first book, *And to Think That I Saw It on Mulberry Street!* With a body of work spanning five decades, Geisel worried some of his work might now be deemed outdated or old-fashioned—especially a book like *The 500 Hats of Bartholomew Cubbins*, which he considered an archaic "literary fairy tale." "If I didn't have a reputation, I couldn't sell it today," he said of *Cubbins*. "Kings and fairy tales got old fashioned. People began walking on the moon and there were no kings."[46]

More seriously, Geisel had recently drawn fire for his use of the derogatory word *Chinaman* in the fifty-year-old *Mulberry Street*—and even he agreed that the term was in poor taste. "That's the way things were fifty years ago," he explained—and in 1978, he had quietly changed the phrase to *Chinese man*. He also tinkered slightly with the art, erasing the character's pigtail, and instructed the Random House production department to remove the character's yellow skin tone ("Now he looks like an Irishman," Geisel said, somewhat unhelpfully.[47]). However, even with Geisel's alterations to the character, *Mulberry Street*'s Chinese man would remain controversial. In 2017, a *Mulberry Street* mural at the Dr. Seuss museum in Springfield would draw sharp criticism for containing the offending character and would eventually be replaced with a Seussian montage.

Critics also revived the observation that very few Dr. Seuss books contained female protagonists—and those that *did* contain female characters portrayed them either as villains—such as the lazy bird Mayzie in *Horton Hatches the Egg*—or lacking in imagination, such as the sister in *The Glunk That Got Thunk*. Geisel, who considered himself a feminist, tried to lay low, but couldn't resist carping about what he considered sanctimonious nitpicking. "I'm in favor of women's lib," he said, "but a lot of members of women's lib have decided that they're going to clean up everything."[48] When critic Alison Lurie took Ted to task in *The New York Review of Books* for sexism, Geisel couldn't resist pointing out that most of his characters were simply fantasy creatures—and "if she [Lurie] can identify their sex, I'll remember her in my will."[49]

While he couldn't pull the transaction off in time to make it part of Dr. Seuss's fiftieth anniversary, Bernstein and Random House completed their acquisition of Vanguard in 1988, obtaining an impressive five-hundred-title backlist that included works by Saul Bellow and Joyce Carol Oates. But Bernstein always said he had purchased Vanguard for one reason: he wanted the two Dr. Seuss books the company had published five decades ago. With the acquisition of *Mulberry Street* and *Bartholomew Cubbins*, Random House officially owned the entire Dr. Seuss catalogue. "That was really the main reason I did it," Bernstein said proudly.[50]

Even as others were celebrating his life and work, Ted was in perpetual agony. Despite increasingly stronger doses of medication, Geisel was in constant pain from the surgeries to his neck and jaw. In late 1987, he canceled a planned trip to Baltimore for the opening of the touring "Dr. Seuss: From Then to Now" retrospective, citing health problems. His doctors continued to urge him to undergo treatment in a hyperbaric chamber to speed his recovery and noted that there were now chambers large enough to seat eight—Ted wouldn't have to lay on his back in the coffin-sized enclosure that so frightened him. In 1988, Audrey even managed to get Ted to the University of San Diego Medical Center, where he could visit the room-sized chamber and hear from doctors, who enthused about its ease and effectiveness—but Ted defiantly walked out in the middle of the discussion. Audrey pled with him to reconsider, but Ted wouldn't budge. "All you're offering me is logic," he growled.[51]

The only room in which the pain ever seemed to abate was his studio, where he could lean back in his chair, looking out at the ocean, or existing in silent conversation with the loyal Theophrastus, waiting for inspiration. But it was harder now to come up with ideas; he would rummage through his bone pile over and over again, looking for possibilities in discarded drawings or half-developed manuscripts, without much luck. After taking on doctors in *You're Only Old Once!* he briefly considered going after lawyers, relishing the idea of mocking the profession that had permitted *Liberty* magazine to—in his opinion—steal his work in the name of a petty profit. But the more he wrote and drew, the more he realized he was only getting "angrier and angrier . . . I found I was being mean. I knew that wouldn't work."[52] Next, he worked at a story about a little boy with a square balloon, but couldn't figure out where it was going, either. "I've got an idea here, and an idea here," he wrote to Ted Owens in frustration, "but I have no idea in the world how to make them connect."[53]

In March of 1988, Geisel turned eighty-four. He was feeling old and feeling tired; friends thought he was looking frail. Geisel likely knew his next book might well be his last—but despite his constant aches and pains, he wasn't fixated on death or dying. Instead, he wanted his final book to be a benediction—a book that embodied the one theme, he said, that ran through all of his books, starting with that very first moment Marco set foot on Mulberry Street.

Hope.

• • • •

Geisel would spend much of 1988 and early 1989 in the Tower and at his desk, working slowly on the book he would come to call *Oh, the Places You'll Go!* His workday had shortened slightly again—most mornings, he wouldn't sit down in his studio until at least ten—but for Ted, old habits were the best habits; he couldn't imagine doing a book any other way, no matter how tired he might get. "You have to put in your hours, and finally you make it work," he said plainly.[54] Pages still went up on the wall for him to lean over and squint at, hands thrust into his back pockets, and the trash can still overflowed with crumpled drawings and discarded pages of typed manuscript.

From the opening page, Geisel was there to greet his readers warmly, then take them by the hand for an expedition through endless possibilities:

> Congratulations!
> Today is your day.
> You're off to Great Places!
> You're off and away!

"The theme is limitless horizons and hope," he explained—and perhaps knowing this would be his final journey with his readers, *Oh, the Places You'll Go!* is a tour de force of Seussian architecture and Seussian characters, with subtle nods to work from his six-decade career. Smiling elephants resembling Horton march across the page; oddly bent houses, castles with soaring arches, and mazes of roads crisscross the landscape. Dragon-like creatures pop out of manholes, while gigantic Hakken-Kraks yowl from the ocean. There were even pages that seemed to recall his magazine work from the 1920s and 1930s, with men in derby hats and long dark coats standing in line while being watched by a cow, and small black cats—straight out of his *Life* magazine cartoons—studiously eyeing a fishing hole. On another page, bearded men play fantastic instruments, similar to those in *The 5,000 Fingers of Dr. T.* Elsewhere, struts resemble the fanciful letters from *On Beyond Zebra*.

As the book's main character, a little boy in yellow with a stocking cap, overcomes slumps, negotiates the Waiting Place, and conquers fears of being alone, Geisel cheers him—and the reader—on wildly, ending the book on a note of triumphant encouragement that Ted had written and rewritten countless times, until he had it just right:

> . . . you're off to Great Places!
> Today is your day!

Your mountain is waiting.
So . . . get on your way![55]

While Geisel was finishing up *Oh, the Places You'll Go!* in early spring 1989, he called Cathy Goldsmith and asked her to come to the Tower to help him with the book's final layout. Goldsmith lived out of the Tower's guest room as she and Ted spent their days with his pages spread out on the floor of his studio, checking his colored pencils against the Random House color charts, and marking every circle and squiggle with the appropriate color number, "until even my eyes hurt," said Goldsmith.[56] As Goldsmith helped Ted pack his completed manuscript into an oversize box for transport back to New York, Geisel gently informed her that he wouldn't be coming to Random House to deliver the book or read it himself. She left the Tower with tears stinging her eyes; it was clear the book was Dr. Seuss's goodbye. "It seemed so clear that he was not knowing where he was going to go pretty soon," she said.[57] As she boarded her plane back to New York, a flight attendant asked if she could take the large box Goldsmith was carrying. Goldsmith refused, aghast at the idea of handing over her precious cargo.

As Ted wrapped up *Oh, the Places You'll Go!*, Audrey was moody and slightly depressed. Ted worried that he was to blame; he knew he could be testy when finishing a book. "She's mad at me for something," Ted whispered to Janet Schulman over the phone. "I can't find out what."[58] But Audrey assured him that things were fine, even as she began taking antidepressants. As the summer of 1989 wore on, Audrey found it difficult to remember things, and privately, she was concerned she might be developing Alzheimer's. Her mood blackened, and she began taking Prozac and sleeping until nearly noon—a sure sign that something was wrong with the normally lively and active Audrey. Finally, at the urging of her daughters, she agreed to undergo an MRI, where doctors discovered a benign tumor lodged between her skull and her brain.

Audrey went in for surgery in January 1990 to excise the tumor and was immediately herself again. "I had been in such total anguish and now I was better, just like that!" she recalled, snapping her fingers.[59] Watching Audrey recover in her bed at Scripps Clinic, with her head wrapped in an enormous turban of bandages, Ted was overcome with emotion. Jed Mattes, Ted's agent, fondly recalled how Audrey had always been able to "unobtrusively anticipate [Ted's] needs so he never had to be aware of them."[60] Seeing Audrey helpless, Ted was now determined to take care of her as best he could—and every day he would visit her, dressed in his best suit and bow tie, bringing her a feather. "If you don't deserve a feather in your cap today, you never will," he would tell her as he inserted that day's feather into her turban.[61] By the end of her hospital stay, her turban was filled with brightly colored feathers sticking out in all directions.

●●●●

Shortly after Cathy Goldsmith delivered *Oh, the Places You'll Go!* to Random House, Michael Frith dropped by for a visit. As he stuck his head into the offices of the juvenile division, editor Janet Schulman beckoned him over. "You should see what Ted just sent," she said, and pointed him toward the newly delivered manuscript. Frith slowly started reading through the pages and felt a catch in his throat. "Do you know what this is?" he said to Schulman. "It's his valedictory. He's saying goodbye to us."[62]

So he was. And when *Oh, the Places You'll Go!* was published in early 1990, most critics and readers seemed to sense it, even if some weren't quite sure how they felt about the book itself. One of the first and most widely circulated reviews, by Scripps Howard News Service writer Fredric Koeppel, seemed determined to be unimpressed, calling the book "slack and unimaginative," and complaining that "the illustrations [are] typically Seussian but pale imitations of his best work"[63]—a sure sign Koeppel had missed at least part of the point of the book. Alison Lurie, writing in *The New York Review of Books*, issued an overanalyzed and overwritten critique, disparaging the book as "the yuppie dream—or nightmare—of 1990 in cartoon form." Lurie further dismissed the book as encouraging children to pursue wealth and fame, rather than helping others, defeating tyrants, or calling out blowhards. "Who is buying this book?" she finally asked. "My guess is that its typical purchaser—or recipient—is aged thirty-something, has a highly paid, publicly visible job, and feels insecure because of the way things are going in the world."[64]

How wrong she would be, as Susan Stark of Gannett News Service—in another widely reprinted review—would immediately assert. As Stark saw it, *Oh, the Places You'll Go!* had "both the depth and levity that seem likely to make it one of everyone's favorites. It also has the greatest thematic breadth of any book in the entire extraordinary Seuss canon. This may well be a summing up on his part, his farewell with a flourish," continued Stark. "If so, he's surely going out in the high style to which he has made us all joyfully, gratefully accustomed."[65]

Most readers and critics saw the book exactly as Frith and Stark had—as Dr. Seuss's final and beneficent words of encouragement and support for anyone, at any age, anxious to make their way in the world. As a result, it would regularly be given as a gift at graduations, read aloud at weddings, tucked into care packages for new college students, or signed by colleagues for a promoted or retiring coworker, making it both a perennial bestseller as well as one of the bestselling Dr. Seuss books of all time. On publication, it would race to the top of the *New York Times* adult fiction bestseller list and linger in the top twenty-five for two years, selling more than a million copies in that time. "This proves it!" Geisel said giddily, "I no longer write for children, I write for people!"[66]

Producers at Tri-Star Productions immediately approached Geisel about turning the book into a full-length animated feature, and Ted would take several meetings with executives at the Tower to discuss fleshing his relatively short book out into a ninety-minute movie. Producers envisioned the film as a mash-up of every Dr. Seuss book, using all of his characters—an idea Geisel loved—and sweetened the deal with a promise that he could write several songs. But Ted's enthusiasm for the project began to wane with every passing week; he just simply couldn't find the energy to work on it at the rapid pace envisioned by Tri-Star. The project would be back-burnered and then abandoned for good.

That summer, after years of gentle nudging by Bob Bernstein and others, Geisel finally agreed to work with two longtime friends, the journalists Neil and Judith Morgan, on his authorized biography. Ted enjoyed sitting with them as they sorted through files of old artwork and manuscripts, and foraged through the archives at UCLA, but he dreaded the idea of being interviewed. His speech was now permanently slurred due to the damage to his jaw, and Geisel worried the Morgans wouldn't be able to understand him.

Still, beginning in December 1990, Geisel sat for nearly eight months of extended interviews, with the Morgans asking him questions about his Springfield childhood, his days at Dartmouth and Oxford, and his early years with Helen as a cartoonist and advertising man in New York City. To his surprise, he enjoyed talking about old times and old friends—and the Morgans, to his delight, seemed to have little problem understanding him. He was also intrigued by the laptop computers the Morgans used to type up their notes; after seventy years of pounding away on a typewriter, he wondered aloud whether he would even be able to learn to use a computer at his age.

As they wrapped up one of their final interviews in the summer of 1991, the Morgans asked Geisel if there was any moral or message he wanted to leave with his readers that he didn't think he'd included in any of his books. After sixty years and more than forty books, was there anything left Dr. Seuss wanted to say? At their next session, Geisel handed them a scrap of paper with his distinctive printing on it:

Any message or slogan? Whenever things go a bit sour
in a job I'm doing, I always tell myself, "You can do better
than this."

The best slogan I can think of to leave with the kids of the
U.S.A. would be: "We can . . . and we've *got* to . . . do
better than this."[67]

Then, thinking better of it, he had darkly crossed out *the kids of*, thereby ensuring his message was addressed to everyone. "I no longer write for children," he'd insisted. "I write for people."

• • • •

"Am I dead now?" Ted playfully asked Audrey.[68] She assured him that he most certainly was *not*—but in early September 1991, he informed his secretary, Claudia Prescott, that he was done signing books and done sending Cat Notes. Any mail left in the Tower would have to be returned to Random House to be answered by form letter. It was then that Prescott understood: despite Audrey's reassurances, Ted knew he was dying. "Claudia, you *are* going to stay on, aren't you?" he asked. Prescott promised that she would and told him she'd come by to check on him.

He was also done with hospitals. "He declared no more treatments, no more trips," said Judith Morgan. "He was so tired of being put in a car and taken out for checkups and attempts to prolong everything and he said he just wanted to quit going to the doctor."[69] Geisel had no intention, then, of taking his last breath in a sterile hospital room, in an unfamiliar bed. He knew where he wanted to die: the one place that he loved the most—the one place on Earth that he truly hated to leave. It wasn't Springfield, nor was it New Zealand, nor any of the other exotic locations he'd visited in his eighty-seven years.

It was his studio in the Tower at the top of Mount Soledad.

The well-worn sofa in Ted's studio—the one where he would writhe when stuck for ideas, or where he would sit for hours reading mysteries and biographies, waiting for his brain to kick-start—was converted into a bed. Here Geisel would sleep most of the day, even as the sunlight came streaming in through the windows and the waves of the Pacific Ocean crashed on the beach below. Audrey would serve as his nurse during the days, handing the evening shift off to a night nurse. Some afternoons, Geisel's doctor, Ruth Grobstein, would sit with him, talking with him long into the night.

His youngest stepdaughter, Leagrey, now thirty-three, came to stay in the Tower as well, quietly chatting with him and watching over him as he slept. In his old age, Geisel admitted that his views of children had changed. "I'm a failure in enough things that I would like to go on and make them better," he said. "I would be a more amenable, lovable person than I am now. I probably would like children better than I do now; individually, I can handle them, but in mass . . . they terrify me."[70] Over the last twenty years, Geisel had cultivated a warm and loving relationship with Lark and Leagrey—a relationship that was all the more special because he'd had to work at it. One late September afternoon, as he sat with Leagrey, he took Theophrastus—his companion and muse since childhood—down from his perch near the desk. "You will take care of the dog, won't you?" he asked as he pressed the well-loved stuffed dog into his daughter's hands.[71]

As she'd promised, Claudia Prescott came to check on Ted on Monday, September 23. She found him sleepy, dropping off even as they tried to have a conversation. "We can do this later," Prescott told him softly. "Yes, I'm not going to die tomorrow," Ted said sleepily.

"He was in denial," recalled Grobstein. "He really believed in magic."[72]

The next day, Ted drifted in and out of consciousness throughout the day. Audrey sat near him, quietly talking with him even as he slept. Around ten on the evening of Tuesday, September 24, 1991,

Theodor Seuss Geisel died peacefully in his sleep in his studio in La Jolla. He was eighty-seven years old.

• • • •

While Theodor Geisel may be gone, Dr. Seuss, of course, goes on.

At the time of Geisel's death in 1991, Dr. Seuss had published forty-eight books in more than twenty languages—and several more Dr. Seuss books, discovered in his bone pile by Audrey and Cathy Goldsmith, would be published after his death, including *Daisy-Head Mayzie* and *What Pet Should I Get?* In the years immediately after Ted's death, Audrey would capably take the reins of the Dr. Seuss organization, aggressively keeping the Dr. Seuss brand at the forefront of pop culture, and fiercely protecting his legacy right up until her own death in December 2018. "You use it or you lose it," Audrey said of the Dr. Seuss brand. "If we're not out there—if we don't keep up the reminders and remembrances—you fall off. And as long as I'm here, that isn't going to happen."[73] And so, Audrey would approve of and license not only new merchandise, but also sign off on Broadway musicals based on and inspired by his work—including the 2000 show *Seussical!*, a long-running and reliable staple of regional theaters—as well as new live-action and animated movies inspired by books like *The Cat in the Hat* and *The Lorax*. On Audrey's watch, Dr. Seuss would suddenly seem to be nearly everywhere, in every form of media and social media, a ubiquitous and unavoidable part of pop culture, yet still as familiar as family.

But for Ted, it had always been the books that mattered most—and nearly thirty years after his death, books by Dr. Seuss still sell as well and as fast as ever, rivaled only by the Harry Potter books by the brilliant J. K. Rowling—Geisel's natural heir, as she reignited the same love for books in today's young readers that Dr. Seuss had first sparked to life with *The Cat in the Hat* fifty years earlier. At a time when parents and teachers were concerned children's minds had been lost to television forever, Dr. Seuss had made reading exciting again. Even today, in a world of Xboxes and iPhones, Dr. Seuss *still* holds their attention.

It hadn't always been that way. Dr. Seuss didn't arrive in the imaginations of children fully formed; rather, he had evolved slowly from a mere pseudonym, a means to an end, signed in distinctive print at the bottom of single-paneled cartoons and then at the bottom of advertisements for insecticides and motor oil. His arrival on the children's book scene in 1937—when Geisel was already well into his thirties—was a monetary calling more than a moral one. It took World War II—and the tutelage of Frank Capra—to turn Dr. Seuss into the crusader and storyteller who arrived at the Utah writer's conference in 1949, angry at "Bunny books" that spoke down to children and treated them like a mere commodity. It was there in Salt Lake City that Dr. Seuss put his finger on his true voice and his calling, articulating that the best books for children were those that took them seriously as readers and valued them as people. "Too many writers have only contempt and condescension for children," Geisel said later, "which is why they give them degrading corn about bunnies."[74]

It was a cat, however, that would finally form Ted Geisel into Dr. Seuss. With the arrival of *The Cat in the Hat*, written as a challenge to the status quo of turgid children's primers, the landscape of children's books was fundamentally altered—and Geisel had done it while adhering to a careful pedagogy of vocabulary lists approved by parents and consecrated by educators. As the Cat swept the mess he'd made with Thing One and Thing Two out the door, Dick and Jane went out right along with it. Reading—and learning to read—were officially fun. "In all the morass of children's books, Dr. Seuss stands out like a particularly welcome friend," the novelist Shirley Jackson once wrote. "Dr. Seuss makes his own rules, and has managed somehow to cover every step of reading growth from beginning to almost-sophisticated with a rich deposit of nonsense."[75] With Beginner Books in particular, Dr. Seuss had taken pedantics and pedagogies and distilled them through his own unique blend of discipline and coordinated chaos to create something entirely new: books that not only helped kids read, but were also books they *liked* to read and *wanted* to read.

For Ted Geisel—and for Dr. Seuss—that love of reading would

always be more than enough. "I think I proved to a number of million kids that reading is not a disagreeable task," he said. "I think I have helped kids laugh in schools as well as at home[76] . . . [but] the best thing about my books might be that I've never found a child who felt compelled to read them."[77] Ultimately, said Geisel, "I'd prefer they forgot about the educational value, and say it was a lot of fun."[78]

And as for becoming Dr. Seuss? Geisel was content with his legacy. Dr. Seuss, from the moment of his inception, had always been there for one reason.

"Just to spread joy," said Geisel, then broke into a wry smile. "How does that sound?"[79]

ACKNOWLEDGMENTS

While writers often lament that writing is a lonely exercise, one of the wonderful realities of publishing is that many books are still a group effort. This is especially true for biographers, who, out of necessity, rely on the assistance, expertise, advice, and—when needed—unbridled sympathy of others. I've been particularly lucky, because—as one can likely imagine—living in the world of Dr. Seuss over the past three years has brought me into the offices, archives, and living rooms of some wonderfully interesting, talented, and very funny people.

Michael Frith, who for years served as Ted Geisel's editor and aide-de-camp, was always very generous with his time, sitting with me in person, on the phone, and over e-mail, where he patiently responded to "just one more question." His frank stories and funny memories helped bring many of the behind-the-scenes moments colorfully to life, and I am grateful to him for explaining some of Ted's obscure jokes, as well as for generously providing me with copies of the word lists and number-coded color charts that Ted wielded so deftly in his work.

As a biographer, I'm always grateful to those who've explored my subject before—and with Dr. Seuss, I was extremely fortunate to get to know Judith Morgan, who was very generous with her time, as well as incredibly kind about sharing her work and her resources. Her and her late husband's book, *Dr. Seuss & Mr. Geisel*, remains an invaluable resource, and I so appreciate having her unique insights, opinions, and commentary on the life and work of Ted Geisel.

I also appreciate the time and courtesy I was shown by Christopher Cerf, who, in addition to talking with me about his parents, also pointed me toward several valuable archival resources; and by Robert Bernstein, whose admiration of Geisel was infectious.

I'm also indebted to a number of Dr. Seuss scholars who had a working familiarity with the archival materials available and generously shared with me their insights and opinions—and, in some cases, their research—as I did my own archival exploring. In particular, I appreciate the help of Dr. Philip Nel, who I could count on not only for assistance in running down and acquiring documents but also for a frank opinion on Ted's work. I'm also especially grateful to Dr. Charles D. Cohen for the awe-inspiring detective work he's done in tracking down Ted's work and influences, particularly from the early part of his career (you can read all about it in his seminal work, *The Seuss, the Whole Seuss, and Nothing but the Seuss*). Cohen's careful research sent me looking in other places I hadn't known about, and his input, encouragement, and enthusiasm helped make this a better book.

This book was also improved by the assistance of countless writers, researchers, librarians, and archivists everywhere, including: Ken Plume and Jake Friedman, who provided invaluable help and insight regarding the collaborations of Dr. Seuss and Chuck Jones; Bob Batchelor, for his help with the history of the Signal Corp; Sonja Williams, for her insights on Dr. Seuss and racism; and the archivists and researchers at the Rauner Special Collections Library at Dartmouth, the collection of Random House/Vanguard/Bennett Cerf papers at Columbia University, and the Mandeville Special Collections at the University of California, San Diego. I also thank Susan Brandt at Dr. Seuss Enterprises in La Jolla for her kindness. In Ted's hometown of Springfield, Massachusetts, I was very fortunate to have the help of Kathleen Simpson and Joanie Muratore-Pallatino with the Springfield Museums, as well as the aid and encouragement of Roger Bunce, who showed me around the house on Fairfield Street.

One of the most enthusiastic supporters of this project is my extraordinary editor at Dutton, John Parsley. From the moment we hatched this project over lunch, he's been its greatest fan and my biggest advocate, keeping me focused on narrative, asking the right questions, and gently helping me sort out things at those times when what I was *trying* to write was not actually what I *wrote*. Patient almost to a fault, he's helped me run traps and troubleshoot, kept us on schedule and on target, and his Zen-like demeanor always makes everything better. I appreciate everything about you, John—and my thanks to your family for letting my pages take over more than a few of your weekends.

I'm always grateful, too, for the professional and personal support of my wonderful agent, Jonathan Lyons, who's had my back for more than a decade now. Smart, kind, and perpetually calm—and there are times I don't make that easy—I can always count on him to check in at just the right times, with all the right questions and all the right answers. As always, I thank his wife, Cameron, and his boys, Roan, Ilan, and Finn, for sharing him with me.

This book was well cared for by the terrific team at Dutton, and I'm grateful for every one of them. In particular, my thanks to Cassidy Sachs, Marlene Glazer, Madison Forsander, as well as to copyeditor Nancy Inglis, who saved my bacon more times than I can count. Any errors that remain are mine.

I'm truly fortunate to have the support and encouragement of so many friends, who were excited about this project from day one. My thanks to Angela, Michael, Jazmyn, and Ivy Drayden, Mike and Cassie Knapp, Gail and Dave Noren, Scott Phillips, John Schilling, Loren Monroe, and Marron and Mike Nelson.

I also know I could always count on the love and enthusiasm of my parents, Elaine and Wayne Miller; and my brother, Cris; his wife, Rebecca; and their boys, Dyson and Jacob. And I especially want to thank my amazing and brilliant daughter, Madison, for always being there for me, even when she's 500 miles away. Love ya, kid.

Finally, none of this would have been possible without the love and support from my extraordinarily patient wife, Barb, who put up with two long years of messes on the tables, walking Grayson by herself, and eating dinner alone. I love you tons. You're my favorite.

—FREDERICKSBURG, VIRGINIA, FEBRUARY 2018

SELECTED BIBLIOGRAPHY

Berenstain, Stan and Jan. *Down a Sunny Dirt Road: An Autobiography*. New York: Random House, 2002.

Berg, A. Scott. *Lindbergh*. New York: Berkley, 1998.

Bernstein, Robert L. *Speaking Freely: My Life in Publishing and Human Rights*. New York: The New Press, 2016.

Cerf, Bennett. *At Random: The Reminiscences of Bennett Cerf*. New York: Random House, 2002.

Cohen, Charles D. *The Seuss, the Whole Seuss, and Nothing but the Seuss: A Visual Biography of Theodor Seuss Geisel*. New York: Random House, 2004.

Cott, Jonathan. *Pipers at the Gates of Dawn: The Wisdom of Children's Literature*. New York: McGraw-Hill, 1983.

Dr. Seuss Enterprises. *The Secret Art of Dr. Seuss*. New York: Random House, 1995.

Fensch, Thomas, ed. *Of Sneetches and Whos and the Good Dr. Seuss: Essays on the Writings and Life of Theodor Geisel*. Jefferson, North Carolina: McFarland & Company, Inc., 1997.

Harris, Mark. *Five Came Back: A Story of Hollywood and the Second World War*. New York: Penguin, 2014.

Held, Jacob M., ed. *Dr. Seuss and Philosophy: Oh, the Thinks You Can Think!* Lanham, Maryland: Rowman & Littlefield, 2011.

Jones, Chuck. *Chuck Reducks*. New York: Warner, 1996.

MacDonald, Ruth K. *Dr. Seuss*. Boston: Twayne, 1988.

McBride, Joseph. *Frank Capra: The Catastrophe of Success*. New York: Simon & Schuster, 1992.

McKinnon, Robert J. *Stepping Into the Picture: Cartoon Designer Maurice Noble*. Jackson, Mississippi: University Press of Mississippi, 2008.

Milkman, Paul. *PM: A New Deal in Journalism, 1940-1948*. New Brunswick (New Jersey): Rutgers University Press, 1997.

Minear, Richard H. *Dr. Seuss Goes to War: The World War II Editorial Cartoons of Theodor Seuss Geisel*. New York: New Press, 1997.

Nel, Philip. *Dr. Seuss: American Icon*. New York: Continuum, 2004.

_____. *The Annotated Cat: Under the Hats of Seuss and His Cats*. New York: Random House, 2007.

_____. *Was the Cat in the Hat Black?* New York: Oxford, 2017.

Pease, Donald E. *Theodor Seuss Geisel*. New York: Oxford, 2010.

Raines, Rebecca Robbins. *Getting the Message Through: A Branch History of the U.S. Army Signal Corps*. Washington, D.C.: Center of Military History, United States Army, 1996.

Schiffrin, Andre. *Dr. Seuss & Co. Go to War: The World War II Editorial Cartoons of America's Leading Comic Artists*. New York: The New Press, 2009.

Strahan, Derek. *Lost Springfield Massachusetts*. Charleston, South Carolina: History Press, 2017.

Stofflet, Mary. *Dr. Seuss from Then to Now: A Catalogue of the Retrospective Exhibition*. New York: Random House, 1986.

NOTES

Please note that TSG indicates Theodor Seuss Geisel.

Chapter 1. Minnows into Whales

1. Dan Carlinsky, "The Wily Ruse of Doctor Seuss: Or, How Ted Geisel Has Done Real Well," *Magazine of the Boston Herald American*, March 4, 1979.
2. Sally Hammond, "Dr. Seuss: The Man Who Stole Boredom," unidentified clipping, c. 1969, Rauner Special Collections Library, Dartmouth College.
3. T. A. Geisel's backstory takes a bit of detective work to decipher, as both his date of birth and date of emigration have been reported incorrectly by various sources. While many cite his birth date as 1840, his emigration from Germany to the United States as occurring in 1867, and his U.S. citizenship as becoming official in 1872, the dates I've provided here were self-reported by T.A. on several passport applications. (See his 1911 and 1914 applications, for example.) Other information comes from a document titled "The Geisel Families of Springfield, MA," by Christopher C. Broderick, held at the Springfield Museum Historic Library.
4. Hammond, "Dr. Seuss: The Man Who Stole Boredom."
5. See "Successful Springfield Industries, No. X, Kalmbach & Geisel's Massive Brewery," *Progressive Springfield*, c. 1910, Springfield Museum Historic Library.
6. Ibid.
7. T.A. and Christine's first child, Bertha, was born in 1872; a second daughter, Christiena, died in 1873 at less than two months old. The next child, Emma Louise, was born November 1, 1874. See Christopher Broderick's "The Geisel Families of Springfield, MA."
8. Adolph A. Geisel was born in Springfield on July 17, 1881, while Christine Cornelia Geisel was born October 11, 1888. Adolph, who would have a successful career as a car dealer and hotelier/restaurateur, died September 4, 1962. Christine died March 2, 1965. See "The Geisel Families of Springfield, MA."
9. See "Theodor R. Geisel, Born Here, Combines Athletic with Civic Interests," *Springfield Union/Springfield Republican Magazine*, July 21, 1929.
10. "Just What the Doctor Ordered . . . Green Eggs and Ham for the Cat in the Hat," *Star Sports & Magazine*, May 8, 1976.
11. See *Twelfth Census of the United States.*
12. TSG, "Non-Autobiography," quoted in Judith and Neil Morgan, *Dr. Seuss & Mr. Geisel: A Biography* (New York: Random House, 1995), 8.
13. For more information, see Derek Strahan, *Lost Springfield Massachusetts.* (Charleston, South Carolina: History Press, 2017), 77–79.
14. See Morgan and Morgan, *Dr. Seuss & Mr. Geisel,* 6
15. See "T.H. [*sic*] Geisel, Parks Boss 30 Years, Dies," *Springfield Republican*, December 10, 1968. Also Morgan and Morgan, *Dr. Seuss & Mr. Geisel,* 8.
16. See the notice in the *Springfield Republican*, March 4, 1902.
17. TSG, "Non-Autobiography," quoted in Morgan and Morgan, *Dr. Seuss & Mr. Geisel,* 6.
18. There is some disagreement on Marnie's given name. While the Morgans report it as Margaretha, other sources—such as the Seuss genealogy in the Springfield Historical Society—cite her name as either Margaretha or Marguerita.

Handwritten census data entries from 1910 and 1920 seem to support the spelling as Margaretha.

19. Morgan and Morgan, *Dr. Seuss & Mr. Geisel*, 9.

20. TSG, "Non-Autobiography," quoted in Morgan and Morgan, *Dr. Seuss & Mr. Geisel*, 9.

21. Ibid., 17.

22. Ibid., 13.

23. The German population was estimated as somewhere around 1,200 in 1915, while the population of Springfield in 1910 was 88,926. See *Thirteenth Census of the United States*.

24. TSG, "Non-Autobiography," quoted in Morgan and Morgan, *Dr. Seuss & Mr. Geisel*, 11.

25. Ibid.

26. Ibid., 7.

27. Robert Sullivan, "Oh, the Places He Went!" *Dartmouth Alumni Magazine*, Winter 1992.

28. See Rob Wilder, "Catching Up with Dr. Seuss," *Parents*, June 1979.

29. Jonathan Cott, "The Good Dr. Seuss," from *Pipers at the Gates of Dawn: The Wisdom of Children's Literature* (New York: Random House, 1983), in Thomas Fensch, ed., *Of Sneetches and Whos and the Good Dr. Seuss: Essays on the Writings and Life of Theodor Geisel* (North Chesterfield, VA: New Century Books, 2015), 110.

30. *The Hole Book* wasn't Newell's only novelty act. There was also *The Slant Book* (1910), which was cut at an angle, and *Topsys & Turvys* (1893), in which an illustration could be rotated 180 degrees to make a different, recognizable illustration—such as a drawing of an ostrich that, when turned upside down, appears to be a drawing of an elephant.

31. "The Books That Made Writers," *New York Times*, November 25, 1979.

32. See Arthur M. Winfield, *The Rover Boys in the Mountains*, 1902.

33. TSG, "Non-Autobiography," quoted in Morgan and Morgan, *Dr. Seuss & Mr. Geisel*, 7.

34. See "Geisel on the Park Board; Mayor's Announcement Made at Meeting of City Council," *Springfield Republican*, September 28, 1909.

35. See front-page photos in the *Springfield Republican*, May 26, 1907.

36. C. Robert Jennings, "Dr. Seuss: 'What Am I Doing Here?'" *Saturday Evening Post*, October 23, 1965.

37. Carlinsky, "The Wily Ruse of Doctor Seuss."

38. Sullivan, "Oh, the Places He Went!"

39. "Interview with Theodor Robert Geisel," *Springfield Herald*, June 22, 1967.

40. Clifford Jordan, "Dr. Seuss," *Dartmouth Alumni Magazine*, October 1962.

41. Sullivan, "Oh, the Places He Went!"

42. Morgan and Morgan, *Dr. Seuss & Mr. Geisel*, 13.

43. Ibid., 7.

44. See the May 7, 1911, ad in the *Springfield Republican*, p. 25.

45. Morgan and Morgan, *Dr. Seuss & Mr. Geisel*, 7.

46. TSG, "Non-Autobiography," quoted in Morgan and Morgan, *Dr. Seuss & Mr. Geisel*, 10–11.

47. Ibid., 16.

48. Ibid., 15.

49. Dr. Seuss, *And to Think That I Saw It on Mulberry Street* (New York: Random House, 1964), 3.

50. TSG, "Non-Autobiography," quoted in Morgan and Morgan, *Dr. Seuss & Mr. Geisel*, 18.

51. See T. R. Geisel's draft registration card, 1918.

52. TSG to Whitney Campbell, October 1, 1926. Quoted in Morgan and Morgan, *Dr. Seuss & Mr. Geisel*, 19.

53. Morgan and Morgan, *Dr. Seuss & Mr. Geisel*, 17.

54. Robert Siegel and Art Silverman, "During World War I, U.S. Government Propaganda Erased German Culture," NPR, *All Things Considered*, April 7, 2017.

55. "Roosevelt Bars the Hyphenated," *New York Times*, October 13, 1915.

56. Wilder, "Catching Up with Dr. Seuss."

57. E. J. Kahn, "Children's Friend," *The New Yorker*, December 17, 1960.

58. Jennings, "Dr. Seuss: 'What Am I Doing Here?'"

59. See the front page of the *Springfield Republican*, May 2, 1918.

60. See "Roosevelt Here; Strong for the War; Wants to Fight Turkey; For Armament After Peace," *Springfield Republican*, May 9, 1918.

61. Morgan and Morgan, *Dr. Seuss & Mr. Geisel*, 22.

62. Carlinsky, "The Wily Ruse of Doctor Seuss."

63. Charles D. Cohen, *The Seuss, the Whole Seuss, and Nothing but the Seuss: A Visual Biography of Theodor Seuss Geisel* (New York: Random House Books for Young Readers, 2004), 25.

64. *Central Recorder* 3, No. 4, October 24, 1919.

65. *Central Recorder* 2, No. 12, February 17, 1919.

66. Cott, "The Good Dr. Seuss."

67. Sidney Edelberg, "Dr. Seuss Comes from Springfield," *Springfield Herald*, June 22, 1967.

68. *Central Recorder* 3, No. 9, November 26, 1919.

69. TSG, "Non-Autobiography," quoted in Morgan and Morgan, *Dr. Seuss & Mr. Geisel*, 19.

70. Ibid., 23.

71. Donald Freeman, "The Nonsensical World of Dr. Seuss," *McCall's*, November 1964.

72. Cott, "The Good Dr. Seuss." Like many of Ted's stories, this one changes in the telling over the years as well. In some versions of the story, his father would curse, "Damn them! Damn them!" and rise to the position of president the day Prohibition went into effect. See "Just What the Doctor Ordered . . . Green Eggs and Ham for the Cat in the Hat," *Star Sports & Magazine*, May 8, 1976.

73. TSG, "Non-Autobiography," quoted in Morgan and Morgan, *Dr. Seuss & Mr. Geisel*, 23.

74. Ibid.

75. Ted's five-string banjo, an Orpheum No. 1, is now on display at the Wood Museum of Springfield History.

76. See program for minstrel show, April 29, 1921, Rauner Special Collections Library, Dartmouth College.

77. William C. Hill to Dartmouth Committee on Fellowship, February 19, 1925, Rauner Special Collections Library, Dartmouth College.

78. *Central Recorder* 4, No. 11, January 7, 1921.

79. See *Pnalka*, 1920–1921, p. 12.

80. Edward Connery Lathem, "The Beginnings of Dr. Seuss: A Conversation with Theodor S. Geisel," *Dartmouth Alumni Magazine*, April 1976.

81. Hilaire Belloc, "The Microbe," *More Beasts (For Worse Children)*, 1910 (reprinted Oxford City Press, 2010).

82. Clifford Jordan, "Dr. Seuss," *Dartmouth Alumni Magazine*, October 1962.

Chapter 2. The Slob Generation

1. Daniel Webster, *Dartmouth v. Woodward*, Statement before the U.S. Supreme Court, March 10, 1818.
2. Leon Burr Richardson, *History of Dartmouth College*, 2 vols. (Hanover: Dartmouth College Publications, 1932), 2: 769.
3. Judith and Neil Morgan, *Dr. Seuss & Mr. Geisel: A Biography* (New York: Random House, 1995), 27.
4. Judith and Neil Morgan, "Dr. Seuss & Theodor Geisel," untitled clipping, UCSB archives, 1994.
5. Edward Connery Lathem, "The Beginnings of Dr. Seuss: A Conversation with Theodor S. Geisel," *Dartmouth Alumni Magazine,* April 1976.
6. See "Two Arguments Against Matrimony" and "The Pied Piper," *Jack-O-Lantern,* Vol. XIV, No. 6, October 1921; "The Fatted Calf," *Jack-O-Lantern,* Vol. XIV, No. 4, January 1922.
7. Morgan and Morgan, *Dr. Seuss & Mr. Geisel*, 28.
8. Ibid.
9. Ibid., 31.
10. Ibid.
11. See "Pity the poor sailors on a night like this," *Jack-O-Lantern,* Vol. XV, No. 3, February 1923.
12. Robert Sullivan, "Oh, the Places He Went!" *Dartmouth Alumni Magazine,* Winter 1992.
13. Lathem, "The Beginnings of Dr. Seuss."
14. Ibid.
15. Ibid.
16. Ibid.
17. See "Who's Who in Bo-Bo," *Jack-O-Lantern,* Vol. XVI, No. 3, November 1923.
18. Lathem, "The Beginnings of Dr. Seuss."
19. See "Zimkowitz 14–Zimkowitz 10," *Jack-O-Lantern,* Vol. XVI, No. 2, October 1923; "Zimkowitz ex-'27 to Wed Greater-Boston Girl," *Jack-O-Lantern,* Vol. XVI, No. 4, December 1923; "Interviews with Famous Ski Jumpers," *Jack-O-Lantern,* Vol. XVI, No. 5, January 1924.
20. Lathem, "The Beginnings of Dr. Seuss."
21. Clifford Jordan, "Dr. Seuss," *Dartmouth Alumni Magazine*, October 1962.
22. "The B. and M. Timetable—A Book Review," *Jack-O-Lantern,* Vol. XVI, No. 10, June 1924.
23. Lathem, "The Beginnings of Dr. Seuss."
24. Joe Harrington, "College Boy 'Least Likely to Succeed' Has It Made," *Boston Globe,* January 22, 1961.
25. Lathem, "The Beginnings of Dr. Seuss."
26. "A Crusader Flares," *The Dartmouth* 46, No. 68, December 10, 1923.
27. "William Jennings Bryan Opposes Evolutionist," *The Dartmouth* 46, No. 68, December 10, 1923.
28. TSG, "Non-Autobiography," quoted in Morgan and Morgan, *Dr. Seuss & Mr. Geisel,* 32.
29. Morgan and Morgan, *Dr. Seuss & Mr. Geisel,* 33.
30. Ted probably wrote the notice himself. See *Jack-O-Lantern,* Vol. XVI, No. 10, June 1924.
31. TSG to Whitney Campbell, April 19, 1926. Quoted in Morgan and Morgan, *Dr. Seuss & Mr. Geisel*, 34.

32. "Vote for Somebody," *Jack-O-Lantern*, Vol. XVII, No. 2, October 1924.
33. See *Jack-O-Lantern*, Vol. XIV, No. 5, February 1922.
34. "The Old Chivalric Faith—," *Jack-O-Lantern*, Vol. XVII, No. 4, December 1924.
35. Lathem, "The Beginnings of Dr. Seuss."
36. Ibid.
37. "Dartmouth Defeats Jacko Eleven, 13–7," *The Dartmouth* 46, No. 40, November 1, 1924.
38. Joe Harrington, "College Boy 'Least Likely to Succeed' Has It Made," *Boston Globe*, January 22, 1961.
39. "Mr. John Keats Sees the Elgin Marbles for the first time," *Jack-O-Lantern*, Vol. XVII, No. 7, March 1925; "Peinture sans Fard," Ibid.
40. Harrington, "College Boy 'Least Likely to Succeed' Has It Made."
41. Morgan and Morgan, *Dr. Seuss & Mr. Geisel*, 34.
42. Ibid., 35–36.
43. Lathem, "The Beginnings of Dr. Seuss."
44. Charles D. Cohen, *The Seuss, the Whole Seuss, and Nothing but the Seuss: A Visual Biography of Theodor Seuss Geisel* (New York: Random House Books for Young Readers, 2004), 55–56.
45. Colin Dangaard, "Dr. Seuss Reigns Supreme as King of the Kids," *Boston Herald American*, November 21, 1976.
46. Lathem, "The Beginnings of Dr. Seuss."
47. Morgan and Morgan, *Dr. Seuss & Mr. Geisel*, 37.
48. Professor Hewette Joyce to Committee on Graduate Instruction and Fellowships, March 13, 1925, Rauner Special Collections Library, Dartmouth College.
49. W. B. Pressey to Committee on Fellowships, March 14, 1925, Rauner Special Collections Library, Dartmouth College.
50. M. S. Sherman to Committee of Fellowships, February 19, 1925, Rauner Special Collections Library, Dartmouth College.
51. Lathem, "The Beginnings of Dr. Seuss."
52. Clifford Jordan, "Dr. Seuss," *Dartmouth Alumni Magazine*, October 1962.
53. R.P.M., On the Firing Line, *Springfield Union*, July 6, 1925.
54. Theodor Scuss Geisel, "The curriculum of this university," On the Firing Line, *Springfield Union*, July 18, 1925.

Chapter 3. Strange Beasts

1. Tolkien, the new Rawlinson and Bosworth Professor of Anglo-Saxon, taught courses in *Beowulf*, Anglo-Saxon literature, and Germanic philology. Ted never mentioned Tolkien by name, but given his fluency in German and his comment about being bogged down by "High German and Gothic," he may indeed have taken Tolkien's course.
2. Edward Connery Lathem, "The Beginnings of Dr. Seuss: A Conversation with Theodor S. Geisel," *Dartmouth Alumni Magazine*, April 1976.
3. Ibid.
4. TSG, "Non-Autobiography." Quoted in Morgan and Morgan, *Dr. Seuss & Mr. Geisel* (New York: Random House, 1995), 42.
5. TSG to Whitney Campbell, August 1926, Rauner Special Collections Library, Dartmouth College.
6. Ibid.
7. See invitation of Viscountess Astor to T. S. Giesel [sic], March 1925, Special Collections Mandeville Library, UCSD.

8. Bob Warren, "Dr. Seuss, Former Jacko Editor, Tells How Boredom May Lead to Success," *The Dartmouth*, May 10, 1934.
9. Lathem, "The Beginnings of Dr. Seuss."
10. Judith and Neil Morgan, *Dr. Seuss & Mr. Geisel: A Biography* (New York: Random House, 1995), 57.
11. Ibid., 45–46.
12. E. J. Kahn, "Profiles: Children's Friend," *The New Yorker*, December 17, 1960.
13. Morgan and Morgan, *Dr. Seuss & Mr. Geisel*, 45.
14. C. Robert Jennings, "Dr. Seuss: 'What Am I Doing Here?'" *Saturday Evening Post*, October 23, 1965.
15. Ibid.
16. Morgan and Morgan, *Dr. Seuss & Mr. Geisel*, 45.
17. Lathem, "The Beginnings of Dr. Seuss."
18. Ibid.
19. Ibid.
20. Ibid.
21. Dan Carlinsky, "The Wily Ruse of Doctor Seuss: Or, How Ted Geisel Has Done Real Well," *Magazine of the Boston Herald American*, March 4, 1979.
22. Ted Geisel to Whit Campbell, July 30, 1926, Rauner Special Collections Library, Dartmouth College.
23. Lathem, "The Beginnings of Dr. Seuss."
24. TSG to Whitney Campbell, April 20, 1926, Rauner Special Collections Library, Dartmouth College.
25. Ibid.
26. Ibid.
27. Ibid.
28. Ibid.
29. TSG to Whitney Campbell, July 30, 1926.
30. TSG to Whitney Campbell, April 20, 1926.
31. TSG to Whitney Campbell, July 30, 1926.
32. Warren, "Dr. Seuss, Former Jacko Editor, Tells How Boredom May Lead to Success."
33. Lathem, "The Beginnings of Dr. Seuss."
34. Carolyn See, "Dr. Seuss and the Naked Ladies: Blowing the Lid Off the Private Life of America's Most Beloved Author," *Esquire*, June 1974.
35. Helen Palmer to Christine Burrows, August 4, 1926. Quoted in Morgan and Morgan, *Dr. Seuss & Mr. Geisel*, 56.
36. TSG to Whitney Campbell, July 30, 1926.
37. Ibid.
38. TSG to Whitney Campbell, August 11, 1926, Rauner Special Collections Library, Dartmouth College.
39. Ibid.
40. Ibid.
41. Morgan and Morgan, *Dr. Seuss & Mr. Geisel*, 51.
42. Jonathan Freedman, "Nearing 80, Dr. Seuss Still Thrills Young, Old," *San Diego Tribune*, February 24, 1984.
43. Ibid.
44. "Non-Autobiography," quoted in Morgan and Morgan, *Dr. Seuss & Mr. Geisel*, 52.
45. TSG to Whitney Campbell, October 2, 1926, Rauner Special Collections Library, Dartmouth College.

46. Ibid.
47. Ibid.
48. Ibid.
49. TSG to Whitney Campbell, January 7, 1927, Rauner Special Collections Library, Dartmouth College.
50. George Kane, "And, Dear Dr. Seuss, the Whole World's in Love with Yeuss," *Rocky Mountain News*, February 15, 1976.
51. Carolyn See, "Dr. Seuss and the Naked Ladies: Blowing the Lid Off the Private Life of America's Most Beloved Author," *Esquire*, June 1974.
52. Judith Martin, "Dr. Seuss: Good Times with Rhymes," *Washington Post*, November 15, 1971.
53. Jennings, "Dr. Seuss: 'What Am I Doing Here?'"
54. Sally Hammond, "Dr. Seuss: The Man Who Stole Boredom," unidentified clipping, c. 1969, Rauner Special Collections Library, Dartmouth College.

Chapter 4. The Flit

1. TSG to Alexander K. Laing, May 1927, Rauner Special Collections Library, Dartmouth College.
2. TSG to Whitney Campbell, April 13, 1927, Rauner Special Collections Library, Dartmouth College.
3. Ibid.
4. Ibid.
5. Edward Connery Lathem, "The Beginnings of Dr. Seuss: A Conversation with Theodor S. Geisel," *Dartmouth Alumni Magazine*, April 1976.
6. Ibid.
7. Ibid.
8. The second Seuss to appear in *The Saturday Evening Post* would be the 1964 prose piece titled, "If at First You Don't Succeed—Quit!"
9. Lathem, "The Beginnings of Dr. Seuss."
10. Ibid.
11. See "Norman Anthony, Editor of Ballyhoo, Dead at 74," *New York Times*, January 22, 1968.
12. George Kane, "And, Dear Dr. Seuss, the Whole World's in Love with Yeuss," *Rocky Mountain News*, February 15, 1976.
13. Judith and Neil Morgan, *Dr. Seuss & Mr. Geisel: A Biography* (New York: Random House, 1995), 63.
14. TSG to Whitney Campbell, December 1927, Rauner Special Collections Library, Dartmouth College.
15. Ibid.
16. Ibid.
17. Lathem, "The Beginnings of Dr. Seuss."
18. "The Waiting Room at Dang-Dang," *Judge*, September 15, 1928.
19. Dr. Seuss, compiled by Mary Stoflett, *Dr. Seuss from Then to Now: A Catalogue of the Retrospective Exhibition* (New York: Random House, 1987), 21.
20. Jonathan Freedman, "Nearing 80, Dr. Seuss Still Thrills Young, Old," *San Diego Tribune*, February 24, 1984.
21. See *Judge*, December 3, 1927.
22. TSG, "Non-Autobiography," quoted in Morgan and Morgan, *Dr. Seuss & Mr. Geisel*, 61.

23. Sally Hammond, "Dr. Seuss: The Man Who Stole Boredom," unidentified clipping, c. 1969, Rauner Special Collections Library, Dartmouth College.
24. See Ellen NicKenzie Lawson, *Smugglers, Bootleggers, and Scofflaws: Prohibition and New York City* (New York: State University of New York, 2013), 83.
25. TSG to Whitney Campbell, March/April (?) 1928, Rauner Special Collections Library, Dartmouth College.
26. Ibid.
27. Ibid.
28. Bob Warren, "Dr. Seuss, Former Jacko Editor, Tells How Boredom May Lead to Success," *The Dartmouth*, May 10, 1934.
29. Dan Carlinsky, "The Wily Ruse of Doctor Seuss: Or, How Ted Geisel Has Done Real Well," *Magazine of the Boston Herald American*, March 4, 1979.
30. Ibid.
31. Warren, "Dr. Seuss, Former Jacko Editor, Tells How Boredom May Lead to Success."
32. TSG to Campbell, March/April (?) 1928.
33. Ibid.
34. Ibid.
35. Lathem, "The Beginnings of Dr. Seuss."
36. Typical of Ted, there is also a version of this story that does *not* mention Mrs. Cleaves. In that version, Ted simply sent his cartoon off to Flit to see if there might be any interest in having him take on an ad campaign. See Warren, "Dr. Seuss, Former Jacko Editor, Tells How Boredom May Lead to Success."
37. TSG to Campbell, March/April (?) 1928.
38. See "The exterminator-man forgets himself at the flea-circus," *Judge*, March 31, 1928.
39. See *Life*, May 31, 1928, p. 30.
40. Charles D. Cohen, *The Seuss, the Whole Seuss, and Nothing but the Seuss: A Visual Biography of Theodor Seuss Geisel* (New York: Random House Books for Young Readers, 2004), 110.
41. Lathem, "The Beginnings of Dr. Seuss."
42. Freedman, "Nearing 80, Dr. Seuss Still Thrills Young, Old."
43. "Ough! Ough! Or Why I Believe in Simplified Spelling," *Judge*, April 13, 1929.
44. The term *nigger in the woodpile* was slang of the era for "a concealed motive or unknown factor affecting a situation in an adverse way." See definition for *nigger in the woodpile* in *Shorter Oxford English Dictionary*, 5th ed., Vol. 2 (New York: Oxford University Press), 2002.
45. "Non-Autobiography," quoted by Morgan and Morgan, *Dr. Seuss & Mr. Geisel*, 70.
46. Jonathan Cott, "The Good Dr. Seuss," in *Pipers at the Gates of Dawn: The Wisdom of Children's Literature* (New York: Random House, 1983).
47. See "Forgotten Events of History," *Life*, July 1930.
48. Carolyn Robbins, "Passing of Dr. Seuss's Niece, 'Peggy the Hoofer,' Puts Spotlight on Springfield Childhood," *Springfield Republican*, March 7, 2015.
49. Mike Salzhauer, "A Carnival Cavort with Dr. Seuss," *Dartmouth Review*, February 2, 1981.
50. Warren, "Dr. Seuss, Former Jacko Editor, Tells How Boredom May Lead to Success."
51. "Gay Menagerie of Queer Animals Fills the Apartment of Dr. Seuss," *Springfield Union-News*, November 28, 1937.
52. The first book to feature Ted's art, the collection of Flit cartoons, had only a limited release.

53. Alexander Abingdon, compiler, *Boners: Being a Collection of Schoolboy Wisdom* (New York: Viking Press, 1931), 15.
54. "Schoolboy Wisdom," *New York Times*, March 1, 1931.
55. See Jennifer Schuessler, "Inside the List," *New York Times Sunday Book Review*, December 12, 2008.
56. Lathem, "The Beginnings of Dr. Seuss."
57. E. J. Kahn, "Profiles: Children's Friend," *The New Yorker*, December 17, 1960.
58. Lathem, "The Beginnings of Dr. Seuss."
59. Ibid.
60. Ibid.
61. TSG, "Non-Autobiography," quoted in Morgan and Morgan, *Dr. Seuss & Mr. Geisel*, 72.
62. Carolyn Robbins, "Memoir Reflects Geisel Family Life in Springfield Before Dr. Seuss Books Written," *Springfield Republican*, September 6, 2015.
63. TSG, "Non-Autobiography," quoted in Morgan and Morgan, *Dr. Seuss & Mr. Geisel*, 68.
64. Walter Winchell, "On Broadway," *Scranton Republican*, February 12, 1931.
65. Judith Martin, "Dr. Seuss: Good Times with Rhymes," *Washington Post*, November 15, 1971.
66. TSG to Harold Rugg, 1932, Rauner Special Collections Library, Dartmouth College.
67. "Czar of the Insect World," *Vanity Fair*, December 1931.
68. Morgan and Morgan, *Dr. Seuss & Mr. Geisel*, 74.
69. Ibid.
70. Cott, "The Good Dr. Seuss."
71. Warren, "Dr. Seuss, Former Jacko Editor, Tells How Boredom May Lead to Success."
72. TSG to Andy Gump Fepp, quoted in Philip Nel, *Dr. Seuss: American Icon* (New York: Continuum, 2003), 70.
73. Dr. Seuss, compiled by Mary Stofflet, *Dr. Seuss from Then to Now*, 35.
74. Lathem, "The Beginnings of Dr. Seuss."
75. Ibid.
76. See Cohen, *The Seuss, the Whole Seuss, and Nothing but the Seuss*, 124.
77. Ibid.
78. A. S. Brown, "When Dr. Seuss Did His Stuff for Exxon," *The Lamp*, Spring 1987.
79. E. J. Kahn, "Profiles: Children's Friend," *The New Yorker*, December 17, 1960.
80. Lathem, "The Beginnings of Dr. Seuss."
81. Carlinsky, "The Wily Ruse of Doctor Seuss."
82. Ibid.
83. Swedish American Line brochure, circa April 1936.
84. C. Robert Jennings, "Dr. Seuss: 'What Am I Doing Here?'" *Saturday Evening Post*, October 23, 1965.
85. Dr. Seuss, compiled by Mary Stofflet, *Dr. Seuss from Then to Now*, 29.
86. Ibid.

Chapter 5. Brat Books

1. Dr. Seuss, compiled by Mary Stofflet, *Dr. Seuss from Then to Now: A Catalogue of the Retrospective Exhibition* (New York: Random House, 1987), 29.
2. Edward Connery Lathem, "The Beginnings of Dr. Seuss: A Conversation with Theodor S. Geisel," *Dartmouth Alumni Magazine*, April 1976.
3. "Making Our Daughters Less Irritating," *Judge*, November 24, 1928.

4. Judith Martin, "Dr. Seuss: Good Times with Rhymes," *Washington Post*, November 15, 1971.

5. Bliss Street is in fact on the *west* side of Springfield, across the Connecticut River from Mulberry Street.

6. Lathem, "The Beginnings of Dr. Seuss."

7. Judith and Neil Morgan, *Dr. Seuss & Mr. Geisel: A Biography* (New York: Random House, 1995), 81.

8. Lathem, "The Beginnings of Dr. Seuss."

9. Mike Salzhauer, "A Carnival Cavort with Dr. Seuss," *Dartmouth Review*, February 2, 1981.

10. Lathem, "The Beginnings of Dr. Seuss."

11. Ibid.

12. See the dedication page of pretty much any printing of *And to Think That I Saw It on Mulberry Street*.

13. Morgan and Morgan, *Dr. Seuss & Mr. Geisel*, 83.

14. Evelyn Shrifte to TSG, August 31, 1937, Vanguard Press Papers, Columbia University.

15. See *Publishers Weekly*, August 28, 1937.

16. See "Crazy Doings on Mulberry Street Told in Book That Is Hard to Beat," *Springfield Union-News*, October 3, 1937.

17. "Books," *The New Yorker*, November 6, 1937.

18. Lathem, "The Beginnings of Dr. Seuss."

19. *Dartmouth Alumni Magazine*, December 1937.

20. Jonathan Cott, "The Good Dr. Seuss," in *Pipers at the Gates of Dawn: The Wisdom of Children's Literature* (New York: Random House, 1983).

21. Lathem, "The Beginnings of Dr. Seuss."

22. See Morgan and Morgan, *Dr. Seuss & Mr. Geisel*, 85.

23. See Ted's 1960 draft of "Brat Books." Emphasis in original, Special Collections Library, UCSD.

24. Dr. Seuss, *And to Think That I Saw It on Mulberry Street*, 14.

25. Don Freeman, "Dr. Seuss at 72—Going Like 60," *Saturday Evening Post*, March 1, 1977.

26. See Robert Cahn, "The Wonderful World of Dr. Seuss," *Saturday Evening Post*, July 6, 1957.

27. "Nut Stuff," *Sales Management*, January 1, 1939.

28. Notes for *Alumni Magazine*, March 1938, "Brief Biographies," Rauner Special Collections Library, Dartmouth College.

29. Cynthia Gorney, "Dr. Seuss at 75: Grinch, Cat in the Hat, Wocket and Generations of Kids in His Pocket," *Washington Post*, May 21, 1979.

30. TSG, unpublished interview with Edward Connery Lathem, 1975. Quoted in Morgan and Morgan, *Dr. Seuss & Mr. Geisel*, 87.

31. Gorney, "Dr. Seuss at 75."

32. Ibid.

33. *Dartmouth Alumni Magazine*, January 1939.

34. See the dedication page of any edition of *The 500 Hats of Bartholomew Cubbins*.

35. Morgan and Morgan, *Dr. Seuss & Mr. Geisel*, 91. Emphasis in original.

36. Cahn, "The Wonderful World of Dr. Seuss."

37. Bennett Cerf, *At Random: The Reminiscences of Bennett Cerf* (New York: Random House, 1977), 18.

38. TSG, unpublished interview with Edward Connery Lathem, 1975. Quoted in Morgan and Morgan, *Dr. Seuss & Mr. Geisel*, 98.

39. TSG to E. J. Kahn Jr., E. J. Kahn papers, New York Public Library. Cited in Morgan and Morgan, *Dr. Seuss & Mr. Geisel*, 93.

40. Bennett Cerf to TSG, December 19, 1938, Random House records, Columbia University Libraries.

41. E. J. Kahn, "Profiles: Children's Friend," *The New Yorker*, December 17, 1960.

42. Gorney, "Dr. Seuss at 75."

43. "Dr. Seuss," *Wilson Library Bulletin*, November 1939.

44. Bennett Cerf to TSG, February 1939. Bennett Cerf papers, Columbia University Libraries.

45. Diane Clark, "He Is Waking Children to a World of Words," *San Diego Union*, December 19, 1976.

46. Ibid.

47. Carolyn See, "Dr. Seuss and the Naked Ladies: Blowing the Lid Off the Private Life of America's Most Beloved Author," *Esquire*, June 1974.

48. Kahn, "Profiles: Children's Friend."

49. Cerf, *At Random*, 123.

50. Dr. Seuss, *The King's Stilts* (New York: Random House, 1939), 17.

51. "Gay Menagerie of Queer Animals Fills the Apartment of Dr. Seuss," *Springfield Union-News*, November 28, 1937.

52. TSG to Lew Miller, 1939. My thanks to Michael Frith for sharing his copy of this correspondence.

53. "The King's Stilts . . ." *New York Herald Tribune Books*, November 12, 1939.

54. Ellen Lewis Buell, "The New Books for Younger Readers," *New York Times*, October 15, 1939.

55. Robert Sullivan, "Oh, the Places He Went!" *Dartmouth Alumni Magazine*, Winter 1992.

56. Lathem, "The Beginnings of Dr. Seuss."

57. TSG and Ralph Warren, United States Patent 2,15-,853, filed May 19, 1938. See Cohen, *The Seuss, the Whole Seuss, and Nothing but the Seuss*, 368 n. 45.

58. Cahn, "The Wonderful World of Dr. Seuss."

59. Ibid.

60. See Cohen, *The Seuss, the Whole Seuss, and Nothing but the Seuss*, 2.

61. Digby Diehl, "Q&A Dr. Seuss," *Los Angeles Times West*, September 17, 1972.

62. "Matilda, the Elephant with a Mother Complex: A Dr. Seuss Fable," *Judge*, April 1938.

63. TSG to Louise Bonino, October 1939. Random House records, Columbia University Libraries.

64. Dr. Seuss, *Horton Hatches the Egg* (New York: Random House, 1940), 18.

65. Cahn, "The Wonderful World of Dr. Seuss."

66. Sullivan, "Oh, the Places He Went!"

67. Cerf, *At Random*, 85.

68. Bennett Cerf to Miss Frances Pindyk, April 11, 1940, Columbia University Special Collections.

69. Alexander Laing, *Dartmouth Alumni Magazine*, December 1940.

70. TSG, undated draft of letter to "Mr. Americus Vesputius Fepp," Rauner Library Special Collections, Dartmouth College. It's unlikely Ted was literally working on *Horton Hatches the Egg* as the Nazis occupied Paris. Paris fell on June 14, 1940, and *Horton* was published only a few days later.

71. *New York Journal-American*, February 17, 1939.

Chapter 6. Cockeyed Crusader

1. See "Our Story," Naragansett Beer website, www.narragansettbeer.com /our-story.
2. "Rome Talk Is Near; Spanish Negotiator Not Expected to Agree to War with Britain," *New York Times*, September 30, 1940.
3. "Gayda Accuses FDR of Offensive Against Axis," *The Bee* (Danville, Virginia), November 1, 1940.
4. "Gayda Warns U.S. Japan Won't Allow Convoys to Ireland," *Portsmouth Herald*, December 28, 1940.
5. See "Virginio Gayda Says . . ." *PM*, January 30, 1941.
6. Ibid.
7. TSG, undated draft of letter to "Mr. Americus Vesputius Fepp," Rauner Special Collections Library, Dartmouth College.
8. A. Scott Berg, *Lindbergh* (New York: Putnam, 1998), 402.
9. Jonathan Freedman, "Nearing 80, Dr. Seuss Still Thrills Young, Old," *San Diego Tribune*, February 24, 1984.
10. TSG, undated draft of letter to "Mr. Americus Vesputius Fepp."
11. Franklin D. Roosevelt State of the Union Address, January 6, 1941. This was also the famous "Four Freedoms" speech. See Roosevelt's reading copy of the speech, archived at https://fdrlibrary.org/documents/356632/390886/readingcopy.pdf/.
12. Berg, *Lindbergh*, 417.
13. Ibid.
14. Freedman, "Nearing 80, Dr. Seuss Still Thrills Young, Old."
15. Some thought that, given *PM*'s use of photography, it stood for "Photo Magazine." Others thought it simply referred to the fact that it was published in the afternoons.
16. Paul Milkman, *PM: A New Deal in Journalism, 1940-1948* (New Brunswick: Rutgers University Press, 1997), 34.
17. Ibid., 37-38.
18. Judith and Neil Morgan, *Dr. Seuss & Mr. Geisel: A Biography* (New York: Random House, 1995), 101.
19. TSG, undated draft of letter to "Mr. Americus Vesputius Fepp." The contract itself, however, for four cartoons a week, wouldn't be signed until May. See notice in the May 22, 1941, *Springfield Newspapers Report*.
20. Ibid.
21. "Talk talk talk talk talk talk talk," *PM*, May 8, 1941; "Ho hum! No chance of contagion," *PM*, May 15, 1941.
22. *PM*, June 2, 1941.
23. "Said a bird in the midst of a Blitz," *PM*, June 23, 1941.
24. *PM*, June 18, 1941.
25. TSG to Evelyn Shrifte, September 8, 1941, Random House records, Columbia University Libraries.
26. TSG, undated rough notes on *PM*, Rauner Special Collections Library, Dartmouth College.
27. See Berg, *Lindbergh*, 427.
28. Ibid., 428.
29. *PM*, September 18, 1941.
30. *PM*, September 22, 1941.
31. *PM*, October 1, 1941.
32. See Berg, *Lindbergh*, 428.

33. TSG, undated rough notes on *PM*, Rauner Special Collections Library, Dartmouth College.
34. Letter quoted in Richard H. Minear, *Dr. Seuss Goes to War: The World War II Editorial Cartoons of Theodor Seuss Geisel* (New York: New Press, 1999), 23.
35. Ibid.
36. *PM*, November 28, 1941.
37. Minear, *Dr. Seuss Goes to War*, 183.
38. *PM*, December 9, 1941.
39. Robert C. Jennings, "Dr. Seuss: 'What Am I Doing Here?'" *Saturday Evening Post*, October 23, 1965.
40. Milkman, *PM: A New Deal in Journalism, 1940-1948*, 21.
41. TSG, undated rough notes on *PM*, Rauner Special Collections Library, Dartmouth College.
42. Milkman, *PM: A New Deal in Journalism, 1940-1948*, 20.
43. Robert Bendiner to TSG, October 29, 1942, Rauner Special Collections Library, Dartmouth College.
44. Thomas Sancton to TSG, October 29, 1942, Rauner Special Collections Library, Dartmouth College.
45. "Malice in Wonderland," *Newsweek*, February 9, 1942.
46. "Holmes as Pacifist Offers to Resign," *New York Times*, December 15, 1941.
47. *PM*, January 13, 1942.
48. See "Letters to and from the Editor," *PM*, January 21 and 28, 1942.
49. See *PM*, January 21, 1942.
50. "A Slap's a Slap," Alan Walker, *The Text Message Blog*, National Archives website, November 22, 2013. Retrieved at https://text-message.blogs.archives.gov/2013/11/22/a-slaps-a-slap-general-john-l-dewitt-and-four-little-words/.
51. *PM*, February 13, 1942.
52. *PM*, March 30, 1942.
53. Milton S. Mayer, "The Case Against the Jew," *Saturday Evening Post*, March 27, 1942.
54. Ralph Ingersoll, "An Editorial Answer to the *Saturday Evening Post*," *PM*, March 27, 1942. I am deeply indebted to Charles D. Cohen for his research on this matter in his superb *The Seuss, the Whole Seuss, and Nothing but the Seuss* (New York: Random House Books for Young Readers, 2004).
55. *PM*, April 1, 1942.
56. *PM*, April 14, 1942.
57. *PM*, June 11, 1942.
58. *PM*, June 30, 1942.
59. *PM*, December 24, 1941.
60. Morgan and Morgan, *Dr. Seuss & Mr. Geisel*, 98.
61. *PM*, January 20, 1942.
62. *PM*, January 21, 1942.
63. *PM*, March 24, 1942.
64. *PM*, July 20, 1942.
65. "Protest from Down Under," *PM*, December 18, 1942.
66. "Gerald L. K. Smith Still in Business; Rightist Continues to Print Anti-Semitic Tracts," *New York Times*, October 11, 1964.
67. Morgan and Morgan, *Dr. Seuss & Mr. Geisel*, 101.
68. Ibid., 102.
69. TSG, undated rough notes on *PM*, Rauner Special Collections Library, Dartmouth College.

70. *PM,* January 19, 1942.
71. *PM,* March 21, 1942.
72. *PM,* April 7, 1942.
73. Helen Geisel to Evelyn Shrifte, July 26, 1942. Quoted in Morgan and Morgan, *Dr. Seuss & Mr. Geisel,* 105.
74. Ibid.
75. Terry Bell, "Hitler and 'Quick, Henry the Flit' Shaped the Saga of Dr. Seuss," *NZEE* (New Zealand), June 7, 1976.

Chapter 7. SNAFU

1. Sally Hammond, "Dr. Seuss: The Man Who Stole Boredom," unidentified clipping, c. 1966, Rauner Special Collections Library, Dartmouth College.
2. Jonathan Freedman, "Nearing 80, Dr. Seuss Still Thrills Young, Old," *San Diego Union,* February 24, 1984.
3. Mark Harris, *Five Came Back: A Story of Hollywood and the Second World War* (New York: Penguin, 2014), 235.
4. Judith and Neil Morgan, *Dr. Seuss & Mr. Geisel: A Biography* (New York: Random House, 1995), 106.
5. Edward Connery Lathem, "Beginnings of Dr. Seuss: A Conversation with Theodor S. Geisel," *Dartmouth Alumni Magazine,* April 1976.
6. *PM,* January 5, 1943.
7. Rough draft, "Re: PM Political Cartoons," Rauner Special Collections Library, Dartmouth College.
8. Joseph McBride, *Frank Capra: The Catastrophe of Success* (New York: Simon & Schuster, 1992), 455.
9. Frank Capra, *Frank Capra: The Name Above the Title: An Autobiography* (New York: Macmillan, 1971), 326.
10. McBride, *Frank Capra,* 474.
11. See Ted's notes for *The 25er,* June 8, 1945, Rauner Special Collections Library, Dartmouth College.
12. Morgan and Morgan, *Dr. Seuss & Mr. Geisel,* 109.
13. Ibid., 108.
14. McBride, *Frank Capra,* 453.
15. Ibid., 456.
16. Ibid., 475.
17. Ibid., 474
18. Ibid.
19. Ibid., 454.
20. Ibid.
21. Ted's notes for *The 25er,* June 8, 1945.
22. Judith Martin, "Dr. Seuss: Good Times with Rhymes," *Washington Post,* November 15, 1971.
23. TSG to Harold Rugg, November 23, 1943, Rauner Special Collections Library, Dartmouth College.
24. "This is Ann!" pamphlet (U.S. Government Printing Office, 1943).
25. TSG to Harold Rugg, November 23, 1943, Rauner Special Collections Library, Dartmouth College.
26. McBride, *Frank Capra,* 470.
27. Ibid., 475. Ted would tell this story many times. This is the most concise.

28. TSG, "Non-Autobiography." Quoted in Morgan and Morgan, *Dr. Seuss & Mr. Geisel*, 109.

29. Damien Love, "Happy Birthday, Ray Harryhausen (June 29, 1920–May 7, 2013): An Interview with the Titan of Stop-Motion Animation," *Bright Lights Film Journal*, June 29, 2014.

30. Cohen, *The Seuss, the Whole Seuss, and Nothing but the Seuss*, 249.

31. Harry McCracken, "Interview with Maurice Noble," *Animato* 21, 1991.

32. Ibid.

33. *Private Snafu: Coming!!*, directed by Chuck Jones, 1943.

34. Richard Corliss, "That Old Feeling: Seuss on First," *Time*, March 2, 2004.

35. *Private Snafu: Gripes*, directed by Friz Freleng, 1943.

36. Ibid.

37. Harris, *Five Came Back*, 236.

38. "Chuck Jones on animating World War II training films with Dr. Seuss," Emmy TV Legends Interviews, Television Academy Foundation, 1998. Retrieved at www .youtube.com/watch?v=Zh_OY0XYGmI.

39. Morgan and Morgan, *Dr. Seuss & Mr. Geisel*, 107.

40. Ibid., 112.

41. Notes on "Officer's Qualifications Note Sheet." I am grateful to Phil Nel for providing this information.

42. See Ted's cartoon "Can you deny that these statuettes were made at the expense of the United States government?" Army Cartoons Folder, Oversize MC 12703 Folder 35, Mandeville Special Collections Library, UCSD.

43. *Private Snafu: Rumors*, directed by Friz Freleng, 1943.

44. See Army Cartoons Folder, Oversize MC 12703 Folder 35, Mandeville Special Collections Library, UCSD.

45. Ted's notes for *The 25er*, June 8, 1945.

46. *PM*, December 30, 1942.

47. Morgan and Morgan, *Dr. Seuss & Mr. Geisel*, 111.

48. *Your Job in Germany*, 1945.

49. Robert Kupferberg, "A Seussian Celebration," *Parade*, February 26, 1984.

50. TSG World War II diary, quoted in Morgan and Morgan, *Dr. Seuss & Mr. Geisel*, 112.

51. Ibid., 113.

52. Ibid.

53. Ted's notes for *The 25er*, June 8, 1945.

54. Philip Nel, *Dr. Seuss: American Icon* (New York: Continuum, 2003), 60.

55. TSG World War II diary, quoted in Morgan and Morgan, *Dr. Seuss & Mr. Geisel*, 113.

56. TSG World War II diary, quoted in Nel, *Dr. Seuss: American Icon*, 61.

57. Cohen, *The Seuss, the Whole Seuss, and Nothing but the Seuss*, 268. As Cohen also explains, the camp Ted toured was "mostly a slave-labor camp. However, later reports would confirm that the gas chamber . . . was used to supply bodies to the Strasbourg University Institute of Anatomy, which paid the gas bill."

58. *Your Job in Germany*, 1945.

59. Digby Diehl, "Q&A: Dr. Seuss," *Los Angeles Times West*, September 17, 1972.

60. Ibid.

61. Ibid. Emphasis added.

62. Morgan and Morgan, *Dr. Seuss & Mr. Geisel*, 113.

63. McBride, *Frank Capra*, 496.

64. E. J. Kahn, "Profiles: Children's Friend," *The New Yorker*, December 17, 1960.

65. Freedman, "Nearing 80, Dr. Seuss Still Thrills Young, Old."

66. Morgan and Morgan, *Dr. Seuss & Mr. Geisel*, 114.
67. Ibid.
68. Kahn, "Profiles: Children's Friend."
69. Morgan and Morgan, *Dr. Seuss & Mr. Geisel*, 114.
70. McBride, *Frank Capra*, 499.
71. Ibid., 497.
72. Ibid., 499.
73. Hal Humphrey, "Zoo's Who? Dr. Seuss, That's Who," *Coronet*, December 1964.
74. Ibid.
75. Ibid.
76. Morgan and Morgan, *Dr. Seuss & Mr. Geisel*, 115.
77. Kahn, "Profiles: Children's Friend."
78. Morgan and Morgan, *Dr. Seuss & Mr. Geisel*, 115–16.
79. See Geisel's letter awarding his Legion of Merit, Mandeville Special Collections Library, UCSD.

Chapter 8. A Good Profession

1. "Honor Milland, Joan Crawford; Best Picture 'Oscar' to 'Lost Week-End'; Joan Crawford and Ray Milland Win 'Oscars,'" *Chicago Daily Tribune*, March 8, 1946.
2. Jonathan Freedman, "Nearing 80, Dr. Seuss Still Thrills Young, Old," *San Diego Union*, February 24, 1984.
3. Digby Diehl, "Q&A: Dr. Seuss," *Los Angeles Times West*, September 17, 1972.
4. Judith and Neil Morgan, *Dr. Seuss & Mr. Geisel: A Biography* (New York: Random House, 1995), 118.
5. Ibid., 119.
6. Ibid., 141.
7. See Charles D. Cohen, *The Seuss, the Whole Seuss, and Nothing but the Seuss: A Visual Biography of Theodor Seuss Geisel* (New York: Random House Books for Young Readers, 2004), 297.
8. Morgan and Morgan, *Dr. Seuss & Mr. Geisel*, 121.
9. Terry Bell, "Hitler and 'Quick, Henry the Flit' Shaped the Saga of Dr. Seuss," *NZEE* (New Zealand), June 7, 1976.
10. Elmo Williams, *Elmo Williams: A Hollywood Memoir* (Jefferson, NC: McFarland, 2006), 69.
11. Ibid., 70.
12. TSG to *Dartmouth Literary Magazine*, circa December 1947, Rauner Special Collections Library, Dartmouth College.
13. Diane Clark, "He Is Waking Children to a World of Words," *San Diego Union*, December 19, 1976.
14. "McElligot's Pool," *New York Times*, November 16, 1947.
15. Rob Wilder, "Catching Up with Dr. Seuss," *Parents*, June 1979.
16. Bosley Crowther, "'Design for Death,' Factual Film About the Japanese, Opens at Victoria—'Bad Sister' Also Arrives," *New York Times*, June 11, 1948.
17. Williams, *Elmo Williams*, 70.
18. Max Miller, "Max Miller," *Tribune-Sun* (San Diego, CA), November 20, 1948.
19. Ibid.
20. See any version of Dr. Seuss, *Thidwick the Big-Hearted Moose*.
21. Mike Salzhauer, "A Carnival Cavort with Dr. Seuss," *Dartmouth Review*, February 2, 1981.

22. Reviews reprinted in Thomas Fensch, *The Man Who Was Dr. Seuss: The Life and Work of Theodor Geisel* (The Woodlands, Texas: New Century Books), 2000, pages unnumbered.

23. "Books," *Dartmouth Alumni Magazine*, undated clipping, c. 1948, Rauner Special Collections Library, Dartmouth College.

24. Reviews reprinted in Fensch, *The Man Who Was Dr. Seuss*.

25. From here until page 209, unless otherwise noted, all quotes are taken from Ted's handwritten notes for "Mrs. Mulvaney and the Billion-Dollar Bunny, an Address, with Drawings on a Blackboard," by Dr. Seuss, c. 1949, Mandeville Special Collections Library, UCSD.

26. Arthur Gordon, "The Wonderful Wizard of Soledad Hill," *Woman's Day*, September 1965.

27. Morgan and Morgan, *Dr. Seuss & Mr. Geisel*, 124.

28. Ibid., 125.

29. "Spur Toward Comic Books Blamed on Parents' Laxity," *Salt Lake Tribune*, July 8, 1949.

30. Morgan and Morgan, *Dr. Seuss & Mr. Geisel*, 126.

31. Ibid.

32. Ibid.

33. Letter to Harold Rapp (?), January 27, 1950, Rauner Special Collections Library, Dartmouth College.

34. Morgan and Morgan, *Dr. Seuss & Mr. Geisel*, 123.

35. Ibid., 122.

36. Ibid., 123.

37. "Children's Books: Bartholomew and the Oobleck," *Boston Globe*, December 4, 1949.

38. T.R.C., "For the Younger Element: Bartholomew and the Oobleck," *Press and Sun-Bulletin* (Binghamton, NY), October 23, 1949.

39. Polly Goodwin, "Books for Children," *Chicago Tribune*, November 13, 1949.

40. See 1949 Dartmouth Alumni form, Rauner Special Collections Library, Dartmouth College.

41. TSG's handwritten notes for "Mrs. Mulvaney and the Billion-Dollar Bunny."

Chapter 9. A Person's a Person

1. See Dr. Seuss, *If I Ran the Zoo* (New York: Random House, 1950).

2. "Jelly Tot, Square Bear-Man!" *Newsweek*, October 8, 1951.

3. Arthur Gordon, "The Wonderful Wizard of Soledad Hill," *Woman's Day*, September 1965.

4. Diane Clark, "He Is Waking Children to a World of Words," *San Diego Union*, December 19, 1976.

5. "Let's Talk About Books," *Kingsport Times-News* (TN), July 2, 1950.

6. Dr. Seuss, *If I Ran the Zoo*, 16.

7. P.G., "If I Ran the Zoo" by Dr. Seuss, *Chicago Tribune*, November 12, 1950.

8. "Book on Zoo Bright, Funny," *Akron Beacon Journal* (OH), November 5, 1950.

9. See TSG's handwritten notes for "Mrs. Mulvaney and the Billion-Dollar Bunny, an Address, with Drawings on a Blackboard," by Dr. Seuss, c. 1949, Mandeville Special Collections Library, UCSD.

10. Or perhaps *McCoy*. There doesn't seem to be a consensus on the pronunciation, which Gildersleeve slurs through. The narration in the *Gerald McBoing-Boing* cartoon, however, sounds distinctly like *McCloy*.

11. Judith and Neil Morgan, *Dr. Seuss & Mr. Geisel: A Biography* (New York: Random House, 1995), 130.

12. Ibid., 131.

13. Dick Bothwell, "McBoing-Boing Creators Busy with More Cartoons," *Tampa Bay Times*, April 24, 1951.

14. Sydney J. Harris, "Extra! New Idea in Movie Cartoons!" *Akron Beacon Journal* (Ohio), April 6, 1951.

15. See Carolyn Robbins, "Passing of Dr. Seuss's Niece, 'Peggy the Hoofer,' Puts Spotlight on Springfield Childhood," *Springfield Republican*, March 7, 2015.

16. Morgan and Morgan, *Dr. Seuss & Mr. Geisel*, 144.

17. Stanley Kramer would also have *Death of a Salesman* (1951), *The Sniper* (1952), and *The Member of the Wedding* (1952) in production at around this time.

18. Morgan and Morgan, *Dr. Seuss & Mr. Geisel*, 137.

19. Elaine Dutka, "Stanley Kramer: Acclaimed Movies Focused on Social Issues," *Los Angeles Times*, February 20, 2001.

20. Donald Spoto, *Stanley Kramer, Film Maker* (New York: G.P. Putnam, 1978), 149.

21. Eleanor Quin, "The 5000 Fingers of Dr. T." Retrieved at www.tcm.com /tcmdb/title/75073/The-5000-Fingers-of-Dr-T/articles.html.

22. Helen Palmer to Barbara Palmer Bayler, May 11, 1952, cited by Morgan and Morgan, *Dr. Seuss & Mr. Geisel*, 133. Barbara was the daughter of Robert Palmer, her only brother.

23. Ibid., 134.

24. Ibid.

25. Ibid.

26. Stan and Jan Berenstain, *Down a Sunny Dirt Road: An Autobiography* (New York: Random House Books for Young Readers, 2002), 147.

27. Quin, "The 5000 Fingers of Dr. T."

28. Charles D. Cohen, *The Seuss, the Whole Seuss, and Nothing but the Seuss: A Visual Biography of Theodor Seuss Geisel* (New York: Random House Books for Young Readers, 2004), 294–95.

29. Spoto, *Stanley Kramer, Film Maker*, 149.

30. TSG, "Non-Autobiography." Quoted in Morgan and Morgan, *Dr. Seuss & Mr. Geisel*, 134–35.

31. E. J. Kahn, "Profiles: Children's Friend," *The New Yorker*, December 17, 1960.

32. Hal Humphrey, "Zoo's Who? Dr. Seuss, That's Who," *Coronet*, December 1964.

33. Morgan and Morgan, *Dr. Seuss & Mr. Geisel*, 135.

34. Ibid., 137.

35. TSG, ". . . But for Grown-Ups Laughing Isn't Any Fun," *New York Times*, November 16, 1952.

36. Ibid.

37. Ibid.

38. Ibid.

39. Ibid.

40. Michael J. Bandler, "Dr. Seuss: Still a Drawing Card," *American Way*, December 1977, emphasis added.

41. "Macy's Parade Has '5,000 Fingers' Float," *Tampa Bay Times* (St. Petersburg, FL), January 11, 1953.

42. Morgan and Morgan, *Dr. Seuss & Mr. Geisel*, 135.

43. Ibid.

44. Morgan and Morgan, *Dr. Seuss & Mr. Geisel*, 136.

45. Quin, "The 5000 Fingers of Dr. T."
46. Terry Bell, "Hitler and 'Quick, Henry the Flit' Shaped the Saga of Dr. Seuss," *NZEE* (New Zealand), June 7, 1976.
47. Morgan and Morgan, *Dr. Seuss & Mr. Geisel*, 136.
48. C. Robert Jennings, "Dr. Seuss: 'What Am I Doing Here?'" *Saturday Evening Post*, October 23, 1965.
49. "Japan's Young Dreams," *Life*, March 29, 1954.
50. Bell, "Hitler and 'Quick, Henry the Flit' Shaped the Saga of Dr. Seuss."
51. Ibid.
52. David Sheff, "Seuss on Wry . . . with Lots of Relish," www.davidsheff.com /dr-seuss/.
53. Morgan and Morgan, *Dr. Seuss & Mr. Geisel*, 135.
54. Bell, "Hitler and 'Quick, Henry the Flit' Shaped the Saga of Dr. Seuss."
55. Ibid.
56. "The 5,000 Fingers of Dr. T," *Variety*. Retrieved at https://variety.com/1952/film /reviews/the-5-000-fingers-of-dr-t-1200417405/.
57. Bosley Crowther, "The Screen in Review: '5,000 Fingers of Dr. T.' with Hayes, Mary Healy, Tommy Rettig, Is at Criterion," *New York Times*, June 20, 1953.
58. Cohen, *The Seuss, the Whole Seuss, and Nothing but the Seuss*, 294.
59. TSG, "Non Autobiography," quoted by Morgan and Morgan, *Dr. Seuss & Mr. Geisel*, 138.
60. Morgan and Morgan, *Dr. Seuss & Mr. Geisel*, 133.
61. Jennings, "Dr. Seuss: 'What Am I Doing Here?'"
62. Ibid.
63. Ibid.
64. She wouldn't represent him long. After Jackson failed to find a publisher for *On the Road* and two other books, Kerouac quickly returned to friend and fellow writer Allen Ginsberg as his representation.
65. Morgan and Morgan, *Dr. Seuss & Mr. Geisel*, 140.
66. Ibid.
67. "Books for Young Readers," *Philadelphia Inquirer*, April 12, 1953.
68. Dorothy Garey, "Children's Books," *Hartford Courant*, April 26, 1953.
69. Walt Kelly, "A La Peter T. Hooper," *New York Times*, April 5, 1953.
70. Kahn, "Profiles: Children's Friend."
71. Morgan and Morgan, *Dr. Seuss & Mr. Geisel*, 144.
72. Ibid., 143.
73. Ibid., 142.
74. Kahn, "Profiles: Children's Friend."
75. Morgan and Morgan, *Dr. Seuss & Mr. Geisel*, 142–43.
76. Ibid., 145.
77. Sheff, "Seuss on Wry . . . with Lots of Relish."
78. TSG's handwritten notes for "Mrs. Mulvaney and the Billion-Dollar Bunny, an Address, with Drawings on a Blackboard," by Dr. Seuss, c. 1949, Mandeville Special Collections Library, UCSD.
79. Sheff, "Seuss on Wry . . . with Lots of Relish."
80. Ibid., emphasis in original.
81. Ibid.
82. Morgan and Morgan, *Dr. Seuss & Mr. Geisel*, 145.
83. TSG, "Final shooting script for TV Ford Foundation telecast attempting to explain something to teenagers of the country about Contemporary Art," 1954, Mandeville Special Collections Library, UCSD.

84. Ibid.
85. Kahn, "Profiles: Children's Friend."
86. TSG, "Final shooting script for TV Ford Foundation telecast."
87. Ibid.
88. Morgan and Morgan, *Dr. Seuss & Mr. Geisel*, 146.
89. Ibid., 147.

Chapter 10. A Literary Straitjacket

1. Judith and Neil Morgan, *Dr. Seuss & Mr. Geisel: A Biography* (New York: Random House, 1995), 148.
2. Ibid. The Morgans cite the initial diagnosis as "Neuronitis acute," which is likely a transcription error.
3. Ibid., 150.
4. Ibid., 149.
5. Ibid., 150.
6. Ibid.
7. Ibid.
8. Ibid.
9. Polly Goodwin, "The Junior Books," *Chicago Tribune*, October 10, 1954.
10. Charles A. Brown III, "Dr. Seuss for Kids? He's Adults' Delight," *Star Tribune* (Minneapolis, MN), September 19, 1954.
11. Goodwin, "The Junior Books."
12. Warren T. Greenleaf, "How the Grinch Stole Reading: The Serious Nonsense of Dr. Seuss," *Parents*, May 1982.
13. Robert C. Jennings, "Dr. Seuss: 'What Am I Doing Here?'" *Saturday Evening Post*, October 23, 1965.
14. Morgan and Morgan, *Dr. Seuss & Mr. Geisel*, 151.
15. Ibid.
16. John Hersey, "Why Do Students Bog Down on First R?" *Life*, May 24, 1954.
17. Description of the Newbery Medal from the Newbery Medal homepage, retrieved at www.ala.org/alsc/awardsgrants/bookmedia/newberymedal /newberymedal.
18. This quote, as well as the brief history of children's primers, is courtesy of Jonathan Cott, in the chapter "The Good Dr. Seuss," from *Pipers at the Gates of Dawn: The Wisdom of Children's Literature* (New York: Random House, 1983).
19. Joseph B. Treaster, "Zerna Sharp, 91, Dies in Indiana; Originated Dick and Jane Texts," *New York Times*, June 19, 1981.
20. Caption on illustration for Hersey, "Why Do Students Bog Down on First R?"
21. Hersey, "Why Do Students Bog Down on First R?"
22. Rudolf Flesch, *Why Johnny Can't Read* (New York: HarperCollins, 2000; reprint of 1955 edition), 6–7.
23. Morgan and Morgan, *Dr. Seuss & Mr. Geisel*, 154.
24. Ibid.
25. See "566 Get Degrees and Dartmouth's 186th Graduation," *Boston Globe*, June 13, 1955.
26. "Honorary Degrees Awarded to Eleven," *Dartmouth Alumni Magazine*, Summer 1955.
27. Cott, "The Good Dr. Seuss."
28. Dr. Seuss, *On Beyond Zebra!* (New York: Random House), 28.

29. See, for example, Helen S. Canfield, "Young Reader's Delight," *Hartford Courant*, November 13, 1955.
30. Jane Cobb, "On Beyond Zebra," *New York Times*, November 13, 1955.
31. "The Gregarious Reader," *Boston Globe*, October 23, 1955.
32. Cott, "The Good Dr. Seuss."
33. Robert Cahn, "The Wonderful World of Dr. Seuss," *Saturday Evening Post*, July 6, 1957.
34. Ibid.
35. TSG, "How Orlo Got His Book," *New York Times*, November 17, 1957.
36. Cott, "The Good Dr. Seuss."
37. TSG, *If I Ran the Circus* (New York: Random House, 1956), 17.
38. TSG, *If I Ran the Circus.*
39. Jim Marcus, "Seeking Seuss in Springfield," *Yankee Traveler*, November–December 1995.
40. Maude French, "If I Ran the Circus," *Dartmouth Alumni Magazine*, December 1956.
41. Diane Clark, "And There, but for the Grace of Dr. Seuss, Goes the Grinch: He Is Waking Children to a World of Words," *San Diego Union*, December 19, 1976.
42. William B. Hart, "Between the Lines," *Redbook*, December 1957.
43. TSG, "The Hoobub and the Grinch," reprinted in *Horton and the Kwuggerbug and More Lost Stories*. Emphasis in original.
44. Clark, "And There, but for the Grace of Dr. Seuss, Goes the Grinch."
45. George Kane, "And, Dear Dr. Seuss, the Whole World's in Love with Yeuss," *Rocky Mountain News*, February 15, 1976.
46. Norman Bell, "Dr. Seuss and His Wonderful World of Whimsy," *Tampa Bay Times*, July 1, 1956.
47. Robert Sullivan, "Oh, the places He Went!" *Dartmouth Alumni Magazine*, Winter 1992.
48. "'Somebody's Got to Win' in Kids' Books: An Interview with Dr. Seuss on His Books for Children, Young and Old," *U.S. News & World Report*, April 14, 1986.
49. Ibid.
50. Ibid.
51. TSG's personal notes on *Cat in the Hat*. Emphasis in original, Mandeville Special Collections, UCSD.
52. Cott, "The Good Dr. Seuss."
53. Anne Commire, ed., "Geisel, Theodor Seuss," in *Something About the Author*, Vol. 28 (Detroit, MI: Gale Research Company, 1982).
54. Morgan and Morgan, *Dr. Seuss & Mr. Geisel*, 138. *The Cat in the Hat* would be among the last books Commins would edit; he would die in 1958 at age sixty-six.
55. Colin Dangaard, "Dr. Seuss Reigns Supreme as King of the Kids," *Boston Herald American*, November 21, 1976.
56. Ibid.
57. Cahn, "The Wonderful World of Dr. Seuss."
58. Cott, "The Good Dr. Seuss."
59. TSG, *The Cat in the Hat.*
60. *The Cat in the Hat* contains a total of 1,626 words, and 236 unique words. Only thirteen words were not on the approved list, including *nothing* and *plaything*.
61. Betsy Marsden Silverman, "Dr. Seuss Talks to Parents About Learning to Read and What Makes Children Want to Do It," *Parents*, November 1960.

62. Beverly Beyette, "Seuss: New Book on the Tip of His Tongue," *Los Angeles Times*, May 29, 1979.
63. Elizabeth Blair, "All Things Considered: How the Grinch Stole Christmas!" NPR, December 23, 2002. Retrieved at http://news.npr.org/programs/morning/features/patc/grinch/index.html.
64. Jeff Lyon, "Writing for Adults, It Seems, Is One of Dr. Seuss's Dreams," *Chicago Tribune*, April 15, 1982.
65. Ted and Helen's conversation was captured by and quoted in Cahn, "The Wonderful World of Dr. Seuss."
66. Dan Carlinsky, "The Wily Ruse of Doctor Seuss: Or, How Ted Geisel Has Done Real Well," *Magazine of the Boston Herald American*, March 4, 1979.
67. Sally Hammond, "Dr. Seuss: The Man Who Stole Boredom," untitled clipping, c. 1966, Rauner Special Collections Library, Dartmouth College.
68. Lyon, "Writing for Adults, It Seems, Is One of Dr. Seuss's Dreams."
69. Morgan and Morgan, *Dr. Seuss & Mr. Geisel*, 158.
70. Ibid.
71. Ibid.
72. Ibid., 157.
73. Ibid., 158.
74. Random House press release, April 19, 1957, Rauner Special Collections Library, Dartmouth College.
75. "Hooray for Dr. Seuss!" *Chicago Tribune*, May 12, 1957.
76. Diane Clark, "He Is Waking Children to a World of Words," *San Diego Union*, December 19, 1976.
77. See William L. Earle, "Man Who Draws Wacky Animals Quit Oxford on Advice of a Girl," *Daily Independent Journal* (San Rafael, CA), November 19, 1957.
78. Cott, "The Good Dr. Seuss."
79. Clark, "He Is Waking Children to a World of Words."
80. Alfred Jacoby, "Dr. Seuss & Mr. Geisel: How to Capture a Child's Fancy," *San Diego Union*, June 7, 1956.
81. "Dr. Seuss' 'Cat in the Hat' Appeals to First-graders," *Los Angeles Times*, December 1, 1957,
82. Cott, "The Good Dr. Seuss."
83. Ibid.
84. "Hooray for Dr. Seuss!"
85. Dorothy Barclay, "See the Book? It is Made with 6-Year-Old's Words," *New York Times*, April 15, 1957.
86. Cott, "The Good Dr. Seuss."
87. Hilliard Harper, "The Private World of Dr. Seuss: A Visit to Theodor Geisel's La Jolla Mountaintop," *Los Angeles Times Magazine*, May 25, 1986.
88. See the cover of *Redbook*, December 1957.
89. Polly Goodwin, "Some Christmas Books for Santa's Biggest Following," *Chicago Tribune*, December 1, 1957.
90. "Book Review: TV Stars Bare Their Secrets," *Independent Press-Telegram* (Long Beach, CA), December 22, 1957.
91. Lyon, "Writing for Adults, It Seems, Is One of Dr. Seuss's Dreams."
92. Arthur Gordon, "The Wonderful Wizard of Soledad Hill," *Woman's Day*, September 1965.
93. TSG, *How the Grinch Stole Christmas!*
94. Arthur Gordon, "The Wonderful Wizard of Soledad Hill."

95. Elizabeth Blair, "All Things Considered: How the Grinch Stole Christmas!" NPR, December 23, 2002. Retrieved at http://news.npr.org/programs/morning /features/patc/grinch/index.html

96. Robert Kupferberg, "A Seussian Celebration," *Parade*, February 26, 1984.

97. While *Peyton Place* had been published in 1956, it was still dominating *The New York Times* bestseller list for the better part of 1957.

98. Kahn, "Profiles: Children's Friend."

99. In Phyllis Cerf's 2006 obituary in the *New York Times*, it would be reported that she and Ted had shared a desk at the McCann-Erickson advertising firm during the 1930s. The real story is that Ted, who preferred working at home, maintained only a drawer of materials at the firm. That drawer was in her desk.

100. Morgan and Morgan, *Dr. Seuss & Mr. Geisel*, 156.

101. Cynthia Gorney, "Dr. Seuss at 75: Grinch, Cat in the Hat, Wocket and Generations of Kids in His Pocket," *Washington Post*, May 21, 1979.

Chapter 11. Beginner Books

1. Lewis Nichols, "Then I Doodled a Tree," *New York Times Book Review*, November 11, 1962.

2. "Beginner Books: New Trade Learn-to-Read Juveniles," *Publishers Weekly*, June 2, 1958.

3. Jonathan Cott, "The Good Dr. Seuss," in *Pipers at the Gates of Dawn: The Wisdom of Children's Literature* (New York: Random House, 1983).

4. Cynthia Gorney, "Dr. Seuss at 75: Grinch, Cat in Hat, Wocket and Generations of Kids in His Pocket," *Washington Post*, May 21, 1979.

5. TSG, "How Orlo Got His Book," *New York Times Book Review*, November 1957.

6. Carol Gelber, "A Few Well-Chosen Words for Children Make Dr. Seuss' New Book a Delight," untitled and undated clipping, circa 1958, Mandeville Special Collections.

7. Beginner's Book Word List. Emphasis in original. My thanks to Mike Frith, who let me copy the word list contained in his personal files.

8. TSG, "How Orlo Got His Book."

9. "Cindy's Creator Is Brief," *Detroit Times*, November 5, 1958.

10. Judith and Neil Morgan, *Dr. Seuss & Mr. Geisel: A Biography* (New York: Random House, 1995), 159.

11. Clifford Jordan, "Dr. Seuss," *Dartmouth Alumni Magazine*, October 1962.

12. Morgan and Morgan, *Dr. Seuss & Mr. Geisel*, 163. Emphasis in original.

13. Ibid., 163–64.

14. TSG, "Making Children Want to Read," *Book Chat*, Fall 1958.

15. Frank Dostal, "Another Dr. Seuss: The Cat in the Hat Comes Back," *Democrat & Chronicle* (Rochester, NY), October 26, 1958.

16. "Beginners Thru 3D Grade—A Bonanza for All," *Chicago Tribune*, November 2, 1958.

17. Glenn Edward Sadler, "Maurice Sendak and Dr. Seuss: A Conversation," *The Horn Book*, September/October 1989.

18. Rob Wilder, "Catching Up with Dr. Seuss," *Parents*, June 1979.

19. See Richard Minear's introduction to *Yertle the Turtle*, in *Your Favorite Seuss*, compiled by Janet Schulman and Cathy Goldsmith (New York: Random House, 2004), p. 190.

20. Cynthia Gorney, "Dr. Seuss at 75: Grinch, Cat in the Hat, Wocket and Generations of Kids in His Pocket," *Washington Post*, May 21, 1979.

21. Morgan and Morgan, *Dr. Seuss & Mr. Geisel*, 163.
22. Gorney, "Dr. Seuss at 75: Grinch, Cat in the Hat, Wocket and Generations of Kids in His Pocket."
23. Stefan Kanfer, "The Doctor Beloved by All," *Time*, October 7, 1991.
24. C. Robert Jennings, "Dr. Seuss: 'What Am I Doing Here?'" *Saturday Evening Post*, October 23, 1965.
25. TSG, *Yertle the Turtle and Other Stories* (New York: Random House, 1958), 19.
26. Cott, "The Good Dr. Seuss."
27. Morgan and Morgan, *Dr. Seuss & Mr. Geisel*, 163.
28. E. J. Kahn, "Profiles: Children's Friend," *The New Yorker*, December 17, 1960.
29. Jordan, "Dr. Seuss."
30. Robert Bernstein, *Speaking Freely: My Life in Publishing and Human Rights* (New York: New Press, 2016), 62.
31. "The One and Only Dr. Seuss and His Wonderful Autographing Tour," *Publishers Weekly*, December 8, 1958.
32. Don Freeman, "Dr. Seuss from Then to Now," *San Diego Magazine*, May 1986.
33. "The One and Only Dr. Seuss and His Wonderful Autographing Tour."
34. Bernstein, *Speaking Freely*, 62.
35. Morgan and Morgan, *Dr. Seuss & Mr. Geisel*, 161.
36. Frank Graham, "Dr. Seuss Is on the Loose," untitled and undated newspaper clipping, c. 1958, Rauner Special Collections Library, Dartmouth College.
37. Kahn, "Profiles: Children's Friend."
38. Morgan and Morgan, *Dr. Seuss & Mr. Geisel*, 164.
39. Bennett Cerf to TSG, March 3, 1959, Columbia University Libraries.
40. Ibid.
41. Much of the description of the Beginner Books office is based on the author's interview with Michael Frith, as well as reminiscences of Stan and Jan Berenstain, *Down a Sunny Dirt Road: An Autobiography* (New York: Random House Books for Young Readers, 2002), 142–43.
42. Ted added that his full name was "Dr. Outgo Schmierkase."
43. Morgan and Morgan, *Dr. Seuss & Mr. Geisel*, 165.
44. Kahn, "Profiles: Children's Friend."
45. "'Somebody's Got to Win' in Kids' Books: An Interview with Dr. Seuss on His Books for Children, Young and Old," *U.S News & World Report*, April 14, 1986.
46. Gelber, "A Few Well-Chosen Words for Children Make Dr. Seuss' New Book a Delight."
47. Colin Dangaard, "Dr. Seuss Reigns Supreme as King of the Kids," *Boston Herald American*, November 21, 1976.
48. Peter Bunzel, "The Wacky World of Dr. Seuss," *Life*, April 6, 1959.
49. Morgan and Morgan, *Dr. Seuss & Mr. Geisel*, 162.
50. TSG, *Happy Birthday to You!* (New York: Random House, 1959).
51. "'Somebody's Got to Win' in Kids' Books."
52. Morgan and Morgan, *Dr. Seuss & Mr. Geisel*, 173.
53. Ibid.
54. Kahn, "Profiles: Children's Friend."
55. Robert Sullivan, "Oh, the Places He Went!" *Dartmouth Alumni Magazine*, Winter 1992.
56. Kahn, "Profiles: Children's Friend."
57. Ibid.
58. Morgan and Morgan, *Dr. Seuss & Mr. Geisel*, 173.

59. Jordan, "Dr. Seuss."
60. Morgan and Morgan, *Dr. Seuss & Mr. Geisel*, 164.
61. Ibid., 129.
62. Ibid.
63. Ibid., 165.
64. Betsy Marden Silverman, "Dr. Seuss Talks to Parents," *Parents*, November 1960.
65. Cott, "The Good Dr. Seuss."
66. Morgan and Morgan, *Dr. Seuss & Mr. Geisel*, 166.
67. "'Somebody's Got to Win' in Kids' Books."
68. Morgan and Morgan, *Dr. Seuss & Mr. Geisel*, 169.
69. See Morgan and Morgan, *Dr. Seuss & Mr. Geisel*, 320, n. 169.
70. Kahn, "Profiles: Children's Friend."
71. Morgan and Morgan, *Dr. Seuss & Mr. Geisel*, 170.
72. Frank Dostal, "Author-Illustrator Duo Scores in Tot's History," *Democrat and Chronicle* (Rochester, NY), March 6, 1960.
73. Maude French, "One Fish Two Fish Red Fish Blue Fish," *Dartmouth Alumni Magazine*, October 1960.
74. Review taken from promotional materials for *One Fish Two Fish Red Fish Blue Fish*. See, for example, the full page insert in the *Chicago Tribune*, November 6, 1960.
75. Melva G. Chernoff, "Books," *Argus Leader* (Sioux Falls, SD), April 3, 1960.
76. "'Somebody's Got to Win' in Kids' Books."
77. See advertising matter for *Green Eggs and Ham*.
78. The fifty unique words were *a, am, and, anywhere, are, be, boat, box, car, could, dark, do, eat, eggs, fox, goat, good, green, ham, here, house, I, if, in, let, like, may, me, mouse, not, on, or, rain, Sam, say, see, so, thank, that, the, them, there, they, train, tree, try, will, with, would, you.* The most used word was *not*, which Ted repeated eighty-two times.
79. Elizabeth C. Mann, "Bountiful Reading of All Kinds for Beginners," *Chicago Tribune*, November 6, 1960.
80. Maude French, "Green Eggs and Ham," *Dartmouth Alumni Magazine*, December 1960.
81. "Literary Luggage: Give Books for Christmas," *Poughkeepsie Journal*, November 27, 1960.
82. Judith Frutig, "Dr. Seuss's Green-Eggs-and-Ham World," *Christian Science Monitor*, May 12, 1978.
83. "He Makes C-A-T Spell Big Money," *Business Week*, July 18, 1960.
84. Dan Carlinsky, "The Wily Ruse of Doctor Seuss: Or, How Ted Geisel Has Done Real Well," *Magazine of the Boston Herald American*, March 4, 1979.
85. Robert Kupferberg, "A Seussian Celebration," *Parade*, February 26, 1984.
86. TSG, "Writing for Children: A Mission," *Los Angeles Times*, November 27, 1960.
87. Ibid.
88. Bennett Cerf, Columbia University Oral History Research Office, Notable New Yorkers: Bennett Cerf, Session 10. Available online at www.columbia.edu /cu/lweb/digital/collections/nny/cerfb/toc.html.
89. See Ernest Havemann, "No More a Headache, Book Business Booms," *Life*, May 12, 1961.
90. See "Random House to Buy Beginner Books," *Publishers Weekly*, August 8, 1960.
91. Cerf, Columbia University Oral History Research Office.
92. Jordan, "Dr. Seuss."
93. Morgan and Morgan, *Dr. Seuss & Mr. Geisel*, 168.

94. Sullivan, "Oh, the Places He Went!"
95. Michael J. Bandler, "Wearing the Hat: Dr. Seuss' Characters Live On, Thanks to the Woman Who Fans the Fantasy," *Chicago Tribune*, November 20, 1994.

Chapter 12. The Work

1. Stan and Jan Berenstain, *Down a Sunny Dirt Road: An Autobiography* (New York: Random House Books for Young Readers, 2002), 136.
2. Ibid.
3. Ibid., 144.
4. Ibid., 145.
5. Ibid., 146.
6. Ibid.
7. Ibid., 150.
8. Ibid.
9. Ibid., 144.
10. Ibid.
11. Ibid., 151.
12. Ibid., 153.
13. Judith Morgan, interview with the author.
14. Morgan and Morgan, *Dr. Seuss & Mr. Geisel*, 173.
15. Ibid.
16. "Dr. Seuss Remembered," *Publishers Weekly*, October 25, 1991.
17. Clifford Jordan, "Dr. Seuss," *Dartmouth Alumni Magazine*, October 1962.
18. Lewis Nichols, "Then I Doodled a Tree," *New York Times Book Review*, November 11, 1962.
19. E. J. Kahn, "Profiles: Children's Friend," *The New Yorker*, December 17, 1960.
20. "Oldest City Employee, Geisel, 81 on Tuesday," *Springfield Union*, June 24, 1960.
21. "Dr. Seuss' 'Sneetches', Mice, Owls, 'How to Ooze'" *The Courier-Journal* (Louisville, KY), November 12, 1961.
22. Jordan, "Dr. Seuss."
23. Morgan and Morgan, *Dr. Seuss & Mr. Geisel*, 176.
24. Nichols, "Then I Doodled a Tree."
25. Frank Graham, "Dr. Seuss Is on the Loose," untitled and undated newspaper clipping, c. 1958, Rauner Special Collections Library, Dartmouth College.
26. TSG notes, cited in Morgan and Morgan, *Dr. Seuss & Mr. Geisel*, 176.
27. Ibid., 176–77.
28. Jordan, "Dr. Seuss."
29. Bennett Cerf, Columbia University Oral History Research Office.
30. "Dr. Seuss Remembered."
31. Morgan and Morgan, *Dr. Seuss & Mr. Geisel*, 177.
32. Bennett Cerf, Columbia University Oral History Research Office.
33. Berenstain, *Down a Sunny Dirt Road*, 157.
34. Ibid., 158.
35. Ibid., 162.
36. Ibid., 163.
37. Ibid., 164.
38. Peter Bunzel, "The Wacky World of Dr. Seuss."
39. Morgan and Morgan, *Dr. Seuss & Mr. Geisel*, 172.
40. "The 25th Anniversary of Dr. Seuss," *Publishers Weekly*, December 17, 1962.
41. Arthur Gordon, "The Wonderful Wizard of Soledad Hill," *Woman's Day*, September 1965.

42. Morgan and Morgan, *Dr. Seuss & Mr. Geisel*, 180.
43. Ibid., 178.
44. Ibid., 179.
45. Ibid.
46. See Random House press release, "News About a Brand New Kind of Book," 1963, Rauner Special Collections Library, Dartmouth College.
47. "Dr. Seuss Gets 'Indorsement' by Expert, 6," *Indianapolis Star*, June 16, 1963.
48. Rome Neal, "Dr. Seuss: Fun with Words," *CBS Sunday Morning*, March 4, 2004.
49. Gordon, "The Wonderful Wizard of Soledad Hill."
50. C. Robert Jennings, "Dr. Seuss: 'What Am I Doing Here?'" *Saturday Evening Post*, October 23, 1965.
51. Robert Cahn, "The Wonderful World of Dr. Seuss," *Saturday Evening Post*, July 6, 1957.
52. Shirley Jackson, "His Personal Prescription," *San Francisco Examiner*, November 10, 1963.
53. Bennett Cerf, Columbia University Oral History Research Office.
54. Morgan and Morgan, *Dr. Seuss & Mr. Geisel*, 179.
55. Ibid.
56. Michael Frith, interview with the author.
57. *An Awfully Big Adventure: The Making of Modern Children's Literature* [Dr. Seuss]. Produced and directed by Roger Parsons. London: BBC, 1998.
58. Bennett Cerf, Columbia University Oral History Research Office.

Chapter 13. Stink. Stank. Stunk.

1. Stan and Jan Berenstain, *Down a Sunny Dirt Road: An Autobiography* (New York: Random House Books for Young Readers, 2002), 168.
2. Jonathan Cott, "The Good Dr. Seuss," in *Pipers at the Gates of Dawn: The Wisdom of Children's Literature* (New York: Random House, 1983).
3. Michael Frith, interview with the author.
4. Morgan and Morgan, *Dr. Seuss & Mr. Geisel*, 166.
5. Kathryn Ringrose, "Interview with Dr. Roger Revelle, May 15–16, 1985," University of California, San Diego 25th Anniversary Oral History Project Interview. Retrieved at https://library.ucsd.edu/speccoll/siooralhistories/2010-44-Revelle.pdf.
6. Donald Freeman, "The Nonsensical World of Dr. Seuss," *McCall's*, November 1964.
7. "Just What the Doctor Ordered . . . Green Eggs and Ham for the Cat in the Hat," *Star Sports & Magazine*, May 8, 1976.
8. Judith Morgan, "Mrs. Theodor Geisel Dies; Author, La Jolla Leader," *San Diego Union*, October 24, 1967.
9. Judith Morgan, interview with the author.
10. Judith Frutig, "Dr. Seuss's Green-Eggs-and-Ham World," *Christian Science Monitor*, May 12, 1978.
11. Ibid.
12. Morgan and Morgan, *Dr. Seuss & Mr. Geisel*, 188.
13. Judith Morgan, interview with the author.
14. Ibid.
15. Ibid.
16. Michael J. Bandler, "Wearing the Hat: Dr. Seuss' Characters Live On, Thanks to the Woman Who Fans the Fantasy," *Chicago Tribune*, November 20, 1994.

17. Judith Morgan, interview with the author.
18. Ibid.
19. TSG, *I Had Trouble in Getting to Solla Sollew*.
20. Morgan and Morgan, *Dr. Seuss & Mr. Geisel*, 182.
21. Ibid., 186.
22. Michael Frith, e-mail to the author.
23. Morgan and Morgan, *Dr. Seuss & Mr. Geisel*, 187.
24. Neil Morgan, "A Troublesome Crew Before Solla Sollew," *San Diego Union*, October 17, 1965.
25. Paula Leibson, "Just Browsing," *El Paso Times*, May 16, 1965.
26. TSG, *Fox in Socks*, 1965.
27. See TSG to "Chuck," July 24, 1967, Rauner Special Collections Library, Dartmouth College.
28. Morgan and Morgan, *Dr. Seuss & Mr. Geisel*, 188.
29. Bob Bernstein, interviewed by Andrew Albanese, "Human Rights Watcher: PW Talks with Former Random House Editor Bob Bernstein," *Publishers Weekly*, May 13, 2016.
30. See Opal Crandall, "Dr. Seuss Storybook Characters Provide Fanciful Fun for 1,400 at Charity Ball," *San Diego Union*, February 7, 1966.
31. Dorothy O'Toole, "Dr. Seuss Ball Delights Adults; Story Book Setting is Created," *San Diego Tribune*, February 7, 1966.
32. Ibid.
33. Leslie Raddatz, "Dr. Seuss Climbs Down from His Mountain . . . to Bring the Grinch to Television," *TV Guide*, December 17, 1966.
34. "Skeptical Dr. Seuss," *Miami Herald TV Preview*, December 11, 1966.
35. Chuck Jones, *Chuck Reducks: Drawing from the Fun Side of Life* (New York: Warner Books, 1996), 266.
36. Morgan and Morgan, *Dr. Seuss & Mr. Geisel*, 189.
37. Ibid.
38. Jones, *Chuck Reducks: Drawing from the Fun Side of Life*, 267.
39. Hal Humphrey, "Special Visit with the Whos," *Los Angeles Times*, December 1966.
40. Morgan and Morgan, *Dr. Seuss & Mr. Geisel*, 189.
41. Jones, *Chuck Reducks: Drawing from the Fun Side of Life*, 266.
42. Ibid., 255.
43. Ibid., 275.
44. Morgan and Morgan, *Dr. Seuss & Mr. Geisel*, 189.
45. Jones, *Chuck Reducks: Drawing from the Fun Side of Life*, 276.
46. Morgan and Morgan, *Dr. Seuss & Mr. Geisel*, 190
47. Robert J. McKinnon, *Stepping Into the Picture: Cartoon Designer Maurice Noble* (Jackson: University Press of Mississippi, 2008), 156–57.
48. Jones, *Chuck Reducks: Drawing from the Fun Side of Life*, 271.
49. Ibid., 270.
50. See TSG notes for *How the Grinch Stole Christmas!* Mandeville Special Collections Library, UCSD.
51. This is the way Jones spells it. See Jones, *Chuck Reducks: Drawing from the Fun Sude of Life*, 270.
52. Ibid., 270.
53. See *How the Grinch Stole Christmas!* recording scripts, Mandeville Special Collections Library, UCSD.
54. Ibid.

55. Mark Arnold, "He's Grrrrreat! The Thurl Ravenscroft Interview," originally published in *Hogan's Alley* 14, 1994. Reprinted at http://cartoonician.com /hes-grrrrreat-the-thurl-ravenscroft-interview/.

56. Ibid. Ravenscroft's contribution—as critical to the song as the lyrics themselves—would mistakenly go uncredited, an oversight Geisel found embarrassing.

57. See TSG's handwritten notes in his copy of *How the Grinch Stole Christmas!* Mandeville Special Collections Library, UCSD.

58. McKinnon, *Stepping Into the Picture*, 158.

59. Ibid.

60. Jones, *Chuck Reducks: Drawing from the Fun Side of Life*, 266.

61. Jack Gould, "'The Grinch' a Bit Short of Expectation," *New York Times*, December 19, 1966.

62. Hal Humphrey, "'Grinch' Disappointing Christmas Special," *Los Angeles Times*, December 19, 1966.

63. Cynthia Lowry, "Seuss' 'Grinch' Great on Teevee," *Tampa Times*, December 19, 1966.

64. Richard K. Shull, "Commercially Speaking About Christmas Spirit," *Indianapolis News*, December 19, 1966; Sandra Hinson, "Walt's Own Show Fitting Tribute to Disney," *Orlando Sentinel*, December 19, 1966; Harry Harris, "Seuss Makes Debut on CBS with Story of 'How the Grinch Stole Christmas,'" *Philadelphia Inquirer*, December 19, 1966.

65. Donald Freeman, "Seuss' Grinch a TV Triumph," *San Diego Union*, December 20, 1966.

66. Judith Morgan, interview with the author.

67. Ibid.

68. Many newspapers picked up the UPI account of Ted's arrest. See, for example, "Drunk Driving Charge Laid to Kids' Author," *Springfield Leader & Press* (Springfield, MO), March 26, 1967.

69. "Dr. Seuss Was Soused?" *Santa Rosa Press Democrat*, March 26, 1967.

70. Jones, *Chuck Reducks: Drawing from the Fun Side of Life*, 262.

71. See "Memo to Chuck Jones from Nick Iuppa," February 6, 1967, Mandeville Special Collections Library, UCSD.

72. Norma Lee Browning, "TV Sets Movieland Party Scene," *Chicago Tribune*, September 20, 1967.

73. Robert Bernstein, *Speaking Freely: My Life in Publishing and Human Rights* (New York: New Press, 2016), 63.

74. Morgan and Morgan, *Dr. Seuss & Mr. Geisel*, 193.

75. Ibid., 194.

76. Ibid.

Chapter 14. I Intend to Go On Doing Just What I Do

1. Judith Morgan and Neil Morgan, *Dr. Seuss & Mr. Geisel: A Biography* (New York: Random House, 1995), 197.

2. Ibid.

3. Helen's suicide note is in the archives of the Office of the Medical Examiner, County of San Diego. Cited in Morgan and Morgan, *Dr. Seuss & Mr. Geisel*, 195.

4. Ibid., 195.

5. Ibid., 198.

6. Ibid., 197–98.

7. Al Perkins to Edwin Pease, October 24, 1967, Rauner Special Collections Library, Dartmouth College.
8. Neil Morgan, "Mostly Morgan," *San Diego Tribune*, October 31, 1967.
9. "Dr. Seuss: Rhymes and Reasons," *Biography*, A&E Television, Peter Jones Productions, November 30, 2003.
10. Ibid.
11. Judith Morgan, interview with the author.
12. "Dr. Seuss: Rhymes and Reasons."
13. Morgan and Morgan, *Dr. Seuss & Mr. Geisel*, 201.
14. Ibid., 201.
15. Joyce Wadler, "Public Lives: Mrs. Seuss Hears a Who, and Tells About It," *New York Times*, November 29, 2000.
16. Morgan and Morgan, *Dr. Seuss & Mr. Geisel*, 201.
17. Judith Morgan, interview with the author.
18. Hilliard Harper, "The Private World of Dr. Seuss: A Visit to Theodor Geisel's La Jolla Mountaintop," *Los Angeles Times Magazine*, May 25, 1986.
19. Morgan and Morgan, *Dr. Seuss & Mr. Geisel*, 202. While the Morgans refer to *The Hand Book* as a Beginner Book, there would never be a Beginner Book by that name. More likely, Perkins's book would be reconfigured as the Bright and Early Book *Hand, Hand, Fingers, Thumb*, which was published in 1969.
20. Ibid.
21. Helen Paske, "Does Dr. Seuss Live Here?" *Sunday Times* (NZ), May 9, 1976.
22. Wadler, "Public Lives: Mrs. Seuss Hears a Who . . ."
23. Charlene Scott, "At Springfield's New Dr. Seuss Museum, a 'Perfect' Tribute to the Best-Seller's Life and Career," WBUR, June 2, 2017.
24. Morgan and Morgan, *Dr. Seuss & Mr. Geisel*, 203.
25. Michael Frith, interview with the author.
26. Ibid.
27. Ibid.
28. Morgan and Morgan, *Dr. Seuss & Mr. Geisel*, 199.
29. J.B., "Beginning Beginners," *Cincinnati Enquirer*, December 5, 1968.
30. "Some New Books for the Juniors," *Daily Independent Journal* (San Rafael, CA), November 2, 1968.
31. Morgan and Morgan, *Dr. Seuss & Mr. Geisel*, 205.
32. "The Seuss and the Suit," *Newsweek*, December 1968.
33. Sidney E. Zion, "'Dr. Seuss' Loses a Copyright Suit: Court Rules Company Has Right to Produce Dolls," *New York Times*, December 17, 1968.
34. Michael Frith, interview with the author.
35. Richard F. Shepard, "Dr. Seuss Beasts Trample Word List," *New York Times*, October 17, 1968.
36. Michael Frith, interview with the author.
37. Morgan and Morgan, *Dr. Seuss & Mr. Geisel*, 205.
38. Colin Dangaard, "Dr. Seuss Reigns Supreme as King of the Kids," *Boston Herald American*, November 21, 1976.
39. Susan Berman, "Real-Life Seuss Welcomes Kids to 'Hoos,'" *Dayton Daily News*, September 29, 1971.
40. Pauline Ray, "Persons: Slow Geisel Shows How Sly Seuss Grows," *New Zealand Listener*, June 5, 1976.
41. Carolyn See, "Dr. Seuss and the Naked Ladies: Blowing the Lid Off the Private Life of America's Most Beloved Author," *Esquire*, June 1974. Ted would never reveal what the proposal for the dirty book had been about.

42. Morgan and Morgan, *Dr. Seuss & Mr. Geisel*, 209.

43. Ibid., 208.

44. Donald Freeman, "The Nonsensical World of Dr. Seuss," *McCall's*, November 1964.

45. Morgan and Morgan, *Dr. Seuss & Mr. Geisel*, 209.

46. Tom Green, "Dr. Seuss Bulldozes Bulldozers," *Courier-Post* (Camden, NJ), February 7, 1972.

47. Cynthia Gorney, "Dr. Seuss at 75: Grinch, Cat in the Hat, Wocket and Generations of Kids in His Pocket," *Washington Post*, May 21, 1979.

48. Jonathan Cott, "The Good Dr. Seuss," in *Pipers at the Gates of Dawn: The Wisdom of Children's Literature* (New York: Random House, 1983).

49. Gorney, "Dr. Seuss at 75."

50. Cott, "The Good Dr. Seuss." Curiously, in another interview, he would claim he had also been inspired by watching Kenyan workmen cutting down trees on the African plains. Also see Berman, "Real-Life Seuss Welcomes Kids to 'Hoos.'"

51. Gorney, "Dr. Seuss at 75."

52. "'Somebody's Got to Win' in Kids' Books: An Interview with Dr. Seuss on His Books for Children, Young and Old," *U.S. News & World Report*, April 14, 1986.

53. Gorney, "Dr. Seuss at 75."

54. Morgan and Morgan, *Dr. Seuss & Mr. Geisel*, 210.

55. "She Brings Colour to Seuss Books," *Evening Post* (NZ), May 10, 1976, Mandeville Special Collections Library, UCSD.

56. Gorney, "Dr. Seuss at 75."

57. Dick Kleiner, "A Rounder Cat in a Rounder Hat," *Times-News* (Burlington, NC), March 10, 1971.

58. Jim Korkis, "Cartoon Research," Animation Anecdotes #24, January 15 ,2016. Retrieved at http://cartoonresearch.com/index.php/animation-anecdotes-245/.

59. Earl Wilson, "Allan Sherman Is 'Weigh Behind,'" *Philadelphia Daily News*, March 2, 1971.

60. Tom Green, "Cat in the Hat Survived Coast Quake," *Times Herald* (Port Huron, MI), March 5, 1971.

61. Ursula Vils, "Dr. Seuss: A Message for Adults," *Los Angeles Times*, August 30, 1971.

62. Ibid.

63. Morgan and Morgan, *Dr. Seuss & Mr. Geisel*, 212.

64. Jeff Lyon, "Writing for Adults, It Seems, Is One of Dr. Seuss's Dreams," *Chicago Tribune*, April 15, 1982.

65. Barbara Zimmers, "Trash Is My Bag," *Jackson Hole News*, September 30, 1971.

66. Alison Lurie, "The Cabinet of Dr. Seuss," *New York Review of Books*, December 20, 1990.

67. Morgan and Morgan, *Dr. Seuss & Mr. Geisel*, 278.

68. Cott, "The Good Dr. Seuss."

69. Lyon, "Writing for Adults, It Seems, Is One of Dr. Seuss's Dreams."

70. Janet Schulman and Cathy Goldsmith, eds., *Your Favorite Seuss* (New York: Random House Books for Young Readers, 2004), 190.

Chapter 15. You'll Miss the Best Things If You Keep Your Eyes Shut

1. William Robbins, "Random House Will Leave Mansion for a Skyscraper," *New York Times*, August 19, 1968.

2. *The New York Times* mistakenly reported that he was in attendance.

3. Henry Raymont, "Cerf Rites Draw Friends of 2 'Worlds,'" *New York Times*, September 10, 1971.
4. Judith Morgan and Neil Morgan, *Dr. Seuss & Mr. Geisel: A Biography* (New York: Random House, 1995), 216.
5. Ibid., 218.
6. Michael Frith, interview with the author.
7. Michael Frith, e-mail to the author, September 25, 2018.
8. Michael Frith, interview with the author.
9. Michael Frith, e-mail to the author.
10. Michael Frith, interview with the author.
11. Digby Diehl, "Q&A: Dr. Seuss," *Los Angeles Times West*, September 17, 1972.
12. Michael Frith, interview with the author.
13. Jo-Ann Greene, "Illustrator Roy McKie Recalls His Collaboration with Late Dr. Seuss," *Publishers Weekly*, February 23, 2013.
14. Morgan and Morgan, *Dr. Seuss & Mr. Geisel*, 220.
15. Clarke Williamson, "Grinding Your Ax Softly on TV," *Paducah Sun* (Paducah, KY), April 9, 1972.
16. See press release "Anti-Litter Organization Gives Award to Dr. Seuss," November 12, 1971, Rauner Special Collections Library, Dartmouth College.
17. Robert Bernstein, *Speaking Freely: My Life in Publishing and Human Rights* (New York: New Press, 2016), 63.
18. Morgan and Morgan, *Dr. Seuss & Mr. Geisel*, 216.
19. "She Brings Colour to Seuss Books," *Evening Post* (NZ), May 10, 1976.
20. Jonathan Cott, "The Good Dr. Seuss," in *Pipers at the Gates of Dawn: The Wisdom of Children's Literature* (New York: Random House, 1983).
21. Beverly Beyette, "Seuss: New Book on the Tip of His Tongue," *Los Angeles Times*, May 29, 1979.
22. Art Buchwald, "Richard M. Nixon Will You Please Go Now," *Washington Post*, July 30, 1974.
23. Helen Paske, "How Dr. Seuss Helped Art Oust Dick," *Sunday Times* (New Zealand), May 9, 1976.
24. Morgan and Morgan, *Dr. Seuss & Mr. Geisel*, 221.
25. Colin Dangaard, "Dr. Seuss Reigns Supreme as King of the Kids," *Boston Herald American*, November 21, 1976.
26. While Geisel had collaborated with plenty of other illustrators, none of those books were credited as being written by Dr. Seuss; they were LeSieg books or, more recently, Rosetta Stone.
27. Michael Frith, interview with the author.
28. Morgan and Morgan, *Dr. Seuss & Mr. Geisel*, 225.
29. Cott, "The Good Dr. Seuss."
30. Morgan and Morgan, *Dr. Seuss & Mr. Geisel*, 231.
31. Ibid.
32. Ibid., 227.
33. Joyce Wadler, "Public Lives: Mrs. Seuss Hears a Who, and Tells About It," *New York Times*, November 29, 2000.
34. Morgan and Morgan, *Dr. Seuss & Mr. Geisel*, 230–31.
35. Ursula Vils, "Dr. Seuss: A Message for Adults," *Los Angeles Times*, August 30, 1971.
36. Donald Freeman, "Dr. Seuss at 72—Going Like 60," *The Saturday Evening Post*, March 1, 1977; www.saturdayeveningpost.com/2016/02/dr-seuss-72-going-like-60/.

37. Dighy Diehl, "Q&A: Dr. Seuss," *Los Angeles Times West,* September 17, 1972.
38. Dangaard, "Dr. Seuss Reigns Supreme as King of the Kids."
39. "She Brings Colour to Seuss Books."
40. "'Somebody's Got to Win' in Kids' Books . . ."
41. Neil Mercer, "The Wacky World of Dr. Seuss," *West Australian* (Perth, Australia), May 16, 1976.
42. Jack Webb, "Dr. Seuss Has a House on a Hill and 100 Hats Without Any Cats," *Cincinnati Enquirer,* October 11, 1974.
43. Elizabeth B. Moje and Woan-Ru Shyu, "Oh, the Places You've Taken Us: *The Reading Teacher's* Tribute to Dr. Seuss," *The Reading Teacher,* May 1992.
44. See Elma Otto to E.C. Lathem, October 30, 1975, Rauner Special Collections Library, Dartmouth College.
45. Freeman, "Dr. Seuss at 72."
46. Kane, "And, Dear Dr. Seuss, the Whole World's in Love with Yeuss."
47. Cott, "The Good Dr. Seuss."
48. Dangaard, "Dr. Seuss Reigns Supreme as King of the Kids."
49. "Just What the Doctor Ordered . . . Green Eggs and Ham for the Cat in the Hat," *Star Sports & Magazine,* May 8, 1976, unattributed clipping, Mandeville Special Collections Library, UCSD.
50. Morgan and Morgan, *Dr. Seuss & Mr. Geisel,* 227.
51. "She Brings Colour to Seuss Books."
52. See TSG notes on Australian trip, 1976, Mandeville Special Collections Library, UCSD.
53. See the *Christchurch Star* (Christchurch, NZ), May 8, 1976, and *North Shore Times Advertiser* (Auckland, NZ), May 6, 1976, Mandeville Special Collections Library, UCSD.
54. See TSG itinerary, Australian trip, 1976, Mandeville Special Collections Library, UCSD.
55. "She Brings Colour to Seuss Books."
56. "The World Loves His Zany Characters," *Standard News Advertiser* (Southland, NZ), June 2, 1976.
57. Ibid.
58. "Do You Like Green Eggs and Ham . . . ?" *The Press* (Christchurch, NZ), May 6, 1976.
59. "Dr. Seuss Flies on for Crusade," *Melbourne Sun* (Australia), May 10, 1976.
60. "'I Can't Draw—I Just Doodle' Claims Dr. Seuss in the City," *Christchurch Star* (New Zealand), May 6, 1976.
61. Mike Gibson, "How Dr. Seuss Got Rid of Richard Nixon," *Sydney Sun* (Australia), May 11, 1976.
62. "Do You Like Green Eggs and Ham . . . ?"
63. Morgan and Morgan, *Dr. Seuss & Mr. Geisel,* 232.
64. Donald Freeman, "Dr. Seuss from Then to Now," *San Diego Magazine,* May 1986.
65. "Phyllis Jackson, 69, Agent for Many Major Writers at Two Talent Companies," *New York Times,* March 22, 1977.
66. TSG, cited in Morgan and Morgan, *Dr. Seuss & Mr. Geisel,* 233–34.
67. Cott, "The Good Dr. Seuss."
68. Cynthia Gorney, "Dr. Seuss at 75: Grinch, Cat in the Hat, Wocket and Generations of Kids in His Pocket," *Washington Post,* May 21, 1979.
69. Eugene Hotchkiss III, "Dr. Seuss Keeps Me Guessing," The Humanity Initiative, 2004. Retrieved at www.humanity.org/voices/commencements/dr.seuss-geisel-lake-forest-college-speech-1977.

70. Cited in Morgan and Morgan, *Dr. Seuss & Mr. Geisel*, 214.
71. Ibid.
72. Digby Diehl, "Q&A: Dr. Seuss."
73. Morgan and Morgan, *Dr. Seuss & Mr. Geisel*, 219.
74. Judith Frutig, "Dr. Seuss's Green-Eggs-and-Ham World," *Christian Science Monitor*, May 12, 1978.
75. See TSG, *I Can Read with My Eyes Shut!* (New York: Random House, 1978).
76. Judith Frutig, "Dr. Seuss's Green-Eggs-and-Ham World."
77. Morgan and Morgan, *Dr. Seuss & Mr. Geisel*, 246.
78. TSG, quoted in Philip Nel, *Dr. Seuss: American Icon* (New York: Continuum, 2004), 16.
79. TSG, "Small Epic Poem (Size 2¾ B)," *The San Diego Union*, June 19, 1978.
80. "Dr. Seuss: Rhymes and Reasons," *Biography*, A&E Television, Peter Jones Productions, November 30, 2003.

Chapter 16. A Few Years Longer

1. Cynthia Gorney, "Dr. Seuss at 75: Grinch, Cat in the Hat, Wocket and Generations of Kids in His Pocket," *Washington Post*, May 21, 1979.
2. Ibid.
3. The most common form letter was a pre-printed Cat Note reading: "Dear ___. Your letter made me and my cat very happy. Thanks and best wishes from your friend, Dr. Seuss." A second—also signed by Dr. Seuss—featured a creature with enormous fuzzy ears, apologizing that he has 30,0000 animals that all need their whiskers clipped, which was taking all his time. The third, signed by the Cat in the Hat, read: "Dr. Seuss is out of town. . . . building something called a Thnidd, and until the Thnidd is finished, I am answering all of Dr. Seuss's mail."
4. TSG to David Reid, December 26, 1979, Mandeville Special Collections Library, UCSD.
5. Helen Paske, "Does Dr. Seuss Live Here?" *Sunday Times* (NZ), May 9, 1976.
6. Judith Morgan and Neil Morgan, *Dr. Seuss & Mr. Geisel* (New York: Random House, 1995), 236.
7. Sybil Steinberg, "What Makes a Funny Children's Book?" *Publishers Weekly*, February 27, 1978.
8. Beverly Beyette, "Seuss: New Book on the Tip of His Tongue," *Los Angeles Times*, May 29, 1979.
9. Ibid.
10. TSG, *Oh Say Can You Say?* (New York: Random House, 1979).
11. Beyette, "Seuss: New Book on the Tip of His Tongue."
12. Morgan and Morgan, *Dr. Seuss & Mr. Geisel*, 240.
13. Gorney, "Dr. Seuss at 75."
14. Beyette, "Seuss: New Book on the Tip of His Tongue."
15. Ibid.
16. Donald Freeman, "Dr. Seuss at 72—Going Like 60," *Saturday Evening Post*, March 1, 1977.
17. Sam Burchell, "Architectural Digest Visits Dr. Seuss," *Architectural Digest*, December 1978.
18. Gorney, "Dr. Seuss at 75."
19. Ibid.
20. Ibid.
21. Mike Steeler, "Children's Theatre Coup: Seuss Work Adapted for Stage," *Minneapolis Tribune*, April 20, 1980.

22. Peter Vaughan, "Young Playwright Doctors Seuss Book," *Minneapolis Star*, April 18, 1980.
23. Carole Nelson, "Kids All Know Who Dr. Seuss Is; His Books Rhyme, and No Excuses," untitled clip, circa April 1980, Mandeville Special Collections Library, UCSD.
24. "Seuss' '500 Hats' Made Magical," *St. Paul Sunday Pioneer Press*, April 20, 1980; Peter Vaughan, "For Heady Fun, Try '500 Hats,'" *Minneapolis Star*, April 22, 1980.
25. For a reflection on TSG's views on posterity, see Morgan and Morgan, *Dr. Seuss & Mr. Geisel*, 266.
26. Jonathan Cott, "The Good Dr. Seuss," in *Pipers at the Gates of Dawn: The Wisdom of Children's Literature* (New York: Random House,1983).
27. Charlotte Leonard, ". . . And the Very Deserving Winner Is . . . Dr. Seuss," *The Journal Herald* (Dayton, OH), February 9, 1980.
28. Joan Weller, "Dr. Seuss Finally Makes It with Award from Librarians," *Ottawa Journal*, March 10, 1980.
29. Description of award taken from American Library Association website. Retrieved at www.ala.org/alsc/awardsgrants/bookmedia/clla/about. The award would be renamed the Children's Literature Legacy Award in 2018.
30. Morgan and Morgan, *Dr. Seuss & Mr. Geisel*, 241.
31. Mike Salzhauer, "A Carnival Cavort with Dr. Seuss," *Dartmouth Review*, February 2, 1981.
32. Jeff Lyon, "Writing for Adults, It Seems, Is One of Dr. Seuss's Dreams," *Chicago Tribune*, April 15, 1982.
33. Morgan and Morgan, *Dr. Seuss & Mr. Geisel*, 229.
34. "Dr. Seuss: Rhymes and Reasons," *Biography*, A&E Television, Peter Jones Productions, November 30, 2003.
35. Morgan and Morgan, *Dr. Seuss & Mr. Geisel*, 244.
36. Mary S. Reed, "Titles for Youngsters and Yuletide," *Jackson Sun* (Jackson, TN), November 18, 1982.
37. Lyon, "Writing for Adults . . ."
38. Gordon Smith, "Children's Writers Worry as Publishers Play It Safe," *Los Angeles Times*, December 10, 1982.
39. Ibid.
40. "'Somebody's Got to Win' in Kids' Books: An Interview with Dr. Seuss on His Books for Children, Young and Old," *U.S. News & World Report*, April 14, 1986.
41. Smith, "Children's Writers Worry as Publishers Play It Safe."
42. Morgan and Morgan, *Dr. Seuss & Mr. Geisel*, 248.
43. Ibid., 259.
44. Carla Waldemar, "Yes, There Really Is a Dr. Seuss," *Twin Cities Readers*, April 24, 1980.
45. Cott, "The Good Dr. Seuss."
46. Ibid.
47. "Dr. Seuss Remembered," *Publishers Weekly*, October 25, 1991.
48. TSG, *The Butter Battle Book* (New York: Random House, 1984).
49. Morgan and Morgan, *Dr. Seuss & Mr. Geisel*, 250.
50. Jonathan Freedman, "Nearing 80, Dr. Seuss Still Thrills Young, Old," *San Diego Union*, February 24, 1984.
51. Morgan and Morgan, *Dr. Seuss & Mr. Geisel*, 250.
52. Ibid., 251.
53. Ibid.
54. Ibid., 252.

55. Ibid.
56. Ibid., 249.
57. Ed Koch to TSG, March 2, 1984, Mandeville Special Collections Library, UCSD.
58. Eden Ross Lipson, "Children's Books: Dr. Seuss' Bleak Polemic," *New York Times*, February 26, 1984.
59. Morgan and Morgan, *Dr. Seuss & Mr. Geisel*, 253.
60. Ellen Goodman, "Dr. Seuss Needs a Good Dose of Hope," *Democrat and Chronicle* (Rochester, NY), April 24, 1984.
61. Ibid.
62. Jennifer Crichton, "Dr. Seuss Turns 80," *Publishers Weekly*, February 10, 1984.
63. Kathy Hacker, "The Ordinary Guise of the Extraordinary Dr. Seuss," *San Francisco Examiner*, April 18, 1984.
64. Rick Wilson, "A Chilling Message for Adults Wrapped in the Guise of Children's Literature," *Times Herald* (Port Huron, MI), April 29, 1984.
65. "Dr. Seuss: Rhymes and Reasons" documentary.
66. Colin Dangaard, "Dr. Seuss Reigns Supreme as King of the Kids," *Boston Herald American*, November 21, 1976.

Chapter 17. Off and Away

1. "4 papers win 2 Pulitzers each, 'Ironweed' is favored in fiction," *Baltimore Sun*, April 17, 1984.
2. David Shaw, "Times Gets Public Service Pulitzer; Conrad Also Wins," *Los Angeles Times*, April 16, 1984.
3. "'Dr. Seuss' Wins Special Pulitzer Citation," *Ithaca Journal*, April 17, 1984.
4. "'Dr. Seuss' Calls Pulitzer Citation 'Amazing,'" *Marshfield News Herald* (Marshfield, WI), April 17, 1984.
5. Judith Morgan and Neil Morgan, *Dr. Seuss & Mr. Geisel: A Biography* (New York: Random House, 1995), 255.
6. Michael Frith, interview with the author.
7. "'Dr. Seuss' Calls Pulitzer Citation 'Amazing.'"
8. "Dr. Seuss: Pulitzer Triumph in Battle Against Illiteracy," *Town Talk* (Alexandria, LA), April 17, 1984.
9. Morgan and Morgan, *Dr. Seuss & Mr. Geisel*, 261.
10. Jay Mathews, "Dr. Seuss: His New Book Is for Adults . . . and About Himself," *Washington Post*, March 2, 1986.
11. Melissa Balmain, "Princeton Awards 1,599 Degrees," *Central New Jersey Home News* (New Brunswick, NJ), June 12, 1985.
12. Melissa Weiner, "Dr. Seuss Brightens Princeton Ceremony," *Philadelphia Inquirer*, June 12, 1985.
13. "Dr. Seuss: Rhymes and Reasons," *Biography*, A&E Television, Peter Jones Productions, November 30, 2003.
14. David W. Dunlop, "Waiting in Fotta-fa-Zee," *New York Times Book Review*, March 23, 1986.
15. TSG, back cover copy to *You're Only Old Once!*
16. Michael Frith, interview with the author.
17. "Dr. Seuss Remembered," *Publishers Weekly*, October 25, 1991.
18. Dr. Seuss, *Dr. Seuss from Then to Now: A Catalogue of the Retrospective* (New York: Random House, 1987), 65.
19. Morgan and Morgan, *Dr. Seuss & Mr. Geisel*, 266.
20. See Mathews, "Dr. Seuss."

21. See Random House newspaper ads, such as *Los Angeles Times Book Review*, March 2, 1986.
22. Donald Freeman, "Dr. Seuss from Then to Now," *San Diego Magazine*, May 1986.
23. "Book Report: Hailing Dr. Seuss," *Washington Post*, March 23, 1986.
24. Edward Sorel, "The Shape That He's In: You're Only Old Once!" *New York Times*, March 23, 1986.
25. Mathews, "Dr. Seuss."
26. Ibid.
27. Jonathan Cott, "The Good Dr. Seuss," in *Pipers at the Gates of Dawn: The Wisdom of Children's Literature* (New York: Random House, 1983).
28. Mathews, "Dr. Seuss."
29. Alan L. Adler, "Green Eggs and Ham Were Just Starters for Author Theodor Geisel," *Santa Cruz Sentinel*, May 21, 1986.
30. Morgan and Morgan, *Dr. Seuss & Mr. Geisel*, 267.
31. Warren T. Greenleaf, "How the Grinch Stole Reading: The Serious Nonsense of Dr. Seuss," *Principal*, May 1982.
32. Leonard Felson, "Colleges Across State Honor New Graduate," *Hartford Courant*, May 19, 1986.
33. Elsie Osterman, "Dr. Seuss: The Man Who Brought to Life Horton the Elephant, Yertle the Turtle and the Cat in the Hat Is Working on 'a Picture Book for Adults,'" *Morning Call* (Allentown, PA), February 6, 1986.
34. Ibid.
35. The Springfield Museum—which now owns the house—is working carefully in the bedroom, peeling back old wallpaper and peering at exposed plaster, to determine if this claim is true. So far they've come up empty.
36. Jan Tarr, "They Saw Seuss on Mulberry," *Hartford Courant*, May 21, 1986.
37. Larry Rohter, "After 60 Years, Dr. Seuss Goes Back to His Roots," *New York Times*, May 21, 1986.
38. Hilliard Harper, "The Private World of Dr. Seuss: A Visit to Theodor Geisel's La Jolla Mountaintop," *Los Angeles Times Magazine*, May 25, 1986.
39. Dan Carlinsky, "Dr. Seuss From A to Z: His Prose and His Art Still Warm a Kid's Heart," *Cincinnati Enquirer*, February 17, 1986.
40. Harper, "The Private World of Dr. Seuss."
41. Ibid.
42. Ibid.
43. Judith Morgan, interview with the author.
44. Morgan and Morgan, *Dr. Seuss & Mr. Geisel*, 274.
45. Gina Cioffi, "It's a Happy Holiday Bowl for Dr. Seuss," *San Diego Union*, December 18, 1986.
46. Carole Nelson, "Kids All Know Who Dr. Seuss Is, His Books Rhyme, and No Excuses," untitled and undated clip, Mandeville Special Collections Library, UCSD, Box 9, Folder 16.
47. Morgan and Morgan, *Dr. Seuss & Mr. Geisel*, 276.
48. Digby Diehl, "Q&A: Dr. Seuss," *Los Angeles Times West*, September 17, 1972.
49. Morgan and Morgan, *Dr. Seuss & Mr. Geisel*, 286.
50. Robert Bernstein, interview with the author.
51. Morgan and Morgan, *Dr. Seuss & Mr. Geisel*, 279.
52. Ibid., 265.
53. Ibid., 279.
54. Ibid.
55. TSG, *Oh, the Places You'll Go!* (New York: Random House, 1990).

56. Morgan and Morgan, *Dr. Seuss & Mr. Geisel*, 281.
57. "Dr. Seuss: Rhymes and Reasons" documentary.
58. Morgan and Morgan, *Dr. Seuss & Mr. Geisel*, 282.
59. Ibid., 283.
60. Ibid., 258.
61. Ibid., 283.
62. Michael Frith, interview with the author.
63. Fredric Koeppel, "New Dr. Seuss Effort Lacks Usual Luster," *Poughkeepsie Journal*, January 28, 1990.
64. Alison Lurie, "The Cabinet of Dr. Seuss," *New York Review of Books*, December 20, 1990.
65. Susan Stark, "New Book on the Loose from Inimitable Dr. Seuss," *Florida Today* (Cocoa, FL), February 11, 1990.
66. Morgan and Morgan, *Dr. Seuss & Mr. Geisel*, 283.
67. See TSG's handwritten notes "We've Got to Do Better!," Mandeville Special Collections Library, UCSD.
68. "Dr. Seuss: Rhymes and Reasons" documentary.
69. Judith Morgan, interview with the author.
70. Morgan and Morgan, *Dr. Seuss & Mr. Geisel*, 286.
71. Ibid., 287.
72. Ibid.
73. James R. Hagerty, "Audrey Geisel Defended and Extended the World of Dr. Seuss," *The Wall Street Journal*, December 28, 2018.
74. Cott, "The Good Dr. Seuss."
75. Shirley Jackson, "His Personal Prescription," *San Francisco Examiner*, November 10, 1963.
76. Robert Cahn, "The Creator of Horton, Thneeds, and Truffula Trees," *Christian Science Monitor*, October 17, 1991.
77. Digby Diehl, "Q&A: Dr. Seuss," *Los Angeles Times West*, September 17, 1972.
78. Craig Piechura, "Just Call Dr. Seuss the New Mother Goose," *Southfield Eccentric* (Southfield, MI), November 26, 1979.
79. Carla Waldemar, "Yes, There Really Is a Dr. Seuss," *Twin Cities Readers* (Minneapolis, MN), April 24, 1980.

INDEX